CASE STUDIES IN ECONOMIC ANALYSIS

Edited on behalf of the Economics Association by
Peter Maunder, *Lecturer in Economics,*
Loughborough University

A new series of teaching materials published by Heinemann Educational Books for the Economics Association. The case studies, which are suitable for both university and A level courses, give practical exemplifications of different issues in major areas of economic analysis. The student's editions contain the case studies, a series of discussion or essay questions, and guidance on further reading. The teacher's editions contain, in addition, notes on the discussion questions and more detailed background information on the case studies.

1. Case Studies in Competition Policy
K. Blois, J. Howe and P. Maunder

Nine case studies on: the monopoly situation (British Oxygen), the oligopoly situation (Brooke Bond Tea), vertical integration (BMC/Pressed Steel); restrictive price agreements (glass containers), resale price maintenance (domestic eletrical appliances), and conglomerate mergers (Unilever/Allied Breweries, Rank/De la Rue, British Match/Wilkinson Sword).

2. Case Studies in Cost Benefit Analysis
P. Barker and K. Button

Five case studies on: the Victoria Line, the Cambrian Coast Railway, the Morecambe Bay Barrage, the resiting of Covent Garden, and the Third London Airport.

HEINEMANN EDUCATIONAL BOOKS LTD

D1471808

Case S

CASE STUDIES IN COMPETITION POLICY

Economics Association Teaching Materials Project

CASE STUDIES IN ECONOMIC ANALYSIS

Series Editor: W. Peter J. Maunder

A series of detailed case studies designed to
enhance an understanding of real-world issues
for the student taking a degree course,
professional examination or Advanced level G.C.E.
in Economics

1. *Case Studies in Competition Policy* by Keith J. Blois, W. Stewart Howe and W. Peter J. Maunder
2. *Case Studies in Cost-Benefit Analysis* by Kenneth J. Button and Peter J. Barker
3. *Case Studies in Regional Economics*, by Kenneth J. Button and D. Gillingwater
4. *Case Studies in Competition*, by W. Peter J. Maunder, Peter J. Barker and Keith J. Blois

CASE STUDIES IN ECONOMIC ANALYSIS

1

CASE STUDIES IN COMPETITION POLICY

by

Keith J. Blois

*Department of Management Studies,
Loughborough University*

W. Stewart Howe

*Department of Accountancy and Economics
Dundee College of Technology*

W. Peter J. Maunder

*Department of Economics
Loughborough University*

PERTH TECHNICAL COLLEGE

STAFF LIBRARY

Published by Heinemann Educational Books
on behalf of The Economics Association

Heinemann Educational Books Ltd
LONDON EDINBURGH MELBOURNE TORONTO AUCKLAND
HONG KONG SINGAPORE KUALA LUMPUR
IBADAN NAIROBI JOHANNESBURG
LUSAKA NEW DELHI

ISBN 0 435 84469 5
Teacher's Guide ISBN 0 435 84470 9
© Economics Association 1975

First published 1975

338.6048

Published by
Heinemann Educational Books Ltd
48 Charles Street, London W1X 8AH
Typeset in Great Britain by
Preface Ltd, Salisbury, Wilts
and printed in Great Britain by
The Pitman Press, London and Bath

Contents

In the Teacher's Guide only teacher's notes on the case studies begin on
p. 77.

Introduction

British competition policy since the war was first enshrined in the 1948 Monopolies and Restrictive Practices (Inquiry and Control) Act which set up the Monopolies and Restrictive Practices Commission. Whatever the effectiveness of this body in changing events in the industries it was asked to study by government, there can be no doubting its value in providing insights into the nature of competitive conduct throughout a range of British industry. Later government legislation — i.e. the 1956 Restrictive Trade Practices Act and the 1966 Prices and Incomes Act — also resulted in statutory bodies which in their various ways have generated valuable material on the workings of British business enterprise.

The aim of these six case studies is two-fold. Firstly, they aim to make more well-known to students than has often hitherto been the case the valuable teaching material available from the activity of these government-created bodies and institutions concerned with competition and ensuing economic issues. Secondly, they seek to involve the student in considering questions and issues arising from the material extracted from the chosen sources.

The sources are certain Reports of the Monopolies Commission and the National Board for Prices and Incomes and the Judgements of the Restrictive Practices Court. One case study draws on original research on the impact of the 1964 Resale Prices Act.

THE CONTENT OF THIS BOOK

The first study is of the classic monopoly situation found by the Monopolies Commission in 1956 to exist in the industrial gases industry. The dominance of British Oxygen in this industry and its implications for the public interest make this an obvious choice for study of the monopoly problem.

The second case study, the tea industry, was chosen to portray competition in an industry whose market structure is oligopolistic. Given the increasing tendency for British industry to become more concentrated into fewer units, this case typifies the public policy problem of ensuring effective competition.

Dramatic changes in market structure come about through amalgamation and merger. The third study examines the motives behind the British Motor Corporation's bid for the car body firm of Pressed Steel in 1966.

Case 4 is a study of the glass container industry, an industry that tried to defend a price agreement before the Restrictive Practices Court in 1961. The Court hearing provides an interesting study of managerial attitudes towards the desirability of competition at this time.

Case 5 is concerned with the impact of the 1964 legislation affecting resale price maintenance. It focuses on the forces affecting price determination in the domestic electrical appliances industry and draws on the first detailed study made of this trade.

The final study is concerned with the problem of multi-product companies and uses the first studies of the Monopolies Commission of conglomerate mergers to indicate the issues involved.

The sources used are not new ones to exploit for case studies. What is claimed to be different about this package is the rigour of each of the case studies in its selection of material, the questions set for discussion and the preparation of teachers' notes. Not all case studies offer the 'answers' to qualitative questions or give notes bringing the teacher up to date with events since the Report was published or Judgement was given. These studies offer *both* these aids in the Teacher's Handbook published separately by Heinemann Educational Books.

Thus in each of the four case studies there are four parts. Firstly there is the material extracted from one of the three sources cited above. Then follows about a dozen questions requiring the student to think about the facts and issues contained in the case study. In the Teacher's Handbook the third section provides the teacher with information on events in these industries since the time of the Report by the Monopolies Commission or N.B.P.I. or the Judgement by the Restrictive Practices Court. The intention here is in part to give the teacher an up-to-date picture of the situation in case students ask how events have changed since the Report or Judgement! However it is not just intended that the teacher be appraised of the present situation to meet such questions but also to give him further material for class use if he wishes. For example, the Teacher's Notes for the glass container study gives data on the packaging materials and raises the question of externalities. We have here the real-world issues of defining markets, competition from substitute products and pollution. The Teacher's Notes thus attempt to broaden the picture of events in the light of more recent events and put the case study in perspective. Finally there are some suggested answers to the questions. It is stressed that the questions may lead to students offering alternative conclusions and analyses to those in this section which may be quite legitimate in the light of the information in the case study. The answers are thus not intended to be exhaustive, but consider the major 'Points intended to be raised from the questions.' This final section is headed as in this quotation rather than 'Answers' to avoid misconceptions on this score.

The final question on each case study is similar and aims to get the student to consider the effect of the Monopolies Commission or N.B.P.I. or Restrictive Practices Court on the industry. This permits a class of students to compare the results of the investigating bodies where they have been split up into sub-groups.

The diagnostic powers required for using these studies are those possessed by capable Advanced level students. However, it is students reading Industrial Economics at degree level for whom these studies are essentially written. Students preparing for the finals of professional examinations will, we hope, also find this gives them a feel of the workings of some of our present and past major organs of economic investigation.

Each of the studies can be read by students prior to class discussion of the questions or alternatively begun from scratch. In the latter case a double lesson, typical of Sixth Form teaching, should be found adequate to cover one case. The studies can of course be set to students individually and written rather than oral answers sought.

Acknowledgements

This text is part of the series of teaching aids that Derek Lee suggested for sponsorship by The Economics Association. The structure of these case studies for undergraduate use has been designed and edited by Peter Maunder. Both gratefully acknowledge the help and valuable comments of other members of The Economics Association, notably Raymond Ryba, Malcolm Bradbury and Peter Chapman.

CASE STUDY
1. A Monopoly Situation: the British Oxygen Co. Ltd.

The British Monopolies and Restrictive Practices Commission (established under the Monopolies and Restrictive Practices (Inquiry and Control) Act, 1948)* had been at work for eight years and had already presented sixteen Reports before it published the results of its inquiry into the operations of the British Oxygen Co. Ltd. (B.O.C.).[1] The basic facts of this case up to 1956 are drawn largely from the Commission's Report on the industrial and medical gases industry.[2] The case of B.O.C. and its activities as the principal U.K. supplier of oxygen, dissolved acetylene and propane was that of a classic monopolist. Indeed, writing subsequently, a contemporary member of the Commission (though one not involved in this particular inquiry) referred to the industry as 'the most clearly defined case of pure monopoly where the producer had not been content to rely on advantages of scale but had pursued a deliberate policy over many years of suppressing competition'.[3] In 1954 B.O.C. accounted for 96.2% of U.K. oxygen supplies and 92.2% of dissolved acetylene; and the company was responsible for the distribution of 58.8% of propane.[4] There were not in 1954 any significant imports in this market and this remains true today. The buyers of the products are 'industrial users' — the steel, shipbuilding and engineering industries together taking between one-third and one-half of total output.[5]

B.O.C.

This firm had been established originally in the last decade of the nineteenth century, and as the industrial gases market expanded after 1918 the firm had consolidated its hold on the U.K. market through acquisition of competitors, of oxygen plant suppliers, and oxygen plant interests of those users who had previously produced for their own

*With the passing of the 1973 Fair Trading Act the Commission's title was changed to the Monopolies and Mergers Commission.

1

consumption. For example, the Commission itself gave the following data relating to acquisitions by B.O.C.[6]

(a)   Oxygen/dissolved acetylene suppliers:
       1896   The Birmingham Oxygen Co. Ltd.
       1899   The Manchester Oxygen Co. Ltd.
       1906   Linde British Refrigeration Co. Ltd.
       1909   The Scotch·and Irish Oxygen Co. Ltd.
       1909   British Liquid Air Ltd.
       1914   The Knowles Oxygen Co. Ltd.
       1930   Allen-Liversidge Ltd.
       1932   Oxygen Industries Ltd.
       1934   British Industrial Gases Ltd.
       1934   Hydrogen, Oxygen and Plant Co. Ltd.

(b)   Oxygen plant suppliers:
       1929   Liquid Air Ltd.
       1934   Oxhycarbon Ltd.

(c)   Firms producing oxygen solely or mainly for own use which
       either sold their plant to B.O.C. or closed their plant:
       1928   The Plymouth Oxygen Co. Ltd.
       1928   The Caledon Shipbuilding & Engineering Co. Ltd.
       1930   The Steel Supply Co. Ltd.
       1930   George Cohen Sons & Co. Ltd.
       1934   Edgar J. Rees Ltd.
       1935   G. A. Harvey & Co. (London) Ltd.
       1939   The Hughes Bolckow Shipbreaking Co. Ltd.
       1944   Thos. W. Ward Ltd.

In addition to these acquisitions, B.O.C. had used the technique of subsidiary 'fighting' companies as a means of eliminating competition. A fighting company is a subsidiary which is used by its parent deliberately to under-price – geographically or in terms of an individual product – competitors on a selective basis. B.O.C. used this device to eliminate Saturn Industrial Gases Ltd. Saturn established oxygen production facilities in the late 1930s at Teeside, Clydeside and Tyneside. In recognition of such competition B.O.C. in 1938 established Industrial Gases (Scotland) Ltd. whose oxygen and dissolved acetylene prices were some 2% below B.O.C.'s national average. After

B.O.C 's general adoption of a system of national prices in January 1940, flexibility was retained in the North-East and in Scotland in respect of individual customers such as shipyards and large engineering firms. Prices of oxygen and dissolved acetylene were already 25p and 45p per cubic foot respectively below prices quoted in England; and B.O.C decided that Industrial Gases (Scotland) Ltd. should 'step in and cut further' in order 'definitely [to] restrict the operations of our opponents' in Scotland and the North-East. Some few years later B.O.C. almost came to the point of acquiring Saturn.[7]

Furthermore, in relations with its customers B.O.C. adopted the principle of exclusive dealing. The use of B.O.C. capital equipment involved customers in having to use B.O.C. gas. Exclusive dealing thus relates to a requirement that a customer buy *all* of its requirements of a category of goods from a particular firm or group of firms. If the supplying firm(s) is a monopolist in some products but faces competition in other product areas, then provision of the goods in which it is a monopolist may entail purchasers in exclusive dealing and thus the purchase of such a firm's products even in those product areas where it is *not* a monopolist. (Thus a firm with a monopoly in computer hardware (i.e. the central machine) may stipulate exclusive dealing and force purchasers to buy its software (i.e. tapes, discs, etc.) even where there are competing software suppliers.)

The Commission also noted that so far as technological progress was concerned, B.O.C. had a history of acquiring technical knowledge through acquisition of patent licences rather than the carrying out of its own research and development work. This had applied to the original oxygen production processes and also to later developments.[8] The Commission felt that although B.O.C. was currently (1954) spending a total of £348,000 on research (about 2½% of income), the results of this were seen as progress on existing products and processes rather than in basic discoveries.[9]

THE MONOPOLIES COMMISSION'S REPORT

In the light of the findings which are highlighted above, it is not surprising to discover that the conclusions of the Commission were not unduly favourable to B.O.C. Almost all of the customer firms whom the Commission contacted had no criticisms to make of the level of prices charged by B.O.C., although it was admitted that 'the absence of competition made it impossible for them to assess the reasonableness or otherwise of B.O.C.'s prices'.[10] In fact as part of its inquiry in this case the Commission questioned a considerable number of every category of user of oxygen and dissolved acetylene. Of those who responded to a questionnaire survey, 45.6% expressed general satisfaction as to B.O.C.'s supply arrangements and the general level of prices. Some complaint was received regarding B.O.C.'s 'full-for-empty' policy involved in cylinder distribution of oxygen (a policy amended by the time of the Commission's Report). But a group of customers did point out that the general absence of competition in the market made it difficult for them to judge the reasonableness or otherwise of B.O.C.'s prices. One firm made it a policy to support Saturn Industrial Gases Ltd. 'as we well realise what might happen if they went out of existence'; another firm which also bought from both Saturn and B.O.C. considered that it 'owed a good deal to having an alternative source of supply which has had a considerable effect on the price of oxygen, dissolved acetylene and propane'; and various other respondents felt that they were more or less in the hands of B.O.C. as regards price, and in some cases felt that B.O.C.'s gas prices could be reduced in the light of the company's high profits.[11]

It was in fact on the question of profit levels that the Commission criticised B.O.C. It found that B.O.C.'s rate of return on capital employed was 23% in 1954 as against *The Economist* average for manufacturing industry for that year of 17.2%.[12] The Commission found this to be an excessive figure for six reasons:

(i) B.O.C. enjoyed a monopoly position.
(ii) The firm's product was essential to its customers.
(iii) B.O.C.'s products were a small part of its customers' total costs.
(iv) Fluctuations in demand for B.O.C.'s products were slight.
(v) The need for replacement capital in the industry was low.
(vi) Because of low risk B.O.C. could operate with a low ratio of financial reserves.[13]

Since the Commission could find no evidence of excessive costs on the part of B.O.C., it concluded that the high returns indicated excess profits. The Commission pointed out that if the company's return on capital employed had been limited to 15% in 1954, then prices could have been reduced by 7%.

Further practices which the Commission criticized were the control of tonnage oxygen plant (i.e. plant producing oxygen on a large scale), the extent to which B.O.C. had followed a policy of acquiring competitors, the firm's use of 'fighting' companies, the exclusive dealing contracts which B.O.C. had with some of its customers, and the extent to which the company had bought most of its technical knowledge through acquiring patent rights and licences rather than undertaking its own research.

Thus the Commission was critical of the way in which B.O.C. had refused or was reluctant to supply oxygen plant to customers as opposed to supplying oxygen itself, of the way in which B.O.C. had eliminated competition by corporate acquisition and by selective price reductions, and of the extent to which B.O.C. had been dependent upon 'external' sources of research. The Commission was also critical of the restrictive nature of B.O.C.'s contracts with its customers, e.g. the exclusive dealing provisions discussed above.

The body of these criticisms were built into the Commission's final recommendations:

1. B.O.C. should publish its prices.
2. Prices should only be varied according to the method of supply and quantity involved in dealing with each customer.
3. B.O.C. should not use the 'fighting' company as a competitive weapon.
4. Some parts of B.O.C.'s contracts with its customers were over restrictive, and should be amended.
5. The Board of Trade should review B.O.C.'s cost and price structure periodically so as to prevent unduly high profits being earned. The Commission rejected any formal limitation of the company's profits.[14]

These recommendations were evidently felt to embody a solution appropriate to the degree of monopoly power which B.O.C. quite clearly possessed in terms of market share and influence on other producers, and to the degree to which the Commission was almost unanimously agreed that the firm had abused this monopoly position as indicated by the level of profits and the steps which the company had taken to maintain this position.

Can these recommendations be justified in the light of the content and conclusions of the Report? With regard to the first of the points above, publication of prices enables (potential) competitors to see what they are 'up against' in terms of price competition. Especially if there are standard national prices, or if these vary systematically according to method and/or quantity of the product supplied, then a competitor may selectively under-price by region or product and thus gain a foothold in the market. The dropping of restrictive clauses in contracts would also have the effect of reducing the 'barriers to entry' in a market. With regard to the last of the Commission's recommendations mentioned above, it is interesting to note that the Commission's view was that a formal limitation of profits would have been administratively complex to negotiate and police; would have meant rigidity and interference in the day-to-day management of B.O.C.; and, in the Commission's own words, might have deprived B.O.C. of 'adequate incentives to continued and increasing efficiency'.

ACTION ON THE REPORT

The outcome of the Commission's recommendations was a series of negotiations between the company and the then Board of Trade. As a result of discussions between B.O.C. and the Board it was agreed that the company would cease taking over other firms for the purpose of consolidating its monopoly position; that B.O.C. would cease to employ the technique of 'fighting companies'; that the firm should relax its exclusive buying arrangements whereby use of B.O.C. equipment was linked to exclusive purchase of B.O.C. gas; that B.O.C. should adopt and publish a national scale of prices, varying according to quantity taken and method of supply, with only exceptional cases (including those customers being supplied with oxygen by pipe on a tonnage basis) being dealt with on a basis other than this; that contracts for the supply of oxygen should be for no longer than one year and at rates identical to non-contract supply; and that the company would cease placing restrictions on the supply of gas plant.[15]

In fact, however, B.O.C. was released from most of the undertakings by August 1962. The company's own justification was couched in the following terms in a subsequent Annual Report.

The pattern of oxygen supply and its cost are in fact very different now from what they were in 1952/1954, the period reported on by the Monopolies Commission.

The strong competition in tonnage oxygen for many years, now applies to gaseous and liquid oxygen for all types of user, and to a widened range of industrial gases. The undertakings which we gave in 1958 to maintain published price lists, and not to have contracts for longer than one year, or for exclusive supply including other gases, were grossly unfair when our competitors were not so bound.[16]

The President of the Board of Trade claimed that these changes were intended 'to free the company from handicap in competing with other suppliers without prejudicing the position of the consumers concerned'.[17] Nevertheless, comment in the press was adverse following this decision. *The Economist*, which had almost gone so far as to suggest a legal breaking up of the company, thought it 'an odd sort of fair play that gives back to the giant of the industry the power to use a pricing system whose abuses had been specifically condemned in the Monopolies Commission's Report';[18] while *Cartel* thought that:

When the barriers to entry into an industry are as formidable as massive investment and an established network of distribution make them for oxygen production, it is shortsighted of the Board of Trade to remove whatever slight restrictions on B.O.C.'s commercial activity offer assistance to its sole competitor. . . . The omission of a divestiture power from the monopoly legislation is also again shown to be a major deficiency. If B.O.C. had been split up in 1956 conditions of entry for new enterprises might well have been less onerous than they are today.[19]

Whatever the wisdom of the government's change in policy there can be no doubting the change in the supply of industrial gases brought about by the entry of Air Products Ltd. It was this one new entrant that was responsible for transforming this market and making it much more competitive in both a price and marketing sense. It had commenced operations in 1957 as a newly-found subsidiary of Air Products and Chemicals Inc. of the U.S. It was able to undercut the published prices of British Oxygen and offer attractive terms to major users on long-term contracts. British Oxygen felt its room for competitive manoeuvre to respond to the new competitor was severely limited by the undertakings agreed in 1958. The release from these came after strong pressure from B.O.C. on the government to lift them due to Air Product's successful growth into a formidable competitor.

Critical comments of B.O.C.'s behaviour following the release from its undertakings appeared. Professor C. K. Rowley has made reference to these but has offered no further evidence.[20] Disappointingly, the Board of Trade itself in 1963 merely observed:

There have been a certain number of complaints about the British Oxygen Company's changes in policy following the relaxation of the undertaking. The Board of Trade have taken note of these.[21]

The above facts, therefore, provide an outline of the action taken by the U.K. anti-trust authorities following the Commission's Report. It should be noted that the Commission could not take independent action and had to rely upon the Board to implement its recommendations.

REFERENCES

1. A good general source on the Monopolies Commission is C. K. Rowley, *The British Monopolies Commission*, Allen and Unwin, 1966.
2. See Monopolies and Restrictive Practices Commission *Report on the Supply of Certain Industrial and Medical Gases*, H.M.S.O., 1956 (H.C.P. 13) (hereinafter *Industrial and Medical Gases*).
3. G. C. Allen, *Monopoly and Restrictive Practices*, Allen and Unwin, 1968, p. 119.
4. *Industrial and Medical Gases*, paras. 20–21.
5. *Industrial and Medical Gases*, para. 107.
6. *Industrial and Medical Gases*, para. 31.
7. See *Industrial and Medical Gases*, paras. 52–3.
8. See *Industrial and Medical Gases*, paras. 24–6.
9. See *Industrial and Medical Gases*, paras. 211–2 and 245.
10. *Industrial and Medical Gases*, para. 110.
11. *Industrial and Medical Gases*, paras. 107–12.
12. *Industrial and Medical Gases*, para. 158.
13. *Industrial and Medical Gases*, para. 261.
14. *Industrial and Medical Gases*, para. 280.
15. See *Board of Trade Journal*, 28 March 1958, pp. 746–7.
16. B.O.C. *Annual Report*, 1963.
17. 667 H. C. Deb. (5th Ser.), 13 November 1962, col. 31.
18. *The Economist*, 17 November 1962, p. 700; also 5 January 1957, pp. 59–60.

19. *Cartel*, January 1963, p. 10.
20. See C. K. Rowley, op. cit., p. 364.
21. See Monopolies and Restrictive Practices Acts, 1948 and 1953, *Annual Report by the Board of Trade to 31 December 1962*, H.M.S.O., 1963 (Cmnd. 143), para. 9.

QUESTIONS FOR DISCUSSION

1. To what extent was B.O.C.'s behaviour up to the mid-1950s typical of the 'classic monopolist'? Would one have expected it to behave in any other way?

2. Why did many of B.O.C.'s customers apparently think that the level of prices charged by B.O.C. was fair? What approach should customer firms have adopted in this situation?

3. Comment on the six reasons given by the Commission for considering the profit level of B.O.C. to be too high (see page 4).

4. B.O.C. contended that its monopoly position was due to superior efficiency on its part, and that such a monopoly was in the public interest for the following reasons:
   (i) B.O.C. provided a wide geographic coverage through many plants.
   (ii) Monopoly conditions provided for efficient and integrated production and distribution of different gases.
   (iii) Production is capital intensive, plant is costly and in need of constant renewal.
   (iv) Distribution must be prompt but is costly in relation to the value of the basic product: competition would produce unnecessary and inefficient duplication.
   (v) Absolute certainty of supply and high standard of safety are necessary: a monopoly situation has provided for these.
   Discuss each of these arguments.

5. Comment on the rationale of the Commission's final recommendations.

6. What do you anticipate would be the effect of B.O.C.'s release from its undertakings to the Board of Trade?

7. Air Products Ltd. emerged as the main competitor to British Oxygen after 1957. What effect might this have been expected to have on British Oxygen's economic performance?

8. What factors would aid a new entrant into this industry?

9. The frozen food industry has grown rapidly in the past decade or so. What effect might this have had on the industrial gases industry?

10. The technology of steel-making has been changing in recent years. What new process is assuming an increasing importance in manufacturing steel? What impact would you expect this to have on the industrial gases industry?

11. Industrial gases are costly to distribute relative to production costs. A gas cylinder is a bulky item, 160 lbs. in weight, and yet only contains perhaps 25 lbs. of gas. The value of the cylinder itself may be ten times that of its contents. How might the major firms try to reduce distribution costs?

12. What impact had the Commission's Report on the industry?

CASE STUDY
2. An Oligopoly Situation: Tea

On 30 April 1970 Brooke Bond Oxo Ltd. announced an immediate increase of 2d. per ¼lb. – equivalent to a rise of 1p. in decimal currrency – on its teas, stating that such an increase was due to increases in factory costs, the costs of packaging and distribution and an increase in the market prices of imported tea. Within a short period Typhoo Tea Ltd. (Typhoo), Lyons Groceries Ltd. (Lyons) and the Co-operative Tea Society Ltd. (C.T.S.) also announced similar sized increases. As, together with Brooke Bond, these three companies accounted for about 85% of the retail market by volume this meant that effectively the recommended retail price of tea had been increased by 2d. per ¼lb. In consequence, on 14 May the Department of Employment and Productivity requested that the National Board for Prices and Incomes (hereafter called 'the Board') should examine and report on 'the question of the costs, prices and profitability of the tea buying, blending, packing and distribution industry'. The Board reported in August 1970 and its report is the basis of this case study.[1]

THE BACKGROUND TO THE REFERENCE

As indicated above, four companies dominated the market and in 1969 their shares by volume of the retail market were:

Table 2.1

Brooke Bond	43%
Typhoo	18%
Lyons	12%
C.T.S.	12%

Five other companies accounted for the remaining 15% of the market.

11

The retail market accounted for about 80% of the total consumption of tea with the remainder going to the catering trade.

Over 60% of the tea supplied on the British market was bought at the London Public Tea Auctions, with most of the remainder being bought at public auctions in the main producing countries. As a result of a persistent over-supply in world market the prices of imported tea at the London Tea Auctions had fallen over the period 1959–69.

Table 2.2 Annual average prices per lb. of tea at the London Auctions

Year	Old pence (d.)	Equivalent price in new pence (p.)
1959	54.6	23
1960	55.4	
1961	53.2	
1962	53.8	
1963	50.7	
1964	51.5	
1965	50.2	
1966	48.9	
1967	49.8	
1968	47.4	
1969	44.1	18.5

In the first six months of 1970 a number of factors coincided which led to a reverse in this trend of declining imported tea prices. A loss of 40 million lbs. of tea due to a strike in the West Bengal plantation in 1969, strikes in the Calcutta warehouses, adverse weather in Ceylon and voluntary international restriction of exports, resulted in reduced supplies being available with the inevitable result that the price of imported tea rose, in the first half of 1970, 6.9d. per lb. (3p.) above the average price in the same period of 1969. Each of the four companies took a different view of the future of imported tea prices. All expected the market price of imported tea to continue to rise but their estimates of increases to be expected in the latter part of 1970 ranged from 2½d. to 5d. per lb. This was the background to the April 1970 price increase in retail tea prices.

In 1969, the tea itself accounted for 70–80% of total costs but this varied over time and between brands; for example, the cost of the tea for each of the four popular brands varied between 44.62d. (18½p.) per lb. and 51.38d. (21p.) per lb. for the 1/9d. (9p.) per ¼lb. packets. Factory costs and administration, selling and distribution, and advertising, each accounted for approximately one-third of the costs other than tea and its packaging. However, Brooke Bond's total costs were significantly above those of the lowest cost company, and it had particularly high unit costs incurred in selling and distribution. The following figures show the total expenditure on advertising of Brooke Bond, Lyons and Typhoo:

Table 2.3

1966	£3.6 million
Latest financial year prior to August 1970	£4.6 million
1970–71 forecasts	£6.1 million

Note: No allowance has been made for increases in the cost of advertising.

Table 2.4

	Old price s. d.	New price s. d.
Brooke Bond		
P.G. Tips, per ¼lb.	1 9	1 11
Triple Dividend, per ¼lb.[a]	1 9	1 11
Typhoo		
Typhoo, per ¼lb.	1 9	1 11
Lyons		
Quick Brew, per ¼lb.	1 9	1 11
Premium, per ¼lb.[b]	1 9	1 11
C.W.S.		
"99", per ¼lb.	1 9	1 11

[a]Each ¼lb. packet had a 3d. collection stamp for sticking on an 80-space card. When completed, the card could be exchanged for £1 in cash or groceries at the retailers.
[b]Each ¼lb. packet had a 3d. collection stamp for sticking on a 60-space card. When completed, the card could be exchanged for 15s. cash or groceries at the retailers.

In 1970 approximately £500,000 was spent on generic advertising by the tea industry and this is included in the figures above. This generic advertising was aimed at slowing down or reversing the fall in the consumption of tea, annual *per capita* consumption of which had decreased from 10lbs. in 1959 to 8½lbs. in 1970.

The four companies each had at least one brand which was sold at a recommended retail price of 1/9*d*. (9p.) per ¼lb. before the price increase and in each case the price was to be raised by 2d. (1p.) per ¼lb.

THE COMPANIES

Brooke Bond and Co. Ltd. in 1968 merged with Liebig's Extract of Meat Co. Ltd. to form Brooke Bond Liebig Ltd., the largest company in the group being Brooke Bond Oxo Ltd. whose activities include the production and distribution of Fray Bentos and Oxo products as well as the tea business. As a result of this merger Brooke Bond trade marks were vested with Brooke Bond Liebig, and Brooke Bond Oxo Ltd. paid royalties to its parent company for the use of these trade marks. The reorganization and integration of selling and warehousing of tea and Fray Bentos and Oxo products was being developed in 1970. Partly as a result of this the number of different brands of packet tea had been reduced from ten to six. Tea bags are supplied in five packs of various sizes. In 1970 Brooke Bond's traditional method of selling, that of salesmen operating frequent and regular van delivery services to retailers, was continuing. However, with the growth of larger retail outlets the delivery to small retailers was less frequent and larger vans were calling more frequently at the larger outlets (by 1970 sales to multiples – organizations with ten or more branches – were 50% of Brooke Bond's total). Warehouses are now only occasionally used.

Typhoo Tea Ltd. was acquired by Schweppes Ltd. in 1968 for £45 million, of which £31 million represented 'goodwill'. Typhoo is unusual in that it has only ever sold one brand of packet tea. It also sells two packs (4oz. and 8oz.) of tea bags. In 1969 the company operated one tea factory but used rented warehouses and employed independent transport contractors for distribution. About 46% of all its sales were to multiples and 41% to voluntary groups and other wholesalers.

The Co-operative Tea Society Ltd. is jointly owned by the Co-operative Wholesale Society and the Scottish Co-operative Wholesale Society to which most of its sales are made, although individual co-operative retail societies order direct. Deliveries are made by C.T.S.'s own transport, by transport hired from its wholesalers or by outside contractors. The C.T.S. sold nine brands of tea and four packs of tea bags in 1969.

Lyons Groceries Ltd. is owned by J. Lyons and Co. Ltd., and handled sales of tea, coffee, and biscuits using a common selling and distribution system for those product ranges. It owned one tea factory and used its own transport. Eleven of its eighteen brands of tea were sold under the name of Lyons, while the remaining seven were sold under the trade names of two tea companies — Horniman's and Black and Green — acquired in the 1930s. Three packs of tea bags were also marketed.

PROFITS IN THE INDUSTRY

The following figures indicate the profits of each of the companies (though comparison should be undertaken with care owing to differences in the dates of their financial years).

Table 2.5

	Year ended	Profit in pence per lb. (d.)	(p.)	Percentage return on capital
Brooke Bond	June 1970 (estimates)	5	2	19
Typhoo	December 1969	12	5	37
Lyons	March 1970	N/A	N/A	16*
C.T.S.	September 1969	3	1	11

*This figure applied to the total business of Lyons Groceries Ltd.

Brooke Bond argued that the financial calculations should take into account the royalty payments which it makes to its parent company for the use of trade marks, pointing out that this would reduce the rate of return on capital to 16.7%. However, the Prices and Incomes Board felt that it would be wrong to treat these as charges against revenues. Similarly, the C.T.S. payments of dividends to its shareholders were treated as a payment out of profits. Typhoo asked that its capital employed should be taken as £41 million, thus giving a return of 9%. The Board, however, calculated the company's return on capital employed on the basis of excluding the element of goodwill. Its sum of capital employed was thus much lower and hence produced a high — 37% — return on capital. The Board was not prepared to accept the firm's basis, arguing that it was concerned with real resources and not with extra financial burdens that may have fallen on a company as a result of a merger or takeover.

THE BOARD'S CONCLUSIONS

The Board was concerned with two factors. Firstly, the question of whether Brooke Bond was justified in raising its prices by 2d. (1p.) per ¼lb. in April 1970. Secondly, it wished to consider why almost immediately the other companies raised their prices by a similar amount.

The Board noted that Brooke Bond had increased its share of the market from 23% to 43% between 1954 and 1970, and expressed the opinion that this increase in market share had been achieved by 'an overall combination of skilful marketing techniques'.[2] It was noted that Brooke Bond had increased its profits in the year ending 30 June 1970 by a significant measure over 1968 and 1969 when the rate of return on capital was 15% and 14% respectively. In addition, the April 1970 price increase announced by Brooke Bond was felt by the Board to be 'out of keeping with its past record'.[3] It was noted that the company had not changed its retail prices since 1957. In particular it had not reduced prices in 1969 when imported tea prices had fallen sharply. The Board expressed considerable concern over Brooke Bond's forecast increase in the cost of advertising, selling and distribution. It was considered that further economies in Brooke Bond's distribution costs should be achievable. As far as selling and advertising costs were concerned the forecast increases in this area were the result of Brooke Bond's aim to obtain a still larger share of the market. The Board recognized that while pursuit of such an aim could well be in the company's interest it felt there was no evidence that it would lead to lower prices to the consumer and that, at least in the short term, the opposite seemed to be likely.

All four major tea companies actively competed in selling to retailers in the manner of offering various special discounts and promotional allowances. However, the Board noted that in the matter of determining retail prices Brooke Bond was apparently subjected to little competition. In fact, for reasons considered below, Brooke Bond appeared to be the industry's price leader.

The Board's conclusion with regard to the first question stated above was that: 'Brooke Bond could make some savings in its marketing expenditure and, in the absence of any requirement of income for new investment in tea, could accept a reduction in profitability to the levels achieved in the years ending June 1968 and 1969.'[4] Further, it concluded that there should be no question of more price increases in the immediate future and that any significant fall in the market price of imported tea in the future should lead to a reduction in Brooke Bond's price.

When Typhoo, Lyons and C.T.S. were asked why they had increased their prices by the same amount as Brooke Bond, two of them indicated that they had considered not raising their recommended prices at all or by only 1d. (½p.) instead of 2d. (1p.) per ¼lb. However, 'one of the reasons why they had not adopted either course was that their competitive tea would have looked "cheap" and therefore not as good as the other leading brands.'[5] All four companies indicated that they believed that the consumer of tea clearly has difficulty in judging quality, and that recommended retail prices were a necessary guide to the consumer of the quality of the tea in a packet. The companies were very firm in this belief even though as a result of price-cutting by retailers the average price to the consumer of popular brands of tea was less in 1970 than six years previously. Indeed Brooke Bond's P.G. Tips brand, which had a recommended retail price of 1/9d. (9p.) per ¼lb. in 1969, was sold at an average price in shops at 1/6d. (7½p.).

The Board concluded that Brooke Bond was not subject to much competition on its recommended retail prices, the principal reason being that consumers, correctly or not, regard such prices as an 'indication of quality'. In the absence of competition on recommended retail prices, the Board hoped that the tea suppliers would engage in more competition when selling to retailers, feeling that this would be of more immediate and direct benefit to consumers than seemed likely to follow from further increases in advertising expenditure.

THE INDUSTRY SINCE 1970

The major reaction to the Board's report came from Brooke Bond. Its managing director made critical comment on it, stressing cost increases which the company had faced in the years since 1956 when the last price increase occurred. He stated that 'factory costs for packing tea had increased by 70%; packaging materials had increased by 68% and the cost of distribution by 100%. The cost of running a van in 1970 was £550 compared with £258 in 1956.'[6]

Typhoo said that the way the Board had interpreted the figures of costs was 'so unreal that it is not worth commenting'[7] and they also argued that increased costs had warranted the increases.

Interestingly Typhoo and Lyons both stated to the Press that there was no question of their being unwilling to follow Brooke Bond's price rise. This is in contradiction with the Board's statement that: 'Two companies told us that they had considered whether it would be to their advantage not to increase their prices following Brooke Bond's announcement, or alternatively, to increase recommended prices by only 1d. per ¼lb.'[8] The implication is that these were two of the following: Typhoo, Lyons, C.T.S.

Not until March 1974 was there a further increase in the recommended retail price of tea. The annual average prices of tea at the London Auctions have moved as follows:

Table 2.6

	Price per kilo* (p.)
1970	45.67
1971	43.25
1972	42.24
1973	43.29
1973 (last quarter)	46.20
1974 (first quarter)	58.24

Source: the Tea Council.
*It should be noted that in comparison with Table 2 the above data is in new pence and the unit weight now expressed in kilos.

It would, though, be an over-simplification to suggest that the comparative stability of the recommended retail price has resulted from the Board's comments in 1970, for three other major factors have influenced the retail tea market. Firstly, the continuing fall in the consumption of tea in terms of lbs. per head of population. Secondly, the increasing use of tea bags. Thirdly, changes in the relative strengths of the tea manufacturing companies.

1. Falling consumption of tea

Table 2.7 Estimates of annual supplies per head of the population

	1958	1968	1969	1970	1971	1972
lbs.	10*	8.8	8.5	8.7	8.2	8.0

Source: *Marketing Manual of the UK.*, International Publishing Corporation, 1973.
*Believed to be the maximum achieved.

Firms in the industry contribute funds to the Tea Council which promotes tea as a drink by non-brand advertising campaigns, viz: 'Join the Tea Set'.

Table 2.8 The Tea Council budgets and actual expenditure on advertising 1969/70—1973/74 (the Tea Council's Financial Year runs from 1 September to 31 August).

Year	Budget £	Actual Expenditure £
1968—69	650,000	616,981
1969—70	500,000	475,211
1970—71	375,000	275,289
1971—72	No budgeted income	82,863
1972—73	225,000	176,606
1973—74	150,000	

Source: The Tea Council.

2. Growth in the use of tea bags

In 1969 it was calculated that tea bags accounted for about 1½% by weight of the total tea market. By 1972 tea bags accounted for 17% of the market and it was expected that by 1973 they would attain 25%.

3. Changing structure of the tea market

The tea market is in 1974 still dominated by the four companies named in the Board's Report but since the Board's investigation the growth in the use of tea bags had led to an alteration of the position of Tetley. By 1973 Tetley was the brand leader with about 40% of the tea bag market. It was purchased (from the American company Beech-Nut) by J. Lyons Ltd. in October 1972. This raised Lyons to a position of equality in terms of overall tea market share with Typhoo. By 1973 Brooke Bond's share of the whole tea market had thus fallen to about 40%.

REFERENCES

1. National Board for Prices and Incomes, Report No. 154, *Tea Prices*, H.M.S.O., August 1970, (Cmnd. 4456).
2. ibid, p. 16.
3. ibid, p. 17.
4. ibid, p. 17.
5. ibid, p. 9.
6. *The Grocer*, 22 August 1970, p. 4.
7. D. Walker, 'Tea Trade angry at P.I.B. attack on 10% price rises', *Financial Times*, 15 August 1970, p. 1.
8. National Board for Prices and Incomes, op. cit., pp. 8–9.

QUESTIONS FOR DISCUSSION

1. Does the pricing behaviour of these firms fit into the model of oligopoly?

2. If the price of tea is considered by a consumer to be an indicator of quality, what shape would you expect a consumer's demand curve for tea to look like?

3. Assuming that the demand curve for tea is of the typical text-book shape (namely downward sloping to the right), draw a diagram to

illustrate the effect of:
(a) a price increase in tea;
(b) the reduced demand for tea arising from changing customer preferences.

4. Brooke Bond wished to increase its share of the market further. What do you believe would be the result of its achieving this objective, if:
(a) the packet tea market is considered as distinct from the market for tea bags and instant tea?
(b) these are considered to constitute one market?

5. (a) Why did the Board refuse to accept Brooke Bond's argument that its rate of return on capital in 1970 was 16.7% and not 19.3%?
(b) What other illustrations are there in this case of the problems of defining the costs relevant to a particular decision?

6. Why was competition keen between the tea companies when they were selling to retailers, but in determining recommended retail prices no one firm was prepared to sell at a lower price than any other firm?

7. Why was (and is) the recommended price of tea cut by retailers?

8. Comment on the critical reaction of Brooke Bond to the Report.

9. How have imported tea prices changed since 1970 in the light of the tea firms' forecasts given to the Board?

10. Suggest reasons for the falling level of tea consumption in the U.K.

11. How well supported has the Tea Council been by tea firms in undertaking generic advertising campaigns?

12. Why do you think there has been a growth in the consumption of tea bags?

13. What impact do you think the Board's Report has had on the industry?

CASE STUDY

3. Vertical Integration: the acquisition by the British Motor Corporation Ltd. of the Pressed Steel Company Ltd.

INTRODUCTION

On 22 July 1965 it was announced that B.M.C. (the British Motor Corporation Ltd.) had made an offer for the shares of the Pressed Steel Co. Ltd. and that the directors of Pressed Steel were recommending their shareholders to accept the offer. This case study is based on the Report of the Monopolies Commission on this merger.[1]

THE TERMS OF THE REFERENCE TO THE MONOPOLIES COMMISSION

On 20 August 1965, the Board of Trade referred this merger, at that stage still being negotiated, to the Monopolies Commission; thus it was the first case to be referred under the 1965 Monopolies and Mergers Act. The reference was made under the section of the Act which stipulated that cases where the assets taken over exceeded £5 million were included in the terms of the Act, and the Commission was required to determine whether or not the merger operated or might be expected to operate against the public interest, and whether any action should be taken to prevent the public interest being damaged, if necessary including any such recommendations for action within its report. As the reference was not made under the section of the Act concerned with the creation or extension of a monopoly, the Commission did not have to determine whether or not a monopoly would be created or extended as a result of the merger. However, the

22

Commission was free to consider any monopoly aspects of the situation with regard to the public interest.

It was found by the Commission that the assets of Pressed Steel amounted to approximately £55 million gross and £33 million net of liabilities, thus bringing the merger within the terms of the 1965 Act.

The Board of Trade did not use its powers to hold up the merger while the Commission conducted its enquiries. This was because the Commission was required to report back within six months of the date of the reference. This time limit was laid down in the 1965 Act.

Written evidence was collected from all British motor manufacturers who were customers of Pressed Steel, the larger customers of Pressed Steel's refrigeration interests, and the Ministries of Defence and Aviation because of Pressed Steel's ownership of an aircraft company. The Commission offered to receive oral evidence from all the major firms concerned and the Confederation of Shipbuilding and Engineering Unions, but of these parties only B.M.C., Pressed Steel and Rootes Motors Ltd. accepted. Some evidence of a commercially confidential nature was received and of course this was not included in the published report of the Commission.

THE MOTOR INDUSTRY IN THE U.K.

The motor industry occupied a vital position in the British economy in 1965, any fluctuations in its level of output very quickly affecting the activity in the numerous industries supplying it with components, and also in industries supplying the vehicle owner. In 1964 the industry's deliveries of cars and commercial vehicles was £1,264 million (based on net selling price 'ex-works') of which more than one-third were exported. This figure represented 16% of the total U.K. visible exports (including re-exports).

Since 1920, when there were eighty-nine firms manufacturing cars, the number of manufacturers declined to thirty-two in 1946 and to twenty in 1964. However, in 1964 less than 4% of the market was supplied by fifteen of these firms, the remainder of the market being provided for by five firms which have grown large enough to take advantage of the economies of large-scale production in manufacturing cars. These five firms competed with one another in terms of product rather than price.

Table 3.1 shows the actual shares of the market in 1963 and 1964 of the 'Big Five' manufacturers for both cars and commercial vehicles. The 'Big Five' being B.M.C., Ford (wholly U.S.-owned), Vauxhall (wholly owned by General Motors U.S.), Rootes (associated with Chrysler U.S.) and Standard Triumph International (Leyland Motor Corporation).

Table 3.1 Car and commercial vehicle production (units) in Britain in 1964

Manufacturers	Cars	C. Vs.	Total
'Big Five'	1.798,568	384,364	2,182,932
% of total	96.30	82.70	93.60
B.M.C	682,673	152,260	834,933
% of total	36.55	32.76	35.80
Others*	69,072	80,372	149,444
% of total	3.70	17.30	6.40
Total	1,867,640	464,736	2,332,376

*included Leyland.
Source: Monopolies Commission Report, p. 2.

The aim of each of the 'Big Five' with regard to car production was to develop a popular model which could be mass produced, although variations on a basic model were also made available. As far as commercial vehicle production was concerned, the market was split into three categories: light vans, medium trucks, and heavy trucks. Light vans, which accounted for about 60% of the total output, were designed to use sub-assembly parts as made for cars. The trucks in the medium range incorporated some components used in car manufacture but heavy trucks were quite distinct. The 'Big Five' produced all types of commercial vehicle but B.M.C. produced the largest number of vans and Vauxhall, Ford and Leyland were the largest manufacturers of medium and heavy trucks.

A motor vehicle is assembled from thousands of parts, and in Britain there grew up a strong components industry independent of the 'Big Five'. In consequence, by 1965 British-owned motor manufacturers bought a large proportion from 2,000 odd component manufacturers. By comparison with the United States or Europe there has been very little vertical integration, but since the war there have been a number of such mergers. For example, in 1953 B.M.C. had acquired the motor body firm of Fisher and Ludlow Ltd. Both Ford and Vauxhall (owned by General Motors) have exemplified for many years the preference of their American parent companies for being essentially self-sufficient in respect of their car-body requirements. Thus it can be seen that by 1965 Pressed Steel was the only remaining independent supplier of mass-produced car bodies in Britain. Given the unusual character of the British car-body business it was thus not surprising to find Pressed Steel referring to itself as 'the largest independent motor car body and body tool manufacturers in the world'.[2]

THE BRITISH MOTOR CORPORATION LTD.

B.M.C. was formed in 1952 on the merger of the Austin Motor Company Ltd. and Morris Motors Ltd. Its range of products included cars, commercial vehicles, tractors, components for its own use and for sale, Bendix washing machines, domestic hot water radiators and domestic sinks.

Between 1952 and 1964 B.M.C.'s net assets in the U.K. increased by £54 million to £88 million and assets overseas have risen by £10 million to £30 million. Between 1960 and 1964 the group's capital expenditure amounted to £64 million. The number of cars and commercial vehicles produced in 1964 is set out in Table 3.1. B.M.C. had many factories in the Midlands but of its 86,000 employees in the U.K. 11,000 were in development districts such as Liverpool and South Wales.

B.M.C. exported 40% of its production in 1964 and marketed its vehicles in 163 countries but regarded Europe as an especially attractive market. It foresaw the trend towards local assembly and a special packing factory has been opened for 'completely knocked down' (C.K.D.) vehicles. Such vehicles are entirely assembled abroad from the parts exported from the U.K.

B.M.C. produced a large number of variations on a basic model — the 'Mini' range included at least eleven different models — and in total had nearly sixty models. It produced models for nearly every sub-section of the car market.

Pressed Steel was the largest independent supplier of vehicle bodies to B.M.C. other supplies being obtained from other independent suppliers and B.M.C.'s own subsidiaries. It is difficult to estimate what proportion of B.M.C.'s bodies were supplied by Pressed Steel prior to the merger, because the process of body manufacture can be roughly divided into three stages: the pressing, sub-assembly, and body-building. At this time some car bodies were totally manufactured in one plant but other bodies were part-processed in one plant and then taken to another for completion. For instance, a considerable proportion of Pressed Steel's output from its Swindon factory was sent to one or other of B.M.C.'s body manufacturers for further processing. However, it was estimated that in 1964 B.M.C. took 28% by units of its body requirements from Pressed Steel.

As far as other components were concerned, standardized parts such as tyres and windshields were purchased from outside suppliers while parts specific to B.M.C. vehicles were manufactured by B.M.C.

THE PRESSED STEEL CO. LTD.

Pressed Steel was incorporated in 1926, on the initiative of Lord Nuffield, being established and financed by Morris Motors Ltd., the Budd Corporation and J. Henry Schroeder and Co. It was located at Cowley on a site adjoining Morris Motors' works. Morris Motors was not able to take enough of the volume of output required and in 1930, so that other motor manufacturers would be encouraged to make use of Pressed Steel's spare capacity, Morris Motors gave up its dominant position. In 1935 the Budd Corporation withdrew and Pressed Steel became independent. Since its incorporation the capital employed rose from £1½ million to £45 million in 1964 and the number of employees from 500 to 26,000.

In 1934 Pressed Steel formed the Prestcold organization, whose activities were confined to the manufacture of commercial refrigeration equipment and air conditioning units. In 1964 Prestcold exported 20% of its output.

An aircraft manufacturing group called British Executive and General Aviation Ltd. (Beagle) was formed by Pressed Steel in 1960 and this firm made a range of light and executive aircraft.

A fourth interest of Pressed Steel was in the manufacture of railway rolling stock in Linwood, but its production facilities in that area were predominantly concerned with the manufacture of vehicle bodies.

Over 90% of Pressed Steel's turnover at the time of the merger was with the motor industry and most of this was the manufacture of car

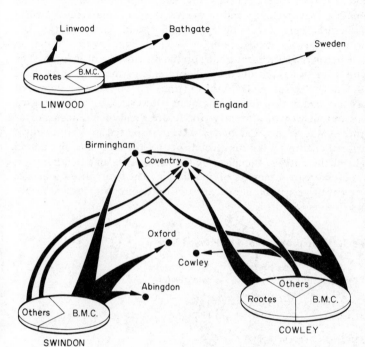

Source: Motors all over the place, The Economist, 31 July 1965, p.459

Fig. 3.1. The location of Pressed Steel's body plants

bodies. It produced car bodies for 40% of all passenger cars manufactured in Great Britain (the body accounting for 35–40% of the unit factory cost of a mass produced car). In addition, the company produced press tools and jigs for sale to all the major British automobile manufacturers and to many overseas manufacturers. It had manufacturing plants at Cowley, Swindon and Linwood, this last mentioned factory being built in collaboration with Rootes in accordance with government policy on the distribution of industry. The Cowley plant was sited on the opposite side of the Garsington Road from B.M.C.'S plant in Oxford, and thus car bodies were conveyed across the road to the car assembly plant. However, over half of Pressed Steel's output went to Coventry (for Rootes) and to Birmingham (for another B.M.C. plant). Car bodies were transported by lorry to these plants rather than by rail on account of the low unit value per pound weight of these items. Complete bodies are mostly 'air'. Rail transport was too expensive a method of 'moving air'. The figure below indicates the extent of geographical movement of car bodies from Pressed Steel's plants.

Table 3.2 The profit record of Pressed Steel

Year to:	Pretax profits (£000's)		As % of capital employed
31.12.59		5,085	23.0
31.12.60		3,174	13.2
31.12.61	Loss	2,510	–
31.12.62	Loss	827	–
31.12.63		2,823	6.2

Source: Company Reports.

Pressed Steel supplied all sizes of car bodies and to a varying degree of finish. Its major customers were B.M.C. and Rootes, each taking approximately 40% of Pressed Steel's output by value. Rootes purchased a more complete – and therefore more expensive – body, so in terms of actual units Rootes took only 27% of Pressed Steel's output whereas B.M.C. accounted for 61%. As was stated earlier, B.M.C. relied on Pressed Steel for part of their body supplies – about one-third – but Rootes, Rover, Jaguar, and Rolls Royce (for standard bodies) were almost entirely dependent upon Pressed Steel. In addition, bodies for the Triumph 2000, Volvo cars, and Ford commercial vehicles were supplied.

THE CASE FOR THE MERGER PRESENTED TO THE COMMISSION

B.M.C. and Pressed Steel said that the case for the merger was contained in the letter of 14 August 1965 sent to all the latter's shareholders.

B.M.C. explained that over the previous twenty years a policy of specialized production of various parts of motor vehicles had been adopted by all the major motor manufacturers and that specialized plants had been set up for the production of these items. It was said that these techniques of specialized production were applicable to body manufacture and that economies could be achieved if plants undertook specialized production of parts of the body of a vehicle rather than complete bodies. In collaboration with Pressed Steel, B.M.C. had in fact already been implementing such a policy at the Swindon plant.

The rationalization of body production on these lines would, in B.M.C.'s opinion, reduce costs and enable it to take full advantage of the economies of scale obtained by 'running high volume through specialized press shops'.[3] Further economies were to be expected in the bulk purchases of materials and through reduction in transport costs. Specialization of production would also result in improved quality, and this would especially result in economies of assembly of C.K.D. units overseas. Advantages were expected from the pooling of engineering, production planning and research activities.

A public assurance was given by B.M.C. to the effect that Pressed Steel would operate as a separate company with the greatest possible autonomy and that its existing goodwill and business relationships with other customers would be maintained. In particular, if a shortage of materials occurred, allocations would be made to all customers on a *pro rata* basis. Pressed Steel would also maintain secrecy of designs and would not discriminate between customers on price. As far as Pressed Steel's other activities were concerned, B.M.C. stated that it did not intend to interfere with them in any way.

Pressed Steel explained that it was dependent upon B.M.C. and Rootes for 80% of its business and that either or both of them might decide to build up their own body-making capacity — this being in line with the industry's trend to vertical integration. It seemed therefore that Pressed Steel might not, in the long run, be able to retain its independence and it had therefore accepted B.M.C.'s offer to protect its employees and shareholders. Keen observers of the situation did in fact make it clear that the merger was always a likely one and that it was indeed a defensive one from the point of view of both Pressed Steel and B.M.C. *The Statist* referred to the B.M.C.–Pressed Steel link as 'one of the stockmarket's oldest bid favourites'.[4] Thus *The Statist* said that: 'The Chrysler influence in Rootes would inevitably lead in course of time to a search for ways of reducing Rootes' dependence upon an outside supplier.'[5] *The Economist* said quite emphatically that 'the bid was inevitable after the Chrysler offer for a substantial part of Rootes last year had introduced another hungry American giant into the British motor scene'.[6] Thus Pressed Steel had legitimate fears for its number of customers in the future; B.M.C. for its part felt the merger would prevent the possibility of having to buy in its major component from an American-owned competitor. B.M.C. indeed stressed the need for a greater degree of integration to strengthen the competitive position against 'large integrated foreign-controlled companies'.[7]

THE COMMISSION'S CONCLUSIONS

The Commission wished to answer two questions:

(a) Were there any fundamental objections to the merger such as to lead to the conclusion that the merger itself was contrary to the public interest and that therefore the *status quo* should be restored?

(b) Were there any other objections such that the merger should be accepted but only subject to conditions safeguarding the public interest?

The Commission found that none of the principal customers of Pressed Steel wished to object to the merger, neither did the Trades Union Confederation concerned. In consequence the Commission found no objection of the fundamental type.

As far as the many economies that B.M.C. expected to obtain were concerned, the Commission accepted that some increase in efficiency was probable, but did 'not think that the benefits would be quite so important as . . . claimed'.[8]

On the other hand, the Commission felt that the main argument against the merger must be based on the risk that it might result in important customers, such as Jaguar, Rover and Rolls Royce, being embarrassed or even put out of business by Pressed Steel's failure to maintain a supply of bodies. However, in considering this question the Commission discussed what would happen if the merger did not occur at this time.

It was felt that in the long run either B.M.C. or Rootes would have set up their own body-making plants, and certainly if Pressed Steel had been taken over by a firm other than B.M.C. — particularly a foreign company — then B.M.C. would have felt obliged to set up additional capacity of its own. This might involve wasteful duplication of resources. In these circumstances the Commission did not feel that Pressed Steel had acted unreasonably in anticipating events and accepting an offer from one of its principal customers.

The Commission commented on the point stressed by B.M.C. that the merger was one between two companies which were British owned and controlled and that any risk that there may have been of Pressed Steel becoming a wholly-owned subsidiary of some foreign company would be eliminated. It said that there might be differing views as to the value to the British economy of investment by foreign firms in manufacturing capacity in this country. It certainly did not seek to criticize the behaviour of foreign vehicle manufacturers who had set up wholly-owned subsidiaries here, but thought that:

B.M.C. may be expected to show more consideration for the needs of Pressed Steel's existing customers than a foreign principal would necessarily feel obliged to do. With Pressed Steel in foreign hands questions might also have arisen about remittances abroad and perhaps about 'rationalization' of Pressed Steel's exports to fit in with a pattern which better suited the policy and the other interests of the foreign principal.[9]

It therefore concluded:

On balance, therefore, we think that in this case there is some appreciable advantage in Pressed Steel being taken over by a British rather than a foreign company.[10]

The Commission examined the assurances offered by B.M.C. and statements made by the Chairman of Pressed Steel about B.M.C.'s attitude to Pressed Steel's relations with other customers. It was concerned when a copy of an internal document, drawn up while negotiations about the merger were still under way, had been made available and was found to be at variance with the public statements about continuity of supplies to customers other than B.M.C. at times of shortage.[11] However, both B.M.C. and Pressed Steel assured the Commission that this document had been entirely superseded by the statement to the shareholders and at the Commission's invitation set out in more specific terms the undertakings given by Pressed Steel in the shareholders' letter.

In conclusion, the Commission expressed regret at the loss of Pressed Steel's independence, but felt that 'the merger does not operate and may not be expected to operate against the public interest.'[12]

THE INDUSTRY SINCE 1965

Since 1965 there have been many significant changes in the structure of the automobile industry in Great Britain. Perhaps most significant was the creation of the British Leyland Motors Corporation (B.L.M.C.) in January 1968. This was preceded by a series of mergers and takeovers by B.M.C. and Leyland Motors.

Thus, in 1966 B.M.C. absorbed the Jaguar group which by this time included Jaguar Cars, Daimler Ltd. (which manufactured cars and bus chassis), Guy Motors Ltd. and Coventry Climax Ltd. In 1967 Leyland, which already owned Standard—Triumph, purchased Rover (apparently partly to counter B.M.C.'s move into the executive car market but also to add to its range of commercial vehicles) which had previously itself purchased Alvis.

In January 1968 Leyland Motors and British Motor Holdings (the name taken after the merger between B.M.C. and Jaguar) merged. This was effectively a take-over by British Leyland owing to B.M.H.'s weak financial and market situation: in 1967 B.M.H. made a loss of £3.28 million and B.M.C.'s market share had fallen from its 'customary' 40% to 34% in 1966, and 35% in 1967.

As far as the other major car manufacturers were concerned, the major changes occurred with regard to Rootes' relationship with Chrysler. As stated earlier, in 1964 Chrysler had purchased the majority of Rootes' capital but only a minority of the equity. Rootes was by then an ailing concern — see Table 3.3.

Table 3.3 The profit record of Rootes Motors

Year to:	Pretax profits (£000's)	As % of capital employed
31.7.59	4,028	17.4
31.7.60	4,410	17.8
31.7.61	1,277	3.8
31.7.62	Loss 2,446	—
31.7.63	416	1.2

Source: Company Reports.

Despite Government-sponsored efforts to keep Rootes in British hands,[13] Chrysler purchased a majority holding in Rootes' equity in 1967, thus creating a situation where over 50% of the U.K. motor industry's unit output comes from American-controlled firms.

In the context of this case study it is striking to note that in 1966 Rootes purchased the Pressed Steel plant in Linwood from B.M.C. This involved an expenditure of about £14 million, some £7.8 million of which was borrowed from the Board of Trade. The interest of Rootes in acquiring Pressed Steel's Scottish plant, although a loss-maker, is intriguing, the more so since six months earlier the company had apparently shown no concern in the Pressed Steel–B.M.C. merger. It must be seen as the expression of the Chrysler philosophy of being a vertically-integrated concern, even though the American parent was not at this time yet in effective control of Rootes. The B.M.C. acquisition of Pressed Steel must have reinforced the new management's determination to reach this goal. The Chairman of Rootes, in his report for 1966 said:

This plant at Linwood is immediately adjacent to Rootes' own Scottish plant and possesses major bodybuilding facilities: all the body requirements of the Hillman Imp range are pressed and assembled there. The provision of major bodybuilding facilities within the Rootes group formed an essential part of Rootes' forward planning referred to in my statement of 22nd November, 1965. The purchase of the Linwood plant afforded the opportunity to pursue this policy and in the view of the Directors of Rootes the acquisition of an established plant of this kind at an acceptable price was much to be preferred to constructing similar facilities elsewhere which would have entailed not only delay but problems of training labour and staff and also much greater capital expenditure and larger initial losses. . . .[14] [He also said:] The plant now owned by Rootes Pressings was formerly one of three major factories, all producing motor car bodies and press tools, which were operated by Pressed Steel as an integrated business and it is not possible to arrive at an allocation of profit or loss properly attributable to the Linwood plant alone; it is accepted, however, that substantial losses were sustained at Linwood in recent years.[15]

This event was not altogether unexpected to the keen observer of the industry. *The Economist* at the time of the B.M.C.–Pressed Steel merger had referred to it as 'merely a prelude to some long-term reverberations.'[16] It had said, on 31 July 1965 that the Linwood plant was only working at about half of capacity and 'would conveniently be used by Rootes to make a new model – if B.M.C. is prepared to sell it a plant that will after all be peripheral to its own requirements'.[17]

The Chrysler influence at Rootes did, in fact, lead in the late 1960s to the company building its own body plant for its Coventry assembly plant. This of course meant that the new Pressed Steel–Fisher Company was faced with the problem of filling capacity formerly used to meet Rootes' orders. Although integration with B.M.C.'s other body-making interests effected economies, the company had the further problem that Leyland announced that it too intended to expand its own body plants. Following the creation of British Leyland, the new organization announced a major expansion of the Cowley assembly plant in May 1969. It had already begun a programme costing £20 million to integrate the Pressed Steel and B.M.C. car assembly plant at Cowley so as to eliminate still further long distance haulage of car body shells.

REFERENCES

1. The Monopolies Commission, *The British Motor Corporation Ltd. and the Pressed Steel Company Ltd: A Report on the Merger*, H.C.P. 46, H.M.S.O., 25 January 1966.
2. *Report and Accounts of Pressed Steel Ltd. for 1964*, cited in *The Statist*, 28 May 1965, p. 1510 .
3. Monopolies Commission Report, op. cit., p. 11.
4. 'Is Pressed Steel going cheap to B.M.C.?', *The Statist*, 30 July 1965, p. 326.

5. 'Keeping B.M.C. British', *The Statist*, 27 August 1965, p. 545.
6. 'Motors all over the place', *The Economist*, 31 July 1965, p. 458.
7. Cited in 'For better for worse', *The Statist*, 20 August 1965, p. 523. (*The Statist* ceased publication in 1967.)
8. *Monopolies Commission Report*, op. cit., p. 16.
9. ibid, p. 16.
10. ibid, p. 16.
11. ibid, p. 17.
12. ibid, p. 18.
13. This is vividly described in G. Turner, *The Leyland Papers*, Pan Books, 1973, pp. 72—6.
14. *Report and Accounts for Rootes Motors for 1966*, p. 1.
15. ibid, p. 5.
16. *The Economist*, 31 July 1965, p. 458.
17. ibid, p. 459.

QUESTIONS FOR DISCUSSION

1. What are the economic arguments usually put forward in support of vertical integration?

2. Which economic arguments were invoked by B.M.C. and Pressed Steel in support of their merger? What relevance had geographical considerations in these arguments?

3. What are the disadvantages of vertical integration?

4. (a) In 1966 Jaguar Ltd. became part of B.M.C. Suggest reasons why this happened.
   (b) Did the merger of Pressed Steel and B.M.C. make it more likely that B.M.C. would be the company who would absorb Jaguar?

5. What would have been the main barriers to either B.M.C. or Chrysler setting up their own body plants in 1965?

6. Suggest reasons why American car manufacturers are more vertically integrated than the British based companies.

7. (a) In the event of either B.M.C. or Rootes setting up their own body plants what would have been the effect on Pressed Steel and the likely consequences?

   (b) In what way would the resulting situation have differed from that described as actually occurring in 1965?

8. In 1930 Morris Motors Ltd. gave up its dominant holding in Pressed Steel so that other car manufacturers would be encouraged to purchase from Pressed Steel. Explain why in 1965 B.M.C. (now owning Morris Motors) should reverse this decision.

9. Comment on the Commission's concern for Pressed Steel's other customers following the merger.

10. What was the non-economic issue that concerned the Commission in this case?

11. How does this case illustrate the fact that mergers have long-term repercussions?

12. What impact did the Commission's Report have in this case?

4. A Restrictive Price Agreement Struck Down: Glass Containers

In common with many other industries, the glass container industry was one where competition between firms after 1945 was restricted, due to the operation of a price agreement. Government policy towards restrictive trade practices changed with the passing of the 1956 Restrictive Trade Practices Act and this case study is based on information brought to light in the Restrictive Practices Court in March 1961. Members of the British Bottle Association tried to defend their agreement and ensure its continuation so as to be an exception to the general new ban on price agreements brought about by the 1956 Act.[1]

THE INDUSTRY IN 1960

There were thirty-two manufacturers in this industry in the U.K. at this time concerned with the manufacture of empty glass containers of a wide variety of design, type, size and purpose. They included containers destined for use as milk bottles, beer and mineral-water bottles, whisky, gin and wine bottles, jam jars, medicine bottles, bottles for perfume and toilet preparations and glass containers for various types of foodstuffs and household commodities. (In the following notes the word 'bottle' will be taken to include all the variations.) There was very little exporting or importing of empty bottles.

Nineteen of the thirty-two manufacturers were members of the British Bottle Association and these nineteen produced 80% of the bottles in the U.K. United Glass Ltd. was by far the largest manufacturer and, together with Allen Glass Ltd. (a member of the Association and a subsidiary of United Glass), produced 37—38% in volume of all the members of the Association, i.e. approximately 30% of the whole U.K. production. Rockware Glass Ltd. was the next largest member of the Association and accounted for 14—15% in value of the total production of the members. The other sixteen members of the Association were smaller in varying degrees. Four of the manufacturers who were not members of the Association were quite large and the largest of these four non-members had the same output by value as Rockware Glass Ltd. The nine other non-members produced relatively few bottles in total.

Several of the thirty-two manufacturers produced other items as well. The smallest member of the Association, for example, was only involved in the manufacture of bottles to the extent of 20% of its total home sales and another member had other non glass-making activities representing 57% of its total home sales. However, most of the members were heavily involved in bottle manufacture and several to the extent of more than 90% in value of their sales. United Glass and its subsidiary had 82% by value of its total production accounted for by bottles.

As far as the industry's customers were concerned, there were a few very large customers and large numbers of small customers. One of the largest members of the Association had twenty customers, out of a total of 2,000–3,000, whose total purchases amounted to 35% of the company's production: 40% of its customers each purchased less than £200 of bottles per year. This situation was not unusual.

The customers, especially the larger ones, used very complex high speed packing and filling machines and any irregularities, even quite small ones, in bottle dimensions could result in costly delays and breakdowns. In consequence, very high quality standards were imposed on the bottle industry and up to 40% of all high-class bottles were rejected by the manufacturers and a 20% rejection rate was quite common for lower quality bottles.

THE ASSOCIATION

Between 1921 and 1935 the bottle industry suffered very badly economically with intense foreign competition and large amounts of excess capacity. In this period prices on many of its products barely covered costs. In 1936 a limited scheme of price agreement was accepted by a number of manufacturers and in 1938 the Glass Container Association was formed and minimum prices were agreed.

During the Second World War a considerable degree of government control was imposed and up to April 1953 there were government price controls. However, in 1949 the Glass Container Association was reconstituted under the name of the British Bottle Association, the object of which was no longer to minimize competition but 'to provide for fair competition on equal terms'.[2]

Nevertheless, such competition did not include price competition, for the Association had an independent chairman whose main function was to receive and study periodic returns from the individual members showing their production costs and profit margins. He then prepared average figures for the members as a whole, including the weighted average profit margin achieved in the manufacture and sale of glass bottles. On the basis of this data it was part of his function to advise the Association as to the desirability and propriety of price increases. The Association's members were not bound to accept the views of the independent chairman, but in fact they never agreed upon an increase in price against the chairman's advice.

Since 1946 the Association's prices had been subject to general increases, apart from adjustments of price in relation to particular types of bottles, on only ten occasions. The increases were:

1947:	January	7½%
	October	5%
1950:	June	2½%
1951:	January	5%
	May	5%
1952:	August	6%
1954:	March	2½% (approx.)
	July	7½%
1955:	October	5%
1957:	June	7½%

Thus between 1955 and 1960 there had been only two general increases in prices, and there had been no general increase in price, despite increasing costs, in the three and a half years after June 1957. It was established in evidence in the Court that the 1960 selling prices were 119% above the selling prices in force immediately prior to September 1939. The percentage increases of costs of labour, raw materials and services involved in the manufacture of glass bottles were substantially greater. Thus, wages in the industry had increased by 270% since September 1939, soda ash by 170%, sand by 200%, coal by 345% and fuel oil by 150%. It is thus apparent that the industry had succeeded in absorbing a considerable measure of increased costs by increased efficiency and production.

In respect of technical progress the industry claimed a creditable record. A lb. jam jar which had weighed 12½oz. in 1920 was 9½oz. in weight in 1945. Two years later the weight was cut to 7oz. and to 5¾oz. by 1960. This lighter product, by economizing raw materials and permitting greater output through faster speeds, benefited glass container firms. Easier handling and economies in transport also accrued to buyers.

THE ASSOCIATION'S AGREEMENT

The Association prescribed a minimum price for each type of bottle, and the types were extremely numerous. Two price lists were maintained by the Association. The first of these related to so-called 'standard bottles' which were bottles of types in general use, and not manufactured solely to the requirements of a particular customer. The second list related to 'special bottles' which, as a very rough estimate, constituted about 30% of the total production of glass bottles in 1960. These were bottles made specially to the requirements of a particular customer, who might or might not have had a registered design for his particular bottle. Special bottles could be supplied by one manufacturer only, or they might be supplied by more than one manufacturer. To avoid this list of special bottles becoming too large, the prices included were only those of bottles which two or more members wanted to manufacture. Prices of bottles manufactured by only one member were however registered with the Secretary.

In most cases there were provisions for quantity discounts. Thus there was a lower price for beer bottles when the order was for 500 gross and over than when the order was for less than 500 gross. In some cases collective rebates were available, i.e. a lower price for quantity purchases was available to the purchaser if his total orders during a twelve-month period exceeded a stated quantity, even though his orders from individual members were below that quantity.

Although the prices were minimum prices, members of the Association seldom quoted above the minimum prices. The manufacturers who were not members of the Association generally followed the Association's prices, although they were not under any agreement to do so.

Certain 'special arrangements' existed between certain customers and suppliers but these arose from historical circumstances. For example, on taking over the bottle production of the subsidiaries of Distillers Co. Ltd., United Glass made special arrangements with Distillers whereby the minimum prices to be fixed by the Association should not be applicable to the sale of glass bottles by United Glass Ltd. to Distillers Co. Ltd. Four other members of the Association also had special arrangements with particular purchasers of glass bottles. These special arrangements applied to something like 15% in value of the total sales of glass bottles by Association members.

The prices agreed by the Association were not directly based on any precise costings of individual types of bottles by all or any of the members. Many of the members had their own standard costing system; but, particularly in view of the vast number of types of bottles, the exceptional production problems, and the variability of the costs from time to time, even of an individual member in relation to the same type of bottle, the Association regarded it as impracticable to base prices of individual types of bottle on any standard costs. The most that could be done towards smoothing out anomalies between the prices of different types of bottles was that those manufacturers who were particularly concerned and experienced with particular 'lines' should form sub-committees or 'groups' to keep that matter under review, and to make recommendations from time to time in order to try to bring prices of different 'lines' into proper relation with one another. As regards profit levels, it had for a considerable time been the aim of the Association to fix minimum prices so as to produce a weighted average profit margin, on turnover, of about 10%.

In fact, the level of 10% was only achieved in six years between 1939 and 1960. In 1939, which was an exceptionally good year, the level was 14.2%. In the years prior to the hearing the figures were:

1954	8.9%
1955	11.4%
1956	9.6%
1957	6.9%
1958	7.5%
1959	6.9%
1960 (to 30.6.60)	8.2%

If one takes the twenty-one years from 1939 to 1959, the weighted average was 9%, though in the late 1950s the average was depressed by the serious but non-recurrent production problems of the largest member.

PRODUCTION PROBLEMS

The bottle manufacturing industry was in 1960, and still is, a 'continuous process' industry, the constituent materials of the glass being molten together at high temperatures in a furnace. Economic production can only be attained when the furnace operates, as nearly as possible, for twenty-four hours in each day and for seven days in each week. Even during holiday periods, such as Christmas, great care needs to be taken to keep to a minimum the cooling off or closing down of the furnace, and if a furnace were to be shut down because of lack of orders, the consequential loss could be serious. Moreover, the up-to-date plant with which many of the members were equipped in 1960 had a very high breakdown point.

Demand for bottles fluctuates throughout the year and the problem of matching capacity to demand was overcome, and still is, by building up stocks in periods of low demand. This enabled the industry to make very full use of its capacity, as is indicated by the following figures which show that the percentage of employment of bottle-making capacity was 99.32% in 1956, 96.82% in 1957, and 94.48% in 1959. The cost of providing the necessary warehouse space for stocks is considerable, especially because of the low value to volume ratio. For example, in the case of the half-pint beer bottles, one cubic foot of space was, in 1960, occupied by a product with a value of only 25p. An additional reason for large stockholdings was that customers had traditionally relied on manufacturers to make deliveries at short notice.

The number of bottles manufactured had risen very rapidly, going from 10,393,000 in 1939 to 22,599,000 in 1959. In 1960 the industry was operating at effectively full capacity and in October 1960 it had stocks of 3,666,000 bottles.

THE ASSOCIATION'S CASE

The Association argued its case under paragraph (b) of Section 21(1) of the Restrictive Trade Practices Act 1956. This section read:

For the purposes of any proceedings before the court ... a restriction accepted in pursuance of any agreement shall be deemed to be contrary to the public interest unless the court is satisfied of any one or more of the following circumstances, that is to say: ... (b) that the removal of the restriction would deny to the public as purchasers, consumers, or users of any goods other specific and substantial benefits or advantages enjoyed or likely to be enjoyed by them as such ...

At the beginning of the hearing the Association stated that the benefits and advantages which the original purchasers of bottles (i.e. unfilled bottles) gained from the Association's Agreement were:

(a) very low prices for glass bottles;
(b) reasonable stability of the prices of glass bottles; and
(c) maintenance and improvement of the quality of glass bottles.

It was further argued that removal of the price restrictions would result in these benefits and advantages being lost in the following way:

(a) at all times the price of bottles would fluctuate sharply;
(b) at times of normal or high demand for bottles the prices of them would be higher than the very low prices maintained by the existing price agreement; whereas
(c) at times of low demand there would be competition of a kind which would result in deterioration in the quality of bottles.

In addition, it was argued that the removal of price restrictions would lead to competition of a kind which would force many members of the Association to leave the industry. If this happened it was predicted that one or more of the members would acquire a monopoly of producing and supplying bottles and in consequence the price of bottles would rise substantially.

On the fifth day of the hearing, Counsel for the Association asked for, and gained, permission to amend the Association's statements. By the eighth day of the hearing the situation was that the Association no longer asserted that at times of high or normal demand prices would be higher without the restriction.

It was necessary for the Association to amend its argument because the witnesses called by the Association had not supported the original arguments put forward by the Association's Counsel. Their evidence in fact indicated that without the price agreement, even in normal demand conditions, prices would fall.

THE COURT'S RULING

The Court ruled that the Association had failed to prove its case and therefore the agreement was struck down. This ruling was based primarily upon an assessment of the balance between the supply and demand of bottles in the forseeable future. The witnesses for the Association did not consider that any other type of container would take the place of glass bottles to such an extent as to affect their forecast of substantial increases in the demand for bottles. The Court's opinion, on the basis of this evidence, was that 'it would require some very special circumstances to bring about a change whereby productive capacity was seriously in excess of demand'.[3]

A particular piece of evidence which obviously impressed the Court was the fact that in 1960, when the hearing was already imminent, a member company of the Association raised £410,000 for new capital to improve their works. In the prospectus used to raise these funds the company predicted an increase in profits in 1961 of £80,000 attributable to these improvements, and in addition the board of the company, when discussing the effect of the possible termination of the agreement, had not envisaged a price war arising.

As well as the above benefits and advantages which the Association argued would be lost to customers, the Court noted that the Association considered that, if the price restriction were abrogated, the following would happen:

(a) the close co-operation of members in research, design, and similar matters would disappear;
(b) members of the Association would no longer produce for stock at times of seasonal low demand;
(c) larger buyers would obtain lower prices and consequently other buyers would pay higher prices; and
(d) purchasers of bottles would no longer obtain prompt delivery at short notice.

However, the Court found little evidence to support these claims without first accepting the possibility of a price war arising. As it had firmly rejected the possibility of such a situation arising, it rejected these propositions.

On profits, the Court felt that these were not unreasonable but was concerned about the use of a weighted average profit figure. It felt that this could shield a wide range of levels of efficiency amongst manufacturers permitting some to earn very high profits on certain ranges. In some cases, though, it recognized that the prices yielded a very low profit margin.

In passing, the Court also noted that in spite of its claim to provide fair competition on equal terms, one purchaser had met a concerted refusal by members of the Association to supply a 'beer' bottle for use as a 'vinegar' bottle. The Court was also hostile to the clause in the Association's agreement which claimed non-liability for defective bottles.

THE INDUSTRY AFTER 1961

Since the whole rationale of the British Bottle Association had gone, members decided to terminate its existence. However, a price information arrangement was set up in its place. The industry thus exemplified the widespread substitution of information agreements for price agreements as a result of the 1956 Act. However, in this case the Glass Container Information Bureau was less successful than many, as although firms circulated details of prices and discounts they in fact tended to sell below these reported levels. Thus it was fairly soon abandoned.

Firms in the industry had not increased prices prior to the Court hearing. But despite rising costs not one firm was in the new environment at first prepared to announce a change for fear of not being followed. However, four months after the Court's Judgement, United Glass, the largest firm in the industry, assumed the role of a price leader by announcing a general increase in prices of glass bottles of 5%. Other firms followed soon afterwards. None the less, competitive pressures broke out since prices of milk bottles and jam jars began to fall (see Figure 4.1). In the case of milk bottles, this is shown in the graph of prices actually paid by a national diary firm. This was partly due to uncertainties by firms in learning again, for the first time in

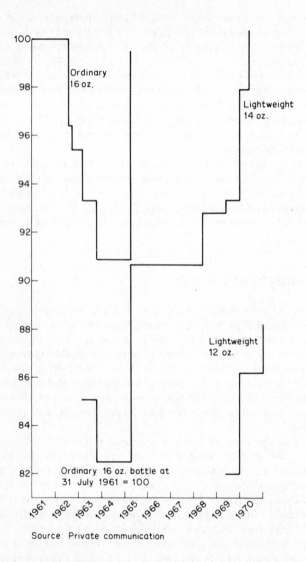

Source: Private communication

Fig. 4.1. One pint milk bottles: prices actually paid by one national dairy firm

many years, how to price — a situation which buyers would use to advantage. In addition there was the *deliberate* lowering of prices by some firms in efforts to broaden the basis of their bottle trade. For example, National Glass Works of York, which specialized in pharmaceutical bottles, decided that the most obvious way of boosting bottle sales to the food industry was to reduce prices.

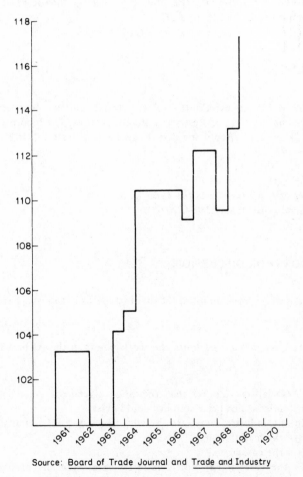

Source: Board of Trade Journal and Trade and Industry

Fig. 4.2. Wholesale price index for glass containers

Price competition was most vigorous between 1962—4, as the graph of wholesale prices shows (Figure 4.2). The Chairman of Rockware Glass declared in 1963 that prices were 'uneconomic' due to 'the problem of price cutting'.[4] His counterpart at United Glass declared that his company had refused 'to accept orders at senseless prices'.[5] The firm of Jackson Glass saw its profits slide from over £250,000 to less than £8,000 between 1962 and 1963 — a fall in the return on capital employed from 14% to 1.5%.

REFERENCES

1. Restrictive Practices Court, *In re British Bottle Association's Agreement,* Reports of Restrictive Practices Cases, The Incorporated Council of Law Reporting for England and Wales, L.R.2. R.P. p. 345—92.
2. ibid., p. 350.
3. ibid., p. 381.
4. *Report of Rockware Glass for 1963,* p. 5.
5. *The Economist,* 9 May 1964, p. 658.

QUESTIONS FOR DISCUSSION

1. What were, in your opinion, the main strengths in the Association's case?

2. What were, in your opinion, the weak points in the Association's case?

3. The Association claimed that the price agreement created conditions under which price stability could exist.
   (a) In any industry, what are the advantages of price stability to:
       (i) the manufacturers?
       (ii) the customers?
   (b) In the case of the Bottle Industry, are there any particular factors which might strengthen these general points?

4. In the event of the price agreement being terminated, the Association considered that its members would come under pressure from large customers to offer them lower prices.
   (a) If you were a large customer, why would you expect to be offered lower prices?
   (b) If you were a bottle manufacturer, what factors would affect your decision as to whether or not to offer large customers lower prices?

5. If a large customer demands prices which are so low that the supplier is unable to make a profit at that price:
   (a) how can the supplier remain profitable if he supplies the customer?
   (b) if the supplier seeks to maintain his profitability by raising his prices to small customers, what effect will this have on the competitiveness of these customers?

6. Price theory suggests that if an industry has excess capacity, then lower prices will result. Such decreases in price will result in lower profits and eventually some firms will leave the industry thus removing the excess capacity.
   Why should the Association create an agreement which amongst other things made this sequence of events less likely in the event of over-capacity occurring in the industry?

7. Why do Figures 4.1 and 4.2 (pages 46 and 47) show a somewhat varied picture of price movements after 1961?

8. What impact would a poor summer and the imposition of purchase tax on alcoholic and soft drinks have on the glass bottle industry?

9. What impact would you think the keener competitive environment in the glass bottle industry after 1961 had on glass bottle firms?

10. What competitive influences from outside the glass bottle industry affect companies within it?

11. Comment on the Court's prediction of the demand for glass containers in the light of the following data.

Table 4.1 Glass Container Output — 1960—71

	Million Units	£m
1960	4469	n/a
1961	4556	n/a
1962	4474	n/a
1963	4564	n/a
1964	4854	53.7
1965	5029	58.4
1966	5170	61.2
1967	5199	61.4
1968	5652	67.7
1969	5865	74.6
1970	6243	85.6
1971	6390	102.1

Source: Glass Manufacturers' Federation.

12. How does the glass bottle industry illustrate the problem of externalities?

13. What impact had the Restrictive Practices Court on the industry?

CASE STUDY
5. Resale Price Maintenance Abandoned: Domestic Electrical Appliances

'Seldom can a government have felt so sure of our profession's support for any drastic intervention in industrial affairs as the British Government could when it proposed to ban this restrictive practice.' P. W. S. Andrews, *On Competition in Economic Theory*, (Macmillan, 1964), p. 127.

INTRODUCTION

Resale price maintenance (r.p.m.) is basically the practice whereby the manufacturer of a product dictates to distributors the price at which his goods shall be resold to final consumers. Where the practice is applied, therefore, the element of price competition at retail is eliminated.

As far as economic theory alone is concerned, the argument *against* r.p.m. has centred around the elimination of direct price competition at retail, and the consequent 'excessive' resort to service competition by distributors and pulling of unnecessary resources of labour into the distributive trades.[1] The case *in favour* of r.p.m. rests upon a wider diversity of grounds. In addition to the suggestion that some consumers themselves favour r.p.m.,[2] it is contended that the distributive-margin-protecting function of r.p.m. may, by preserving the number of retail outlets, increase manufacturers' sales and at the same time give a further service of product availability to consumers.[3] Additionally, such distributor 'protection' is held to encourage the provision of necessary services by retailers; and the prevention of direct retail price competition is held to prevent the undesirable growth of retailing monopolies. Manufacturers and distributors alike are held to suffer from the loss-leader tactics which may be pursued by some retailers under non-r.p.m. conditions. These involve selling goods at 'below-cost',

51

and this is held not only to be an 'unfair' type of retail competition, but also to upset manufacturers' production schedules and in some cases eventually to reduce permanently the demand for products so treated.

Government consideration of r.p.m. in this country did not materialize until some forty years after the practice had become established in the areas of household medicines, books, groceries, tobacco and confectionery over the last decades of the nineteenth century.[4] The earliest government consideration of the practice was, however, purely *ad hoc*, and it was not until 1949 that the first thorough study of r.p.m. − the Lloyd Jacob Report − was published. It was this document which set the pattern of distinguishing between individual and collective r.p.m. schemes − generally condemning the latter but not the former. This dichotomy in the attitude of the government towards r.p.m. was built into Part II of the 1956 Restrictive Trade Practices Act. Under this legislation the law on *individual* r.p.m. was strengthened in favour of the manufacturer, while *collective adoption* of r.p.m. became a registrable restrictive trading agreement, and *collective r.p.m. enforcement* was banned outright. Experience over the next seven or eight years, however, was to show that the prohibition of collective enforcement of r.p.m. was insufficient to curb the impact of the practice; and in the estimation of some, the incidence of r.p.m. had not significantly declined from J. F. Pickering's estimate of one-third of total consumer expenditure in 1956.[5] The result of this dissatisfaction was the Resale Prices Act of 1964 which, in the manner of the 1956 Restrictive Trade Practices Act, in respect of horizontal trading agreements, made *individual* r.p.m. illegal subject to exemption during a period of registration pending a hearing before the Restrictive Practices Court. The grounds or 'gateways' for exemption were that in the absence of r.p.m.:

1. the quality or variety or goods would be substantially reduced, or
2. the number of retail distributors would be substantially reduced, or
3. retail prices would generally and in the long term increase, or
4. goods would be sold under dangerous conditions, or
5. necessary services would no longer be provided.

Experience with this Act has been entirely encouraging so far as the ending of r.p.m. is concerned. Out of 502 classes of goods for which exemption was initially claimed, 250 had been dropped by April 1967; and of the 157 references arising from the original 502 claims, 147 had been dropped by the manufacturers themselves by June 1968 and two cases had been unsuccessfully defended in the Court.[6] The present situation is that r.p.m. is now operated only in those two instances where the Court has specifically allowed it to continue, books and medicaments; that in no other case does r.p.m. operate; and that the Monopolies Commission has itself looked into and basically cast doubt upon other practices which may be substitutes for r.p.m., or which may be held to impede those changes which the ending of r.p.m. was designed to bring about.[7]

THE CASE OF DOMESTIC ELECTRICAL APPLIANCES

The domestic electrical appliances industry in this country was established by the large general electrical manufacturers which grew up in the last decades of the nineteenth century and the early years of the present one. The industry developed both specialist and non-specialist firms. Some firms like A.E.I.[8] by 1960 made a wide range of electrical equipment other than domestic appliances. Others, such as Servis, made just a few products that fall within the definition of this industry. In this study, domestic appliances are defined as including such items as electric cookers, refrigerators, hair dryers, kettles, toasters, vacuum cleaners and washing machines: radio and television sets are excluded.

THE ENDING OF RESALE PRICE MAINTENANCE

Price maintenance really started to become an issue in the field of appliances with the ending of the 1959–60 sales boom. In fact, although the 1950's have been described for the electrical engineering industry as a whole as 'a sellers' market of unparalleled proportions',[9] for domestic appliances Corley considers 'The year 1955 marks a dividing line in the post-war history of the appliances industry. The earlier sellers' market had disappeared and there were signs of increasing consumer resistance.'[10] The boom conditions in this field were encouraged by successive reductions in Purchase Tax in the mid-1950s, and the abolition of hire purchase controls on appliances from October 1958. We shall find in the following pages that the state of demand for appliances was a crucial factor in the ending of r.p.m.

The state of thinking on r.p.m. in the appliance market may be gathered from the following comment of the *Electrical Times* at the beginning of 1960:

> With the Restricted [*sic*!] Practices Court working effectively to destroy orderly trading, economists and politicians are currently canvassing the chances of the Government taking steps to remove the last effective remaining hold by manufacturers on retailing activities, the right to fix resale prices, written into the RTP Act. One argument in favour of this action is that it would introduce more competition in retailing and distribution, with the inference that this would mean lower prices through better efficiency at the cost of some concerns going out of business. However, those who advance this claim too easily assume that all retail goods need as little retail attention as a packet of detergent. In fact, the standard of selling and the standard of after-sales service would both be likely to fall in the cut-throat competition between retailers to give a shade lower marked price on the product. This would be a particularly unwelcome possibility for the electrical industry, where technical service is so important . . . now is the time for the industry to make sure that the advantages flowing from the practice are as widely known as the alleged disadvantages.[11]

Appliance distributors generally saw 'the right of enforcement of resale prices by individual manufacturers as one of the few defences remaining against the worst extremes of price competition',[12] while the National Electrical Contractors' Trading Association considered that the small price reductions which could possibly result in the appliance trade from the abolition of r.p.m. would in no way compensate for the disruption to the trade which would follow.[13]

Just how enthusiastic the manufacturers were in their support for r.p.m. is difficult to know. Jones and Marriott have made an interesting comment in claiming that 'Hotpoint was the only domestic appliance company in the late 'fifties which was not committed to the defence of retail price maintenance'.[14] This would lead one to suppose that all of the other major appliance manufacturers fully supported r.p.m. Certainly, when the 1959–60 appliance boom was just past its peak, it would appear that manufacturers were determined to hold retail prices at maintained levels. In the middle of 1961 the managing director of G.E.C. (Domestic Equipment) Ltd. strongly warned intending price cutters that 'Resale price maintenance is one of the big planks in my platform, and the company will not hesitate to apply for an injunction if any of our appliances are sold below the fixed resale price'.[15] John Bloom's experience at this time was that 'In the home appliances field, most manufacturers were still very severe on anyone trying to sell at a cut price'.[16]

In fact John Bloom played an important role in convincing appliance producers of the unreality of a policy of r.p.m. from the early 1960s onwards. Bloom not only undersold the traditional appliance manufacturers with his Dutch washing machines marketed in this country by Rolls Razor from 1960. He also sold these manufacturers' own appliances at reduced prices from his chain of discount stores which opened in 1962. By 1963 Bloom's company ranked sixth in terms of U.K. home sales; and although Rolls Razor went into liquidation the following year, Bloom had shown price-conscious consumer durable purchasers how much could be taken off the retail prices of most appliances. In the words of *The Economist* it was 'a revolution of which the effects cannot easily be undone'.[17]

One of the most significant factors leading up to the final abandonment of r.p.m. was the poor level of demand for appliances from 1960 onwards. Corley has analysed the true situation (see Table 5.2) and Pickering has gone so far as to claim that 'by 1959 manufacturers of consumer durable goods were beginning to feel the effects of the heavy investment boom of the mid-1950s followed by a falling off in consumer expenditure. This meant that excessive stocks were being carried and manufacturers were powerless to control extensive price cutting in what was virtually a grand clearance sale'.[18]

Table 5.2 Home market for domestic refrigerators (in 000's)

	Home deliveries	Imports	Stocks	Retail sales
1959	832	125	–	957
1960	913	182	500	595

Source: T. A. B. Corley, *op. cit.*, p. 54.

In this context is is not surprising that increased discount selling of appliances should have occurred, involving Tesco, Frazeley Enterprises of Birmingham, Supa-Save, and Grandways. On the question of discounts available to general purchasers, *Which?* commented early in 1961 that 'if you pay the list price for a refrigerator, you may be paying £25 more than you need',[19] while discounts available to members of professional and trade associations were even greater.

An indication of the general size of discount available may be gained from the following data:

Table 5.3 Examples of discount store price reductions, 1961

Appliance	Grandways saving		Supa-Save Saving	
	£ p	%	£ p	%
Hotpoint Iced Diamond refrigerator	7.05	11		
Hotpoint X37 refrigerator	3.00	6		
Hoover vacuum cleaner 652	3.81	10		
Hoover washing machine	6.92	15		
Morphy-Richards steam iron	1.07½	27	46½	12
Morphy-Richards hair drier	61	17	41	11
Morphy-Richards food mixer			85	13

Source: *Which?*, September 1961, p. 236.

In the light of these circumstances it is not surprising that one manufacturer should take the lead in abolishing a practice which was not only being imperfectly implemented at most, but which at current price levels was clearly unrealistic.

Hoover in fact took the first step by abandoning unilaterally its policy of r.p.m. from 1 July 1965. The company explained its change of policy:

Price cutting in a disguised form by means of premium offers and generous trade-in terms, has become widespread ... Direct price cutting by cash discounts is growing, and side by side with this there are offers from some professional associations and trade unions for special discounts for their members ... Meanwhile, with the uncertainty of the outcome, the avoidance of price maintenance grows, to the disadvantage of those who are trying to adhere to agreements. Hoover has therefore decided to end this uncertainty as far as their own products are concerned.[20]

The company would appear to have had little cause subsequently to reverse its views, and the present managing director was later to comment that the result of Hoover's move was that 'prices have found a level that dealers can sell at and consumers want to pay'.[21]

While one can give some emphasis to the state of demand for appliances, and also to the ingenious price-cutting schemes possible in a market where trade-in allowances and free gifts were common, two other factors were crucial: the general growth of appliance discount stores, and the passing of the 1964 Resale Prices Act intended to bring to an end individual r.p.m. It appeared at one time that the existence of r.p.m. itself would prevent the growth of those very outlets which in other fields had contributed to the ending of the practice. This, however, is seriously to underestimate the influence of those discount outlets which were cutting prices, which opened up a new area of price awareness for consumers, where bargains were high-lighted in the popular press and in consumer publications, and which finally impressed upon manufacturers the growing unreality of their 'maintained' prices. Additionally one cannot ignore the impact of the 1964 Act. Appliance manufacturers were free to continue with r.p.m. so long as their products were registered for exemption under the Act. But Hoover admitted that:

The uncertainty of obtaining a favourable decision from the application put forward by the British Electrical and Allied Manufacturers' Association on behalf of its members, and the long time span which must elapse before the case could be adjudicated, were major factors in framing our policy. . . .[22]

Even in January 1964 the *Electrical Times* was voicing general feeling within the industry when it wrote:

The practice of RPM has been much modified in recent years, as collective price-fixing has been outlawed, but the vulnerability to cut-price tactics that domestic electrical equipment trading has suffered in other countries has so far been avoided. Now RPM has followed fair trading codes effectively into history, although the detailed plot of the murder is still to come partly in a RPM Bill expected in some weeks' time, and in a subsequent White Paper. The result is likely to be an initial holiday for shoppers with attractive price reductions but subsequently the disorderly trading and minimum-service retail outlets that have been found elsewhere when RPM has been abolished.[23]

The result of this situation was that although there was no rush of manufacturers immediately to follow Hoover in July 1965, and indeed although injunction activity on the part of other manufacturers proceeded as before, the call for continued r.p.m. in the industry looked weak with a major producer having abandoned the policy. B.E.A.M.A. in fact submitted a Statement of Case to the Registrar in May 1966; but following a partial abandonment of r.p.m. by Electrolux in September of that year, a lack of finance with which to fight the case, and a growing pessimism as to its likely outcome, B.E.A.M.A. withdrew its joint defence. The remaining individual appliance manufacturers declining to submit an alternative defence, a Court Order banning individual r.p.m. in this field came into force very early in 1967.

REFERENCES

1. The economic arguments for and against r.p.m. are brought together respectively in P. W. S. Andrews and F. A Friday, *Fair Trade*, Macmillan, 1960; and B. S. Yamey, *Resale Price Maintenance and Shoppers' Choice*, I.E.A., 1960.
2. On this see L. Sonkodi, 'Do Housewives Prefer Fixed Prices?', *Cartel*, July 1961, pp. 74—7.
3. For a theoretical analysis of this proposition see J. R. Gould and L. E. Preston, 'Resale Price Maintenance and Retail Outlets', *Economica*, August 1965, vol. xxxii, pp. 302—12.
4. Some details of the origin of the practice are given in B. S. Yamey, 'The Origins of Resale Price Maintenance: A Study of Three Branches of Retail Trade', *Economic Journal*, September 1952, vol. lxii, pp. 522—45. An account of government action on the practice is given in W. S. Howe, 'The Ending of Resale Price Maintenance: Implementation of Government Policy', *Economics*, Summer 1973, vol. x., pp. 5—16.
5. See J. F. Pickering, *Resale Price Maintenance in Practice*, Allen and Unwin, 1966, pp. 48—9.

6. See M. R. Dunn, 'Resale Price Maintenance: Restrictionism Defeated', *Journal of the Institute of Bankers*, December 1968, vol. lxxix., pp. 501—11.
7. See Monopolies Commission, *Recommended Resale Prices*, H.M.S.O., 1969, (H.C.P. 100); and *Refusal to Supply*, H.M.S.O., 1970, (Cmnd. 4372). Under the 1973 Fair Trading Act (Sec. 95) agreements on *recommended* resale prices now have to be registered with the Director General of Fair Trading.
8. See G. Walker, 'The Development and Organisation of Associated Electrical Industries Ltd.' in R. S. Edwards and H. Townsend, (eds.), *Business Enterprise*, Macmillan, 1965, p. 312.
9. G. Turner, *Business in Britain*, Eyre and Spottiswoode, 1969, p. 64.
10. T. A B. Corley, *Domestic Electrical Appliances*, Cape, 1966, p. 49.
11. *Electrical Times*, 14 January 1960, pp. 39—40.
12. *Electrical Times*, 28 July 1960, p. 119.
13. *Electrical Review*, 24 January 1964, p. 119.
14. R. Jones and O. Marriott, *Anatomy of a Merger: A History of G.E.C., A.E.I. and English Electric*, Cape, 1970, p. 240.
15. *Electrical Times*, 1 June 1961, p. 886.
16. J. Bloom, *It's No Sin to Make a Profit*, W. H Allen, 1970, p. 85.
17. *The Economist*, 26 July 1964, p. 399.
18. J. F. Pickering, 'The Enforcement of Resale Price Maintenance, 1956—1964', *Public Law*, Autumn 1965, p. 233.
19. *Which?*, May 1961, p. 120.
20. Hoover press release quoted in *Electrical Review*, 2 July 1965, p. 8.
21. *Management Today*, March 1967, p. 44.
22. Hoover Ltd., *Annual Report*, 1965, p. 4.
23. *Electrical Times*, 23 January 1964, p. 117.

QUESTIONS FOR DISCUSSION

1. What reasons might you expect manufacturers to give to support a system of individual r.p.m. in respect of domestic appliances in, say, 1955?

2. What reasons might you expect retailers to give to support a system of individual r.p.m. in respect of domestic appliances in, say, 1955?

3. Comment critically on your answers to the two previous questions.

4. How can r.p.m. be circumvented by retailers while still charging manufacturers' maintained prices?

5. Comment on the role of those retailers who cut prices of appliances in the early 1960s.

6. Could any particular advantage be expected to accrue to Hoover following its initiative in unilaterally abandoning r.p.m.?

7. What were the causes on the supply side bringing r.p.m. to an end in this industry?

8. Why was demand a factor in the demise of r.p.m. in this industry?

9. What would you expect the effect upon the profitability of appliance manufacture to be as a result of the ending of r.p.m.?

10. What impact had the 1964 Resale Prices Act on this industry?

CASE STUDY
6. Conglomerate mergers*: three case studies

The conglomerate company, let alone the conglomerate merger, or merger between two conglomerate companies, is a phenomenon towards which traditional economics and the man in the street may be said to share a common attitude; they cannot fully absorb it into their existing framework of knowledge.[1] In spite of this, and as Mr. Jim Slater (to most people the U.K. incarnation of the conglomerate company) has pointed out,[2] it has to be recognized that most of the largest companies in this country are in fact conglomerates. I.C.I., G.K.N., G.E.C.—English Electric, E.M.I., Reed International, Tube Investments, as well as the companies at which we shall look in some detail below (Unilever, Allied Breweries, Rank Organisation, De La Rue, British Match and Wilkinson Sword) are all to a greater or lesser extent conglomerate firms.

We may define a conglomerate company rather negatively by saying that it is one whose varying product interests cannot be seen as being linked to each other in terms of either a horizontal or vertical market relationship. Thus the American conglomerate Ling—Temco—Vought was typified by its diversified holdings in sports equipment, pharmaceuticals and food-groceries: disparate interests humorously rationalized on the New York Stock Exchange as golf balls, goof balls and meat balls! More rigorously we can distinguish between four different types of conglomerate companies.[3] Firstly, there are the *Giant Conglomerates* – those very large firms such as Unilever which have consciously grown through wide diversification both horizontally and vertically, and also into seemingly unrelated fields. Secondly, there are firms such as the Rank Organisation which can be called *Large*

---

*This term is capable of a number of definitions varying from a merger between two specialist companies whose respective activities are unrelated, to a merger between two conglomerate companies. In practice most discussion centres around the latter category of mergers, or takeovers of specialist producers by conglomerate firms.

Diversifiers, that have grown through branching out in a significant way into a limited number of fairly diverse fields. Thirdly, there are the *Industrial Holding Companies* such as Thomas Tilling and Norcros which have often a very large number of small holdings in a wide variety of unrelated markets: Thomas Tilling, for example, in book publishing (Heinemann), motor car distribution (Volkswagen Distribution Agency) and women's stocking (Pretty Polly). Finally, there are the *Classic Conglomerates* — companies whose only interest in their diversified industrial holdings appears to lie in the financial rationale and opportunities for industrial reshuffling involved: in the U.K. this class of organization has been typified for most by Slater Walker Securities.[4]

The conglomerate firm first became established in the United States where, however, there is now a growing business-world disenchantment and Federal dislike of these organizations, with the Justice Department, if not yet the Supreme Court, taking a stern line on conglomerate acquisitions.[5] The best means of appraising government attitudes towards conglomerates in this country is through an examination of the three Monopolies Commission Reports which have dealt with conglomerate mergers. The firms involved were Unilever and Allied Breweries,[6] the Rank Organisation and De La Rue,[7] and British Match Corporation and Wilkinson Sword.[8]

(i) UNILEVER AND ALLIED BREWERIES: PROPOSED BUT ABANDONED

Unilever has derived its diversified structure from its original constituent companies: Lever Brothers the soap manufacturers, and the Margarine Union established in this country by Jurgens and Van den Berghs in 1927. The merger of these two businesses in 1929 and the subsequent acquisition of further manufacturing and distribution facilities took the firm into the fields of soapless detergents, shampoos and toothpaste, fresh fish, quick-frozen foods, canned and dehydrated foods, instant puddings, cake mix, cheese, and brewing and wines. The Unilever organization in this country (i.e. Unilever Ltd., as opposed to Unilever N.V. in Holland) is thus organized into the following five product groups: Food, Detergents, Toilet Preparations, Chemicals, and Paper, Printing, Packaging and Plastics.[9] The Commission noted that at the time of its inquiry Unilever Ltd. ranked fifth in the league of U.K.

industrial companies, but that even considering Unilever Ltd. and N.V. as one company, and assuming a merger with Allied Breweries, the combined organization would be only the fourth largest in the U.K. industrial league:

Table 6.1 Capital Employed 1968

Unilever Ltd.	£541m
Unilever N.V.	£511m
Allied Breweries	£305m
	£1,357m.

Source: Monopolies Commission *Unilever–Allied*, para. 35.

Allied Breweries Ltd. came into existence in May 1961 to incorporate the capital of Ind Coope Ltd., Tetley Walker Ltd. and Ansells Brewery Ltd. In 1967 Allied was the second largest brewery group in the U.K. with 15.5% of home production. It was also the second largest owner of retail outlets, though the largest owner of off-licence premises. Allied had acquired wine and spirit interests through Ind Coope (Grants of St. James's and Victoria Wine Co.), and had gone further into this field in 1968 with the acquisition of Showerings, Vine Products, and Whiteway's, making itself the largest wine and spirit wholesaler and retailer and also acquiring about 20% of the cider market. Like Unilever, Allied also had a number of overseas interests, both in Africa and in Europe.

A fuller understanding of the proposed merger comes from recognition of its defensive nature. As regards brewing mergers alone, it has been more recently emphasized that: 'With demand stagnant, or at best slowly rising, markets were primarily extended by the purchase of firms, not so much for their breweries but for their tied outlets and distribution areas.'[10] It would appear in the context of this merger that Allied Breweries was aware of its lack of growth potential under existing conditions. The company chairman also stressed at the time, having given particular emphasis to overseas aspects: 'we are held up, particularly in the United States, for example, because we need the sort of expertise and managerial resources that Unilever can offer.'[11] Indeed, it appears to have seemed to some that Allied was attempting to move itself out of a low growth situation by external diversification. To this extent one journalist asked : 'Does it really make sense for

Unilever to put its money into beer and wines, which have the slow growth rates associated with traditional industries?'[12]

The financial press also seemed to feel at the time that the Unilever—Allied proposed merger had been put together in a relatively casual manner. It seems that the respective chairmen of the two companies concered were the prime movers in the affair. Thus:

> Lord Cole and Sir Derek Pritchard began talking about a link between their two companies — Unilever and Allied Breweries — last Monday night. They were in Prichard's flat, not really for that purpose, but simply meeting as old friends with some common business problems.[13]

The Unilever view of the merger put to the Commission was that it would be 'a consolidation of two companies whose activities are related functionally at either the production or marketing level, but whose products are different', and that its acquisition of Allied would be 'a natural extension of Unilever's international food business'.[14] It was held that with the existing overlap in operations, further expansion by both companies, particularly overseas, would be facilitated by a merger. It was, however, stressed by both companies that it was expected that few effects of the merger would be felt in this country, and that the main purpose of the proposed merger was the establishment of an international drinks business based in the U.K. Anticipated benefits to be achieved in this country, however, were joint research in the food and drinks field, economies in transport and distribution, market research and packaging. It was stressed that Unilever's and Allied's retail outlets would not, as a result of the merger, become closed to the products of other food and drinks producers.

The bases of the Commission's conclusions were these: it did not consider that market concentration or barriers to entry into the drinks field would be increased by the merger. This conclusion was based upon the companies' stressing of the international motivation for the merger and not that of expansion in the U.K. drinks market. Other possible public detriments, on which the Commission was satisfied that it had received adequate assurances from the firms, were those of product cross-subsidization and competitive (predatory?) under-pricing, exclusive dealing in respect of the retail outlets of the two firms, and the level of promotional advertising. The Commission also accepted that there might be an improvement in resource use in areas of technical, marketing, management and productivity services following the merger. Both the firms themselves and the Commission felt unable to comment firmly either way on the impact of the merger on the U.K. balance of payments. The Commission, therefore, saw no likely disadvantage arising from the merger and thus concluded that the merger would not operate against the public interest. It is, however, instructive to note the wording of the Commission's conclusions:

> We find that there are some indications that greater efficiency in the use of resources, especially technical and marketing resources, are likely although they do not appear to us to be at all considerable in size. There is, we feel, some risk that little of these benefits will be passed on to the public. On the other hand there is a chance that the exploitation of these efficiencies may cause other brewers to seek greater efficiency themselves and that the resulting stimulation of competition in the industry may eventually bring benefits to the public. So far as public benefits from the proposed overseas operation can be foreseen they seem to us to be small and uncertain. However, we have not found any clear indications of likely damage to the public interest.[15]

(ii) RANK AND DE LA RUE: PROPOSED BUT FORBIDDEN

In this case the Commission was examining two conglomerate companies in a takeover rather than a merger situation. In November 1968 Rank had announced its intention to bid for De La Rue. The Rank Organisation had acquired its diversified character through moving from its original interests in film production and distribution to other leisure activities and leisure hardware, and in 1956 into xerography through the establishment of Rank Xerox.

De La Rue was a considerably smaller company than Rank: 186th in order of capital employed among U.K. companies as opposed to Rank's position as 38th. De La Rue had expanded its initial expertise as high-quality printers (originally founded in 1913); and from this field — where it was strongly established as a printer of bank notes — had expanded into the plastics moulding and industrial laminates market (Formica) and subsequently into water and other domestic heating systems (Potterton).

Table 6.2 Rank Organisation Ltd. Turnover 1967–68 (%)

Rank Xerox Ltd.	41.1
Rank Organisation (other than Rank Xerox)	
Film exhibition, home and overseas	18.2
Film production and distribution	5.2
Film studios and laboratories	2.6
Manufacturing	14.5
Audio visual	4.3
Bowling, dancing and bingo	4.8
Hotels and motorports	4.4
Television rental, relay and retail	3.9
Sundries	1.0
	100.0

Source: Monopolies Commission, *Rank–De La Rue*, para. 12.

Table 6.3 De La Rue Co. Ltd. Turnover 1967–68 (%)

Formica International Ltd.*	52.3
Thomas De La Rue International Ltd.	24.8
Potterton International Ltd.	22.9
	100.0

*40% of this is owned by American Cyanamid Co.
Source: Monopolies Commission, *Rank–De La Rue*, para. 24.

Since the Rank bid was being rejected by De La Rue, the Commission was faced with two conflicting accounts of the projected outcome of the merger. Rank essentially wanted to acquire De La Rue in order to expand the non-Xerox part of its activities; and it claimed that the De La Rue management of the time had not fully exploited the possibilities of its own company. De La Rue's reply to this was that: 'Rank's total lack of experience and understanding of all aspects of this business combined with the complete dissimilarity and in some respects even incompatibility (e.g. bank-note printing and the entertainment industry) of the activities of the two groups must lead to a decrease in the efficiency of De La Rue.'[16] In particular, De La Rue claimed that its special relationship with Cyanamid (through Formica) would be disrupted and become less favourable under Rank control; and this argument was also applied in respect of De La Rue's relationships with the American firm General Electric (computer marketing), and through De La Rue Giori S.A. (bank-note printing machinery). Rank, however, further alleged a failure on De La Rue's part to develop fully its markets in decorative laminates and gas heating appliances — allegations which De La Rue found it more difficult to reject. De La Rue's real defence against takeover was founded, however, upon the security and confidential basis of much of its work — particularly in the international context. It was this loss of identity on the part of De La Rue which it was held would lead to a loss of valuable De La Rue management in the event of a Rank takeover. De La Rue thus claimed that 'management methods and personnel policies in Rank are such as to be unacceptable to a significant proportion of members of top management in the various businesses of De La Rue, and that these people would decline to accept continued employment in the acquired Company, in some cases leaving immediately.'[17]

The Commission, in appraising the situation, did not consider that there would be any adverse effects upon market concentration or barriers to entry if the merger took place. On resource use, the Commission felt that some technical assistance required by De La Rue from Cyanamid, American G.E.C. and Giori of Switzerland might not be so readily available to the company if it was owned by Rank; and it also thought that in the context of the use of marketing resources there might be a loss following any departure of top De La Rue executives consequent upon a Rank takeover. In fact, the Commission's severest reservations on the whole question of takeover were based upon its fears as to the impact of this upon De La Rue senior management. Thus:

We are satisfied that the merger would have serious adverse effects on the present, and in our view efficient, management of De La Rue in the sense that there is a near certainty that several key persons would leave and others, even if they remained, would suffer loss of morale. Because of the different character of the two businesses Rank could not from its own resources make up for loss of management personnel in De La Rue. While in due course replacements would no doubt be found, in the transition period there could be severe loss of efficiency the effects of which could persist for a long time. There is also a serious risk of loss of business, including foreign business and business opportunities, since ... in certain important fields the retention, and increase, of business depends upon the establishment and maintenance of confidence based on personal relations, and the likely loss of key personnel could mean an immediate loss.[18]

Taking account of the particular significance of De La Rue in its own markets — especially those concerned broadly with security services — the Commission felt bound to lay great stress on this factor; and, it would seem, principally for this reason, recommended that the merger of the two companies should not be allowed to take place.

(iii) B.M.C. AND WILKINSON SWORD: PROPOSED AND EFFECTED

The most recent conglomerate merger to have been dealt with by the Monopolies Commission was that involving the British Match Corporation and Wilkinson Sword. This proposed merger was approved by the Commission in October 1973. The two firms involved were international in terms of the geographical spread of their operations, but were both otherwise relatively small. In terms of capital employed, British Match (B.M.C.) was 118th in size in the U.K., while Wilkinson was 493rd. B.M.C. had a virtual monopoly of match production and sales in the U.K. and 1972—73 data were as follows:

Table 6.4 B.M.C. 1972—73

	Turnover		Profits (%)
	£m	%	
Matches	40.8	53.1	74.3
Wood chipboard	9.4	12.2	9.7
Lumber and plywood	4.6	6.0	1.2
Printing and packaging	9.1	11.9	7.6
Miscellaneous	12.9	16.8	7.2
	£76.8m	100.0%	100.0%

Source: Monopolies Commission *B.M.C. — Wilkinson*, para. 13; and British Match *Report and Accounts*, 1973.

The possible decline in the U.K. market for matches (although this accounted for less than 20% of B.M.C.'s total world match sales by volume in 1972–73) had led B.M.C. to pursue a programme of rationalization and possible diversification since the mid-1950s. The latter part of this programme committed the firm to considering U.K. acquisition in similar fields. This form of expansion had not proved uniformly successful, however, and in 1972–73 while the non-match activities accounted for 46.9% of turnover and about half of capital employed, they contributed only 25.7% of profits. In the U.K. these activities include wood chipboard, printing and packaging, pyrotechnics, steel wool and hardware products, ticket-issuing machines, and industrial fans.

At this same time Wilkinson was in a very similar position to B.M.C. Wilkinson was still heavily committed to the field of consumer products. The figures in 1972 were as follows:

Table 6.5 Wilkinson Sword 1972

	Turnover		Return on capital	Profits
	£m	%	%	%
Consumer products	18.1	71.6	31.3	74.7
Hand tools	2.4	9.4	8.1	4.1
Graviner*	4.8	19.0	22.4	21.2
	£25.3m	100.0	26.1%	100.0

*Comprises fire detection, protection and suppression equipment.
Source: Monopolies Commission *B.M.C. – Wilkinson*, para. 24; and Wilkinson Sword *Report and Accounts*, 1972.

At the end of the 1950s Wilkinson had found itself essentially a small engineering firm, and subsequent expansion into international marketing-oriented fields had placed considerable financial and managerial strains upon the company. These problems had made it difficult for the firm to exploit fully its technological advances in the wet shave market such as the polytetrafluorethylene (P.T.F.E.) coated blade in 1961 and the Bonded Shaving System in 1970. As also in the case of B.M.C., Wilkinson's experience in its newer markets was not altogether a happy one as may be seen from the above data.

There was felt to be scope for rationalization of some of the respective interests of B.M.C. and Wilkinson: for example Wilkinson's interests in garden tools and kitchen cutlery, and B.M.C.'s steel wool, soap-filled pads, scourers and kitchen cutlery and gadgets. Also Wilkinson's fire equipment and B.M.C.'s pyrotechnic products such as distress signal flares, signal buoys and tear gas grenades.

These possible gains were, however, regarded as subsidiary to the prospective benefits to both companies from the merger due to increased 'substance'. It was felt that a large international company incorporating a widely known and respected brand name could make a much greater impression in overseas markets and take much greater risks in developing new products. Thus, in the words of the Commission:

We were told that 'substance' included knowledge in depth of the cultural, political, financial and commercial aspects of a particular country; manufacturing experience (not necessarily of the product to be promoted); experience of local participation in management and in labour relations; time spent in acquiring such knowledge and experience; and reputation derived from commercial success. 'Substance' could not, it was thought, be built up by operations conducted solely through agents without a nucleus or network of directly employed personnel. The employment of agents in support of directly employed personnel, for marketing and distribution was not, however, precluded and might indeed be preferable to any attempt to inject a new product into marketing and distribution procedures designed for a different purpose. The benefits which Wilkinson could expect to receive from B.M.C. 'substance' in, for example, ·Brazil (where B.M.C. has been long and is strongly established but Wilkinson has no experience) and South Africa (where B.M.C. has a substantial presence but Wilkinson has a small market share and no 'substance') were therefore fundamental; *nor were such benefits dependent upon sharing marketing systems or distribution channels* although the possibility of such sharing would be explored. *The companies were in agreement that, especially in marginal cases, the presence of enough 'substance' to bear the weight of expansion or diversification was easier to recognise than to define* [author's italics].[19]

Economies were also expected to be achieved in the pooling of research and development facilites and in centralized management.

The Commission's feeling was that since the products of the two firms were complementary, the merger would not result in concentration in individual markets. The emergence of barriers to entry or predatory pricing were also discounted. Continuing its assessment the Commission pertinently commented:

> We consider that the principal public interest issue in this inquiry is whether the merger might turn out to be less successful than both B.M.C. and Wilkinson expect and result in the total resources of the companies being less efficiently used than they would be if the companies remained separate entities. Both companies argued, and indeed it was the core of their case, that the opposite would happen, and that the merger would be beneficial by enabling better use to be made of the joint resources.[20]

But in this connection the Commission found it difficult to foresee the outcome of the merger.

> We had no doubt that if the expectations of the companies were realised, the proposed merger would bring substantial benefits and more efficient use would be made of the combined resources. We considered, however, that it was not self-evident that the expectations would be realised or that we could ignore the possibility that, if the expectations were not realised, consequences damaging both to the merged company and to the public interest might result. In this connection we were concerned about the differences in the fields of activities of the two companies, and about their apparently different management styles, and the fact that, as B.M.C. itself told us, the non-match activities into which it had already diversified 'had, taken as a whole, achieved unsatisfactory profits, exhibited only variable growth potential and posed difficulties of satisfactory management'.[21]

The Commission felt in the end, however, that following a thorough external reappraisal of the company's organization and policies, B.M.C. could improve resource use by its acquisition of Wilkinson. Thus:

> So regarded, the possibility that the joint resources would be less efficiently utilised as a result of the proposed merger appears less likely. Nevertheless, the success of the merger could not be guaranteed, and any benefits from it would have to be won.[22]

Even in the light of the above points, the manner of the Commission's final conclusions should be noted.

> In general, therefore, our view of the benefits claimed for the merger is that while it cannot be regarded as a panacea for all of B.M.C.'s admitted ills or as automatically creating 'a coherent enterprise (operating in the field of consumer goods) capable of achieving substantial growth internationally', there is nevertheless the probability of its leading to at least a reasonable measure of success in this direction.
>
> Even if the merger resulted in no benefits, or no substantial benefits, of the kind claimed for it, it does not follow that it would necessarily be against the public interest. We therefore still need to consider whether, if the merger were not successful, it could be positively damaging in its effects on the use of resources.
>
> The activities of the merged company as a whole could be damaged if friction or incompatibilities were to develop within the merged management. But, as we have indicated, we do not think such a development is likely in this case.[23]

THE COMMISSION'S VERDICTS

The Commission thus did not oppose either the proposed Unilever–Allied Breweries or the British Match Corporation–Wilkinson Sword mergers but was against the Rank–De la Rue merger. In fact the first of these planned amalgamations did not take place due to changes in the relative share prices of the two companies during the period of the Commission's investigation. The very process of the Commission studying the planned merger of Unilever and Allied Breweries thus had a real impact on the turn of events in this case. The then Labour Government accepted the Commission's verdict of opposing the Rank–De La Rue merger, and indeed felt obliged to lay an Order before Parliament to prevent Rank acquiring De La Rue.[24] The British Match Corporation–Wilkinson Sword merger has been effected – the new grouping being called Wilkinson Match.

REFERENCES

1. This is not entirely true so far as economists are concerned: see D. C. Mueller, 'A Theory of Conglomerate Mergers', *Quarterly*

Journal of Economics, November 1969, vol. lxxxiii, pp. 643–59; and J. C. Narver, *Conglomerate Mergers and Market Competition,* University of California Press, 1967, esp. Ch. iv.

2. See Mr. Jim Slater's article 'Conglomerates: case for more mergers' in *Financial Times,* 15 February 1969; also his letter in *The Times,* 9 April 1969.

3. See R. V. Buxton 'Conglomerates in the Cold', *Management Today,* November 1969, p. 94.

4. For a view which contests this image of Slater Walker see R. Winsbury, 'Slater Walker's Non-Conglomerate', *Management Today,* August 1969, pp. 81–7.

5. See J. Martin, 'The great conglomerate bust-up', *The Financial Times,* 4 August 1971.

6. Monopolies Commission *Unilever Ltd. and Allied Breweries Ltd.: A Report on the Proposed Merger,* H.M.S.O., 1969, (H.C.P. 297) (hereinafter *Unilever–Allied*).

7. Monopolies Commission *The Rank Organisation Ltd. and The De La Rue Co. Ltd.: A Report on the Proposed Acquisition of the De La Rue Co. Ltd.,* H.M.S.O., 1969, (H.C.P. 298) (hereinafter *Rank–De La Rue*).

8. See Monopolies Commission *British Match Corporation Ltd. and Wilkinson Sword Ltd.: A Report on the Proposed Merger,* H.M.S.O., 1973, (Cmnd. 5442) (hereinafter *B.M.C.–Wilkinson*).

9. Further details are given in the opening paragraphs of the Commission's Report; and a further source of information is A. D. Bonham-Carter, 'Centralisation and Decentralisation in Unilever' in R. S. Edwards and H. Townsend, (eds.), *Business Enterprise,* Macmillan, 1958, pp. 335–341.

10. J. Mark, 'The British Brewing Industry', *Lloyds Bank Review,* April 1974, p. 33.

11. M. Corina and R. Cowton 'Mighty brew with a strong international flavour', *The Times,* 30 November 1968.

12. 'Unilever–Allied Breweries: throwing up the sponge', *The Economist,* 7 December 1968.

13. M. Southern and J. Amos, 'Now try and tell Stork from bitter', *Unilever–Allied,* paras. 69 and 71.

15. *Unilever–Allied,* para. 124.

16. *Rank–De La Rue,* para. 43.

17. *Rank–De La Rue,* para. 58.

18. *Rank–De La Rue,* para. 98.

19. *B.M.C.—Wilkinson*, para. 46.
20. *B.M.C.—Wilkinson*, para. 71.
21. *B.M.C.—Wilkinson*, para. 74.
22. *B.M.C.—Wilkinson*, para. 81.
23. *B.M.C.—Wilkinson*, paras. 86—8.
24. See the comments of Mr. Anthony Crosland, then President of the Board of Trade, in the House of Commons reported in *The Times*, 11 November 1969.

QUESTIONS FOR DISCUSSION

1. Define a conglomerate company. Give examples of conglomerate firms, other than those in the case studies, with some of the products they make or distribute.

2. 'The conglomerate was and remains one of the most remarkable and ill-understood creations of the past decade'. (J. Thackray, 'The Conglomerate Catastrophes', *Management Today*, June 1971, p. 75.) Why?

3. Why do you think the Commission appeared to be hesitant in its support of the Unilever—Allied Breweries proposed merger?

4. Was the Commission right to place so much stress upon management characteristics in its conclusions on the Rank—De La Rue proposed merger?

5. Why should the Commission have put so much stress upon 'substance' as an advantage of the B.M.C.—Wilkinson Sword merger?

6. What do the three Reports indicate about the Monopolies Commission's thinking on:
   (a) company size?
   (b) efficiency and conglomerate mergers?

7. How may conglomerate mergers raise issues of:
   (a) cross subsidization?
   (b) reciprocal trading?

8. What is the relevance of 'industrial logic' in the context of conglomerate mergers?

9. Is there a specific wider role for conglomerate firms in the U.K. economy, e.g. in promoting competition?

10. Comment on the following data:

Table 6.6 Industrial, Commercial and Financial Mergers Classified by Type of Integration (%)

	1965 (part)	1966	1967	1968	1969	1970	1971	1972	1973 (part)
Horizontal:									
No.	78	76	86	81	80	84	75	65	79
Value	75	84	91	79	83	70	62	40	87
Vertical:									
No.	12	12	5	4	2	1	6	7	5
Value	13	9	4	4	1	—	4	9	4
Diversified:									
No.	10	12	9	15	18	15	19	28	16
Value	12	7	5	17	16	30	34	51	9

Source: J. D. Gribbin, 'The Operation of the Mergers Panel since 1965', *Trade and Industry*, 17 January 1974, p. 71.
Note: This data covers only mergers falling under the Commission's purview in terms of the 1965 Monopolies and Mergers Act: i.e. where a statutory monopoly is created or assets exceeding £5m are acquired.

11. What impact had the Monopolies Commission in these three case studies?

Teacher's Notes

CASE STUDY
1. A Monopoly Situation: the British Oxygen Co. Ltd.

TEACHER'S NOTES

The analysis following a study of the main facts of the case must take account of the situation in the industry since 1956. The main developments have been:

1. Entry of a new firm

Air Products Ltd., a subsidiary of Air Products and Chemicals Inc. of U.S.A., was established in 1957 and by 1972 had an estimated 35% of the U.K. industrial gases market, including 10% of the tonnage oxygen market. This entry followed too closely upon the publication of the Commission's Report for the two events to be unrelated; but assessment of the relative importance of the two factors is thereby complicated. It has been noted that 'the report was far more important than its criticisms, for it coincided with the entry of Air Products ... into the British Market'.[1] One explanation is that B.O.C.'s obligation to publish its prices between 1958 and 1962 gave A.P.L. a chance to establish a foothold in the market by selective undercutting.

2. Steel industry changes

The basic oxygen method of making steel has now replaced the traditional open-hearth system. The new process was virtually non-existent in the late 1950s but now accounts for about one-third of steel-making, and a projected 90% by 1980 — see Fig. 1.1 (page 80). Steel industry oxygen demand rose from 4,671 m. cubic feet in 1958 to 40,550 m. cubic feet in 1970. Centralized purchasing followed national-ization of steel in 1967, and there could be scope for a 'countervailing power' analysis of the situation. This may be consciously in the minds of B.S.C. officials.

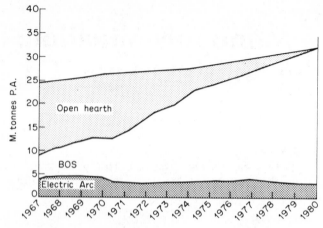

Source: L. Kingshott, Ringing up record profits, British Steel, summer 1974, p.5.

Fig. 1.1. B.S.C. Steelmaking capacity by process

3. Research and development

Considerable mention is made of this in B.O.C. Annual Reports, and from 1960 onwards the firm appears to have decentralized this activity in an effort to improve efficiency. New developments have included the production of liquid hydrogen and liquid helium, developments in 1962 of a computer-control flame-cutting machine, and work in the field of cryogenics (low temperature food preserving, etc.). One must, however, concur with the point which Rowley makes, that while B.O.C. does appear to have become more research-conscious in the 1960s 'whether it was stimulated into activity by the [Commission's] report or by market factors is impossible to judge from available material'.[2]

4. General environment

Comment on the beneficial impact of the Commission's Report has appeared. Some of the management journals have highlighted this. Speaking of the establishment of a management development unit at B.O.C., and of savings of wages in the stock control office of 20%, and reduced stock-carrying levels, one journal commented:

B.O.C.'s interest in inspiring its employees to greater productivity is a direct result of a changed competitive situation. Until a few years ago the company enjoyed a virtual monopoly in the U.K. market. Then an American owned rival entered the scene and captured a significant portion of B.O.C.'s traditional business. B.O.C. responded by re-examining its position and determining to shed its sleepy, complacent image.[3]

But even the above quotation is couched in terms of the total change in the competitive situation as much as the impact of the Commission's Report itself. Again another journal commented:

Having for years been an archetypal blue-chip company, a monopoly run as a public service as much as a commercial company (an attitude symbolised by the presence of Lord Reith, ex-B.B.C., as vice-chairman) British Oxygen had in 1956 found itself under the scrutiny of the Monopolies Commission, forced to make public its costs and prices, and facing the intrusion into its once captive home market of a new and vigorous competitor, Air Products of America. It was, to quote one director, 'Shell-Shocked'.[4]

The comments under this heading can only give a general impression of trends in the industry. What is apparent, however, is that B.O.C. did go through a period of intensified competition in the early 1960s. Reference to the company's own measure of return on capital employed shows the following:

Return on capital employed: (%)

| 1960 | 17.3 | 1962 | 11.5 |
| 1961 | 13.6 | 1963 | 11.3 |

The Annual Reports of this period speak of business obtained against sharp competition in the industrial gases field, of considerably reduced profit margins, of reduced activity in the steel industry keeping tonnage oxygen revenue below expectation, and of demand for all industrial gases and equipment being below capacity. Under these conditions 'compete or die' is industry's choice today. Price agreements are being abandoned, tariffs lowered, new processes introduced, amalgamations arranged, everywhere increasing competition. Competition is a welcome spur to endeavour but its conditions are hard; it leaves no room for easy profits or wages, restrictive practices or obstruction of new methods.[5]

Reference has continued to be made in the accounts to increased competition in the industrial gases market. In 1968 B.O.C. were only able to say that demand for oxygen and acetylene was maintained at the level of the previous year, while in 1971 the B.O.C. Annual Report pointed out that in respect of gases 'Trading conditions remained highly competitive throughout the year with constant pressure on margins. A significant drop in demand from manufacturing industry was experienced in the second half-year when rising costs became a particularly serious problem demanding constant management attention'.[6]

5. Diversification

B.O.C. has in recent years diversified its interests though in areas allied with air products. As a major producer of liquid nitrogen, the company not unnaturally studied the frozen food industry for investment purposes. It was already involved in distributing frozen foods and deep freezers (Food Services Division) and for some time had also been delivering frozen foods to major retail chains like Marks and Spencer in specially equipped vehicles (B.O.C. Transfield Ltd.). It then began a Consumer Products Division and now its King Harry Foods subsidiary makes pizzas. After initial difficulties the 'King Harry' brand range has now proved a success. The Thame factory now also supplies pizzas under own label for Eden Vale, Birds Eye and Bejam.

B.O.C. has also invested in fish farming — it has a trout farm in Cumberland. Again this investment is understandable since the farm uses oxygen to product 6—8 oz. trout on a twelve-month production schedule. The investment is expected to show a return on capital employed of 30—35%.

Given the obvious problems of growth by acquisition in the U.K., it is not surprising that B.O.C. should seek growth overseas. In 1974 it acquired one-third of the common stock of Airco Ltd., one of the three major industrial gas firms in the United States.

6. Some particulars on the industrial gases market

Total sales including both atmospheric and fuel gases in 1972 exceeded £100 million. B.O.C. and Air Products are by far the major companies. Distillers and I.C.I. are, however, important suppliers of carbon dioxide.

Oxygen remains the major part of the market. Tonnage oxygen sales have grown much faster than the industry as a whole — about 17% per annum throughout the 1960s. This is due essentially to demand from the steel industry. The data relating to Question 10 indicates yet further growth being likely as the basic oxygen process of steel-making becomes more widespread.

Nitrogen is becoming widely used by frozen food firms and continuing growth here seems assured.

Helium, like nitrogen, has excellent cold temperature properties which may make it more important in the future for cooling purposes.

Argon, in common with the previous two gases, has inert properties and is widely used in the welding industry.

Butane and *propane* are part of the fuel gas sector of the industry. Shell, B.P. and Esso are important suppliers of the first and Calor Gas is the major firm making propane in bulk and in cylinders.

REFERENCES

1. C. Mansell, 'B.O.C.'s Human Formula', *Management Today*, April 1970, p. 84.
2. C. K. Rowley, op. cit., p. 362.
3. *International Management*, July 1972, p. 31.
4. *The Director*, April 1972, p. 66.
5. B.O.C. *Annual Report*, 1960.
6. B.O.C. *Annual Report*, 1971.

FURTHER READING

The air products industry is not one well known to the laymen for the obvious reason that it is not in the consumer goods sector of the economy. The sources cited in the references provide some items for perusal by those keen to study this industry in more depth. See also:

J. S. Hutchison, 'Development and organisation of the British Oxygen Company Ltd.' in R. S. Edwards and H. Townsend, (eds.), *Business Growth*, Macmillan, 1966, pp. 301–12.

'Profits from the air', *Times Review of Industry*, May 1966.
The Financial Times Survey — Industrial Gases, 17 June 1969.
The Financial Times Survey — Industrial Gases, 24 August 1970.
The Times Special Report — Industrial Gases, 24 January 1972.

These all contain valuable articles on the prospects for each part of the industry. For further details of the properties and uses of various gases, see P. Mylton-Davies, 'Compress to Expand: the World of Industrial Gases', *Sales Engineering* (Journal of the Institute of Sales Engineers), vol. 4, no. 7, August 1971, pp. 11—4, 23—4.

APPENDIX

Table 1.1 B.O.C. Industrial and Medical Gases Sales by Use (1953)

	Oxygen %	Dissolved Acetylene %	Propane %
Steel Industry	35	8	13
Shipbuilders and marine			
engineers	10	16	20
General engineers	12	19	12
Electrical plant			
manufacturers	3	5	1
Car and aircraft			
manufacturers	5.5	9	4
Scrap cutting	7	7.5	27
Public bodies and government			
departments	9.5	10	12
Miscellaneous (including garages)	18	25.5	11
	100.0	100.0	100

Source: *Industrial and Medical Gases*, para. 107.

Table 1.2 Pre-Tax Profits/Capital Employed (%)

	B.O.C.	Air Products
1954	16.5	–
1955	15.0	–
1956	14.0	–
1957	14.1	–
1958	15.1	–
1959	16.6	5.3
1960	17.3	2.3
1961	13.6	5.5
1962	11.5	1.7
1963	11.3	6.3
1964	13.0	8.7
1965	12.8	7.4
1966	10.6	7.4
1967	10.6	9.2
1968	12.1	13.6
1969	11.5	12.9
1970	12.5	15.3
1971	13.1	11.9
1972	13.5	–
1973	14.5	–
1974	15.5	–

Source: Company Annual Reports and Accounts.

POINTS INTENDED TO BE RAISED FROM THE QUESTIONS

1. The main aspects here are B.O.C.'s market conduct and market performance. Firstly one cannot fail to put stress upon consolidation of its monopoly power as evidenced by:
   (i) purchase of potential competitors;
   (ii) 'predatory pricing' through fighting companies;
   (iii) exclusive dealing with some customers.
   As regards market performance it exhibited a poor record of technological progressiveness as exemplified by its acquisition of know-how under licence. This may be associated with the fact that it had no real incentive to offer price competition.

2. B.O.C.'s customers had no basis for comparing alternative prices and in any case had minimal incentive if industrial gas was a small proportion of customer inputs.

No information from which to calculate B.O.C. profit levels was available given the few alternative U.K. sources of supply and the absence of imports.

Supplying one's own requirements was not economical on a small scale for most users.

Firms may not have wished to approach the Monopolies Commission and risk alienating their relationship with B.O.C.

3. (i) B.O.C. was subject to little risk of loss of custom
    (ii) Price had little influence upon demand
    (iii) As in (ii) above
    (iv) Again, little risk involved in operations
    (v) No need for B.O.C. to accumulate large replacement reserves
    (vi) Reduced level of capital to service.

4. Point (i) contains the suggestion that B.O.C. was undertaking geographical cross-subsidization between plants and thus benefiting more distant consumers. Apart from the question of whether such behaviour is efficient in economic terms, there is no reason to suppose that competition would fail to serve geographically remote consumers. Points (ii) and (iv) fail to distinguish between the level of costs under monopoly and the level of prices. Costs *may* be lower for the reasons given under (ii) and (iv), but whether prices are lower or standards of service higher is a different question. One cannot assume this to be the case under monopoly. The Commission had contested point (iii). There is no reason to suppose that monopoly rather than competition should encourage the conditions under point (v) − especially as this product is bought by industrial users.

5. Publication of national prices and a ban on the use of fighting companies could give a competitor a chance to enter a part of the market. This would be a significant point if one part of the market had lower barriers to entry than another. This was so in industrial gases, and allowed Air Products Ltd. to enter the non-cylinder market and so avoid locking up capital. B.O.C. currently has £30 m. invested in cylinders. This figure appears in *Marketing*, May 1973, p. 25.

Prohibition of tying customers financially to one supplier should also reduce entry barriers.

Some informal control of B.O.C. profits may have been deemed necessary if no new competitive entrant into the market was expected.

6. Without a new competitor B.O.C. could have reverted to its previous practices and continued to earn successive profits. These practices themselves have the effect of raising barriers to entry in the market.

7. Customers would have an alternative source of supply, and so competition might increase.

B.O.C. likely to reduce prices nationally and/or increase the rate of technological change: improve efficiency and reduce costs. Presumption that competitive stimulus would improve its performance.

8. Rising demand is a favourable market situation for a new entrant. The industrial gases market overall has grown by over 10% a year in recent years. This certainly must have helped Air Products grow throughout the 1960s. Secondly, a new entrant would be able to build optimum-sized plant, site in the optimum locations and incorporate the best available techniques of production. This would be costly but would permit lower operating costs so as to break into the market and offer attractive prices to the customers of existing firms. Thirdly, many buyers of gases would be inclined to stimulate a new entrant in order to obtain a greater competition in supplies in the future. Since there was in 1956 a monopoly supplier the possibility of a new source of supply would be welcomed by most customers. Apart from price considerations, the strategic point that supplies are not dependent on one source in case of disruption (strikes, fire damage) is also important.

9. Nitrogen is a gas with inert properties. The gas in liquid form has a very low temperature $- 196^{\circ}$C. The frozen food industry has exploited these cryogenic properties of nitrogen in blast freezing fruits, fish and vegetables. The production of nitrogen by the major firms is attractive since it is a by-product in making oxygen. Expenditure on frozen foods has risen rapidly — retail sales rose from £101 million in 1967 to £220 million in 1973 — an average annual growth rate of 24%. The rapidly expanding sale of freezers

should indeed ensure the frozen food industry of booming sales throughout the later 1970s. The two major firms have not unexpectedly thus found sales of nitrogen growing fast — over 20% per annum.

10. **Table 1.4 Steel-Making Processes** (% of total production)

	1950	1960	1970
Open Hearth	88	84	48
Electric Arc	4	8	19
Basic Oxygen	—	—	28
Other Processes	8	8	5
	100	100	100

Source: *Making Steel*, British Steel Corporation, 1972.

As can be seen from the above data the basic oxygen-making process is now responsible for approaching one-third of steel production as these trends continue. Nationalization of steel production since 1967 has made the British Steel Corporation a major oxygen consumer. In 1970 B.O.C. consumed 40,550 m. cubic feet of oxygen, spending in excess of £10 million in this market, while the 1960 comparable volume figure was 9,667 m. cubic feet. Clearly, then, the change in steel production technology will have had a significant impact on the market for oxygen.

11. For bulky delivery rail transport is attractive. B.O.C. announced a 'Plan 70' costing £17 million involving distribution by large cryogenic rail tankers. These tankers take gas from large plants such as at Widnes and final delivery to customers is made by road tanker. For the small customer — the merchant market — there appears, however, no workable alternative to road deliveries of cylinders.

12. The Commission's recommendations were acted upon by the government. They provided the basis for new competition in the industry. Thus the structure of the industry altered with consequent repercussions on B.O.C.'s market performance.

2. An Oligopoly Situation: Tea

TEACHER'S NOTES

1. General Points

Both the price-quality relationship of tea and the question of defining capital employed for two tea firms were key issues that faced the National Board for Prices and Incomes. Its Report is thus of particular interest and indeed one observer concluded that it provided 'enough material for generations of essays on British Capitalism 1970'.[1]

The declining demand for tea is clearly the industry's major long-term problem. Various reasons have been put forward for this

Table 2.9 Principal Advertisers and Brands of Tea (those spending £75,000 or more in 1970, 1971, 1972 or 1973 on television or press advertising).

		(£'000)			
Advertiser	*Brand*	*1970*	*1971*	*1972*	*1973*
Brooke Bond	Dividend	269	272	91	61
	P.G. Tips	446	388	389	423
	T Bags	307	485	387	415
C.W.S.	"99"	114	103		
Ceylon Tea Bureau	Ceylon Tea	166	124		
Cadbury's	Fine Brew	110			
Tea Council		410	121		151
Lyons	Range	80			
	Quickbrew	185	283	316	157
	Quickbrew T Bags	67	359	321	301
Tetley	Teabags	398	554	477	423
Typhoo	Typhoo	418	246	192	352
	Teabags	348	286	559	173
	Total	3634	3607	3341	2749

Source: *Marketing Manual of the U.K.*, 1972, 1973 and 1974, International Publishing Corporation.

decrease in demand, but nobody has a complete and satisfactory explanation. The comment of a tea expert who blamed it on the fact that people (especially young people) were 'Too damn idle to make a proper cup of tea if you ask me',[2] probably has some truth in it, especially when the various and expensive attempts to create an instant tea are recalled (Brooke Bond invested £2½ million in such a project).

Further falls in the consumption of tea have been predicted by the Tea Council, who in 1972 were forecasting a fall of 24% in consumption by 1980 unless some action was taken to arrest the trend. Unfortunately, the Tea Council has been kept short of funds by its members (which include tea growers) and has been unable to continue the quite effective generic advertising campaign it mounted in the 1960s.

Table 2.9 indicates that advertising expenditure on individual tea brands has fallen slightly between 1970 and 1972 but it is clear also that all-industry advertising expenditure has fallen much more sharply. However, the decline in tea consumption has to be kept in perspective for tea is still the major form of drink. For example, in 1968 it was estimated that two-thirds of all proprietary drinks consumed is tea – the remaining one-third including beer, spirits, cordials, coffee, etc., and in 1970 it was considered that one cup of coffee was consumed for every five cups of tea.

The interesting point about tea bags is that they represent a very much more expensive way of buying tea for the consumer as the retail price includes the cost of putting tea into bags and then the bags into packets. (In fact, although in 1969 tea bags represented 1½% of the market by weight, by value they took 3%.) However, consumers are likely to use one tea bag in place of 3 spoons of loose tea and are thus using less tea overall. It follows that the tea companies are attracted by the better profit margins per unit sold offered by tea bags but are well aware of the decreased consumption following their use.

The announcement by Twinings, a speciality tea firm, in September 1974 that it was lauching a range of quality teas in tea bags illustrates this point. Tea bags in 1974 accounted for 30% of total tea sales and Twinings estimate this figure will double by 1980. Even then the proportion will be lower than in other countries such as the U.S. where tea bags account for 90% of total sales. In Canada the figure is 86% and in Germany 68%.

Table 2.10 gives the brand shares both for packet loose tea and tea bags.

Table 2.10 Brand Shares for Tea and Tea Bags

Brand Name		Brand Preference			
			1971		1972
		Tea	Tea Bags	Tea	Tea Bags
Brooke Bond	Dividend	15%		14%	
	P.G. Tips	29%		29%	
	T Bags		27%		20%
C.W.S.	"99"	13%	5%	13%	4–6%
Lyons	Quickbrew	5%		6%	
	Quickbrew T Bags		5%		
Tetley	Tea Bags		33%		38%
Typhoo	Typhoo	21%		24%	
	Teabags		10–12%		14%

Source: *Marketing Manual of the U.K.*, 1972 and 1973, International Publishing Corporation.

2. A note on brand shares

Brand Share information can be collected from consumer surveys in three main forms:

> share of purchasers of brands;
> share of product volume;
> share of spending on the product.

These three methods often give different answers. In addition, there are various bases for these three types of data. For example, the data in the I.P.C. *Marketing Manual of the U.K.* (see Table 2.10), is based on the percentages of purchasers who exclusively or mainly use one brand.

Many companies regard brand share figures as confidential matters and will only lay claim to 'about x% of the market' in public statements. In consequence, when account is also taken of the various methods of measuring brand shares, it is not surprising that reports (in particular press reports) of brand shares are often in conflict with one another and/or add up to over 100% of the market.

3. The attitude of consumers to prices

There is now a considerable volume of evidence which indicates that consumers' perception of the quality of a product is affected by the price of the product. As far as economists are concerned this concept has been developed most fully by André Gabor and his associates of Nottingham University.[3] Their work has included tests in real and hypothetical shopping situations when they collect data which indicates whether or not a consumer is prepared to purchase a product at various prices. From this data they then plot a 'buy-response curve' which indicates for each price the percentage of those interviewed who are prepared to purchase the product over a range of prices. Experience shows that this curve is bell-shaped and approximates to a normal distribution curve near its mean. The shape of this buy-response curve implies that the corresponding demand curve is likely to have a substantial backward-sloping portion in the region of lower prices.

The idea that the price of a product can act as an indicator of quality has long been accepted as luxury ranges of goods such as furs, ladies' hats, cosmetics, etc. However, the work by the Nottingham group indicates that it applies equally well to items such as ladies' stockings, cheaper food items, cleaning materials, etc. Indeed, a recent study showed that housewives in Great Britain would not purchase a yellow-skinned chicken (a normal colour in the United States and Europe) as they associated the colour with age and fatty content. Nevertheless when the chickens were priced 1p. per lb. above the white counterparts they sold quite well. The study concluded that the best hope of marketing these yellow-skined chickens in Britain lay in selling them as a premium product at a higher price.[4]

4. Price increases in 1974

Table 2.6 of the case study (page 18) pointed out that in 1973–74 tea prices at the London Auctions rose rapidly. A number of factors explain this soaring price. Droughts in East Africa and Ceylon cut back output from these sources at a time when Indian crops were reduced due to a severe shortage of fertilizers, in turn the result of the oil crisis. Increasing demand in India itself has also contributed to the hardening of world prices – domestic consumption now accounts for half of India's tea production.

In response to the rising auction price, retail tea prices rose in 1974. Lyons increased the price of its ¼lb. Red Label and Orange Label tea by 1p. in March. Brooke Bond followed in April and Lyons also increased prices of all its range of teas. In May Typhoo adjusted its prices upwards by 8%. Since individual tea firms had to seek permission from the Prices Commission to increase prices, price leadership was inoperable in early 1974.

In September 1974 the Labour Government implemented a subsidy on tea of 2p. per ¼lb. so as to offset another 1p. price increase about to be applied by tea firms. This subsidy was calculated to bring about a reduction of about 0.1% in the retail price index and cost £29 in a full year.

5. Other changes in 1974

In April 1974 the C.W.S. announced that it proposed to build an automated tea factory costing £2.5 million at Crewe. This decision suggests that the C.W.S. is optimistic about demand prospects for its "99" tea bags since the new plant capacity will be four times its output in 1973. The "99" tea bags brand has seen an increase in sales of 100% each year since 1970. The growth in the overall tea bag market has been cited earlier.

In April 1974 Lyons Tetley launched a new low-priced brand of tea — Silver Label. This was seen as filling a gap in the market between tea packeted with a dividend stamp for redemption and popular brands. This was the first new tea brand from Lyons since it had introduced Quick Brew in 1956.

A most significant announcement was made by Brooke Bond in July 1974. This was that as from 28 September it no longer proposed to distribute tea to about 85,000 grocers since they did not purchase a minimum quantity of twenty-five parcels per week. In effect, it meant that these retailers would in future have to purchase their requirements from cash and carry wholesalers. Soaring labour and transport costs were cited as the reason for this decision. It was pointed out that whereas in 1969 it cost £3,500 to keep a van and its driver on the road the cost had risen to £6,500 by 1974. Pressure on margins due to the operation of the price controls must have been an important factor in bringing about the timing of this change in Brooke Bond's policy.

An interesting study of the tea market was made by Mr David Theobald, buying director of Lyons Tetley and chairman of the U.K. Tea Trade Committee, speaking at the American Tea Convention in November 1974. He felt that by 1984 tea bags would account for 80 percent of the market.[5]

REFERENCES

1. N. Faith, 'Any other business', *The Sunday Times (Business News)*, 16 August 1970.
2. Cited in B. Ritchie, 'The tea men's cup of woe', *The Sunday Times*, 30 September 1973.
3. A. Gabor and C. W. J. Granger, 'Price as an Indicator of Quality', *Economica*, February 1966.
4. R. Collins, 'Housewives chicken out of a yellow skin', *The Guardian*, 11 January 1974.
5. D. Theobald, 'Looking into the future of the tea market', *The Grocer*, 9 November 1974, p. 32.

FURTHER READING

There is copious material on tea, particularly on the retailing side, in the grocery trade press, viz: *The Grocer, Supermarketing.* The following sources are deliberately chosen as more readily obtainable ones than from that quarter.

B. Moynahan, 'Brooke Bond's better brew', *Management Today*, March 1967, p. 74.
D. Thomas, 'The Tale of Tetley's tea bag', *Management Today*, September 1968, p. 29.
The Financial Times, 'Report on Tea', 12 July 1972, p. 13.
M. Corina, 'Tea bags stir up competition', *The Times*, 1 November 1972.

For a detailed economic study of tea in an international context see: G. K. Sarkar, *The World Tea Economy*, Oxford University Press, Calcutta, 1972.

POINTS INTENDED TO BE RAISED FROM THE QUESTIONS

1. One possible outcome of an oligopoly situation is indeed that list prices will remain stable because each firm fears that the reactions of competitors will nullify the advantages it seeks to gain by changing its price. The situation described is typical of a price leadership situation where the price changes of a company in the industry are imitated by the other firms in that industry. Competition centres on discounts but list prices remain practically uniform. The bread industry also exemplifies list price uniformity, price leadership and discount competition. (See D. Swann, D. P. O'Brien, W. P. J. Maunder, W. S. Howe, *Competition in British Industry: Case Studies of the Effects of Restrictive Practices Legislation*, Loughborough University, 1974, chapter 2.)

2. The shape of the demand curve would firstly be downward sloping to the right, but below a certain price it would begin to curve back towards the Y-axis, as shown in the diagram.

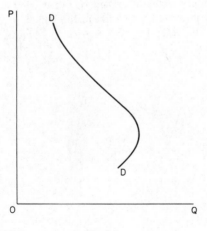

Fig. 2.1

3. (a) The effect of an increase in the price of tea, *ceteris paribus*, would be to reduce demand as indicated in the diagram by a

movement along the demand curve DD. An increase in price from P_1 to P_2 reducing demand from Q_1 to Q_2.

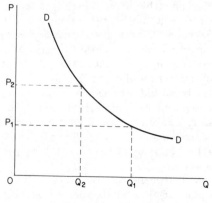

Fig. 2.2

(b) The reduced demand arising from changing consumer preferences is indicated by a shift in the demand curve downwards and to the left. Thus at a price P_1 there is a reduction in demand from Q_1 to Q_2.

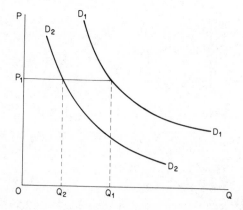

Fig. 2.3

4. If Brooke Bond achieved its objective it would approach the position of a monopolist in the economists' sense. (It was already in 1970 controlling over twice as much of the market as its nearest competitor, and already a monopolist in terms of the existing British monopoly legislation as it controlled more than a third of the market.) Monopolists are liable to become accused of one or more of the following:

  (i) excessive profit making and/or failure to control costs;

  (ii) insufficient investment in Research and Development;

  (iii) attempts to contain existing competition;

  (iv) attempts to discourage new competition.

  (a) In this case Brooke Bond is already accused of (i) by the Board; (ii) would seem to be of little relevance to this product; (iii) is already being pursued by heavy advertising expenditure. In a declining market it is unlikely that new entrants will arise, so (iv) is unimportant.

  (b) Criticism (i) stands. With regard to (ii) Brooke Bond was spending heavily on developing instant tea. Criticism (iii) still applies. In regard to (iv), Tetley Tea had entered the market and established a large market share.

5. (a) Brooke Bond argued that if the payments of the royalties to its parent company for permission to use its trade marks were included, the rate of return on capital would only be 16.7%. As a rough estimate this means that Brooke Bond was paying about £0.5 million per year for use of these trade marks. The Board regarded these payments as internal transfers of funds within the group and not real costs.

  (b) Other illustrations include the claim by Typhoo that the £31 million paid by Schweppes for its 'goodwill' was part of its capital employed. The Board did not agree to this. However, it would seem likely that the figure for goodwill was so high because of undervaluation of the tangible assets of Typhoo. Also there was a debate as to whether or not the C.T.S.'s payments of dividends to its shareholders are a cost against revenue or a payment from profits.

6. When selling to retailers the tea companies are selling to a large number of small shops, and a small number of large organizations such as Tesco. (In 1969, 62% of total grocery turnover was handled

by some 300 purchasing centres.) It is thus crucial for each of the tea manufacturers to offer these large retail organizations attractive discounts off recommended retail prices or else they could lose a large part of their sales to one of their rivals. On the other hand, the retail price recommended by each of the tea firms was similar since none of the firms wanted to be selling at a lower price than anyone else for fear of consumer reaction in terms of perceived low quality.

7. Tea, like sugar and coffee, is purchased frequently by housewives. Consequently, it is an item typically sold at a price below the recommended price by retailers in order to tempt housewives to enter a given supermarket or shop in the hope that she buys all her shopping in the store at the same time. In the jargon of retailing, it is a 'traffic-builder'.

8. No comment was passed on the fact that the price of imported tea, which represents 70—80% of all costs, had fallen over the period 1959—69. Large increases in the on-costs as quoted affect profit margins only slightly; moreover, one would expect increasing efficiency over time to permit rising costs to be partly absorbed so as not to require price adjustments.

9. Imported tea prices have shown no marked upward trend until 1973—74. Thus the tea firms' view that these prices would increase has been confirmed, but not in the years immediately after 1970.

10. Tea faces competition from other forms of drink and in recent years instant coffee firms have spent heavily in promoting their product (see Table 2.11). In fact the consumption of coffee per head of population has risen from 2.71lbs in 1965 to 4.4 in 1972. This development has to some extent been assisted by significant technical developments in the production of instant coffee. For example, in 1954 Nescafe were able to eliminate the carbohydrates that accounted for half the weight of instant coffee and to produce Nescafe with 100% ('pure') coffee. As a result of this the size of the 3s. 6d. tin was reduced to 2oz. thus reducing distribution and storage costs.

Table 2.11 Principal Advertisers and Brands of Coffee (those spending £75,000 or more in 1970, 1971 or 1972 on television or press advertising).

Advertisers	Brand	1970	(£'000) 1971	1972
Brooke Bond	Ground		93	
Nestle	Gold Blend (Instant)	288	141	
	Nescafe (Instant)	510	925	875
	Nescafe Blend 37	106	131	136
	Fine Blend			211
Lyons	Various	64	77	
Ovaltine			128	64
General Foods	Maxwell House	940	837	633
	Birds Eye			660
		1933	2379	2526

Source: *Marketing Manual of the U.K.*, 1972 and 1973, International Publishing Corporation.

11. Table 2.8 in Case Study 2 (page 19) does suggest that the Tea Council has not found great enthusiasm from tea firms in contributing to an all-industry campaign to promote tea. One of the problems of such generic campaigns is the very absence of a brand name associated with the product. This tends to reduce the effectiveness of such advertisements since the consumer does not obviously link the 'message' with a particular brand. The support of the milling–baking companies for the Flour Advisory Bureau ('Use your Loaf', etc.) has also tended to weaken over the years.

12. Tea bags represent a form of convenience food which have grown in popularity with consumers over the past decade or so. They represent a quick method of measuring the quantity required at any one time and make disposal of used tea easy.

13. The report appears to have had very little impact on the industry. The individual firms have maintained intense competition based upon promotional expenditure and none of them reduced their prices even though in 1971, 1972 and 1973 imported tea prices fell from the 1970 figure (see Table 2.6 in Case Study 2 page 18).

CASE STUDY
3. Vertical Integration: the acquisition by the British Motor Corporation Ltd. of the Pressed Steel Company Ltd.

TEACHER'S NOTES

Economies of scale for car bodies

C. F. Pratten has a section on this in his book on economies of scale.[1] His information led him to estimate that the minimum tooling costs in the 1960s for a new steel body for a car would be about £5 million. This assumes that the model has two- and four-door variants and a shooting brake in its range. Although these figures are large they must be considered in the context of the volume of output of the model — for example in 1964 alone 244,000 B.M.C. 1100 cars were produced. Pratten also provides the following data which shows that these costs can be spread either by making many units over a short period or by extending a model run over a longer period of time.

Table 3.4 Index of body costs

Annual Output ('000)	Expected life of basic model		
	2 years	5 years	10 years
25	100	78	70
50	86	70	66
250	64	58	57
500	57	56	55
1,000	56	55	54

Barriers to new competition

The costs and difficulties faced by a company beginning to produce a product new to its production experience are usually seriously under-estimated. Some idea of the magnitude of the problem can be gained by considering the Monopolies Commission Report on the merger between G.K.N. Ltd. and Birfields Ltd.[2] In this Report it stated B.R.D. (a subsidiary of G.K.N.) began to manufacture propeller shafts for cars and commercial vehicles in 1959 and added axle shafts to its range in 1961. It entered this market previously monopolized by Hardy Spicer Ltd. (a subsidiary of the Birfield Group) with the active encouragement of some vehicle manufacturers who were dissatisfied with various aspects of Hardy Spicer's performance. For example, Ford undertook to place 10%, rising to 30%, of its business with B.R.D. for the first two years of B.R.D. production.

In spite of this assistance, the fact that propeller shafts are not extremely complex items, and G.K.N.'s great industrial experience, it was not until 1963 that a profit was made on the venture. Even then it was estimated to be only 1.3% on sales and rose slowly in the following years to 6.7% in 1965.

The supply of other car components

Throughout the past decade strikes among car component firms have highlighted the dependence of car manufacturers on their component suppliers. As stated in the case study, over 2,000 firms supply new or replacement parts to the motor industry. Some 20,000 components are involved in the construction of a car. The previous section indicated how G.K.N. were encouraged to commence the manufacture of transmissions equipment. It has now replaced Hardy Spicer as the dominant supplier of items like propeller and axle shafts, and acquired this company in 1967. The following are leading makers of major items of vehicle components.

The industry has never regarded massive stockpiling of components a viable solution in preventing car assembly lines from grinding to a halt in the event of strikes among component firms. The physical, let alone the financial, problem rules out this possibility. Vertical integration, however, does not necessarily provide any real answer to the problem. If the car maker owns a component subsidiary and labour unrest occurs in the latter it is in no better situation. It is however as an integrated

Table 3.5 Major component suppliers to the motor industry

	Supplier	Market share %
Sheet steel	British Steel Corporation	100
Glass	Pilkington	99.9
Electrical equipment	Lucas	98.0
Pistons	Associated Engineering Group	75.0
Door locks	Wilmot Breeden	70.75
PVC and other plastics	I.C.I.	70
Sparking plugs	Champion	60
Forgings	Guest, Keen and Nettlefold	60
Batteries	Electrical Power Storage Company	50
Tyres	Dunlop	50
Castings	Birmid group	50
Carburettors	Zenith	35
Paints	Berger and Courtaulds	30 each

Source: 'Car makers' revolt', *The Economist*, 11 July 1970, p. 53.

company itself responsible for implementing a labour relations policy that it seeks industrial peace: it can no longer point a finger at the supplier for being unable to supply essential parts. Hence the wage structure of an acquired component concern is of key importance to a car company.

Now the B.M.C. plant at Cowley had a long record of poor industrial relations prior to, and indeed since, the merger with Pressed Steel. By contrast Pressed Steel had a much better reputation, greatly helped by the presence of one trade union rather than a multiplicity as was the case across the Garsington Road. British Leyland has increasingly had to formulate an industrial relations policy and appointed a director to be responsible for the company's policy in this area.

The degree of concentration of component production has increased in the past decade, but this concentration has made the industry more vulnerable than ever to isolated labour disputes. In an effort to increase its choice in buying starter motors and alternators Leyland in 1967 set up a subsidiary, Butec, to manufacture under licence from the Leecheville Corporation of Cleveland, Ohio. It was stimulated to commence manufacture itself owing to supply difficulties due to strikes at Lucas.

Mr. J. Edwards

The 1965 Pressed Steel—B.M.C. merger and the B.M.C.—Leyland merger three years later had poignant repercussions for one person. He was Mr. Joe Edwards. He had been director of manufacture at B.M.C. until dismissed by the company's autocratic boss, Leonard Lord, in 1956. He the . joined Pressed Steel. Following the merger with B.M.C. he became man..ging director of the latter with Sir George Harriman as chairman. Th B.M.C.—Leyland link quickly led to his resignation in April 1968. There could be only one managing director in the new organization — Donald Stokes. Edwards was thus the loser in the situation brought about by the merger. This personal aspect of the merger is revealed by Turner's book.[3]

British Leyland's financial difficulties

British Leyland's decision in December 1974 to ask the government for financial help and to accept a measure of public ownership in return did not surprise any close observer of the company's fortunes. Its cash crisis was the culmination of continual production problems in its Austin—Morris subsidiary due to strikes and losses in output from the operation of the three-day week during the miners' strike. After the B.M.C.—Leyland merger in 1968 the new group found it hard to earn sufficient profits to finance its capital expenditure programmes.

Explanations for the new group's basic problems have not been slow to appear in the financial press. Thus *The Economist* declared:

> The group has too many old-fashioned plants, too many models, and too many of them mini-profit Minis into which the inefficient leviathan of Austin—Morris has drained resources that should have gone into the profitable specialist car or truck and bus divisions. Profitable Jaguar builds 30,000 cars a year, one-tenth as many as Mercedes. And British Leyland has too many workers, producing at half the rate of their continental rivals, not least because they are too often on strike.[4]

The financial performance of the group can be seen from the following data:

Table 3.6 British Leyland's profit record (£m).

Year to September	1964	1965	1966	1967	1968*	1969	1970	1971	1972	1973	1974
Austin—Morris	26	21	19	(5)	11	8	8	(16)	6	10	12
Specialist Car	8	9	8	6		11	3	8	14	18	9
Truck and Bus	10	9	8	6	6	7	8	8	6	9	6
Overseas etc.	8	11	9	9	13	14	9	10	2	12	(5)
Group pre-tax	52	50	44	16	38	40	4	32	32	51	0
Profits lost through strikes					12	15	27	18	12	8	
Profits ex strikes etc.					50	55	31	50	44	59	

*British Leyland formed in 1968. Figures for earlier years are an amalgamation of the profits of formerly independent subsidiaries.
( ) denotes loss

Source: J. Ensor, 'British Leyland's road to Whitehall', *The Financial Times*, 7 December 1974.

REFERENCES

1. C. F. Pratten, *Economies of Scale in Manufacturing Industry*, Cambridge University Press, 1971, pp. 135–6.
2. The Monopolies Commission, *Guest Keen and Nettlefolds Ltd. and Birfields Ltd. A Report on the Merger*, HMSO, 1967, (Cmnd. 3186).
3. G. Turner,*The Leyland Papers,* Pan Books, 1973.
4. 'Stokewagen, beware', *The Economist*, 14 December 1974, p. 64.

FURTHER READING

The motor vehicle industry has a glamour status in the eyes of many laymen. Economists too have not failed to give it their attention. There are the now somewhat dated tests of Maxcy and Silberston (*The Motor Industry*, 1959) and G. Turner (*The Car Makers*, 1963). The following are more recent sources:

D. Rhys, *The Motor Industry*, Butterworth, 1972.
J. Ensor, *The Motor Industry*, Longman, 1971.
G. Turner, *The Leyland Papers*, Pan Books, 1973.
The Economist Motor Survey, 'Cars and Their Components', 23 October 1965.
R. Eglin, 'End of the line for Stokes's dream', *The Sunday Times*, 8 December 1974.
A. Goodrick-Clarke, 'British Leyland's financial millstone', *The Times*, 9 December 1974.

POINTS INTENDED TO BE RAISED FROM THE QUESTIONS

1. The arguments can be summarized as follows:
   (i) Certainty of supplies of materials and services.
   (ii) Prompt revision of production and distribution policies.
   (iii) Better control over product distribution.
   (iv) Tighter quality control.
   (v) Better inventory control.
   (vi) General stability of operations.
   (vii) Decreased marketing expenses.
   (viii) Additional profit margins or the ability to charge lower prices on final products.

2. Of the above arguments, B.M.C. used (i); (ii); (iii) in the sense that production could be more efficiently scheduled to take account of the geographical distribution of factories; and (vi).

3. The problems stemming from integration are essentially as follows:
   (i) Disparities between productive capacities at various stages of production.
   (ii) Lack of specialization.
   (iii) Extension of the management team.
   (iv) Lack of competitive pressures on the costs of intermediate products.

4. (a) The purchase of Jaguar extended the B.M.C. product range to include the executive car range (Jaguar having previously purchased Daimlers) and also heavy trucks and bus chassis.
   (b) As Pressed Steel supplied almost all of Jaguar's car bodies both before and after the merger with B.M.C., there was a natural tie from their point of view, especially with the car body representing such a large proportion of a car's costs. However, this point should not be stressed too much as Rover, also almost entirely supplied by Pressed Steel, was taken over by the Leyland Motor Corporation before it merged with British Motor Holdings — a company created out of B.M.C.

5. The barriers to entry in this case would have been:
   (a) Knowledge of production techniques by the established firm in the fullest sense including the skill and knowledge accumulated by employees at all levels resulting in higher cost operation for the new entrant in the short-term.
   (b) Real economies of scale, making operation at less than the minimum optimum output expensive in terms of cost per unit.
   (c) Also possibly the capital costs involved which might have amounted to at least £15 million in 1965.

6. (i) The larger size of the American market makes the manufacture of components by the car firms economically viable because the volume of cars produced by a single firm is large enough for the firm to gain most of the economies of scale available at each stage of production.

(ii) Both Henry Ford and William Durant (founder of General Motors) believed in a high degree of self-sufficiency. Ford expanded backwards into the production of components while Durant bought an interest in his suppliers.

7. (a) (i) Pressed Steel would have started to operate at well below the break-even level of production and begun to accumulate losses.

(ii) B.M.C. or Rootes (whichever had not set up its own plant) would have needed to take steps to assure itself of continuity of supply of bodies. Such steps obviously could have included a take-over or a merger.

(b) In the actual situation, Pressed Steel was able to discuss the possibility of a merger from a position of financial strength. In the situation described above, it would be very much in the position of a victim and less able to protect the interests of its employees and shareholders.

8. In the context of this question, the following differences and similarities which existed between the situations in 1930 and in 1965 are relevant:

(i) In 1930 Morris Motors was unable to absorb the volume of output required to keep Pressed Steel economic.

(ii) In 1930 Pressed Steel's and Morris's only factories were physically adjacent. By 1965 both B.M.C. and Pressed Steel had several plants and B.M.C. felt that significant production and transportation economies could be made if it had the power to rationalize production in Pressed Steel plants relative to its requirements.

(iii) In 1930 there were several other independent body plants in existence and therefore Pressed Steel was facing intense competition to obtain the business over and above Morris's which was necessary to operate economically. In 1965 Pressed Steel was the only independent mass car body manufacturer and thus faced no competition from other independent body plants. The competition which it did face arose from the possibility that one of its two major customers might set up its own body plant, thus depriving Pressed Steel of a significant proportion of its sales volume and causing it to operate at uneconomic levels of production. B.M.C. feared that if they did not take over Pressed Steel then Rootes might do so, and

B.M.C. would then be purchasing bodies from an ailing firm which would either result in their paying higher prices (due to high unit production costs), or worse still finding that Pressed Steel was likely to face closing down.

9. The Commission was assured that Pressed Steel would operate autonomously and existing customers would be allocated materials on a *pro rata* basis if a shortage arose. However, assurance of physical supplies is one thing: the price paid for them is another. Without engaging in deliberate price discrimination B.M.C.'s ownership could lead to other customers paying at less advantageous prices than itself, even when order volumes were allowed for.

10. The value to be attached to keeping Pressed Steel in British hands. This nationalistic feeling, also relevant in the Chrysler—Rootes link, was explicitly appealed to by B.M.C. in its formal offer document for Pressed Steel. The Commission was clearly sympathetic. One comment on the merger to the Commission said bluntly that it would 'secure the last vulnerable flank of the British-owned part of this country's motor industry'. 'Keeping B.M.C. British', *The Statist*, 27 August 1965, p. 545.

11. The Chrysler link with Rootes cannot fail to be associated with the B.M.C. bid for Pressed Steel. Secondly, the very completion of the merger reinforced Chrysler's intention to become self-sufficient in respect of its body requirements. In turn this put pressure on Pressed Steel to find new business. Leyland, the remaining major customer, was now dependent on a company owned by one of its rivals and it too was stimulated to build its own body plant.

12. It permitted the merger to go ahead thus making B.M.C. a much more vertically-integrated concern. As has been argued above, the indirect effect of this was to hasten the time when other car assembly firms would be similarly integrated. The Commission received assurances from B.M.C. regarding its attitude to Pressed Steel's other customers. However, it can be criticized in the sense that these in practice were not necessarily adequate safeguards for customers of integrated concerns. It is difficult, for example, to believe that owner-customer firms do not do better than secure a *pro rata* proportion of supplies when these are scarce. Moreover, the assurance on price discrimination in the Report did not look very strong.

CASE STUDY
4. A Restrictive Price Agreement Struck Down: Glass Containers

TEACHER'S NOTES

The impact of the 1956 Act on the bottle industry has been previously documented in an article published in *Economics*, the journal of the Economics Association.[1] (Off-print copies of this article are available from the Association.) The article examined the course of technical progress and economic efficiency in the industry resulting from the new competitive environment and the changing structure of the industry as affected by mergers.

A more comprehensive account of these issues is given in the book by D. Swann, D. P. O'Brien, W. P. J. Maunder and W. S. Howe, *Competition in British Industry: Case Studies of the Effects of Restrictive Practices Legislation*, published by the Department of Economics, Loughborough University of Technology, in April 1974. Chapter 2 of this book includes a lengthy examination of the glass container industry since 1961. Given that these two sources are available, no attempt is made here to cover the same ground.

There have in fact been few substantial changes in the industry since the two sources just cited were written.

1. The packaging industry

Question 10 (page 49) was intended to try to make the student appreciate the fact that firms making glass bottles face competition from other manufacturers of packaging materials such as tin cans, plastic and paper. Data on the output of each of the packaging-making trades is not comprehensive. The following data comes from one of the major studies of this sector of the economy.

Table 4.1 Estimated sales of selected packaging materials by value 1967–70.

	1967 £m.	1968 £m.	1969 £m.	1970 £m.
Tinplate containers	137.0	145.0	161.0	180.0
Paperboard boxes and cartons	100.0	112.0	122.0	133.0
Fibreboard packing cases	97.0	114.0	127.0	142.0
Plastics materials	61.0	76.0	90.0	120.0
Glass containers	61.4	67.7	74.6	83.3
Aerosols	13.3	16.6	19.0	24.0
Paper bags and carrier bags	25.0	26.0	27.0	29.0
Paper sacks	n.a.	n.a.	39.0	42.0
Steel drums new	n.a.	n.a.	30.0	33.0
Steel drums reconditioned	n.a.	n.a.	3.5	3.7
Cellulose film	31.6	35.0	37.0	36.0
Aluminium foil	n.a.	n.a.	n.a.	30.0
Collapsible tubes	n.a.	n.a.	n.a.	7.0
Jute bags	n.a.	n.a.	n.a.	20.0
Wooden containers	n.a.	n.a.	n.a.	23.0

Source: R. Mills, *Statistical Review of the Packaging Industry 1967–70*, Packaging Industries Research Association, 1971, p. 1.

Taken as a whole the packaging sector has grown faster in recent years than the overall rate of growth of industrial production. The table indicates that glass containers account for some 10% of the total output by value of all the packaging trades.

The two major glass bottle firms acquired companies making plastic bottles in the early 1960s. Their decision to do so obviously represented a policy of self-protection should sales of glass bottles be threatened from this quarter.

For example, in 1962 United Glass acquired Key Glass, a firm which had not been a member of the British Bottle Association. Key Glass owned a plastics subsidiary which was then one of the largest producers of blow-moulded plastic containers in the country. Rockware had taken a 50% shareholding in Blewis and Shaw, a manufacturer of plastic containers, in 1959, and acquired full control by 1970. Rockware also acquired in 1969 the Marrick Manufacturing Co. Ltd., a firm making PVC containers for the food, beverage, household and toiletry industries.

The glass container firms' diversification policy is understandable.

Entry by existing users of glass bottles into the plastics industry is indeed relatively very easy. A firm that packages in bottles can install a plastic blow-moulding machine at low cost and easily produce for its own requirements, thus making it necessary for the container supplier to take action to provide a more attractive proposition.

Glass has always had certain advantages as a packaging medium such as chemical inertness, transparency and the ability to reseal a glass container for later use. However the industry has been on the defensive from metal cans and plastic containers to the extent that its weight and fragility have been disadvantages compared with these products. Glass had lost ground to polythene-made containers in uses where the likelihood of breakage is high, such as in the kitchen or bathroom. The policy of the major glass firms to win a share of the new markets for plastic bottles was indeed appropriate from their point of view.

2. The environment

Question 12 (page 50) was included as being an excellent illustration of the problem, well-known in economics, of externalities. Widespread discussion in the press and other media on the desirability of one-trip bottles took place in 1971, at a time when concern with general spoiling of the environment was in fashion. Forecasts then made of the increasing problem of litter disposal in an advanced economy like our own added to the ecological aspects of the problem. A report on refuse disposal showed that an average household produced 29.2 lbs. of refuse a week in 1968, of which 10.8 lbs. was paper, 2.6 lbs. metal, 2.7 lbs. glass and 0.3 lbs. plastics. By 1980 it was expected that the weight would increase to 32 lbs. a week, while the volume would increase by 44%.[2]

In many uses the glass container has long been used once only. The main exception until the mid-1960s was in respect of carbonated soft drinks, beer and milk. Changing methods of retail distribution — the increasing importance of self-service supermarkets and off-licences relative to traditional grocery outlets — have now made these three markets for glass containers increasingly ones where the container makes one-trip only. Sales of one-trip carbonated soft drinks rose rapidly in the late 1960s to a total of 290 million units in 1970. The growth in sales of such bottles for beer also rose very fast. The market for the product began in 1967 and rose to 60 million units within two years. Shortages of tin plate following a strike by blast furnacemen at Port Talbot in the summer of 1969 prompted brewing companies to turn even more to glass rather than cans. This example itself indicates the possibility of the substitution of the packaging medium within the whole packaging sector, a point stressed earlier.

One-trip bottles are, by definition, disposed of once their contents have been drunk. Firms selling soft drinks like Cadbury–Schweppes took an ˙indifferent attitude towards the question of bottle disposal until 1971 when they felt obliged to join in serious discussion with conservationists on the question of recycling glass containers. Thus there is now someone with the specific task of seeing that the packaging of Cadbury Schweppes products 'is compatible with the country's environmental interests'.[3] Surveys of the economics of re-using glass containers have been made. On the basis of a pilot scheme at Harlow, United Glass claimed that collection of used glass bottles by itself would not be economical.[4] Similar evidence emerged from another scheme at York tried by Redfearn-National.[5] The figures are not at issue here: what is interesting is the fact that the schemes have been set up at all as a defensive measure by glass container firms to meet criticism that they are not concerned with environmental matters.[6]

Shortages experienced by bottle users in 1973 led to fears concerning the availability of daily milk supplies. Whereas in the late 1960s the average milk bottle used to make 42 trips between the dairy and the home, this average had fallen to only 22 by 1973. The milk trade thus now has to replace 1.5 million bottles each day at a cost of some 3p. each. This alarm in late 1973 concerning the return of milk bottles indicated the importance of the packaging industry in the economy in a very basic way and at the same time the problem of 'the throw-away society'.

REFERENCES

1. W. Peter J. Maunder, 'The Glass Container Industry: a study on the effect of the 1956 Restrictive Trade Practices Act', *Economics*, vol. 9, part 4, Summer 1972, pp. 202–19.
2. K. Gofton, 'The search for tidy rubbish', *The Financial Times*, 27 November 1971, p. 17. The report cited in the text was issued by the Department of the Environment in 1971 called *Refuse Disposal*. It was the product of a working party under Mr. J. Sumner. For a general statement of the problem of refuse disposal see the Green Paper *War on Waste*, published in September 1974.

3. Interview with Mr D. M. Baynes, 'The role of food in the environment', *The Grocer*, 5 October 1974.

4. R. F. Cook, 'Can glass recycling pay for itself?', *United Glass Packaging Forum* No. 17, September 1974.

5. *Glass container recovery: its viability*, a report compiled by Redfearn National Glass Ltd.

6. The Glass Manufacturers Federation issued a report in 1973 called *The Glass Container Industry and the Environmental Debate*.

POINTS INTENDED TO BE RAISED FROM THE QUESTIONS

1. Prices had been increased only ten times over a period of fourteen years. Between 1939 and 1960 prices had been increased by 119% while there had been substantially greater increases in the costs of labour and raw materials. This suggested increasing efficiency of bottle production and the adoption of new technology of manufacture. Profits of firms in the Association, as measured by the overall average figure were invariably below the target figure of 10%, again suggesting a moderate pricing strategy in practice. Capacity had been installed to meet rising demand and worked to full use so that costs per unit could be minimized.

2. Prices were not closely related to costs – anomalies existed. The use of an overall profit target of 10% shielded inefficient firms from the competition of more efficient firms who could, if the agreement ended, produce successfully at lower prices. The production difficulties of United Glass, the major firm, in fact distorted the overall average profit margin. The Association's change in its arguments were not likely to persuade the Court in its favour. The Court was not given a convincing reason why price cutting would break out if capacity was likely to be fully used in future years as demand expanded. Technical progress was continuing despite the possibility of the collapse of the agreement at the hands of the Court. The non-price restraints on competition revealed in the Court hearing were hardly in the spirit of 'fair competition' stressed before the Court.

3. (a) (i) Price stability is advantageous to manufacturers in that it enables them to plan ahead with a greater degree of

certainty than if prices are fluctuating. In particular it makes it less risky for them to use periods of low demand as a time for building up stocks.

(ii) Price stability is advantageous to customers for the same basic reason, namely that it removes one source of uncertainty from all those which affect their planning. Another advantage is that it makes it unnecessary for them to undertake speculative stockholding from the price point of view, although this may still be necessary to meet unforeseeable fluctuations in demand.

(b) The bottle manufacturers argued to the Court that price stability made them willing to hold large stocks of bottles. They did this for two reasons. Firstly many of their customers operated in areas where there were large seasonal fluctuations in output, e.g. jam making. Secondly there was a tradition in the industry that the bottle makers held large stocks so as to be able to meet customers' unexpected fluctuations in requirements.

The manufacturer felt that if there was not price stability they would not be prepared to hold stocks but would have to match their production very exactly to demand. This could only be done by creating more capacity which would be idle for much of the year.

4. In answering this question it is first necessary to decide what is a large customer — is it a big organization in the sense of having a lot of employees? Is it large in the sense that it buys a lot of bottles, or large in the sense that it buys large quantities of a particular bottle?

(a) If a customer takes large quantities of a particular type of bottle in a given period of time, then it might expect a lower price because it would anticipate that the manufacturer would achieve certain economies when manufacturing in volume. On the other hand, if the customer took several different types of bottles which in total represented a large quantity, although manufacturing economies might not apply the supplier might achieve administration and distribution economies.

(b) A supplier, in deciding whether or not to offer larger customers lower prices, will need to estimate the economies it anticipates it would achieve by dealing with a large customer. In general, it would expect to share these economies with the customer.

5. (a) A supplier can, in these circumstances, only remain profitable by earning higher profits on other business and/or increasing its efficiency and thus lowering its costs.

   (b) If the supplier raises its prices to its smaller customers this will increase the smaller firms' costs and thus reduce their competitiveness.

6. Obviously each member of the Association is anxious to remain in business. The price agreement, by reducing the likelihood of a price war developing, means that if the industry ever found itself in the position of having excess capacity the available business would be fixed at a price which on average was profitable. This would make it less likely that any firm would find the financial pressures unbearable and leave the industry.

7. The wholesale price index is based on the list prices of bottle manufacturers and excludes discounts conceded to buyers. Thus a fall in published prices such as occurred in 1963 indicated sharply increased competition throughout the industry going beyond increased discounts. Thus competitive pressures had spread from sections of the industry such as the milk bottle trade mentioned earlier, where prices were already being keenly determined. The first index is then a general one taking in all types of glass bottles; the second relates to one product and one buyer only. One would expect the latter to be more sensitive in so far as it would reflect the competitive pressure exerted by a major buyer.

8. Important factors that contributed towards the strengthening of price competition which occurred in 1962 were the very poor summer of that year, and the imposition of purchase tax on both alcoholic and soft drinks in the Budget. Both led to a drop in demand for bottles for beverages in 1962. This in turn meant that with the presence of surplus manufacturing capacity producers tended to bid down prices.

9. Keener competition would be likely to lead to closure of high-cost plants and stimulate the search to reduce costs of production and distribution as far as possible. Technical progress would be likely to be encouraged since this means for existing products greater output per unit input, and also research into new techniques of production and new products. Thus research and development would be more

crucial than hitherto for the industry's long-term success. Profits of firms would certainly be reduced and be the tangible factor in effecting the remedial measures just suggested. In some cases firms earning lower profits might withdraw from the industry voluntarily or through bankruptcy. Mergers would very likely be expected, resulting in a moderating of the strength of competition.

10. There are competitive forces affecting technical progress of an exogenous character. Increased competition from substitute materials such as paper, tin and plastic in the past decade have been an important factor predisposing management in glass bottles to have been more dynamic and innovative than would have otherwise been necessary to retain existing market shares. Buyers of glass containers too have been increasing their knowledge of their particular market environments through market research. The character of container and pack design has been of growing importance. The strong possibility of substitution for glass by buyers from the glass industry is therefore an important point affecting the total environment in which glass firms operate. To take just the case of milk bottles: the danger to glass container firms specializing in milk bottles of dairies introducing every-other-day deliveries was, after 1961, a strong stimulus to reduce the cost of bottles. The repeated use of milk bottles is cheaper for dairies than the use of single-trip paper or plastic containers and this helps to maintain costly seven-day deliveries of milk. Fewer deliveries would almost certainly cause bottle firms to lose trade as households bought milk in cartons or used milk substitutes packaged in tin containers. We see here clearly the real competitive threat to the industry offered by rival forms of packaging. Competition from paper substitutes has also been an important phenomenon behind them. Light-weighting has reduced the cost of milk bottles by something like 10%, as compared with a decade ago. These technical developments have thus been a necessary and indeed a successful holding operation by the industry in beating off competition from substitutes.

11. The Court could not foresee anything other than rising demand for glass bottles after 1961. Every year after 1962 has in fact seen an increase in the industry's total sales. The average annual growth in terms of physical output between 1962 and 1971 was 4.75%; in respect of value the growth rate was 12.87%. The market situation

has thus not been such as to create conditions for the price war as feared by the British Bottle Association, though the government's periodic deflationary measures throughout the 1960s inevitably affected the rate of increase in demand in particular years. On the other hand 1962 and 1963 were years when demand in particular sectors was sluggish — in 1962 from the beverage industry, in 1963 from food processors. These first years of a free competitive market were then the ones when keen price competition would have been expected. However it is highly arguable whether the term 'price war' is an appropriate description of the actual course of events in those years.

12. The rise in sales after 1966 of the one-trip bottle for beer and also carbonated soft drinks has underscored the issue of the disposal of waste in our society. The publicity attached to the dumping by militant conservationists of several thousand non-returnable bottles outside the Head Office of Schweppes Ltd. in October 1971 illustrates the present-day concern with spoiling the environment. One-trip bottles for carbonated soft drinks grew in importance during the late 1960s since supermarkets were disinclined to collect a deposit at the time of purchase and later repay it to the customer. The one-trip bottle means of course extra business for glass bottle companies even though demand for them comes from brewers and bottlers as a result of the attitude of retail chains.

13. The Court struck down the B.B.A. agreement thus creating a necessary condition for greater competition in the industry. The market environment after 1961 in fact became keener with repercussions for firms in terms of efficiency and technical progress. The Court's verdict was thus a crucial one and can fairly be seen as of distinctive importance in the industry's recent history.

FURTHER READING

In addition to the sources cited in the Teacher's Notes the following are suggested:

The Times Survey: Packaging, 23 June 1972.
The Financial Times Survey: Packaging, 9 May 1973.

5. Resale Price Maintenance Abandoned: Domestic Electrical Appliances

TEACHER'S NOTES

These comprise an account of the main economic changes in the domestic electrical appliances sector since the ending of r.p.m.

1. The industry's market structure

In July 1966 A.E.I. and E.M.I. (the latter through Morphy Richards) established a joint subsidiary company, British Domestic Appliances Ltd. (B.D.A.), to cater for this specialist market. It is from this organization (which was expanded in 1967 and 1968 when G.E.C. brought together A.E.I. and E.E.) that E.M.I. withdrew in 1972 following heavy losses. It has long been recognized by those acquainted with the industry that cross subsidization between the various activities of the general electrical engineering companies occurs. Thus one firm of stockbrokers commented at the end of the 1960s:

> Many appliance subsidiaries have been running at a loss, but because of prestige considerations have been financed from profits from other divisions. This has kept the number of appliance manufacturers at a high level.[1]

As far as market structure itself is concerned, concentration is fairly high in individual appliance sectors.

It is necessary to point out the practice of appliance producers of manufacturing for each other appliances which are marketed under the brand of a company which has not been responsible for manufacture. Figures on the extent of this practice are few, but it has been estimated that English Electric at one time made 30% of all cookers sold through the market, although the English Electric and Revo brands accounted for only 16% of market sales.

Table 5.4 Percentage share of the three largest firms (according to brand).

	1957–61	1959–63	1963–67	1967
Electric cookers	58	56	53	53
Electric refrigerators	42	39	37	37
Washing machines	64	67	68	68
Vacuum cleaners	67	78	83	..
Electric hair dryers	88	82	73	..
Electric kettles	68	75	73	..

Source: Hoare and Co. Investment Research *Domestic Electrical Appliances*, (1969).

Competition in the various appliance sub-markets is at present keen.[2] Additionally, imports now play a considerable part in the British domestic appliance market, and Corley considers that this 'has a significance out of all proportion to its volume, for the appliances industry is no more insulated from external factors than is the general run of British industry'.[3] As far as individual appliance markets are concerned it has been estimated that whereas in 1965 imports accounted for nearly 10% of the home market, as against 5% in 1963, by 1968 this figure had risen to 13%; and a stockbroker's survey of the industry suggested that in respect of that year figures for individual appliances would be as follows: cleaners and polishers 3.2%, laundering appliances 11.2%, and refrigerators 23.8%.

2. The domestic electrical appliances industry without r.p.m.

The most pertinent areas for investigation here are:

    (a) price levels of appliances;
    (b) developments in house branding;
    (c) sales and servicing provision;
    (d) retail distribution;
    (e) manufacturer competition and efficiency.

(a) Prices
Philips, Thorn, B.D.A., English Electric and Electrolux all announced their intention of *recommending* resale prices following the ending of

r.p.m., but it soon became clear that there would be considerable departures from these.

Table 5.5 Domestic appliances prices (1968)

	Recommended Price £. s. d.	Typical Price £. s. d.	Reduction (%)
Upright vacuum cleaner	·32.15.2	29.18. 2	8.7
Cylinder vacuum cleaner	15.11.7	14.14. 8	5.4
Twin-tub washing machine	70. 2.3	62. 4. 4	11.2
Spin dryer	25. 2.0	22. 0.11	12.2

Source: National Board for Prices and Incomes Report No. 73, *The Prices of Hoover Domestic Appliances,* H.M.S.O. 1968, (Cmnd. 3671) para. 10

A later *Which?* survey relating to appliances bought in 1967 revealed the following:

Table 5.6 Prices paid for appliances (1967)

Recommended retail price	33.1%
Discount 10%	20.8%
11%—20%	30.0%
21%—30%	12.5%
30%	3.6%
	100.0

Source: *Which?,* March 1971, p. 72.

In fact in December 1969 B.D.A. announced the ending of *recommended* resale prices in respect of refrigerators — in which they held about 50% of the market — a move which seems to have been made in the light of the severity of domestic and international competition. It is clear that the degree of price-cutting has not diminished, and that discounts of 15%—25% from recommended prices are common. Two further checks are, however, necessary: how have appliances prices moved against *consumer prices in general* and how have prices moved against *manufacturers' costs?*

Table 5.7 Year-on-year price changes (%)

	1964	1965	1966	1967	1968	1969	1970
All Consumer Prices	3.4	4.7	3.5	2.4	4.5	5.3	5.3
Appliance Prices	2.1	1.6	1.4	1.4	4.8	4.6	5.2

Source: *Management Today*, May 1971, p. 26.

Table 5.8 Prices and costs index (1967 = 100)

				*Consumer Product Price**	
	Steel	*Aluminium*	*Copper*	*Twin-tub*	*Cleaner*
1963	105	102	74	118.5	109.3
1967	100	100	100	100.0	100.0
1969	107	123	134	104.3	97.1
1970	121	135	155	106.0	106.8

*based on typical 'going' prices, excluding purchase-tax.
Source: Hoover Ltd. *Annual Report* 1970, pp. 4–5.

The two sets of data indicate that consumer price increases, both generally and in relation to input costs, have been contained in the period since 1965.

(b) House brands

It was suggested that the incidence of house brands might increase with the ending of r.p.m.;[4] but although the Area Electricity Boards and mail order stores such as G.U.S. have adopted such a policy the incidence varies markedly between appliances. On the whole, Area Boards have increased house branding since 1965; but while they pursue this policy in refrigerators (where they have about one-third of the market)...

Given the Electricity Boards' dominant position in the cooker market, it is perhaps surprising that they have not adopted a private label policy here too, but the highly symbiotic relationship of the Boards with the cooker manufacturers has probably rendered this unnecessary as well as potentially embarrassing for the Boards.[5]

(c) Safety and servicing

This was one of the main areas in which supporters of r.p.m. thought that standards would fall in the absence of the practice. The fears would appear to be largely unfounded. This is not to suggest that criticism has not been voiced or is not justified;[6] but two points must be remembered. Firstly, in-guarantee work is now carried out by manufacturers and thus should not be influenced by distributive changes. Secondly, in this context it would seem that it is some of the multiple appliance distributors who are most critical of the conditions in the industry generally, and who are in a number of cases trying to do something about the situation. Thus, Currys has been reported as claiming that: 'The standard of servicing offered is nothing like as good as it should be. The consumer is having a raw deal at the moment'.[7] Furthermore, it would seem that it is not the price-cutting multiples which are necessarily offering the lowest standard of repair work. Speaking of the recent situation, one commentator on the industry noted:

> Playing the discount game used to be a case of taking rock-bottom prices and doing one's own fetching, carrying and transporting. Now multiples and stores are offering even more service, believing less in aggressive price wars than in consistently maintained low prices allied to service. The first consumer requisite of brown or white goods is that they are never out of order.[8]

Not only does this philosophy apply to the better-known multiple appliance distributors, but it is also the code of some of the largest discount stores. A director of one of these emphasized that: 'The fact that we offer discounts makes no difference whatsoever to our after-sales service.'[9]

(d) Retail distribution

Not unnaturally the worst was feared for small appliance distributors following the ending of r.p.m. The President of the Electrical Appliance Association wrote to Mr. Heath at the time of the original r.p.m. Bill protesting against the ' "unfair and hasty decision" which is likely to cause the greatest hardship to thousands of independent retailers whilst doing nothing to reduce the price of goods to the public.'[10] But in fact events were to show that in this particular case price-cutting was to become a characteristic of all sizes of retail outlet. Despite exhortations from trade association secretaries 'not to attempt to meet cut-price competitors on their own ground, but to provide value-for-money merchandise with a dependable repair service',[11] much of the price-cutting in this field has been undertaken by non-multiple organizations, and these appear to have held up their market share in the face of multiple competition. In fact the real growth of multiples took place in this field largely before the ending of individual r.p.m., and the following data shows little change in the situation since that date:

Table 5.9 Household appliance sales — market shares (%)

	Multiples		Electricity Boards	
	1966	1969	1966	1969
Washing machines	26	26	18	20
Vacuum cleaners	17	17	11	18
Electric refrigerators	14	17	29	33

Source: A.G.B.*Audit*, , April 1971, pp. 3—4.

One of the trends which is discernible in the trade is the growth of buying groups of independent distributors. In this way not only have appliance distributors in the independent category shown that they are *willing* to cut prices along with the multiples, but 'they can compete with the threat from the larger buying units by offering goods at competitive prices to the consumer and synonymously staying in business themselves'.[12]

It would thus seem that in this market the independent distributors have been willing and able to promote their own survival against the multiples, and that (as we have pointed out earlier) this has occurred without loss of the quality of service to final consumers.

(c) Manufacturer competition
The setting for this has been a far from buoyant appliances market.

Table 5.10 U.K. deliveries of certain home-produced consumer durables (mn.)

	1966	1967	1968	1969	period change (%)
Vacuum cleaners	0.98	1.07	1.18	1.16	+18.4
Washing machines	0.60	0.62	0.69	0.58	−3.3
Electric irons	1.84	1.70	1.74	1.58	−14.1
Electric blankets	1.50	1.24	1.39	1.36	−9.3
Electric cookers (under 5km.)	0.55	0.62	0.68	0.65	+18.2
Domestic refrigerators	0.81	0.65	0.88	0.86	+6.2

Source: E.I.U. *Retail Business*, June 1970, No. 148, p. 13.

It is not surprising in this context that the industry has been characterized by some redundancy, and that, as the following financial data shows, profitability has if anything declined over the period since 1965.

Table 5.11 Company profits in domestic appliances

	Pre-Tax Profits/Capital Employed (%)				
	1966	*1967*	*1968*	*1969*	*1970*
Bulpitt and Son Ltd.	15.3	16.1	13.5	14.2	11.0
Dimplex Industries Ltd.	33.3	16.2	13.9	23.5	29.1
Electrolux Ltd.	3.9	15.3	25.5	18.5	20.7
Goblin (B.V.C.) Ltd.	12.3	15.8	21.7	15.0	8.5
Hoover Ltd.	16.5	17.3	22.6	16.8	17.8

Source: Company Annual Reports and Accounts.

These figures are subject to the usual caveats involved in using aggregated data relating to multi-product company performance. However, it would seem from others sources that profitability in appliance production is low or negligible. Parkinson Cowan's Fisher-Bendix subsidiary in the domestic appliance field had been making such losses immediately prior to the takeover of this group by Thorn early in 1971 that the firm had recorded overall losses despite some profits made in other sectors of its business.[13] In 1971 the Annual Report of E.M.I. Ltd. dealt with the loss incurred that year by B.D.A. in which E.M.I. (through Morphy Richards) had a 25% stake. During the year ended 31 March 1971, B.D.A. incurred a loss of £2,164,000 (this is assumed from E.M.I.'s 25% share and the burden of losses of £541,000).[14] Though not all manufacturers can be operating on this basis — and the figures previously for the specialist appliance producers show that they are not — it is generally acknowledged that profitability in the industry overall is low.

REFERENCES

1. Hoare and Co. Investment Research, *Domestic Electrical Appliances*, 1969, p. 35.

2. See *Management Today*, April 1968, p. 69.
3. T. A. B. Corley, *Domestic Electrical Appliances*, Cape 1966, p. 120.
4. See *The Financial Times*, 30 June 1965.
5. *Private Label Reviewed*, J. Walter Thompson 1970, p. 11.
6. See Consumer Council *Annual Report* 1969–70, p. 42; and *Which?*, March 1971, pp. 68–86.
7. Quoted in *The Guardian*, 12 January 1972.
8. *The Financial Times*, 11 September 1971.
9. Sales Director of Comet Discount Warehouse quoted in *Leicester Mercury*, 18 October 1971.
10. Quoted in *Electrical Review*, 24 January 1964, p. 119.
11. Michael Keegan of the R.T.R.A. quoted in *Electrical Retailer and Trader*, 5 January 1967.
12. A.G.B. *Audit*, April 1971, p. 4.
13. See *The Financial Times*, 2 April 1971.
14. See E.M.I. Ltd. *Annual Report* 1971, p. 11.

POINTS INTENDED TO BE RAISED FROM THE QUESTIONS

1. Manufacturers would be likely to stress the undesirability of undue price, and thus demand, fluctuations. R.p.m. would give price stability. They would argue that fixed prices encourage service (stockholding, delivery, credit etc.) with the certainty of a guaranteed margin.

   The encouragement of a larger number of distributors leading to increased sales and reduced retailer buying-power would also be relevant. Manufacturers' full control of price levels would be felt important for those products where price is a partial indicator of quality.

2. Retailers would also agree that fixed prices guaranteed an adequate trade margin for proper service provision. They would be likely to stress the need of price stability and the dangers of 'cut-throat' competition.

3. The virtues of price stability would certainly be the key argument for both manufacturers and retailers. The fact that this meant that

direct price competition would not exist needs to be appreciated. Competition is an uncomfortable process and security is inevitably a natural motive for business firms as for individuals. The *levels* of trade margins could give distributors a comfortable living without them in fact giving adequate service to customers.

4. (a) High trade-in allowances (i.e. better than really appropriate prices for the old appliances of customers).
   (b) Subsidized hire-purchase terms (i.e. reduced interest charge).
   (c) Giving of free gifts with new appliances.
   (d) Free service contracts, etc. for extended periods (including labour and parts).
   (e) Extended recognition of trade and professional club membership (e.g. selling at wholesale prices to ordinary members of the public).

5. These appliance distributors:
   (a) Showed that r.p.m. provisions could be evaded without sellers openly breaking the law.
   (b) Showed consumer durable purchasers the savings which were possible.
   (c) Suggested that existing distributive margins protected by r.p.m. were too large.
   (d) Suggested that the price elasticity of demand for appliances in the short run might be quite high.
   (e) Indicated that the correct policy during a relative shortfall in demand against production capacity was a price reduction.
   (f) By increasing their proportion of total appliance sales showed manufacturers how important they were, and that their consequent buying power would be of significance in determining distributive policies in the industry.

6. Hoover would expect to gain (a) from the public which would find open price reductions on Hoover products, and (b) from cut-price appliance distributors who would favour stocking Hoover products upon which alone they could offer legal price reductions. Hoover's importance in the appliance market would be some guarantee against traditional distributors boycotting Hoover products in protest. These distributors would not gain from such a policy.

7. Investment in new plant in the late 1950s had resulted in excess capacity in the industry. Secret price cuts through high trade-in values in a state of over-supply meant the *de facto* end of r.p.m. from 1960 onwards. The second factor related to the supply at the retail level, i.e. the growth of discount store and supermarket selling of appliances. In a situation of over-supply the turnover which these distributors offered was welcome to manufacturers, albeit at cut prices.

8. Demand was sluggish from 1960 onwards. Price theory would suggest that a weakening in the state of demand in relation to capacity is likely to cause competition to increase in intensity. In the case of domestic appliances, government policy — the reimposition of hire purchase controls in April 1960 — reinforced the downward movement in spending on these goods.

9. A squeeze on the profits of manufacturers might be expected.
   (a) The fall in retail prices would eventually work back to reduced manufacturer trade prices if retail margins were not to absorb the whole of the retail price fall.
   (b) The ending of r.p.m. could lead to a fall in the number of distributors, thus to retail buying oligopsony power and to reduced selling prices for manufacturers.

10. The Act had an impact on this industry since manufacturers saw little chance of 'success' in gaining exemption from the main provisions of the Act. Such a process would have been expensive. However the demand and supply factors seem to be more important in explaining the demise of r.p.m. in this industry. Even in the absence of the 1964 Act it seems likely that r.p.m. would have broken down by 1965 due to the increasingly competitive nature of the industry.

FURTHER READING

This study is based on research for a M.Sc. thesis of Loughborough University of Technology submitted by W. S. Howe in July 1972. The thesis was called 'Resale Price Maintenance — History, Theory and Case Studies'. Two industries besides electric appliances were studied —

chocolate and sugar confectionery (where r.p.m. collapsed in 1967 before the Restrictive Practices Court) and pharmaceutical goods (where the court upheld r.p.m. in 1970). The thesis is available on inter-library loan from the Library of Loughborough University.

A survey of the ending of r.p.m. has appeared in *Economics*. See W. S. Howe, 'The ending of resale price maintenance: implementation of government policy', Vol. X, Part 1, Summer 1973, pp. 5–16.

Useful company surveys are:
P. Farrant, 'Hot point at A.E.I.', *Management Today*, July–August 1966, p. 78.
D. Thomas, 'When Frigidaire caught cold', *Management Today*, September 1968, p. 88.
D. Thomas, 'The hard times of Hoover', *Management Today*, March 1970, p. 94.

CASE STUDY
6. Conglomerate mergers: three case studies

TEACHER'S NOTES

1. Government policy towards conglomerate mergers

One could well conclude from an analysis of these three Reports that the Monopolies Commission had put itself in the same category as traditional economics and the man in the street, suggested in the opening paragraph of this study (page 61): that it had failed to understand the nature of the conglomerate company. In fact *The Economist's* first interpretation of the news of the first two Reports was that 'bigness has this Government's blessing and conglomerates in general have not'.[1] Since the Commission sanctioned the merger of the fifth and seventeenth largest U.K. companies (Unilever and Allied Breweries) it could not mean that the Commission had fears over company size alone.

Likewise it was noted that it was not the question of market dominance or barriers to entry to which the Commission took exception in the case of Rank and De La Rue. The Commission appears to have sanctioned the Unilever—Allied merger partly because Unilever had promised to leave Allied in this country virtually untouched and to allow it to continue to operate as a fairly specialized concern, and partly because many of the changes following the merger would take place overseas and would thus have little impact on the U.K. public interest[2] (except for the question of any impact on the balance of payments, on which the Commission was satisfied).

In the case of Rank the reasons which the Commission gave for objecting to the merger can either be seen as being healthfully individualistic and pragmatic, or capricious and unconvincing. One can argue against a lack of fundamental principles or rules (such as the 'gateways' of the 1956 and 1968 Restrictive Trade Practices Acts) on the grounds that decisions on industrial structure should not depend upon the 'unpredictable reactions of individuals in high places, influenced by the fashion of the moment'.[3] But to attempt to lay down

129

specific or even general criteria for government approval of mergers (as the then Board of Trade did to some extent later in 1969[4]), may be in the view of some people to adopt too rigid and inflexible an attitude towards a phenomenon which is only just beginning to be understood at the level of applied industrial economics.[5] But the whole point about the conglomerate merger is that it cannot usually even be explained by reference to some of the rationale associated with horizontal or vertical mergers. The desire to achieve economies of scale or to acquire monopoly power cannot usually or easily be fulfilled in the context of the conglomerate merger. Hindley has suggested that:

> The list of conglomerate mergers is likely to be a particularly fruitful source of mergers which are, in essence, concealed takeover bids. This is precisely because they cannot be explained in terms of 'industrial logic'; so that a probably more correct explanation is relatively unprofitable operation by the managers of one of the firms.[6]

We have seen above that this was in fact one of the reasons put forward by Rank management for their takeover of De la Rue. There is, however, no reason why this should not be an acceptable reason for a merger, and this would put a different complexion upon the 'substance' argument in the B.M.C.–Wilkinson case. Indeed in the context of conglomerate mergers it must become the principal reason. It is just in the context of the conglomerate merger that the concept of 'industrial logic' is most difficult to define. Whatever the details, however, surrounding any particular conglomerate merger case, it must come down to a measure or indication of potential increased efficiency in the new industrial grouping. To this extent the Monopolies Commission will search for those characteristics about potential conglomerate mergers which will bear upon the efficiency — in terms of resource use — of the merged firms. This criterion would largely explain the acceptance of the proposed Unilever–Allied, B.M.C.–Wilkinson mergers, and the rejection by the Commission of Rank's bid for De La Rue.

The interpretation of the government's thinking on conglomerates must however be related in part to their size, and to the influence which they have been held to exert on small sections of their total business. This feature, and the capital gains which it was held could arise in these situations, were the reasons given by Mr. Crosland at the time of the beginning of the Commission's inquiry into these two conglomerate mergers. The fact that the Commission was dealing with a new phenomenon appears to have given it a freedom to move away from its narrower concern previously with resource use. This allowed it to consider the effect on other brewers of the Unilever—Allied merger, the question of 'substance' in the case of B.M.C. and Wilkinson, and the question of the loss of executive manpower at De La Rue. This does not, however, cancel out all of the trenchant criticism which has been voiced at the Commission's conclusions — basically concerning the weakness of the overall analysis in the case of Unilever and Allied, the inappropriateness of the grounds for banning Rank's bid for De La Rue, and the loose and imprecise discussion of 'substance' in the more recent Report.

One issue which has arisen from these cases is that of a merger which has not in fact gone ahead despite a firm initial bid and subsequent Commission approval. In fact, the proposed merger between Unilever and Allied did not take place. Due to an adverse movement in relative share prices in the interim between the initial suggestion of the merger and the publication of the Commission's Report, the two firms decided not to go ahead with their merger but to expand into European and other overseas markets independently. During the period between the original merger proposal and the publication of the Commission's Report, movements of the respective companies' share prices caused their p/e ratios (i.e. the ratio of the current price of a firm's ordinary shares to its most recent equity earnings) to move apart until Unilever had a p/e of under 13 while Allied stood at 17. Movements in this ratio can significantly alter the immediate financial implications of a merger where the link is to be achieved by share exchange. But should this be allowed to interfere with a merger which, it was submitted to the Commission, would confer long-term benefits on shareholders and the national economy?[7]

The question of changes of mind among parties to a merger following a reference to the Commission has arisen in a subsequent case, as has that of incompatible management styles. Boots originally made an offer for House of Fraser in November 1973; but in the light of 'entirely exceptional international and national circumstances' decided in March 1974 that it wished to renegotiate the terms of the bid, which had originally been accepted by House of Fraser and in particular by Sir Hugh Fraser. In this case a change of mind occurred during the period of the Commission's inquiry. Such changes of mind do, however, raise questions concerning the basis of the original merger or takeover decisions, although some would argue that the very reference of a proposed merger to the Commission may be enough to deter some business people from going ahead with a venture. A series of such events did occur in 1973 — that is, bids were dropped following a reference to the Commission. These were Sears—William Timpson, Tarmac—Wolseley Hughes, Glynwed—Armitage Shanks, Whessoe—Capper Neill, and Bowater—Hanson Trust. But this does not explain the case of Unilever and Allied where a proposed merger was dropped following Commission approval.

Another topic which has been raised again by the Commission's Boots—House of Fraser inquiry is compatibility of management in two organizations. We saw that this management incompatibility was significant in influencing the Commission in vetoing the Rank—De La Rue proposed bid. The Commission also came down against the Boots—House of Fraser proposed merger partly on the grounds of animosity between the two management teams following Boots' attempt to withdraw from takeover. It has been questioned in the case of De La Rue whether one could have expected the incumbent management to express any other desire than to leave following an unwelcome takeover; whether this was a consideration to which the Commission should have attached much weight; and whether the national interest in economic efficiency would not anyhow have been served by the departure of some of De La Rue management. Certainly, on this last point *The Guardian*, commenting on the sale in 1973 by De La Rue of its Potterton boiler subsidiary, was strongly critical of the firm's management.

The inept handling of this potentially rich business can only intensify institutional doubts about the quality of De La Rue's management.

Indeed, De La Rue has looked to be badly in need of the attentions of an institutional ginger group for several years now. . . .

There can be few cases in management history when a company has chosen to divest itself of a company with a strong brand name in the middle of a boom. This in itself is worrying for it suggests that De La Rue has too many problems elsewhere to cope with turning Potterton around. Shareholders be warned.[8]

Conglomerate companies and conglomerate mergers are a significant part of the U.K. economy at the present time. The Monopolies

Commission will be forced to look into conglomerate mergers more frequently in the future; thus an analysis of the conglomerate inquiries so far may indicate the principal issues involved in an increasingly important area of government competition policy.

2. Some notes on the companies in the case study

Unilever—Allied Breweries

The collapse of this proposed link was explained by the parties as due to share price movements. While not denying that this factor made negotiation of mutually acceptable terms difficult to achieve, it is also pertinent to point out that there were doubts in both firms about the desirability of the merger. The personal way in which the proposed merger was mooted by the chairman of Unilever contrasted with his company's usual patient and detailed study of possible firms for acquisition. Research on the subject indicates that there was less enthusiasm for the link amongst some senior management in both companies, and the difficulties of agreeing acceptable financial terms based on Stock Exchange quotations indeed appear to have come as a relief rather than disappointment in these quarters.

The period since 1969 has seen Unilever prefer to grow by a more gradual policy of acquisition than by major takeovers. No doubt its failure to acquire Smith and Nephew (makers of 'Nivea' and 'Elastoplast') in 1968 also explains this philosophy. Lord Cole's successor, Dr. E. Woodroofe, was quoted in 1973 as saying that: 'We prefer for the moment to extend our frontiers by the jig-saw approach.'[9] As a response to poor results in 1970, the company overhauled its top management structure and sought better profitability from its constituent parts. These moves suggest the relevance of the economists' terminology of 'managerial slack' and 'X-inefficiency'. Unilever has been the subject of a fascinating major study by Professor Charles Wilson.[10] More basic current information is available from the company's Information Division based at Unilever House, London E.C.4. It is interesting to note that Unilever itself was the result of a defensive merger in 1929 between the English soap-making firm of Lever Brothers and the Dutch margarine company, Margarine Unie, (itself formed in 1927 by the union of Jurgens and Van den Burghs). The use of common raw materials meant the two firms were in competition with one another. The 1929 merger eliminated this competition.

Allied Breweries, as the study indicates, was itself the result of a series of mergers between regional brewing concerns. It made an unsuccessful attempt in 1972 to acquire Trust Houses Forte which was a notably bitter affair resulting in the replacement of Lord Crowther by Sir Charles Forte as chairman of the latter concern.

Rank—De La Rue

Following the struggle to remain independent, De La Rue effected steps to improve its profitability and as with Unilever reorganized its management structure. Loss-making subsidiaries, viz. plastics, were sold off; the sale of the Potterton boiler subsidiary was cited in the note above (page 132).

British Match Corporation—Wilkinson Sword

This merger can be seen as an example of how a large firm can welcome a link with a smaller one since it seeks dynamic new management. Wilkinson Sword built up a reputation for its performance in the highly competitive razor blade market where it faced competition from the much larger film of Gillette. It was Wilkinson which introduced the world's first stainless steel razor blade. Competition between Gillette and Wilkinson has resulted in this product being the subject of a rapid rate of improved technology, i.e. varieties of bonded razors. It is not surprising that given the ability to stand up to keen competition from Gillette the Randolph management felt their skills could be appropriately employed in improving the fortunes of a larger concern. This merger was thus an example of a 'reverse takeover' — the small firm providing the management of the new enlarged company.

3. Conglomerates in the United States

The case study began with a note (page 62) that the anti-trust authorities in the United States have in recent years viewed conglomerate mergers with a critical eye. Doubts about their value in terms of their effects on competition now appear to have been substantiated in a recent study by the Federal Trade Commission.[11] The senior author of the report, Professor S. Boyle, has stated that the report shows that:

Large conglomerate mergers have a substantial anti-competitive effect. They may mask information regarding the profitability of producing the whole spectrum of industrial outputs. They make it impossible for firms, not already in an industry, to determine the profitability of that industry and, perhaps most importantly, they obscure from the sight of the owners of the corporation information which would enable them to judge the quality and effectiveness of corporate managers.[12]

Part of the case that came to be built up against conglomerates by the late 1960s was that they necessarily had a self-perpetuating growth character. This was because for groups like Ling—Temco—Vought and Litton Industries to continue taking over more and more companies, they needed a high price-earnings ratio. To maintain such a ratio they needed growth fuelled by takeovers. The momentum of continual acquisition had to be maintained. But once the successful growth in profits was broken and the Wall Street quotation sagged, then the conglomerate group runs into potential trouble. In the short term profits could be made by selling off unprofitable parts of acquired companies and research and development expenditures. However, too short-sighted a view of profits can prejudice a company's long-term viability. It was for these reasons that the glamour status attached to Ling—Temco—Vought and others of its type faded, and also because of investors' — let alone U.S. policy-makers' — doubts over the desirability of ever-mushrooming corporate groups.

REFERENCES

1. 'Mergers: bigness ain't bad', *The Economist,* 7 June 1969, p. 76.
2. 'It's conglomerates they're after', *The Economist,* 14 June 1969, p. 69.
3. See Samuel Brittan, 'Too much pragmatism in monopoly policy', *The Financial Times,* 31 July 1969.
4. See *Mergers: A Guide to Board of Trade Practice,* H.M.S.O., 1969.
5. One could say that the first real understanding of mergers in this context in the United Kingdom began with Gerald Newbould's *Management and Merger Activity,* Guthstead, 1970.
6. B. Hindley, *Industrial Merger and Public Policy,* I.E.A., 1970, p. 29.
7. One comment on the collapse of the merger said:

   If it really is so enormously important to their future [the companies] should be able by now to give some quantitative indication of the benefits they had expected from their joint development. All this could presumably have been put in detail to institutional shareholders in an effort to make them aware of the extra share values — the boost in the sum over the parts — that might have made an equity bid possible. [It ended its assessment:] When important aims are difficult, you do not just give up — otherwise people start to wonder whether they were really important after all.

'Is Lord Cole a serious beer-buyer?' *The Sunday Times* Business News, 8 June 1969.
8. 'De La Rue: decline and fall', *The Guardian,* 31 October 1973.
9. P. Wiltshire, 'Unilever: the company they don't appreciate', *The Sunday Times,* 27 May 1973. However, the bid in 1973 for the builders' merchants, Ellis and Everard, failed. The public-interest benefits from such an acquisition are questionable. *The Economist* commented at the time that such a bid in the United States would have been referred to the Justice Department on the ground that potential competition from a new entrant was being removed (Unilever had built up its own builders' merchants business from scratch). — 'David and Goliath', *The Economist,* 15 September 1973.
10. C. Wilson, *Unilever, 1945—65: Challenge and Response in the Post-war Industrial Reconstruction,* Cassell, 1968. Wilson has also written an earlier volume, called *The History of Unilever* published in 1954, which dealt with the years from the company's formation in 1929 to 1945.
11. The F.T.C. study was called *Economic Report on Conglomerate Merger Performance.* A summary appeared in *The Financial Times* of 5 January 1973: A. Dicks, 'The conglomerates under fire'.
12. Letter from Professor Boyle in *The Economist,* 3 February 1973.

POINTS INTENDED TO BE RAISED FROM THE QUESTIONS

1. A conglomerate company is one which produces a variety of goods which have no 'market' relationship — i.e. they represent neither vertical nor horizontal integration. For example:
   Reed International — ceramic sanitary ware, paint, stationery, business directories.

Unilever — supermarkets, toilet preparations, detergents, plastics, animal feeds.

E.M.I. — X-ray systems, fire protection equipment, gramophone records, squash courts, public houses.

2. On the surface there is little justification for their formation. But:
   (a) there may be *economies of scale* to be achieved at the general level in the area of finance, managerial expertise, marketing;
   (b) *diversification* into a number of markets may reduce the risk of variability of earnings;
   (c) *cross-fertilization* of ideas and technology between markets;
   (d) absolute size may *increase market power* and give some *protection from takeover.*

3. (a) The Commission does not have to perceive benefit in a merger to give it approval, only absence of detriment.
   (b) The Commission appears to have felt that many of the merger advantages would accrue to the companies involved rather than be passed on to final consumers.
   (c) Many of the effects of the merger would be felt overseas rather than in the U.K.
   (d) Benefits in the U.K. (e.g. increased competition in brewing) would be indirect and perhaps longer term.

4. The Commission considered De La Rue management to be important, and therefore its threatened departure detrimental, because:
   (a) personal management contacts were important;
   (b) confidentiality had to be maintained;
   (c) management styles of the two companies appeared incompatible.

5. This was the area of advantage stressed by the firms because:
   (a) few of the activities of the respective firms were complementary;
   (b) of the lack of real success in separate diversification;
   (c) the success of firms in market-oriented industries was held to be a function of size;
   (d) operating internationally, such advantages of size were held to be necessary in each country.

6. (a) The Commission appears to have had no reservations about company size.

   (b) The loss in efficiency which may have arisen in the case of Rank and De La Rue appears to have related to management incompatibility. It was in this context, as well perhaps as an unfamiliarity with the security printing aspect of De La Rue, that the Commission doubted whether Rank could efficiently manage a joint Rank—De La Rue business. The wide range of business covered by B.M.C. and Wilkinson does not appear to have worried the Commission.

7. (a) Conglomerates *can* subsidize some sections of their operations from surplus profits in others. They could use this technique to under-price specialist firms and thus force the latter out of a market. There is, however, no evidence to suggest that this occurs in practice.

   (b) By insisting that where possible subsidiaries of a conglomerate should trade with each other in obtaining inputs or selling finished goods, the market for certain products could be closed to outside specialist firms. Again, there is no real evidence on the incidence of this practice.

8. The concept of industrial logic relates to the appropriateness, in terms of traditional market relationships, of a combination of activities within one firm. There is, for example, an apparent logic in the process if a firm integrates vertically to its source of input supply or to its distributive channel. Again, it must appear logical if a paint manufacturer also makes wallpaper (same final use market) or a pneumatic tyre producer makes plimsolls and hoses (same raw material involved). The same 'logic' does not apply to firms making books and women's tights (Thomas Tilling). However, such diversification may be defended if each separate activity can be operated on a de-centralized basis, if top management is thus merely concerned with overall financial control and not day-to-day operations at plant level (i.e. it does not require to have expertise in the individual product fields), and the overall purpose of adding activities to a firm is to increase the dividend and capital appreciation per share of the firm. If this is the goal of the firm, and if diversified firms can achieve this goal, then the concept of industrial logic is superfluous.

9. Conglomerate diversification may be a pro-competitive force in the economy if it results in reduced barriers to entry to markets: i.e. if a large conglomerate has the finance to enter a capital-intensive sector which a 'new' firm would not. On the other hand, conglomerates *may* indulge in cross-subsidization of activities: under-pricing of competitors in the short-term may be achieved by selling at a loss, which can be covered by profits from other divisions. If this results in elimination of potential competition, and thus an opportunity for the conglomerate subsequently to increase prices and earn surplus profits, then this aspect of conglomerate diversification may be regarded as uncompetitive and against the public interest.

10. The data shows the increasing significance until the late 1960s of conglomerate mergers. Much of this may be accounted for by the popularity of this form of corporate expansion, based upon the success of the U.S. examples in the mid 1960s. The scope at this time for further significant horizontal merger activity may have been limited, and the early period of the operation of the 1965 Monopolies and Mergers Act may have witnessed a decline in horizontal amalgamation. Nonetheless, this was a period of some significant horizontal mergers: for example, G.E.C.–A.E.I.– English Electric, and Leyland–B.M.C. A significant contribution to the relative size in importance of conglomerate mergers, however, was the reduced popularity of vertical integration. It is unlikely that horizontal mergers will ever cease to be of considerable significance in the U.K. economy, as much scope still remains for concentration in many engineering sectors (including machine tools), construction, textiles and possibly even retailing.

11. The Commission's decisions were all accepted by the government of the day and thus formulated government policy in respect of conglomerate mergers. The verdicts were crucial in effecting the outcome of the planned mergers. The time required to study the Unilever–Allied Breweries merger led to the parties involved deciding to drop their proposed link. Whether they would have successfully completed their negotiations on the merger in the absence of a reference to the Monopolies Commission — before share price movements caused complications — it is impossible to say. What is clear is that the Commission's perusal of the merger in

effect stopped it. By contrast, the British Match Corporation—Wilkinson Sword link was allowed. The Rank—De La Rue merger was ruled as contrary to the public interest and, since the government accepted the Commission's verdict, the latter played the decisive role in determining the outcome in this case.

FURTHER READING

On the impact of conglomerate mergers there is only one detailed study in this country to hand, of Slater Walker's acquisition in 1967 of Greengate and Irwell Ltd. See C. Pratten, 'A case study of a conglomerate merger', *Moorgate and Wall Street*, Spring 1970.

On the companies in the case study, see:

'Europe's second company' (Unilever), *The Economist*, 15 April 1967.
K. Van Musschenbroek, 'Unilever banks on co-ordination', *The Financial Times*, 7 May 1970.
K. Van Musschenbroek, 'Cash conscious Unilever', *The Financial Times*, 8 August 1972.
G. Foster, 'The colossal cares of Unilever', *Management Today*, January 1967.

On the state of conglomerates in the U.S. see:

D. Palmer, 'Rise and fall of the conglomerate image', *The Financial Times*, 28 May 1970.
G. de Jonquieres, 'Conglomerates: a poisoned dart from Congress', *The Financial Times*, 3 November 1971.

The classic study on the subject is:

J. C. Narver, *Conglomerate Mergers and Market Competition*, University of California Press, 1967.

Also recommended is:

J. M. Blair, *Economic Concentration: Structure, Behaviour and Public Policy*, Harcourt Brace Jovanovich Inc. 1972, Ch. 12.

Preface

John first wrote me because *Herzog* had given him some support in his late wife's final illness. He was grieving. We began a correspondence that went on for a couple of years before I actually met him. I think he came to the States first, and I saw more of him later when I went to Israel. On that first meeting I found out a little about him, but not the whole story.

I found him pert, deep, salty—seasoned at sea. I was amazed that he was so much at home in English, and such a Conradian. Like Conrad he was Polish by birth and a seaman. His English, for a Jewish Pole, was faultless. I was attracted by the conjunction: Poland, English and the sea. He was a great reader, which made him immediately sympathetic to me. He'd read Conrad, but not only Conrad. He was steeped in late nineteenth century literature, the Russians and the English.

I also immediately recognized that he was a born story-spinner. In him it was more than a flair; it was a passion—a passion with deep sources in his reading and his life. I was also attracted to

I

the characteristic Jewishness of his story-telling. I have a very wide experience of this.

I immediately recognized traits of my family in him. My father, too, was a European who'd been everywhere and done everything. He had a way of speaking that grated on people and when he met someone from Lodz, he'd say, "Of course I know Lodz, I was there for three months!" My father was a restless man—he had to be to sail in so many directions at once. John, too, at one time. You can tell that his writing began in the long seasons at sea. His secret was that he was a man of letters, therefore incommunicable to most of his companions. That's in his stories, that he is hidden in the ship's company.

He should be read by all good readers because John is full of sympathy and never writes without strong feeling. He's not diffuse. Like so many writers of his generation he's given to art completely.

Why is he not better known? Known at all?

He was never taken up by the big shots. If I say he's a great Jewish writer he'll get thrown into the Jewish box. He's not just that. He wasn't published much? He didn't try very hard. He's a man without strategy who doesn't communicate much outside his stories. But there he has that gift of being able to communicate instantly with those whose antennae are prepared to receive rare frequencies. He's so used to living in dreams he doesn't have any ambitions.

Saul Bellow
Fall, 2002

*John Auerbach passed away in November, 2002,
as this volume was in preparation*

The Publisher would like to express appreciation to
Nola Chilton Auerbach and to Keith Botsford, for their
invaluable assistance in the genesis of this volume

Transformations
Part I

Chapter one

This, he said to himself, you push away.

That's how you have been conditioned; he has nothing to do with you anymore. He can't tell you anything, nor bother you. Not with his memories, not with his advice. Now look at yourself as others see you, as the *Volksdeutscher* on the opposite bench sees you, and the Pole next to him. Yes, that was part of the training.

But they are asleep.

Never mind; just imagine they've opened their eyes, and are staring at you. What do they see?

He remembered his reflection in the barber's mirror. Not in the mirror facing the chair on which he was sitting while the barber worked on his hair, but the other full length one, hanging near the entrance, which showed you full-size. You stood there looking at yourself critically while the barber brushed off the loose hairs from your jacket with a tiny whisk.

That's how they would see you now if they opened their eyes. A young man of medium height, very slightly bent, just enough to suggest negligence or relaxation. With long arms, ashen blond hair, rather small green-blue eyes, a straight long nose, full lips. Square forehead. That's all. They would not see anything else. Nor should they.

But you have to push him away, because eventually he will show up somehow, in a subtle way. He might even give rise to suspicion. To a shadow of suspicion, which is more than enough. That is impermissible; it was not in the contract, it is unfair.

So what do you do with him now? You were not trained to exorcise the dead and you do not know how to deal with him.

Perhaps I should pull the handle, stop the train and let him jump off.

No, it won't work. The only thing you can do, Grabowski decided, is to endure him, and take care that he does not show. Not in your eyes, and not anywhere else.

I hope to God they won't wake up. Also, it is rather dark here.

Pushing him away won't help. It will only upset both of us. Better endure, he said to himself. Show him that you can endure, and make sure you don't disclose anything to anybody.

Still, Grabowski thought, it was unfair.

Unfair? Who the hell was thinking about fairness? Who gives a damn about fairness?

It was on the slow train from Warsaw to Danzig that David Gordon made his penultimate appearance. He would next materialize, in a sense, some time later, on the seashore at Weichselmünde, which is near Danzig. But Grabowski could not have anticipated that while on the train. He was sufficiently annoyed with David's first re-appearance. The Jew was supposed to be dead; he was not supposed to bother Grabowski, who was his creation.

But here he was, and apparently quite confident that none of the four men in the train's dimly lit compartment would notice his presence. A small bulb painted dark blue gave off a very feeble light indeed.

David Gordon was concealed under Grabowski's skin. This

skin, barely a few days old, was still correspondingly thin and tender, but growing rapidly, from minute to minute, in thickness and toughness, and David Gordon evidently considered the protection sufficient.

David wished to recollect certain incidents from his life during the last two years.

Well, let him, Grabowski thought. If he insists on it. Still, it is very unfair. It is contrary to our contract of creation.

David did not bother to argue.

We'll endure, then, Grabowski thought.

He made sure once more that the other passengers—three Poles who, like himself, had volunteered to work for the Germans in Danzig, and their escort, a civilian *Volksdeutscher*—were still sound asleep. They were snoring.

I can spend the night with my creator's ghost, if necessary, Grabowski thought, I can take it, I'll listen and look, if that's what you want.

And to hell with you, I am strong enough, you made me that way.

He settled more comfortably in his corner seat, and once more his eyes wandered over the sleeping men's faces, and over the drab, wooden walls of the compartment. Finally, they rested on a metal plate directly over the window. *Emergency brake: in case of peril, pull the handle. Misuse will be punished in accordance with the Law.*

Perhaps you should have pulled that handle two years ago, Grabowski told Gordon, and to hell with the Law.

7

Chapter two

On the 1st of September 1939, at six o'clock in the morning, David Gordon was crouching with his face buried in the soft, wet earth of the embankment.

This is a strange position to be assumed by a man, especially that early in the morning, though in fact it was a most natural one. Several people on David's left and right were positioned in exactly the same way. David and his compatriots in the trench had assumed the crouching position instinctively, almost automatically, half an hour earlier, and had remained there for what seemed to them a very long time.

David thought, at least in basic reactions and impulses, all humans are equal.

The morning was beautiful and bright, the air was still fresh, but already laden with that peculiar dryness of late summer signaling the hot day to come.

The Second World War had just started, but the thought of it never crossed David's mind, or that of the other occupants of that deep trench on the East Prussian border. They had no time to think

8

of it with their faces buried in the soft earth trying to control the involuntarily movements of their bowels.

The *Stukas*—the German dive-bombers—were at them from the beginning.

The bombing was not very accurate. Not one direct hit was scored in the first hour, but the *Stuka* airplane had a new invention mounted between its wheels: a siren which made a very special noise during the plane's dive. There and then, it was being tested for the first time. In fact, it was the *Stuka*'s main weapon. The shrill deafening whistling tore apart people's nerve centers before the bombs tore apart their bodies and guts.

David was aware of a growing desire to stop hearing and feeling, to stop existing, to do anything to escape from that monstrous shrieking, which was born out of a very high, barely audible note, and swelled rapidly, steadily increasing in volume and force until the entire universe became one shrill whistle, drilling his skull and body. He stuck his fingers in his ears, and saw that others tried it too. It did not help. The all-destroying drilling noise penetrated easily, if not through the eardrums, then through the skull bones.

On and on the bombardment continued. During short pauses David withdrew his face from the earth wall, and looked around. He saw soldiers with wild, dirty faces, mad round eyes, trembling hands. These were not the same people he had known the day before.

He found certain relief in this confirmation that it was not only he who had lost his sanity. And then, again, the high whistle sounded, and while he pressed his face into the earth, it grew and grew, beyond the limits of human endurance, and the earth swayed slightly and pressed on his cheeks, on his eyelids, and lips, in rhythm with the thuds of the bombs' explosions. Then all of a sudden it rushed at him in a thick black wave, and he passed out. His last thought was enormous relief that he was out of it.

In the darkness of the train compartment Grabowski nodded, knowingly.

So that was how they killed you for the first time, eh? Somewhat naive, isn't it? Well, at the age of eighteen a certain naiveté is permissible. Later, one learns that only the chosen ones, the very lucky, manage to get out that easily. And, after all, it was not you who pulled that handle. Misuse will be punished—in accordance with the Law.

He opened his eyes, saw faces above him, and noticed there was no more whistling in the air. He was lying on the bottom of the trench. A man wearing a white armband with a red cross on it was touching his body.

"Move your arms and legs!"

He did, with conscious effort.

"Praised be God! Can you get up?"

He sat up, then stood on his feet. He felt dizzy, leaned against the wall.

"God be praised!"

David recognized Sergeant Zabiegala.

"You're lucky, boy! It only buried you a little bit! Quick, back to your position! They have stopped bombing, they'll attack any moment now!"

It was amazing, the human resilience. The deadly whistle of the dive-bomber was a thing of the past. It had never really happened. The soldiers were functioning again, running, preparing their rifles, loading ammunition.

Zabiegala, the sergeant, was everywhere. He helped to mount the heavy machine gun in its position, he gave a hand with a case of ammunition, ran to the field phone, exchanged a few words with the nervous, adolescent lieutenant, and found time to stop for one moment near David. He gave him a slap on his back:

"Lots of luck, eh, Gordon? Feeling OK now?"

Without waiting for an answer, he ran on.

David peered though a slit in the embankment. The attack had begun: across the field, not more than a thousand yards from them, gray armored cars and tanks were moving.

The tanks, as Sergeant Zabiegala had explained only two days earlier, were not dangerous. Only one in ten was a real tank. The rest were ordinary cars, covered with cardboard and painted.

10

"The Germans," said Zabiegala, "don't have enough steel to produce many tanks, but they were in such a hurry to start this war that they substituted these fakes to scare us. Our intelligence discovered it in time. Who do they think they have now before them? Czechs? Idiots? One good saber-blow by a cavalryman, or one resolute plunge with a bayonet and the thing falls apart. You can also throw a hand grenade at them if they are close enough. They'll burn like candles on a Christmas tree. They'll burn like paper, like goddamn cardboard, which they actually are."

"And remember," Zabiegala concluded his lecture, "the thing the German fears more than anything else is a cavalry charge, or an infantry charge with bayonets. Once they hear your battle cry, filled with real rage, they'll scram."

Thus spoke Sergeant Zabiegala. The soldiers listened in absolute silence, some of them open-mouthed, to increase the absorption capacity of their minds, hanging on to every word that passed through his lips.

Wasn't he the top authority, a professional NCO with 25 years service in the army?

"Once you're in the army, in this regiment, and in this company, I am your father and mother. I am everything to you. You got problems, ask me."

That had been two days earlier, and now the same make-believe tanks the sergeant had been talking about were crawling across the field toward them. They—Zabiegala's soldiers—watched them coolly, their rifles ready, their hearts still thumping a little following the *Stuka* assault, but confident now, without much fear.

"Let them come. We'll show them."

Halfway through the field the tanks stopped, and a short but violent artillery barrage hit the front trench.

The shells came whistling and roaring: they had no psychological effect similar to that of the *Stukas*: but explosions shook the trench, geysers of black earth spurted skywards, and against the deafening noise David heard a strange sound, much weaker, but piercing: the screaming of the wounded.

And ten minutes later, when the shelling had stopped, the terrible human shrieking persisted, high-pitched, and conveying unbearable suffering, pain.

David's neighbor on the right came nearer and said into his ear:

"Lieutenant Grodski is finished. It tore his legs off."

David nodded. The screaming had stopped. His neighbor crossed himself looking skyward. David hoped Sergeant Zabiegala had not been hit. It would be difficult to imagine the continuation of the war without him.

Now the tanks were near, their gun turrets turning, the guns blazing fire, and they were shooting back; shouting and shooting. The roar of the tank engines was ever nearer, and David wondered why none of the cardboard tanks was burning yet. Then he found that he had no more ammunition and turned to get some more. He saw that on his left side there was nobody, and that his neighbor on the right, the man who had crossed himself before, was running, half bent, along the trench. He followed him, and saw others running too, through the connecting trench toward the Second Line. Zabiegala was there, his back against the wall, touching lightly each man's arm as if counting them.

"Quick, quick! On the double, meeting point in the village! Keep running the whole way, quick!"

The village was more than a mile away, and David ran, together with the others; they spread across the field, dashing towards the village whose houses, visible among the trees, were burning fiercely. Clutching his rifle, and not having looked back even once, he reached the village church out of breath.

"There is much running in war," David thought.

David could not have known that he would have to run the whole distance of 200 miles to Warsaw. But Sergeant Zabiegala was there, and said, after regaining his breath:

"Orders from the division—we retreat, temporarily."

Chapter three

After the first twenty-four hours, the order of things changed in a changing world. From then on, they were only running or marching at night. In daytime, they rested in the woods.

"Was it an order from the division? Who had arranged things that way?"

The sky, a hot pale-blue, with a blazing sun, offered no answer, but it was clear that walking in daytime was impossible. War planes, nimble as mosquitoes, evil as horse-flies were flying low, slowly looking for anything crawling on the surface of the scorched earth. They strafed with machine guns columns of fleeing peasants or stragglers. They hunted for small groups of people. They shot at cows and horses and even at single men. They were everywhere, and at any time, from sunrise till dusk.

Only night provided shelter and relief. That was what night had been created for.

David, lying in thick bushes on the edge of the forest, watched the sun rolling down, below the horizon, and simultaneously a red

13

glow, rising in the east and gradually spreading over the sky, as if another dawn had started on the opposite side. The universe was exploding in a strange symmetry: the shiny, starless darkness overhead, the red-purple-violet sunset in the west, the artificial dawn, in more vulgar oranges and yellows, brighter than the real one. In the east and in the north, the glow of villages and towns burning beyond the horizon. David, with wide open eyes, watched this balance of colors in the night sky, and felt, for the first time in his life, his sense of reality questioned. It was an eerie moment, as if he had been transferred into another world, or, into a different life.

"But I am David Gordon, on my way to Warsaw," he whispered.

His comrades, on the edge of the forest, were still asleep. Soon the indefatigable Zabiegala would pass from one to another, shaking them.

"Get up, it is time."

Meanwhile, between dusk and dawn, only David was awake, and the birds terribly confused by the sudden failure of the eternal order of light and darkness.

Then they were marching again, quickly, in a single line, each man following the one in front of him, led by a silent, elderly major, who had lost his unit somewhere. They marched for hours without stopping. The goal was to reach Warsaw as soon as possible.

"There," Zabiegala explained, "we will re-organize, there we will show the swine. They caught us by surprise, by treason, treason and diversion were everywhere, the supplies and ammunition were sabotaged. In Warsaw, yes, we will show them."

The name of the capital was repeated so often that it became unreal, it became the Mecca, the Jerusalem, the magic word. Shattered divisions, defeated battalions, stragglers from non-existing army units, everybody was summoned to Warsaw by order of the Supreme Command.

Magical, David thought, but fitting in a new world where airplanes shoot at cows, and dawn shines every evening.

Quick as they were—"the Polish infantryman can make sixty

miles a day if necessary," Zabiegala had claimed—the Germans on their motorcars and motorcycles were sometimes quicker. They entered a small forest in the early morning, and no sooner had they lain down to rest, when shooting started. Along the road where the Poles had just passed, a long motorcycle column was moving, the riders helmeted, wearing goggles and long field-gray overcoats, in spite of the hot weather. They looked like invaders from Mars.

The Poles took shelter behind the trees, but then shots rang from the forest, and from a ditch, not more than a hundred yards to the left. Looking hard against the rising sun, David tried to see the enemy in the ditch. Zabiegala crawled behind him. "Save ammunition!" he said in a hoarse whisper. David knew they had only ten rounds per rifle.

The short staccato of a machine gun over his head, another volley from the forest, then the thud of a mortar shell. This, David thought, will be the end. Any moment one of their planes will come and finish them off.

Turning his head, he saw the sergeant and the major talking together. Zabiegala nodded and once again started crawling fast behind his men's feet.

"Put on the bayonet," he said, as he passed by David. "We'll charge."

All over the line, men were fixing the bayonets on their rifles. The enemy fire increased from all directions. There was no doubt they were surrounded.

"When I count, one, two, three, charge against the ditch!" shouted Zabiegala.

But when the moment came, nobody moved. They were completely pinned down by enemy fire.

David thought how exact the expression 'pinned down' was. If he lifted his head by two inches, a bullet would hit him.

"Charge, bastards!" yelled Zabiegala.

And then a strange thing happened: the major got up, a revolver in his hand, and roared: "What? You scared of the bullets? All right. I'll show you how to do it. No bullets can touch me!"

He passed through the line of supine men and started walking quickly toward the ditch. "Come on!" he shouted.

An important incident, thought Grabowski, looking through the train window at the impenetrable darkness outside, in David Gordon's life. One has to see a hero in action once in one's lifetime. To read or to hear is not enough. You must see it, then it makes a mark on your soul. A picture. The forest's edge, the explosions, the officer with his revolver walking towards the enemy.

David, jumping up, saw in the corner of his eye other men rising, shouting a battle cry perhaps, not a human sound, a noise a wild animal makes sometimes. The major, as if he were an actor in a slow-motion movie, raised his hand with the revolver and jerked his head up, performed a mad half-pirouette, and fell heavily on the soft, spongy ground. The man on David's left cried: "Jesus!" and fell on his face. But David kept running with the others, yelling and shrieking and clutching his rifle with the bayonet.

Then another unreal thing happened. The Germans in their round helmets and steel-gray uniforms jumped out of the ditch and started fleeing toward the road. David hardly noticed that the shooting had stopped. He ran as fast as he could, saw the Germans mounting their machines and driving off amidst the deafening roar of the engines.

In the evening, Zabiegala, with a face like old leather said: "As I told you. You charge them with bayonets, they flee." He spat between his feet. But a little later, they buried the major and three other soldiers, and David saw the first dead man in his life. The officer's eyes were closed, and his face was light gray. There was no pain, surprise, or horror on it. David experimentally touched the dead man's hand. It was cold, it felt like paper. It was strange to think that he had seen this man moving and talking a short time earlier. He wouldn't have been surprised if the major had sat up, passed a hand over his face, and said in his low, nasal voice: "Call the sergeant, soldier. I want to talk to him."

That no such thing happened revealed a big secret for David: the irrevocability of death. It was frightening.

Chapter four

The train stopped at a small station, and the *Volksdeutscher* moved his strangely elongated head, murmured something, and started snoring again. Grabowski was sorry for the interruption. David Gordon had recollected his first dead man, a Polish officer, whose name he had forgotten. Later, in the Ghetto, he saw many others, almost daily. But the first one, and the awareness of the irrevocability of death, the discovery of the direction of time and human one-way movement, was significant, special. Like the first woman.

But David Gordon in the forest, somewhere midway between the Prussian border and Warsaw, had not slept with a woman yet. He was eighteen and a virgin. He had only just started living and already bad things had come.

Grabowski pressed his face to the windowpane, but all he could see was a tiny paved platform and a wooden hut lit by a solitary blue lantern hanging from a pole. A man stood on the platform with his back to the train.

Grabowski lowered the windowpane and leaned out. He saw

17

further into the darkness the red light of the semaphore. The four men were sleeping, curled up.

I surely don't need all these details of David Gordon's life, thought Grabowski. After all, it is, in our times, a very commonplace life. But all this is a burden to me, and I was not supposed to carry it with me. The war and then the Ghetto, till the day he had enough sense to die, when he threw away that white armband with the blue Star of David on it.

Not yet, David answered. Not yet. Other things were to come, and they were, in a way, the foundation of your existence, Grabowski. Although you will, naturally, in accordance with our planning, forget all of them. Irrevocably. Yes, that is the word, like the irrevocability of the major's death. I do not even remember his name, and I knew it then. He was the first.

Grabowski looked at the other passengers and thought there was a strange sweetness and innocence in sleeping men, no matter which men.

The 'escort,' the *Volksdeutscher*, for instance, must have had a lot on his conscience—if he had any conscience at all. Or the Poles, each one with a load of his own, what they did, what they thought, dreamed. But now, in this moment of suspension, while the train stood in front of the red semaphore light, waiting, they were, with their eyes closed, temporarily released from all of it, from their history, from Time itself, from remembrance. Grabowski envied them.

Zabiegala, David recollected, was never forgotten.

No wonder. Didn't he say himself that he was his soldiers' father and mother?

When the time came, Zabiegala disappeared too. But before their ways parted, Zabiegala did a favor to David Gordon.

The resistance was underway. Soldiers—many soldiers— manned the barricades on the outskirts of the town. The barricades were constructed from cobblestones, overturned trams and buses, and furniture. There were also buildings converted into strong points, and elaborate trenches. The Germans did not want to waste their soldiers in an outright frontal assault. They had time, they waited. Behind the defenders' backs, Warsaw was dying. Without water, food, electricity. Burning. The town was bombed in daytime by low-flying planes, at night by artillery. Days—beautiful September days—were clouded by huge pillars of smoke rising from the burning town. On the front, around the town, there was but little fighting. The ammunition had to run out eventually. The civilian population would reach the limits of suffering. That day could not be far.

David was sitting on the ground floor of an old apartment building, watching a group of soldiers playing cards. He had to be on duty on the barricade at four in the morning but he was not sleepy. During the last few days he had had enough rest to compensate for the week of marching. His feet were in good order again.

He watched the game with interest. One tall, huge soldier seemed to win constantly. David was sure the man was cheating, but could not discover his trick. He always had three against pairs, and a full against three. Once he produced four aces against the four queens of his opponent.

Perhaps sheer luck, David thought, and got up, stretching. Time to turn in. Just then the sergeant came in, glanced at the card players and told David: "Come with me."

David followed him outside the building. Zabiegala stopped, and put his heavy hand on his arm.

"Listen, Gordon, you are from this town, aren't you? Well, it's over."

David said nothing.

"Stand at ease, soldier. All right, Gordon, get some civilian clothes, take off these uniform rags, and go home."

He could not understand.

"Christ, you are dumber than I thought," said Zabiegala in anger. "You are an Israelite, yes? Well, bad times have come for you, this you perceive at least, don't you? It is better for you if you stay home. We'll all be prisoners of war as of tomorrow and God knows what they plan to do with you, with Jews, once they've got you in their claws… Take civilian rags, and scram. That's an order."

"But chief, we're still fighting, aren't we?"

"The capitulation will be signed at midnight. The war is finished."

David looked at him. He was badly shocked.

"Cross my heart, I'm not lying, Gordon. Have I ever told you a lie?"

"Once, with the cardboard tanks."

Zabiegala smiled with great bitterness. "Well, I was being told lies." He looked over David's head into the darkness, and sighed.

"Go, Gordon."

He extended his big hand, and David shook it.

"You were a good soldier," the sergeant said. "Take good care of yourself now. Bad times are coming. Take care!"

He turned abruptly, and went into the house.

A green rocket exploded high in the sky and descended slowly.

Chapter five

His problems under the occupation and during the period of the formation of the Ghetto were on different levels. He had to survive, to feed himself and his mother. Luckily, they did not have to change flats, their prewar apartment was within the planned ghetto borders.

There were but a few possibilities: David found out quickly that he could make a living by teaching children. Schools were closed, and the prevailing mood was that the war would be over next spring, or summer at the latest. Then, everything would be back to normal, in the sense that the schools would re-open, fathers would return to work and provide money, mothers would again give orders to servants and maids, the flats would be clean, the plants watered, meals cooked.

When normalcy returned, it would be a pity for the children to have lost a year. People took private teachers. David, a graduate of '39, gave lessons: four, five, six. More than that, he could not handle. Easy as the work was, in the evening he was dead tired, incapable of doing anything. Straight to bed. The pupils varied in age. The youngest were two girls of eleven, the oldest was Henryk, a spoiled only son of extremely rich parents, aged sixteen. His paramount interest in life was sex: Latin was sheer torture for him. David was paid four zloty an hour to teach him Latin.

The small difference in age was embarrassing. The boy was stupid and indolent.

I must push it at him, by force, thought David. But the boy's father had emphasized that Henryk was a sensitive child, David should avoid quarrelling with him, it could damage his delicate constitution.

"And yet, you shall instruct him in such a way, that he'd be able to pass the exams next year. You understand it, young man?"

He had a shining, bald skull, and looked at David from behind gold-rimmed glasses. The mother, who was also present during this interview, was a small, round woman, very energetic, with slightly protruding dark eyes, which had a defiant, hostile glint in them. Raven black hair, combed back smoothly, and caught in a tight knot at the back of her head.

It was a curse to handle Henryk: but it was his best paid hour, and David was reluctant to throw it away, and waited, till it would die a natural death: of starvation, or lack of blood pressure.

He renewed his pre-war social contacts with Tami, the girl he had dated before the war, and with a gang of boys from the Conservatory and their girls.

Chapter six

The first year of the Ghetto, which had not yet been closed off, was the year David discovered vodka. Supplied to David by his friend Arthur, to whom, in turn, it was supplied by Miss Ada, who was keeping Arthur at the time, and she a spinster of 46.

As a result, Arthur, who was sixteen and who had been an outstanding piano student at the Conservatory before the war, played Tchaikovsky's *Piano Concerto No. 1* in the hall of the *Femina* movie house (which served for a time as a concert hall in the Ghetto) totally and completely drunk. David and three or four other friends, including Barbara, thought he'd never make it from the door to the piano. It is true Arthur stumbled a few times making his way through the orchestra, with a heavenly smile on his childlike face, and with half-closed eyes. It is also true, that he sat down in a second violinist's lap and remained sitting there for a full minute. But it is also true that the conductor, old Neumann, stood quietly, waiting for Arthur, and when Arthur finally arrived at the edge of the podium, Neumann held him gently by his arms, while he made a deep bow. Perhaps it was he who bent him. Arthur landed on his piano stool and played the concerto like a young god.

Nobody in the hall had ever heard a better, more beautiful and technically impeccable performance. People went crazy, applauding endlessly and screaming for an encore. Two German officers, sitting in the third row, looked at each other in amazement. Both music-lovers, they had come secretly to this concert in the Ghetto convinced that as far as performing artists go, few people could match the Jews. It was, of course, a bad risk to sit together with Jews. The two Germans knew they would be severely punished if found there, but the Ghetto was still open, and they took the chance. When they came in and sat down, people all around panicked and started running to the exit. But the elder of the two Germans shouted: "*Halt!* Stop! We only came to listen to the music!" and gradually, the commotion subsided.

After the performance, they applauded wildly with the Jews, and asked for the name of the artist.

"Unknown, absolutely unknown," explained a white-haired Jew.

"Very talented, very gifted," the younger officer kept repeating.

For an encore, off stage, Arthur vomited three times, while Barbara held his damp forehead and David tried to wipe his mouth with real lemon—were there more than a dozen lemons in the whole Ghetto that evening? Finally Arthur opened his pale eyes, tears streaming down his cheeks, and said to Barbara: "Go away you whore," and to David: "Can you give me some coffee? I'm dying for coffee." David had the dark-brown hot brew which served for coffee ready in five minutes, but he had to hold the cup in his own hands, Arthur's were shaking too badly. He took a sip or two, and asked: "How was the concert?" They all told him he had been fantastic, incredible, unbelievable. Arthur closed his eyes again, and sighed. He said he had not the slightest idea what had happened to him, or where he had been from the moment he went on stage until he puked in the artist's room.

"Listen," he told David in a hoarse whisper, "send all these people away, and bring me to Ada. In a rickshaw. I…I cannot walk. Come with me."

People were running through the dark streets, and the rick-shaw-man pedaled at a breakneck speed, for the curfew hour was minutes away. After eight, the Germans shot first, and asked for papers later.

But they arrived in time, and only then did David realize he wouldn't be able to go home himself. It was too late.

He dragged Arthur to Ada's flat on the second floor and knocked on the door: the bell did not work.

When she opened the door a moment later, in her dressing gown, tall and elongated like a saint in an old icon, Arthur said: "Good evening, Madame Ada. I brought a friend with me."

Ada, with her almost transparent face, murmured: "Of course. But he'll have to sleep by himself on the sofa."

Guarding her rights. "What did she think I was, a queer?"

Ada still had two rooms to herself, which was extraordinary in the Ghetto, with an average of four, five people to one room. The Germans had herded half-a-million people into the confined part of the town, and were still sending Jews to the Ghetto from smaller towns and villages. She must have very good connections in the *Judenrat*, thought David.

Arthur, with half-closed eyes suggested: "Shall we have something to drink? It is very cold outside."

Ada, floating over the floor like candlelight, immediately brought three glasses and a bottle.

"Are you sure you want to drink?" asked David.

"That's exactly what I need now."

The room was clean, the furniture smelled of turpentine; if it weren't for the low hissing of the carbid lamp, one could forget about the war and the Ghetto.

She emptied half of her glass in the same ephemeral way she was moving about; one could not see her drinking, her colorless lips just touched the rim of the glass, that was all. David drank his in one gulp; strange that she should still have money for this, as vodka was expensive. Arthur took his drink like medicine, and grimaced: "Madame Ada, don't you have anything to go with it?"

She floated back into the room with a piece of herring. It took away the biting edge from the vodka.

David felt his head spinning slowly around, just one complete revolution. Drinking on an empty stomach, he had hardly eaten anything during the day. He closed his eyes, it was easier that way. He heard Arthur chuckling softly: "This is good, eh, David? I'll tell you what: the gang—our gang—is stupid. Boys and girls alike, but the girls have an advantage. You know what? They have the advantage between their legs."

"Arthur," whispered Ada.

He laughed merrily: "You, too, Ada. You have the same advantage. Even though you do not belong to the gang. You, you are too—too mature for it. Have I expressed myself correctly?"

Ada had huge eyes now, and something flashed up in them, like a reflection of a distant lightning.

"There is nothing to be ashamed of, Ada," Arthur continued. "That is the way things were, and are, in a normal world, which has almost ceased to be."

He lifted high the forefinger of his right hand. "But we are already passing into another one, such as you have never dreamt of. Everything is different in this new world. About that concert tonight, did you see how Rudi was looking at me? Eh? David!"

Arthur had another drink. "You should drink, too, David. It is good. It helps. Now, Rudi knows nothing about it, though he can perhaps move his fingers over the keyboard more quickly than I. He is a goddamn piano-playing machine, Rudi is. And I am sure he makes love to Barbara exactly like he plays piano—technically impeccable. And as quickly."

"Arthur," Ada said. "You should not drink any more now."

"Shut up. If I did not drink you'd lose your advantage, and you know it."

"David, say something. You seldom speak. Open up. Or drink

26

some more. Vodka helps to open up. The same way music sometimes helps me. Not Mozart, though! He is too joyous. Eh, David?"

David looked straight ahead. The whole wall opposite him was crammed with books. He could read some of the spines from where he sat. All, without an exception, were philosophy: Plato. Zeno. Schopenhauer. Socrates. Aristotle. Leibniz. Montaigne. Kant. Fichte. Hume. Bergson. Kierkegaard.

Arthur watched David scan the bookshelves. "They are not hers. They belong to the man who lived here before I came. Ada says he is in Germany."

"Arthur," sorrowful pleading and despair from the woman in her long gown.

"A Polish officer. In a POW camp for the rest of the war. Funny, isn't it? They weren't the types you would connect with these books... Well, I am only his substitute. I don't know why. Perhaps I resemble him. I have never seen his photograph...These are his books."

Ada leaned forward, and put her hand on David's knee. "You can take them, read them; I know you'd take good care of them. He wouldn't mind, I know..."

"Drink, David, Perhaps some day an Ada will find you, and then you'll always have vodka to rely on, to help you, to push you through...I like you more than anybody in the whole gang—and I do not know why. This is a good sign, if you do not know why... when there is no logical explanation. What a pity, you do not play piano. Do you want me to teach you?"

"Yes," Ada's voice was stronger than before, "I know he'd let you read his books and he took with him only Montaigne to the war..."

The book cabinet, the whole wall opposite, seemed to be swinging slowly, rolling gently. He clutched the sides of the chair. Arthur's and Ada' s voices came from afar, from another space. He could not keep his eyes in focus any more, and found Arthur's face on the second shelf, between two fat volumes of Spencer. And yet he was light, weightless, free. He moved his head and everything around him whirled in a maelstrom. Ada, elongated enormously in her pale gown, curved like a rainbow, Arthur with his serene smile and the face of a sleeping child, rows of books, the table with the carbid lamp on it, upside down…

"It is all right, lie down," he heard Ada's voice, soft and soothing.

He closed his eyes and felt somebody spread a blanket over him.

Chapter seven

All those are," inquired Grabowski in the darkness of the train compartment, "what you call milestones? All right, I accept the first dead man, the first woman, the discovery of booze."

"Not only milestones as far as you are concerned," answered David. "Those are components out of which you were constructed. And don't forget those books. My God, the books! Books," David confided, "have always been our real, true, honest curse. If we did not read, everything would be different."

David had to keep the two groups always apart. They had nothing in common. Arthur and all those young, cynical and sophisticated intellectuals, incessantly busy with themselves, music, and Jakov Wassermann—in that order. And Tami, sweet Tami, and her proletarian circle of husky, ugly, Yiddish-speaking young workers. During this period, having rejected, with an impatient gesture, Wassermann, Kellerman, and Proust on one side, and *Lenin's Collected Works, Volume 2* and the *Short History of the Russian Communist Party* pushed on him by Tami, on the other, David chose to read Conrad. Conrad was very much in vogue. What else could be read in a time of absolute despair?

29

He found, like many others, much to relish in Conrad's treatise, hints of how to fight on after you have lost the fight. Man against his fate, always losing but never giving up. What could be more suitable to these circumstances? What else could one do, to preserve even an illusion of one's human dignity, but to follow this advice: *usque ad finem*?

David wrote in his notebook: *The ultimate alternative to suicide is a powerful medicine, a potent weapon. I keep it as such, and nobody can take it away from me. Meanwhile, I can delude, cheat myself, and tell myself I am just probing the limits of endurance.*

Tami and her new Ghetto friends had, apparently, no such problems. The working class would prevail, and Paradise on earth was just round the corner. It was as inevitable, the final victory, as the next sunrise. The powerful Socialist State next door was a guarantee for that. True, meanwhile it watched the convulsions of the old, dying order, its disintegration, its agony throes, with a quiet, objective detachment, confident in its invincible power.

"We are nothing, dust," said Tami. "Our very existence has no meaning at all; history goes its own course. Inevitability of the historical process."

David smoked a thin *Junak* cigarette to kill the gnawing hunger in his stomach and wished Yoske and Chaim and Moshe would go to hell so he could then sit near Tami on the couch and pass his hand over her long, stockinged legs; which, admittedly, was not much, but better than nothing. But these young workers loved to be with their newly converted Tami. They looked at her with eyes full of love, devotion, like Catholic women lifting their tormented faces to Christ on the cross in a church. And she shone in this company, basking in the Sun of the Brotherhood of the Working Class.

Moshe, the red-haired boy with a big, hooked nose, had a black eye and ugly scratches on his face. A few days earlier he had worked on a bad *placowka*. It was an SS unit of some kind, and a German had beaten him up badly. David had to admit that he had taken it very stoically, hadn't made much fuss about it.

If that maid-screwing Henryk does not make any progress

with his Latin his father will dismiss me; I'll have to join a work crew outside the Ghetto—a *placowka*—as well, thought David. And why not? I might earn more there.

The Germans, naturally, paid nothing. Theoretically, every able-bodied Jew in the Ghetto had to work ten days monthly for the Germans, otherwise his ration cards would not be stamped and valid. But whoever still had some money in the Ghetto bought himself out of it by paying another Jew to go to work in his place. A new profession was created: a *placowkarz*. You just had to remember your new name each time, and give the right card for stamping. The working places were outside the Ghetto, usually with various units of the army stationed in and around the town.

Some places were "good," the Germans were relatively decent, the work was not too hard, and with a bit of luck you could smuggle in some food on your way back to the Ghetto: cauliflower and potatoes in your trousers. Other *placowkas* contained fear in their very names: SS-Praga Totenkopf. Gestapo Headquarters, Shucha Street. Sometimes Jews had to wash the blood off the floors and walls of the torture chambers.

The other boy, Yoske, with pimples on his face, did not work outside: he was running a rickshaw, a passenger tricycle, and it was enough to feed himself, his sister, and his old mother. Tami's mother worked as a cook in the community kitchen, making thin soup out of straw; and Tami herself gave lessons to children aged nine or ten. The house smelled of cabbage and of garbage, which, uncollected, piled up on the staircase and in the yard.

David, hungry, and desperately clinging to Conrad's heroes' patterns of behavior, was in love with Tami, who had long, golden hair, tiny budding breasts, and a boy's body. She also had huge, luminous, gray eyes, and when she was not quoting Lenin, she stroked David's unruly hair, and let him touch her, though she would not let him make love to her.

He was confused, desperate, had never had a woman yet, but remained absolutely reluctant to embrace the Marxist faith.

"Sometimes I think you betray me with these boys."

"Silly, you know I am a virgin. I plan to give myself to the first Soviet soldier I meet."

"Why? They'll never come here; they are Germany's best friends."

"They'll be the liberators of mankind, you'll see."

"We'll never see. Look around you; hundreds of people dying every day from typhus, from starvation."

He looked at her in despair, but her eyes saw other things. Whatever problems she had with herself, she stripped them of all importance. What counted was the supreme dream of the coming millennium.

He withdrew into himself. Artaphernes, Darius, and the old wars of theirs, fought thousands of years ago. Their bones must have turned to dust long, long ago, but somebody had recorded their existence, so that Henryk, in the Warsaw Ghetto, *Anno Domini* 1940, might learn about it. For his benefit; but he preferred the maid's cunt.

The book I want to write about this Ghetto, would anybody read it in a thousand years from now? Very doubtful! And how did it feel to be a slave pulling an oar on one of Artaphernes' ships? Chained to that oar, whipped by a slave driver? We are not chained yet, but there is a wall around the Ghetto, and armed guards at every gate. And Tami keeps her virginity for a Soviet soldier. Sure, Conrad's heroes fought their battles against Fate in other surroundings altogether. So did Artaphernes, his sailors and his slaves. But does it really matter? Transfer them here, and put a white armband with the ancient Star of David on their arms. Well, how do they look now? I cannot work it out properly. I am too hungry.

So lock it out. Forget it.

Instead, dream of the empty whiteness of a hospital in a Far-Eastern port; curtains flowing slowly, doors and windows open. Dark-red and purple evenings in far-off harbors, sails furled on feluccas. A boat rocking gently near a wooden pier.

The world was quiet, for once.

The sun was setting, and it touched briefly with gold the windowpanes of the six-floor tenement building opposite. The other world might exist, after all…

Tami put her childish hand on David's arm: "What an incorrigible dreamer you are, David sweet. Wake up. Let's go to the community kitchen, get some soup."

Chapter eight

Professor Diener had taught, one afternoon a week before the war, Jewish history and religion to the "chosen" ones, the twelve or fifteen Jewish pupils of the State *Gymnasia*. There were nine such schools for boys and eight for girls in pre-war Warsaw, and in each class one or two Jews were tolerated.

Professor Diener caught David on Smecza Street, which was as ugly and crowded as any other street in the Ghetto.

"David," he said, "I'll tell you a secret I have discovered, a great secret: The world hates Jews!"

Out of sheer respect for his former teacher David said nothing. Diener's black coat was a bit torn, and shining with old age. His eyes were clear, and the forehead was still bulging, like in those days, making an impression of hidden wisdom, great brainpower. But David thought that the professor had never been very interesting in his lectures, and with the suffering of the Ghetto on top of everything, the old man had simply gone senile.

Passers-by were pushing them every moment, and David wanted very much to say goodbye and go on his way, but Diener held on to the button of his coat. Old Jewish pre-war joke about three Jews holding each other by the buttons of their coats, and discussing on the street, come true, the Jewish quality of self-derision.

If only a German truck stopped, and they'd start hunting people, we'd have to run, and I'd lose him.

"Not the world as it is, I mean," Diener explained. "The world is beautiful, but indifferent: to Jews, to the *goyim*. To animals as well. What I mean is, I had that notion, that all people hate Jews. Jews hate Jews as well, but that, as Kipling used to say, is another story. You'll ask me, in what sense do people hate Jews, and I'll tell you, I do not know. They hate religious Jews, and non-observant Jews, and atheistic Jews, rich Jews, and poor ones. Patriots of their countries, and Zionists. They hate us in a biological way, and yet there is no biological difference, no basis for it. That is the paradox, and I cannot solve it, and it kills me. Listen," he twisted David's button, "they hate circumcised Jews, and the very few that are not circumcised. I know personally two of these. Would you believe it? What is it? Why?

"So I was lying in bed—it is much warmer that way—and thinking, maybe it is the name, the sound of it: linguistics, acoustics, and aesthetics, you got it, David?"

He is insane, thought David. Hunger has unhinged his brain. Next, he'll run amok through the streets. Or perhaps not, he is not the type. He'll lie down on the street, cover himself with a newspaper and wait for death.

But Diener talked quietly, with no trace of passion, just the polite interest of a scholar working in research.

"Listen to the collection: Zyd, Yevrey, Juif, Jude, Jew; all those do not sound too pleasant, do they? In Italian, it is entirely different, you don't know Italian, do you, David? Well, I do. It is Ebrei, and it has a nice sound. I hear Italians are no anti-Semites, not even now, under Mussolini. But then I kept thinking—that's about the only thing I still can do now, to think—yes, but Italians hated Jews too, four, five hundred years ago. Why, the very name Ghetto, they invented it, it is of Italian origin. So this theory isn't any good, either..."

35

David thought the old man would let him go. But Diener hadn't finished yet. "On the other hand, I have considered the possibility of inherited paranoiac traits in our race. But we are not even a race! And why do Jews hate each other? Eh?"

The hand, which had held David's overcoat button, dropped.

Pity on the old man. He really was perplexed with these problems. His face showed it; sunken cheeks, gray skin, bags under his eyes.

"What are your problems, David?" Diener asked, with kindness.

Four years ago he had asked the same question and in the same tone.

The answers were different.

"The wall," David said. "Logic, reason. I have been reading Kant, Hegel. They do not make any sense. Do not apply to the times we are living in, apparently."

"Ethics?" inquired Diener.

"No, no. That is on another planet altogether."

"Try Spinoza."

"I have, in the beginning. I have no use for it here, now."

Diener seemed to be in a hurry, all of a sudden.

"Yes, yes," he said. "These are difficult times, very extraordinary times. Still, we might live to see light again, don't you think?"

"No," David said frankly.

"Well, you should, you should, my boy." He put his hand on David's arm. "There is a God up there. He bestowed on mankind the blessing of hope."

"Goodbye, professor," David answered.

Chapter nine

The gang was not really his. He was not a musician himself, and had only met them while waiting for Tami at the Conservatory. She was in the sixth year in professor Lefeld's piano class, when the war started. A Jewish joke, she recognized the piano class as such and renounced it with a fervor equal only to her previous acquiescence to her mother's wishes.

But they had accepted him, and that was how he had met Arthur, Rudi, Bubi, and their girls. The girls did not play any musical instruments; playing an instrument was not absolutely necessary, as it was in Tami's case. The Jewish upper middle class in Warsaw could afford the eccentricity of not sending their daughters to the Conservatory, if the daughters themselves did not insist on going. However, for the lower class—to which Tami's mother belonged—it was an imperative. Parents ate shit and often lived in half-slums, north of Leszno street, denying themselves the essentials of life, while trying desperately to push their children into Polish State Schools, to which they were sometimes accepted—no more than one or two to a class of forty—after tortuous *concourse* exams. Two hundred candidates

37

competed for forty vacant places. They were admitted on the sheer merit of their intelligence, or with the help of powerful connections, which were only rarely available. When David sweated his way in through two essays, *"Poland's struggle to become a sea-power in the 17th century"* and *"Elements of Patriotic Thought in the Work of Polish Eighteenth Century Poets,"* his parents kissed him. He was a good son. With his tidy Jewish mind, he showed those *goyim* what he knew, and how to write Polish. "He has good style," the professor of Polish literature said dryly to his mother.

Rudi and Arthur were already accomplished pianists when the war broke out; Bubi, a very promising violinist. Barbara was taking private dancing lessons with Mme. Borova. Martha's father was one of the most famous translators from German; Wassermann in Polish was his work as well as Zweig's *Sergeant Grisha*. Yet Martha did not bask in her father's fame. By the age of 17 she had a slim volume of her own very vanguard poetry, a private, limited edition. She wrote poems, watched her father's third wife and ninth mistress fighting it out with keen, cool eyes, and carved a line on the gold band of her ruby ring for every lover of her own. In 1940, she had eight lines on that ring.

"Watch out for that one," Arthur said, speaking slowly and with half-closed eyes, as if he were going to fall asleep at any moment, "watch out, David. When she is through with somebody, only bleached bones are left."

Martha overheard him. "Sometimes I crunch the bones as well, to get to the marrow."

"She is a regular little slut, this one," Arthur said.

This she pretended not to hear.

A strange way to kill time, David thought. But there is little else to do. I could continue with Berdyaev at home, but Berdyaev leaves me cold. I flared up when I started, that's always what happens to me in the beginning, and after the first few chapters, I cool off. But what do you expect of them? To give you a ready made recipe how to live your life in the Ghetto?

Well, I admit something like that was what I was yearning for.

There is Baruch Spinoza, who gives neat answers to a lot of questions, and Bergson. And before that I had Kierkegaard, but he was a difficult one. Perhaps they do give remedies for one's *Weltschmerz*, but most of these concepts do not apply to this situation. It is very unique, even in the long history of the human race. An Adolf Hitler seldom repeats himself: However, you can make historical comparisons; that is legitimate. Not very useful, though. Tomas de Torquemada as compared with Schickelgruber. Find Freudian parallels.

"This chatter does not bother you," Arthur said, "and that is good. I also can shut myself out, if I have a good melody in my head. But when they put a record on the gramophone, it is more difficult."

Renia, Bubi's girl, and Barbara were doing just that. Two couples started dancing a slow dance. Martha looked out the window.

"Hey, I think they are hunting in the neighborhood, people are running like mad. Better stop that music."

"They cannot hear it from up here on the sixth floor."

Martha lifted the needle from the record. They all crowded at the window, except David.

"Here! The truck is here! They are loading them in now!"

What would Berdyaev have to say seeing this? Or, any of them? If any one of them were forced to witness this, they'd have to take a position, a stance. He challenged them, the philosophers: "It is the year of the Lord 1941, a truck stops in the middle of a street, and four or five helmeted and armed men start catching people, passersby, indiscriminately, and force them up on the truck. It is already jammed with people, and they push in still more. Frightened people, wearing white armbands with a blue Star of David. Now they drive off. Where to? If they are lucky, they'll have to perform some menial work, and will be released later. If they are less lucky, they will never return. One never knows.

David placed a row of philosophers at the windows of Martha's apartment and let them look on; determinists and indeterminists. Make your own judgment.

"They are off—the truck has left."

Martha returned to the gramophone and placed the needle back on the record: Fred Astaire and Ginger Rogers, music from a 1939 movie—before the war.

"Why don't you dance?" Martha asked. "Shall I invite you?"

"After that?"

She looked at him; she had very long, curled lashes.

"Ah," she said finally. "Ah, good. So you are one of those types. I guessed so. OK. Shall I make you a drink?"

"Please."

She was back with the glass in a moment, and sat down near him.

"How callous, how brutal all of us have become," David said.

She shrugged: "How could it be otherwise? You are exposed to it daily, and it comes in heavy doses. It is infectious like typhus,"

"And these people still dancing—unbelievable!"

"What do you expect them to do? Tomorrow, why tonight, it can happen to any of us."

"That is no justification."

But Martha was extremely composed, cool.

"You must forget it, and live from one hour to the next. If I make plans at all, they are for the next ten minutes. That's the only way."

Martha turned her head so that he saw her in profile. It was a pretty face, too pretty perhaps: the short, narrow nose, full but straight lips (who said that Jews had a drooping lower lip?) and clear eyes shaded by long lashes. Seen like this, it was a face cut out from some ad for cosmetics or toothpaste. But the short, straight line, running from the left corner of her mouth toward the round chin spoiled the effect. It was out of place. It gave a hint of a cynical attitude, or of disillusionment, too much wisdom or knowledge in a girl of 20. The line was barely visible on the smooth surface of her skin, and yet it robbed the whole picture of purity and destroyed the impression of youth. There was too much hardness in it. As if she purposefully exposed herself to his examination, she looked at him, unsmiling, and said: "You know what drives me crazy in this Ghetto? Downstairs, just at the corner, a beggar sits on the street. He is crying and shouting like all the beggars here, but every time I pass there, he tries to clutch with his paws at my legs, my skirt. You can say thousands of Ghetto beggars do the same. That's the truth. But this one's touch makes me physically sick. I don't know if I've ever hated anybody as much, in my whole life, as I hate this beggar. And it's not only his touching me, it's his whole performance, his professional frenzy, the curses and pleading. He uses them alternately, beating the pavement with his fists, tearing open his rags, exposing his sores, the rolling of his eyes, his mouth foaming—it's all acting. There is such an immense meanness in him. Oh, he must be very clever. I never give him a cent. Once, I kicked him to free myself from his tentacles. He has more arms than the goddess Kali, the bastard."

David said: "You don't believe that he is hungry?"

"Of course he is. Who isn't? But he's not human."

"That's what the Germans say."

"Ah, David! If he only sat there silently, with his hand extended…"

"Would you give him a coin? A piece of bread?"

The vertical line from the corner of her mouth deepened.

"Do you give anything to any beggar?"

"I have nothing to give. But some people give."

"Another thing, they have been hunting people around this corner innumerable times, but they never touch him, the Germans. But twice I saw them taking snapshots of him."

You cannot die for every beggar, David thought, because you'd have to die ten thousand times daily. But perhaps something dies inside you, every time you pass a hungry beggar. It accumulates, it builds up. Perhaps she has seen more beggars than I have, and as a result, the line has grown on her face.

The others had started teasing Arthur. David could never stand teasing. As a child, he would run home in tears, because one child had teased another. It didn't hurt so much if they teased him; he'd answer with anger, it would end in a fight, or not, and that was it. But with others, it caused him no end of suffering.

41

He was in particularly bad shape by then: the manhunt in the street, the gramophone, Martha collecting lovers on her golden ring and playing cool and protective with him. He could do nothing to prevent the others, who had had enough dancing, from continuing their teasing game.

"Admit it," Rudi said, "that if it were not Tchaikovsky, you could not have played it."

"Not under those conditions," added Barbara.

"I admit it," Arthur said.

"It is only bombastic shit you can play when you're drunk."

"I did not know I was playing at all."

"Anyhow, I am not the one to judge if you have talent or not, but you certainly have guts—when drunk." said Renia.

Arthur turned his head like a blind man, and slowly raised his heavy eyelids.

"Arthur has everything," Barbara said, "not only guts."

He smiled. "You should know, Barb. Who am I to deny it?"

She threw him a vicious look. They had been living like a married couple for three months before Ada took him to her apartment.

"But even that and guts are not enough, when it comes to music. It is music we are talking about?"

David's throat was dry and hot. "Hell, Rudi, what have you got against Arthur tonight?"

"Ho-ho! Look who's talking! Silly, it's just a sport. We're all good friends here, aren't we, Arthur? Where is your sense of humor, philosopher?"

"And while on the subject of humor, how is your mysterious book coming along?"

"Shit."

"I don't believe it. I always thought you'd write a great book, David. And now that you're working outside, and you have become a regular *placowkarz*, you've got so much more experience than we poor fellows, sitting here, and doing nothing."

At least I took them off him, David thought. They had left Arthur in peace.

"Listen, Rudi. Do you know why I started working on *placowkas*? Because a student of mine had no interest in Latin, and his father fired me. He was only interested in cunts."

The whole company roared with laughter. Barbara squealed: "I almost peed in my drawers from that," and another wave of laughter followed.

"Well, couldn't you give him instruction in that field?"

"Lack of experience."

"David, give Barbara the address of your former pupil."

Something badly out of order there. But they did not seem to sense it. Easy with passing judgments on the world, on the Ghetto.

"David," Rudi, still laughing, sat down next to him, stout, round-faced, well-dressed, "I'll give you an address of an academy—of a university. Send your student there. Or, listen to my advice—go, and study yourself."

Chapter ten

Everybody gives me advice, Barbara, Martha, Rudi, Arthur, Tami. The philosophers. Conrad. Well, Conrad merely suggests, and that is much better. But even so, I am flooded with advice. I cannot use any of it. I must find my own way. I have given up on finding a sense of reality. Perhaps such a thing does not exist at all. Mother, for instance, does not give advice, and does not accept any reality. She lives serenely in the past, and refuses categorically to be dragged along with time or history. She finds this way convenient. Tolerable.

David's father, a clerk in a transportation firm, died in 1936.

They had been living ever since on the insurance money, and after 1939, on whatever David earned. She did not find it disturbing in any way. She succeeded in closing herself completely inside herself, and yet it did not prevent her from doing her daily chores effectively: she cleaned the house, mended clothes, cooked. She was active, she functioned normally; only her body, never big since the war, seemed to shrink. The creases on her delicate face, running from the corners of her eyes toward the silver-white of her temples, had multiplied, and this gave her a smiling appearance.

David tried sometimes to engage her in conversation, to discuss the situation. This was when they started resettling people prior to the forming of the Ghetto. It was useless. She listened carefully, looking aside, and nodding slightly, but at a certain moment, David understood that she had not been listening at all; she must have been engaged the whole time in some inner dialogue with herself, or with David's father, perhaps.

"Are you listening, Mama?"

"Of course."

"Well, what do you say about it?"

"We'll do as you said, David."

"But, Mama,"

"Perhaps we should approach Blaustein to give father a raise, or, at least an advance."

Blaustein was the manager of the transportation firm in which David's father had worked; they hadn't heard from him since the war. Somebody once told David that he had escaped to Vilna, and then to America, in 1939.

She got up. "Have to look at the supper. Did you want to ask anything else, David? Come with me to the kitchen, we can talk there."

They had just this one room and the kitchen, which, when cooking—or, rather the heating up of the soup which David would bring from the community kitchen—was finished, served as David's room. He made his camp bed in the middle of it. On all the walls he had pinned up huge maps of various war fronts.

He had cut out these amazingly detailed maps from old illustrated magazines from World War I, stacks of which were hidden on the bottom shelf of the huge bookcase with a glass door that stood in the long, dark corridor leading from the front door to the living room.

The maps were absolutely relevant again after 25 years. What had undergone a radical change was the concept of time. In 1914 the maps of Verdun and its forts, Douaumont, and Vaux, appeared weekly for a year and more. In 1940, Verdun was in the news one day,

45

and never reappeared. Hitler's armored columns ripped through it, and before the din of the caterpillars on the pavement died away, the place was forgotten. The one million dead from the old war buried in shallow graves must have grinned.

In the bookcase were enormous stacks of these magazines. First the Russian ones, on thick, stiff, glistening paper, and a black, two-headed eagle on each cover, and then the German and Austrian ones. Solid paper must have been a peculiarity of Czarist Russia. The Austrian publications were printed on tissue-thin sheets. One of them, richly illustrated, had captions under each photograph, as idiotic as the Austro-Hungarian Empire, in ten languages. A young, mustached officer in leather boots leaning against the wing of a biplane in a dramatic way: *Lieutenant Rahm and his airplane.* The same sentence repeated ten times, in Polish, Hungarian, Czech, Slovakian, Italian…David could not suppress a smile.

The Russian magazines were full of Cossacks who distinguished themselves in battle, and were awarded the St. George Cross. The Germans relied still mostly on drawings and paintings by unknown artists, showing in heavy colors gory details of fighting, wounded and dying Englishmen and Frenchmen in red trousers.

All the other shelves were jammed with cloth- and leather-bound books. David's father had collected Russian classics: the complete Tolstoy, Turgenev, Dostoevski, Chekhov. On the front page was printed *Dozvolenno Tsenzuroy,* indicating the censors had approved. At that time, they still called things by their proper names. *Annals of Ogoniok* from 1912, 1913.

David smiled handling the *Complete Works of Henryk Sienkiewicz* in Russian translation. The man had received a Nobel Prize for *Quo Vadis.* Martha's comment: "The most illustrious piece of shit and kitsch ever written." Various *Histories of Civilization, Histories of Discoveries, Histories of Mankind, Astronomy* by Flammarion, all heavy, solid volumes, indestructible, not like the books of today. Occasionally, the paper would acquire a yellowish tint; otherwise time had not touched them.

German classics with golden lettering on the covers, in twisted

Gothic alphabet: Goethe, Schiller. Thick librettos and notes of over one hundred operas. A music-lover. Searching for treasures in the dark corners of the cabinet, David regretted he had not known his father better. *Show me your books and I'll tell you who you are.* The distant past, when David's father was his age; the books had been part of his father's world, another proof that Time was marching on, in one direction. Books seemed to be losing value in the new world. Nobody, except him, paid any attention to the ancient bookcase in the dark corridor. Nobody took interest in Ada's former lover's philosophy library. She dusted the books twice weekly. "Why?" he asked. "He loved them so much," she whispered, "I want them in good order when, if—if he comes back."

But they both knew it would never happen. It would be a miracle. And yet David had witnessed miracles, incomprehensible, improbable in the pattern of a world of stone.

Chapter eleven

They were like small cracks on the face of a granite cliff.

One morning on Nalewki Street, David joined a crowd, watching a group of SS-men torturing three Jews across the street. The men were lined up against the wall, one of them gaunt and tall, the two others short. They had beards, and all three were dressed alike, like a team of clowns.

One could not know what their crime was; perhaps they had not stepped aside, into the gutter, to make way for the Germans on the sidewalk; perhaps they had not bowed low enough.

They stood against the wall, as much alone as a man in the moment of his death, their heads bare except for the little black skullcap, the yarmulke. The wind moved their beards.

One of the SS-men was talking to them. What he said must have been funny, for the other Germans laughed aloud. Then, in a quick movement, the joker took out a lighter and set the tall Jew's beard on fire.

A cry of pain as the man clutched his beard, trying to extinguish the flame. The German hit him hard across the face; David could hear

48

the slap from where he stood. Next, the Jew standing in the middle was addressed. David heard the hard staccato of the German words; the Jew's answer was inaudible, but he could see his lips moving. He, too, was slapped, hard. The SS-man had leather gloves on his hands. The Jew's black skullcap fell on the pavement. The German kept shouting, the Jew bent his knees, picked up the cap, and replaced it on his head. Another slap followed, and the skullcap fell again. Blood gushed from the Jew's face. He swayed, regained balance after a moment, and bent clumsily again. He smoothed the skullcap on his head with both hands, and the German hit him again in the face, with force. Then, deliberately, he swept with his other hand the skullcap off the man's bald head. *"Fanatisches Judenschwein!"*—Fanatic Jew-pigs!

His whole body shaking—David could see it—the old Jew bent down and groped blindly on the ground. He retrieved finally the black piece of cloth, and again replaced it on his head.

In expectation of the next blow, David felt his stomach rise to his throat.

But then another German, apparently an officer, stepped out of the group and put his hand on the first one's arm.

"Genug, Helmuth," he said in a loud voice. "Leave him be."

They stood, shaking, the three old Jews, one with half of his beard burnt, the other with a blood-covered mask instead of a face, the third one untouched physically, pale, motionless. All three with covered heads, as ordered by their God, they stood still, even after the group of Germans had leisurely walked away, talking in loud voices.

Then, two of the victims disappeared quickly, as if the pavement swallowed them in shame; the third Jew touched his head once more, to make sure his skullcap was there, and collapsed slowly.

"I was sure he'd kill him," a man said to David, "nothing enrages them more than stubbornness, defiance."

"Defiance?"

"Well, he kept replacing that goddamn yarmulke of his again and again, didn't he?"

"Yes. He did. Well, I guess he had no choice."

49

The man looked at him quickly, searching, with hard eyes. Probing my sanity, David thought. The man nodded, tapped with his forefinger on his forehead, and quickened his step. "A bit crazy yourself, eh?" he said.

Home, in the kitchen, David relived the miracle.

Let's be cool about it, let's look at that logically. Like Professor Diener. There was something terrifying, something defying any logic in the predicament of these three bearded Jews. Even as seen against the whole bloody and tiresome history of this people. Similar things must have happened. If you believed in what was written in the Bible, Jews had a hard time as slaves in Egypt: but crazy Jewish tradition has it that it was forbidden to curse the ancient Egyptians because they had given the Jews both shelter and bread. The Inquisition? Expulsion from Spain? Good. Either you got baptized, or you left the country. In a moment's notice.

This was something that had never happened before—there were no alternatives. Baptism or leaving were not offered as ways of escape, salvation. Hitler's credo was simple: you will not be allowed to live out your days till you die; you must be destroyed before that. A paradox? It surely is, but it does not change anything. Jews must cease to exist, this was the rule, the reality, the only one, the valid one, to which all logic was subject, David remarked.

Therefore, late in the evening, he spent in the light of the carbid lamp two hours struggling with the *Critique of Pure Reason*.

He got up when his eyes were smarting so much that he could not read any more, and walked around in the kitchen, where his camp bed stood. He looked at the maps covering the walls. Thick, jagged, black front lines, twenty-five years ago. At that moment, the whole continent was in the clutches of Evil. Two points of resistance, he noticed: in the upper left corner of the map of Europe, on an island, people stubbornly refused to submit, and fought on. The bearded Jew against the wall in Nalewki Street knew but little about it. He was at the bottom of the abyss, and found it necessary to comply with the strict orders of his God, refusing to accept orders from another Master.

David rubbed his forehead, stopped pacing the wooden boards of the floor, and faced his own bookshelf. Conrad, Cervantes, Montaigne, and borrowed from Ada: Kant, Hegel, Hobbes, Fichte, Kierkegaard...

He sighed. What a volume of thought! What medicines for the suffering human soul! But none a remedy for the present sickness. Hardly a palliative. David, much disturbed, sick at heart, picked up a book at random.

He stretched out on his bed, and started reading. Another book dealing with Evil, a book he had read once, long ago, before the war. In another world, another existence. He had hardly understood it then. He opened the first page.

Call me Ishmael.

Chapter twelve

So it was the work on a *placowka*. Jews had stopped teaching their children with hired teachers. Nobody needs your knowledge, your brains anymore, you must make your living with your muscles. The Ghetto was closed for good, only people working on *placowkas* were going out, escorted, or transported on army trucks.

The early winter mornings on the square in front of the old community building on Grzybowska Street, were a Gothic tale. The world stood still in frozen darkness, intense, and deep: the three-story brick house loomed high with its rows of blind windows. The ground floor was lit with petrol and carbid lamps, and in the space in front of it, on unpaved hard ground of frozen mud, hundreds of Jews were milling around.

A few army trucks stood nearby; they turned on their headlights occasionally, cutting the darkness with bright yellow corridors of light, bringing into visible existence groups of men huddled together for warmth. A few torches made from rags soaked with petrol were smoldering.

Heads of groups were calling names, trying to assemble their men. *"Luftwaffe* A-3 here! *Okecie! Okecie! Praga, Wehrmacht One!"*

Columns were slowly formed, men lining up in rows, three deep, were counted and recounted. The group leaders collected the work cards, scribbled names with pencils on lists, ran to-and-fro searching for the German NCO who would take the men to work, on trucks or by foot.

David groped in darkness in search of Weiss. Weiss, Tami's friend Moshe had told him, could give you a good *placowka*, where they would not beat you, the work was not too hard, and you could possibly buy a few vegetables during a break, and try to smuggle them back to the Ghetto. Sometimes you could get leftovers from the Germans.

People murmured among themselves in low voices, mostly in Yiddish, which David could understand, but hardly spoke. It was bitter cold, and waiting on this square in darkness people kept stamping their feet and rubbing their hands. Shouldering his way toward the office, David thought that this slave market did not fit any image he had in his mind. Slaves in leatherbound volumes of the *History of Discoveries* or *History of the New World* in Russian, richly illustrated with woodcuts and engravings, were naked. Those were warm countries. The slaves were colored, their skin was red or black. These here were Jews, white people. In most grotesque rags, fattened with strings to keep them warm.

In the crowded office, Jewish officials were going over the lists at the wooden table. A few Germans stood impatiently, waiting for their men. Their uniforms were spotless, shoes polished, they were clean-shaven.

"Man, move on! Do it quicker! I've been waiting for twenty minutes!" a tall air force sergeant barked. Another NCO slapped his boots with a riding crop. "Why can't you learn some order? Is it so difficult to have your men ready when we come?"

The men at the table sweated in spite of the cold, working feverishly, and re-doubled their efforts.

"*Luftwaffe* 5 is ready!"

One of the men at the table handed a list to a group leader: "Katz, take your men quickly, the officer is waiting!"

David stuck his head in, inquired timidly after Weiss.

"That's me," answered a short, broad man with a very pale face and hooked nose, "what do you want?"

"My name is Gordon, David Gordon. Moshe K. sent me to you."

"Moshe? Gordon? Aha," he seemed to recollect something, "well, you're late, the *Luftwaffe* 5 and the Printing House are gone. Also the Headquarters. I'll send you to Praga if I can, it isn't bad either, wait outside. What's your working name today? Give me your card. Dunski? Josef Dunski you are today, and for the next five days, remember! Wait outside, I'll call you."

Once more outside the darkness was as frozen as before. A group-leader's muffled voice repeated: "Three, four, left! Left!" as he tried to keep his men in step. Some detachments were marching away. A double beam of a truck's headlights moved slowly over the marching men, over the brick wall; the truck loaded with workers, backing up.

But there were still more people in the square, whom he could not see. He heard them talking, cursing, coughing, sneezing.

He craved feelings of brotherhood with these people. Common fate. Tami would say, the fraternity of the proletariat. Nothing, he thought. He searched his soul truthfully. Nothing at all. He told himself he was becoming a very cold-blooded bastard. It occurred to him that the torture of being closed in the Ghetto exceeded by far the nuisance of standing at five in the morning in this big square, surrounded by hundreds of fellow slaves. But he hardly shared anything with anybody. Not with Tami, not with Martha and that gang.

David badly wanted a cigarette to kill the first pangs of hunger this morning, but restrained himself. His five cigarettes had to last the whole day.

"Dunski! Gordon! That is, Dunski, come here. Go to this group. It is SS Unit 212, go with them. Group leader Cohen."

Weiss jumped out of the office and found David in the darkness. "Listen," he said in a hoarse voice, "don't be afraid. They are SS, but it is not a bad *placowka*, really. You can even get food from them. And they finish at five, on the hour. That is the truck, over there. That means no check up at the Ghetto gate when you come back. Good luck. *Nu*, go!"

Chapter thirteen

He dug a ditch for the first three hours. After that, an SSman came over, hooked his thumbs in his belt, and watched the Jews working there for five full minutes. Then he came up to David and two others, and lightly touched their arms.

"You," he said quietly, "and you, and you. Come with me."

He led them to a shed, which he wanted to convert into a garage.

"The floor must be smooth," he explained. "Take these stones, and throw them on a heap outside. But in good order. Even stones must be well ordered where a German is living."

At twelve o'clock a young bespectacled soldier called out: "Lunch break!" Half an hour later he took two men with him. They came back, bringing with them a pail of thick soup.

David learned that a man working on a *placowka* should have a spoon, a fork, and a tin plate with him. Just in case. "It happens once a month, perhaps, that you get some food from them," explained Herschel, the man who lent him his things, "but you must have it—just in case. You see what happened: they did not like their soup, the dogs had already been fed bones; so, instead of throwing the soup away, somebody said: 'Give it to the Jews.' As nobody protested, they gave it. But mind you, they were satisfied with the work. This group is not bad, good workers. A week ago, we had some older people, and the Germans fell into rage. Don't ask me how it was. Not one of the whole group escaped without bruises and scratches. Then they took the two oldest ones and made them stand there—over there, you see?—with a brick in each hand, for an hour. I ask you, how long can a man stand like that, even a strong, young man, like you or I? Five, ten minutes? Fifteen? They dropped the bricks after a few moments. The *Scharführer*—that is, their officer—came running and screaming, and we thought he'd kick the old Jew to death. He kept kicking him with his boots for I don't know how long. The other one fell unconscious immediately, and they took him away; but we brought the first one home, to the Ghetto with us. He surely died, no discussion about it, he was spitting blood, they must have broken his ribs."

Herschel stopped, spit, and lit half a cigarette. "And today they give us soup. So don't forget to bring your kit next time. Are you coming tomorrow?"

"Yes," David said. "I'll be coming every day. How much do they pay you?" Herschel took from his breast pocket several work cards.

"I have no fixed prices. This one gives me twenty zloty, this one, Mandelblatt, he is poor and sick, and I take only ten from him. Kirsch pays me sixteen, he is not a millionaire, either. And this is my own. You have for the whole month, too?"

"Only for two weeks, but I think I can easily get more."

"Sure. A lot of Jews prefer paying us to work for the Germans, especially when they can afford it. Well, that's how we make our living. Come, let's go back to his garage."

In a way he found it funny that they should pay him for working instead of them. Tami had definite opinions about it: "You are getting your free lessons in socialism. These bourgeois Jews pay for your muscles, for your energy. They do not use their own; they are smarter than you. They have money."

David had objections. "I think they are simply afraid; the names of some of these *placowkas* are frightening: *Gestapo-Schucha, SS-Sonderstelle*. I do not think they are smarter, or weaker than I. They are simply scared. I admit there is a certain amount of risk in the life of a professional *placowkarz*. But not much more than in any Jew's life in the Ghetto. Anyhow, they are paying me because I dare, and they dare not. That's all there is to it."

"Romantic nonsense! Perhaps they are afraid of the Germans, but they are mainly afraid of work! Remember this! They have never worked, and they hate work. Their business is to exploit other people's toil... Now, in Russia, for instance, he who does not work does not eat, did you know that?"

"I've read about it," David answered coolly, "and first of all, I do not believe it; and second, what is work? Believe me, I work harder than on a *placowka*, when I work trying to understand that German Fichte. Or Kant, another German."

"I agree with you, that thinking is work," Tami said, "if it is the right thinking."

"Well, what about mine?"

She looked at him seriously, and then started smiling.

"You. You are a crazy creature and your thinking is crazy. But that does not matter so much, because you work—now you even work with your hands—and because I love you."

"What if I were rich and would not have to work at all?"

She grew serious again. "I don't know if I could love you then, David. I do not think I could. A man who does not work—with his hands or with his brains—is a parasite. No, I don't think I could love a parasite."

A wave of inexplicable sadness descended on David and suddenly the whole world became dark gray; even Tami's splendid golden hair, rich and soft, lost its luster.

What was this huge shadow, he pondered, depriving him of the most elementary will to live?

Only one wish persisted, clear and strong, the wish to cease to exist. With that attitude, even Tami could not serve as an incentive to life. Life was not worth living. And somewhere, still, he was desperately searching for a motive.

What about serving some moral purpose? Like, say, fighting Evil. He checked the suggestion precariously, hesitatingly, from all sides, like a man handling a broken vessel that he had glued together, and was not at all sure the pieces would hold.

There could be something to it, although it would involve solving a lot of problems: defining the nature of Evil, the means and ways of the struggle, the application of rational and irrational methods. It would be a torturous road probing his sense of reality—if such a thing existed.

In spite of all that, it could provide a possibility of purpose, a cause, a *raison d'être*. The only possible one, perhaps. Also—and he saw it clearly—this solution had a built-in negativity in its nature. Fighting evil is fighting against and not fighting for.

Grabowski, speeding to Danzig on the night train, pragmatic, and richly endowed with that sense of reality his creator badly missed, could not refrain from some critical observations. What a sissy that David was! What a mess all these philosophical books produced in his mind! What confusion! What self-pity! Masochistic orgies fanning the consuming fires of pain; the pleasures of endless microscopic studies of the dissection of one's suffering; and the constant claims on fate, on his bad luck. Of course, anybody caught up in this Ghetto could honestly be called a bad-luck man—lots of people were sharing that same fate.

After a while, Grabowski thought, one became insensitive to the suffering of others; and a little bit later, one grew indifferent to one's own. Then, it was easy to die. Germans were great as cultivators of indifference; they knew how to bring people to that stage by scientific methods. Great philosophers and great inventors. One could conquer the whole world in this way. David, in his inexcusable childish naiveté, could never understand how the same people who had produced Kant and Schopenhauer had also given birth to Hitler, and then rallied to him with such enthusiasm. Well, Grabowski concluded, at least David had had the good sense to die at the right moment and to produce me.

Chapter fourteen

Rudi, who had crossed, like so many others, to the other side, to Bialystok, in October 1940, and returned four months later, never tired of relating his experiences in the country of the Red Star from which the Salvation would come. Memories of this trip haunted him.

When he set out from Warsaw, he had in his pocket a recommendation from the Conservatory's Rector. A most promising young pianist, it said. A rising star on the firmament of Polish music. Rudi had plans.

Through Bialystok to Lvov. From there, the letter would carry him to Moscow. In Soviet Russia, whatever was going on, the artist, the musician, was in the top echelon. Everybody knew it.

But the trip proved a catastrophic failure right from the beginning. First, he was robbed of all his possessions crossing the border.

Polish peasants living along the frontier dividing the territories under the German and the Russian occupation grew rich during this period of mass wanderings. Rudi contributed his part.

Once across the border, intercepted by a band of Mongol soldiers in torn and stained uniforms, under the command of a young, puff-cheeked lieutenant, Rudi and his group of stragglers had their first experience on the Soviet soil.

"Where to?" the young, fat officer on horseback demanded.

"Bialystok, Lvov, lieutenant."

"Where from?"

"Warsaw."

"Why did you cross the border illegally?"

People in the group hesitated. Wild looks of the soldiers with their rifles and bayonets at the ready confused them. Someone dared to speak out.

"There are Fascists there. Impossible to live."

The lieutenant smiled in a not unfriendly way.

"What will you do in Bialystok?"

Again there was an awkward pause. It seemed impossible to explain how life under German rule was. The investigation took place on a huge field, the wind was blowing, cream-colored clouds swam swiftly over the pale blue sky. "Help to build Socialism!" one bold man said.

Again, the officer smiled. The morning was fresh, one could actually start building Socialism on a day like that. He liked the answer. "Help to build Socialism," he repeated. "I'll let you go to Bialystok," he said. "But you must go as a group. Report there to the Provisional Government."

Rudi continued for twenty kilometers with the group until he thought his legs would not carry him any longer. But then the Mongol soldiers helped them move with rifle butts. Rudi was shaking while telling about this brutality. "They behaved exactly like the Germans. They did not discriminate against the Jews; but they cursed in a most horrible way. 'Fuck your mother's cunt, the fucking dumb whore that brought you unnecessarily into this world.' And so on."

Martha laughed aloud: "How ingenious!"

"Very ingenious. I never heard the same word repeated in say, five minutes: except *cunt*, which reappeared every second."

"A pity you did not take notes. It would be interesting to analyze the curses from all angles."

"I had no time," said Rudi tartly, "I was too busy trying to avoid those rifle butts."

"And the officer?"

"The officer slapped his horse and rode away; he lost interest in us."

Bialystok was jammed with huge crowds of refugees from the German side. They bivouacked on the streets, and in the fields surrounding the town. Official buildings were decorated with slogans: *Long live the victorious Red Army! Under Stalin's leadership, on to the victory of Socialism!* Food was supplied to the town by the peasants from the vicinity, but sold at absurd prices. The black market flourished. Twice daily, at an unspecified time, a train was provided to carry people out of the town. And every evening, there was entertainment: a propaganda film, free of charge.

It took Rudi a week to fight his way to the Government House to get the document authorizing him free passage on the train to Lvov. But to get the document was one thing, and to get a place on the train was another. Only a few lucky, strong ones procured places inside the carriages. Hundreds of others swarmed on the roofs, or hung on to the sides of the carriages, grabbing windows, ladders, door handles. Before the train pulled out, a final free-for-all, desperate battle was fought: those who remained on the platform trying to storm the train, those on the train kicking them off, clutching to their places with all their strength.

Rudi somehow figured that his pass entitled him to a place inside the train, and stopped a uniformed Russian railway man, asking him for assistance. The man frowned and read aloud: "As a refugee, entitled to free railway passage", and shook his head. "This is absurd," he said. "The Provisional Government cannot issue such passes. This is a Soviet State Railway. And, anyhow, where is the round stamp?"

Before Rudi had a chance to protest or argue, the man had torn the paper into tiny pieces, and let them fall through his fingers.

Rudi said: "I felt I could kill the swine on the spot. I saw red, literally. But the railway man calmly opened the holster, drew out a big Nagan revolver, and said: "I'll count till five. If you do not disappear by then, I'll shoot you."

Crying with rage, Rudi disappeared into the crowd; disappearing, at least, was not a difficult task. He spent the night on the platform. The next morning he fought bravely, and won a place on the roof of the last carriage. An elderly man tried to drag him off at the last moment. "I kicked him in the face," Rudi said. –"I must have hurt him, he screamed like mad on the platform." But by then the train pulled out, the locomotive spitting out billows of black, acrid smoke.

Rudi, the pianist, lit a cigarette, and lingered awhile silently over his memories. Then he said, "The worst of it, as I remember, was the smell of the Soviet Union. Human sweat, unwashed bodies, dirty rags, straw, tar. Then the propaganda. Banners, slogans, portraits of leaders everywhere. Lectures by political officers."

He watched one *politruk* tell an audience of mostly peasants: 'Remember, you were living in a feudal society. Everything belonged to the lord. His was the cattle, the fields, your labor, and even your girl on your wedding night.'

All the illiterate peasants laughed like mad, for they had never heard about such a thing, and some were courageous or stupid enough to shout:

'No, no, that business about the girl cannot be true!'

The *politruk* was confused, the poor thing. 'No?' he said. 'Then you must have had an exceptionally good lord. Here it is written that it was so.'

He lifted a pamphlet high in his hand, so that they all could see. "Their horrible newspapers, the *Pravda* and the *Izvestia*. Lies, lies. Clumsy, idiotic explanations of their war against Finland. I could not bear it any more. And there was no chance to get out of there, to Moscow. They claimed that in Moscow everything was different but I couldn't get there."

64

Rudi was silent for a moment. "You know what their test was for distinguishing a disguised bourgeois from a peasant or a proletarian, a worker? They made them take off their pants. If the drawers were clean, the suspected man was an officer, or factory owner, or a *pan*. He was doomed. That was that." David listened with concentration. It must have been really bad there. As bad as here? Prison walls, the horrible stench of the Ghetto. Starvation. Disease. And the many loudspeakers spitting Nazi propaganda in an unceasing flow. The propaganda was not the least of his problems. Six times daily, poison was released from these big, funnel-shaped loudspeakers. They repeated endlessly, a million times, hammering it into human skulls, that Germany was winning the war on all fronts, that this was the reality, the only reality, that everything would remain as it is, forever and ever. For a thousand years to come. For eternity.

Then, the announcements: "By the order of the Governor… by the order of the district chief of the police… it is strictly forbidden… it is forbidden, under the penalty of death… the curfew hour is set earlier… the following bandits were executed yesterday… a warning… a reminder… punished… death…"

An endless flow. No man's nerves could stand against it. The papers only supplemented it, the German language *Warschauer Zeitung*, and the Polish rag, the *Kurier*. For a very short time, even a special paper for the Ghetto was published. It said, in its editorial: *In the new European and World order, after Germany's final victory, there will be, no doubt, also a rational final solution of the Jewish problem…*

The man, who wrote these words could not have known. He was just having a vision. Jewish people have always been blessed with prophets. Besides, his was rational thinking. His only fault was that he had not listened carefully to the supreme leader of the German people. But Hitler was always consistent: not in one of his numerous speeches did he neglect to mention that the enemy No. 1 was, is, and will always be the Jew, until he perishes from the face of this planet.

65

Chapter fifteen

David found that he earned more working on a *placowka* than teaching. The best thing about it was that it was outdoor work. Also, it provided variety. The worst was the acute awareness of being a slave, of working for the Germans for nothing, only because you had to; the exposure to abuse, nakedness before brutality. A whim of a corporal could keep you working long after darkness fell; the sickening realization of one's total vulnerability, impotence, nothingness.

These feelings could not be eliminated, much as he tried. He found adapting himself to the psychology of slavery impossible. And yet, many people, many good people he was working with, had made this adaptation. There was no stoic philosophy as a basis for Herschel's thinking, just simple, fatalistic submission. He envied Herschel. He envied Tami and her worker-friends, and he knew he could never become one of them. There was a threshold he could not pass, in spite of his attempts. He labeled this inability of his, for a time, *The Intellectual Curse.*

In March, he was assigned by pure chance to the best job he'd had so far. It was in the building of the former Polish General Staff on

Napoleon Square. In the basement of the building was a big central heating system. A Polish janitor, Jan Sulczynski, was in charge of it. David was his assistant. His job was to bring coal in a wheelbarrow from a heap in the backyard to the cellar: Sulczynski would then throw a few shovels of coal into each of the four furnaces. At three in the afternoon the Pole used to drag out the ashes, and David removed them in the same wheelbarrow. Once a week he loaded the ashes on an army truck. The entire heating system was automatic, and required no attention from either of them.

Sulczynski spent his days dozing on a bench. Every few hours, two Germans—an officer and a soldier—came down to the basement. The soldier carried a big load of papers and maps. Neither would say a word. Silently, he nodded at David and the Pole. David opened the furnace door, and the soldier threw the papers into the flames. The door remained open until every piece of paper was consumed. The two Germans stayed till the end of this operation. Then the iron door was banged closed, and the two would leave without a word. Sulczynski went back to his bench and stretched out his legs. Like a big, old cat. David almost expected him to meow at any moment. The Pole said: "They have a school for staff officers up there and they burn here the papers and the maps with which they study." Why does he offer me this piece of information? Has this any special meaning? David wondered.

"As for me," Sulczynski said, "I have decided to spend most of this war on that bench. It is comfortable."

He stretched his legs and arms.

"That is why I applied for a helper," he said. "I considered it too much work to haul the coal from the yard, and dragging ashes, and all that. I could not lie so much on the bench before. So I said to the lieutenant, Sir, I need a helper. You want to keep this place clean, and in good order, don't you? And he kind of nodded, considered this, and said, 'I do not think I can get another paid Polish worker, it says one janitor on the personnel list, but I think I can get some Jews from the Ghetto. They cost nothing.' One, I said. One is enough. And so you came here. It is not hard work, is it?"

67

"No, not at all," David said. "The only trouble is there are no shops around here and I would like to buy some potatoes and vegetables to bring home."

Sulczynski said: "Well, you cannot have a nice soft job like this, and potatoes."

David, leaning on the shovel, thought the man was nuts. Let us play nuts, then. Two are better than one. He asked: "Were you in the army, Mr. Sulczynski? In September 1939, I mean."

"What makes you ask me?"

"Just because I was, and I thought you resemble somebody I knew there."

"Where were you?"

"The 36th Infantry Regiment."

"Then it was not me. I was in the 21st Warsaw's Children."

He watched David with his yellow half-closed cat-eyes, and David felt uncomfortable.

"I can bring you some potatoes and cauliflower tomorrow, if you want," Sulczynski said.

"Thank you. That would be very good indeed."

"Don't mention it."

He turned on the bench with his back to David.

David peered through a round hole in the furnace door at the fire inside. The fire was beautiful. The fire was fascinating. Red and white tongues leaped, jumped, flowed, consuming the coal, biting the furnace walls.

As a child, he had loved to look at fire in the big brass tubular stove, while nanny was preparing to bathe him in the old-fashioned bathtub on four crooked legs. He remembered it and was surprised. How old was he then? Four? Five? It was long, long ago. But some people worshipped fire. For good reason, too. David was full of understanding for this.

"Listen," he heard Sulczynski's voice. "You want a piece of advice?"

"Sure, I never reject advice."

"What is your name?"

"Gordon."

"Gordon? That's not a Jewish name."

"Plenty of Jews with that name, Mr. Sulczynski."

"Good. Listen, Gordon. Don't stay in the Ghetto. Beat it. It is a bad place to stay in."

David stood silent, astonished, between the fire and the Pole on the bench.

"Now I will sleep a bit," Sulczynski said. "Don't forget to wake me up when you hear the Germans coming."

"Do you drink, Mr. Sulczynski?"

The yellow eyes became mere slits. "Have you ever seen anybody in this country that does not?"

Next morning they shared the vodka David had brought with him. He got it from Arthur who had an unlimited supply. "The bitch keeps me drunk the whole time," he laughed. "That is in our contract. I tell you, David, I intend to persuade Martha's father to translate Wassermann's book about Ada. Wassermann should have written about her. It is wrong that he has not written such a book yet. This is real stuff for Wassermann. *Fall Maurizius Roman* is nothing. No, no, take it! You need it as much as I, and there is more than enough of the stuff!"

So he drank the vodka with Sulczynski, feeling more stable, occasionally glancing at the fire imprisoned and roaring in the furnaces, his thoughts clearer, ideas developing suddenly and being immediately controlled by quick brain action, the brain, fed with vodka, working smoothly, unhesitatingly, no grinding of gears or stoppages. Only once during that hour did Sulczynski interrupt the silence. The bottle was empty.

"You remember my advice, Gordon?"

"Yes, Mr. Sulczynski."

"Good then. Remember. Throw away the bottle."

He worked there for ten days. When he came into the cellar on the eleventh day, the Pole was not there. A young German soldier in fatigues stood in front of the boilers.

"What do you want here?"

"I… I work here."

"No. I work here now, if you call this work. There's not enough to do here for a child let alone a grown man."

"The Polish janitor…"

"There's no more Polish janitor. Get the hell out of here."

And that was the end of the *placowka* in the German School for Staff Officers. But David remembered Sulczynski for a long time.

Chapter sixteen

War was raging in the world, fought by soldiers, airmen, sailors, underground fighters and guerillas. Planned by leaders, generals, officers, its battles were reported with a generous dose of lies, by propaganda and official communiqués, through radio and the papers.

But the real planning was done in the backyard of the old, drab big apartment house in which David was living. Or, at least that was the impression anyone would have had watching the tenants gathering there every morning at ten o'clock. Sometimes real information could be obtained there—and only there—if you were admitted to the Inner Cabinet.

David, whenever he did not go to work on the *placowka*, would join the meeting or content himself with watching it from the kitchen window. He was, of course, too young to have a say in the proceedings, but was tolerated by the Members.

The undisputed head of this body was Mr. Blum, who, with a cigar stuck in his bulldog face, so closely resembled Churchill that his leadership was tacitly and unanimously accepted by all others right from their first meeting early in 1940, which means even before the other Churchill became Prime Minister.

Mr. Blum had been, before the war, the owner of one of the biggest fur shops in Warsaw. A wealthy man, he occupied a large apartment on the fourth floor. Short, stocky, with a round belly, and always wearing a fashionable dark felt hat at a slight angle, a silver-knobbed cane in his hand, he would open the meetings emitting rings of heavy smoke from a long, black cigar clamped in his mouth. On another day, he had told David, piercing him with a pair of small, incredibly blue, and very cold eyes: "I have, praised be God, a stock of these cigars, to last me through the war."

David smiled: "Depends how long this war is going to last." There was no smile on Blum's face: "It does not. Even if it lasts five years or more."

The other members of the cabinet—Sommerfeld, Gryn, Shapiro and Levy—remained silent, till Blum opened the meeting, starting with a survey of the Ghetto black market taken the day before.

"The Hard, mostly gold coins, remained stable. The Soft went up by four points, which is very, very remarkable."

The black market in dollars—gold coins and bank notes—directly reflected the war situation. This was the axiom of their thinking; anyone foolish enough to question this basis, would be denied, immediately, the right to participate in the daily meetings. And yet, looking at them from his kitchen window, Tami's words rang in David's ears: "What are we? Nothing, dust." Indeed, any one of them, all serious middle-aged men, had a touch of the morbid and the grotesque about them, the result of the white armband on their sleeve which exposed each one to daily mortal danger just by walking down the street or sitting at home or lying in bed. Just breathing the air. Living. David chuckled. *Living is hazardous to your life.* A nice formulation. But one seldom thinks about it. One goes on breathing, eating what there is to eat, moving one's arms and legs. Talking. Urinating. Acting. Reacting. Discussing the situation.

At some point, Blum had probably identified himself with

Churchill. Perhaps only half-consciously, but even this was sufficient to make these daily meetings almost real. A serious exchange of views. They were still sober enough not to make any decisions, unlike the unfortunate King Rumkowski in Lodz Ghetto.

They played their parts well. Tall, thin Sommerfeld—formerly of Sommerfeld *&* Zurkiss, wholesalers in grain, with patches of diseased skin on his face, like burnished copper—was the foreign minister. The information supplied by him in a voice monotonous like an autumn rain, was usually a balanced mixture of wishful thinking and irresponsible gossip. But occasionally, he would dip his hand into his pocket, and, having assured himself with a quick glance that nobody outside the tight cabinet circle was looking, would produce a small sheet of paper covered with very fine hand writing. *BBC, London, last night.*

They put their heads closer together, listening eagerly; like prisoners in a cell listening to any sound coming from outside the prison. The possession of a radio receiver was, naturally, punishable by death.

The news was not good. Germany was victorious on all fronts. But even the confirmation of it, from London, gave them some hope. Facts were reviewed and commented on from every angle. And, what was most important, the other side did not think about surrender. They were absolutely resolved to fight on, as the other Churchill, in London, announced. If necessary, from America, from their overseas territories.

Blum bit on his cigar, very grim, and said nothing. He looked down at the end of his walking cane, which he pressed hard against the pavement. Others were silent. Finally, Gryn sighed: "Do you know how long a war like this can last? Perhaps ten years."

Sommerfeld, an educated man: "There have been longer wars in history: a thirty year war, a hundred year war."

"Thank you. It is very good that they are going to fight Hitler, but we have a poor chance to see the end of it."

"They'll starve us out." This from Shapiro, who was dealing in black-market food.

Levi, the supplier of local gossip said in a hushed voice: "Gentlemen, they say next week somebody is coming to Warsaw…"

"Who?"

"A very high-ranking official. I heard two versions of it. One said it was Miller, the Gestapo head, the other…" he lowered his voice still more; they had to bend their heads to hear him whisper.

"Himmler himself."

"I do not think it has any direct connection with us here in the Ghetto," said Blum.

"What, then?"

Gryn said, "They have started a new wave of repressions against the Polish intelligentsia. I heard they arrested hundreds of doctors, lawyers, engineers."

Blum looked at him with cool contempt: "You think Himmler would come to Warsaw because of a few hundred Polish doctors? Laughable!"

"But they keep shooting the Poles like rabbits! I heard from an absolutely responsible source that a new list of executed Poles was published three days ago."

"I saw it," David said.

They turned to him. Blum studied him in silence for a long moment.

"You saw it?"

"On my way to the *placowka*. A list of 24 names. Polish bandits executed for criminal acts against the German Army."

"We are, naturally, the worst off," said Sommerfeld, "but nobody could claim they treat the Poles with silk gloves either."

They nodded. They exchanged more gossip. They yearned to hear some good news from each other, one good word, some hope.

They were still here, still functioning, running households, still with their families, with some food, some money, some hidden valuables perhaps; still thinking rational thoughts, but each one of them had an eerie feeling, that the pavement under his feet might open at any moment and swallow him up.

Sommerfeld said, "Have you heard this one? A rabbi was

praying yesterday in a *shul*: 'Dear God, we have been your Chosen People for more than five thousand years; perhaps You choose now another one?'"

They laughed a little, half-heartedly. The tension was eased for a few seconds; but the catastrophic feeling persisted.

Chapter seventeen

Toward spring 1941, David Gordon thought he could finally bring some kind of order into the complex problems of his life.

Fichte, Kant, Spinoza, and Schopenhauer were shelved; Kierkegaard survived on the kitchen table for another week.

An unusual calm, a clarity of mind, came to him suddenly one April morning. He opened the window and looked up. The tiny square of sky above was pale blue. He stayed at the window, his mind free of thoughts, for some minutes. David sat down, opened his notebook, and wrote on a new page: *The theory of life in 1941. Force is the only way of dealing with this situation. There is no other alternative.*

He closed the notebook. The thing one had to do was fight and never mind what all these philosophers said about violence.

Very soon the 'cabinet' would meet down in the yard; he did not feel like watching them today. He followed the track of his thoughts: for a Jew, closed in the Ghetto, there are two possibilities of fighting. The first, right here on this territory. This precluded a priori any chance of victory. However, a considerable number of Germans could be killed, which was of no little importance.

The other way is to escape, in order to join any group fighting the Nazis. No matter what group, in Poland, or abroad.

A strange urge took hold of him. He took out a big-scale city plan of Warsaw with the borders of the Ghetto marked on it with thick black lines, and spread it on the table. He was a commander-in-chief. He tapped the map with a pencil.

Arms, men, ammunition, food. None were available here. Not just for General David Gordon, but for any general. Never mind. Let us play. Where would you make your strong points? What are your lines of defense? Of communication? Arrows of attack?

Attack? But that was out of the question, even in a war game, in play! Behind the enemy units, behind these thick black lines was Polish Warsaw and what would the Jews from the Ghetto do there? What could be the objective of an attack?

So please, General David, do not attack. Defense, concentrate on defense.

I should have Zabiegala here, thought David. Zabiegala would help.

But you don't have him. You have nothing. Make the defense from nothing, then.

A minefield would be a nice thing to start with. Armored cars torn to pieces, exploding. I would not have the minefield right at the Ghetto gate. No sir. We'll lay it back, as far as the Solna Street crossing: or even further still, till Karmelicka. Strict orders: We do not open fire until at least a company of Germans is inside the Ghetto. Along Leszno, with scouts almost reaching the minefield. Then, at a signal: Fire! From this block, from that, and from that, simultaneously. Hand grenades, rifles—ah, if you had two or three machine guns...

He marked the blocks with his pencil.

What pleasure that imaginary battle gave him! What satisfaction!

Gratification of desires, he noted in his notebook, *means killing Germans.*

Your men, General Gordon, have to be hand picked. The half-a-million Jews here are no army. Nobody thinks of fighting.

77

They prefer to push one day into another, trembling at the sound of soldiers' boots at night. Like you, yourself. Hoping against hope that they'll survive somehow. By a miracle. Some hope that the Red Army will march in. Some hope for the impossible. Hundreds of thousands physically exhausted, starved out, weak, morally finished. Many no longer have the strength for hoping anymore. There were legions of living dead.

I wonder if I could find a thousand able-bodied men here.

David wrote: *A minimum of physical strength is required to maintain hope. Some authorities maintain it is possible to fight without hope. This means that the concept and virtue of resistance are of a higher moral order than hope itself.*

Too many philosophical books, David sighed. In the latter instance, I should take the biggest kitchen knife, or this axe, go straight to the Ghetto gate, kill the gendarme, and let myself be killed a moment later. This is morally a very acceptable way of suicide.

Drops of sweat were on his face. The old alternative of a 'quiet' suicide by using a razor blade in a basin of warm water seemed more tempting, a delicious, peaceful death.

David opened the kitchen cabinet. Behind a stack of white porcelain dishes reserved for holidays and special occasions—unused since the beginning of the war—stood a half-full bottle of vodka. Arthur had brought it to him some time ago.

"You should have some kind of painkiller," he explained. "I pinched it from Ada, naturally."

"She won't notice? And you? You won't miss it?"

"Don't be stupid. You must have a drop of it always handy. Otherwise it is difficult to survive. I know, I have tried."

David poured himself a full glass and drank. I cannot leave Mother. Not in order to fight, not for anything. Not even for suicide of any kind, I'd have to be a different man.

Tentatively—what kind of man?

You'd have to be ruthless. Yes, ruthlessness is the quality: to be able to disregard completely the suffering of others and one's own.

78

Free of remorse, of regret, of sorrow, of conscience. Free of memories—which means practically newborn.

What else? As free of any emotions as possible. Cunning. Sly.

David was not General Gordon any more, but the Creator of a new man. A man? He smiled. This is a monster I am creating, a homunculus. If you want to make something—or somebody—equal to this task, stripping it of the essential human qualities was absolutely imperative. In fact, that was what the Germans were doing.

And look how successful they were! As far as he was concerned, personally, the process had started on the 1st of September 1939, and had made substantial progress. He was not the same person he had been in August 1939.

Well, riding on that track, why not accelerate it?

The monster, David thought, had to be nihilistic in philosophical terms. He also had to be fearless. Fear was erosive stuff, consuming people from within, like cancer. Destroying their defense instincts. If his creature had to survive outside the Ghetto, he must be able to look at the face of the vilest Gestapo torturer, to look him straight in the eyes, and to laugh at him.

Very excited, David took another glass of vodka. He wiped his lips with the back of his hand. The outline, the framework existed. He had to work out many, many details to complete it. To put meat and muscles on it. He had to destroy the hope of survival. Survival was not necessary—fighting Germans was the Supreme Good.

Mother came in quietly a few times and escaped noiselessly.

He should have stopped her saying: Mama, I am leaving you.

She surely would have nodded and said, better consult father.

Or asked, innocently, why?

"Because your son has disappeared. I am not your son."

"David has disappeared? Strange. Then, he'll be back soon. Nobody, nothing disappears, really. Temporarily, yes, but not for good. Yesterday, I searched for my glasses for half an hour. I was sure that I had left them there, on the table. I have an iron memory but when I needed them, they were not there. I just waited patiently for half an hour, and there they were again, on the table where I had left them. Patience."

"But mother, I am going to be another person!"

"Then it won't be you, if you are another person." David helped himself to another vodka. Discussing his plan with mother would not do.

The real question is, can you, or can you not? Do you really want to risk everything? To destroy everything? Even memory?

Grabowski, in the train, which was now speeding steadily north as if to make up for the time lost previously on countless little stops and stations, grimaced; to tell the whole truth by memory was difficult. Most difficult of all, and never completely one hundred percent successful. Perhaps it required more training. David Gordon was a smart man and quite strong-willed, and he had worked out the stages of death and rebirth skillfully. Everything had run smoothly as planned, except for the memory aspect.

After the idea was conceived, he began working seriously, systematically, taking pains to smooth out the smallest details. He even took care that David did not die a virgin. Dorka was helpful and co-operative, for twenty zloty.

After the stagnation of many months, things started happening.

But even then, he found in himself an overwhelming compulsion to share his great idea with somebody else—no other than Tami.

She listened motionless, and her eyes did not move from his face.

"I have been spending endless hours on it; days and nights. This is my only real, full-time occupation."

"You used to spend much time with Arthur, Rudi, Martha, all that gang."

"I have never spent much time with them and now even less than ever. I am working out the details."

He stopped. He had a habit of lowering his head at the end of a sentence, and raising it again at the beginning of the next one.

"Tami, I have not told this to anybody. You are the only person who knows about it—about what is going on in my head."

"And your friend Arthur?"

"He knows nothing. Perhaps he feels something, for he is the most sensitive man I have ever met, but I am not even sure of that. Besides that woman keeps him drunk almost constantly."

Tami suddenly leaned over and put her hand on his. A thin, transparent child's hand. She was dying of anemia, or starvation, he thought. Probably both.

"I have the basic elements solved," he told her. "They are mental, not physical."

With much contempt, Tami, 19 years old, and a hot convert to the Marxist creed, repeated: "Mental? In your head?"

"Absolutely. You see, Tami, it is not the physical examination that finishes off ninety-nine per cent of the Jews who try to escape to the Aryan side. Not the physical features; not their faces, noses, lips. It is the fear in their eyes, the fear they are unable to conceal, to control mentally. The secret of success or failure is here." He tapped his forehead with his finger.

"The mental connection between the persecuted and the potential persecutor. They work on the same wavelength; that is what destroys the victim. Horses, dogs, all animals know when a man is afraid of them. So do the Nazis, the policemen, the informers. The blackmailers. How do they know? If you change the wavelength of your brain, they can do nothing to you. When I discovered this, it was like a revelation. It changed my approach, it changed everything."

She eyed him with a sad detachment.

"I cannot change myself physically," David said. "I cannot add that foreskin to my penis which was cut off twenty years ago without asking me if I approve; though some Jews do just that—beauty cor-

81

rection. Did you know that? It is absurd, nonsense. I can do better than that. I can make myself appear to them in such a way, that even the meanest, the most suspicious bastard among them would not dream I might be circumcised."

"Is that within man's mental powers? What about emotions which are uncontrollable?"

"One has to learn to control them. Nothing is uncontrollable. It does not come easily, but it can be mastered."

"And you have mastered it?"

"Not yet. It is very difficult. I have to keep training myself."

Tami withdrew. He saw she was thinking hard.

"These are strange things you are telling me, David. I am afraid this experiment, this training, could change you, permanently, into an inhuman creature. A monster. Something like, well you know, the Dr. Jekyll and Mr. Hyde story."

"When it is over, when I have achieved my aim, I'll forget all about it."

"Some things are irreversible, David."

"Nothing is irreversible."

"Historical process. Time. Death."

He inclined his head. "The last two, perhaps, but the human mind keeps fighting against them. It has always fought since the beginning of time. Hence, the ideas of resurrection, of reincarnation, and fantasies about travel in time. The idea of irreversibility is repulsive to people."

Tami said: "David, do you believe in fate?"

"Well, I do to a certain degree—let's say almost. But that has nothing to do with it. And I know what you are aiming at, with your historical necessity and inevitability, and all that stuff. But let me tell you something. Even if this thing of mine, this transformation I am trying to achieve; even if I knew it were irreversible, even if I knew that I'd remain like this forever, changed, I still would take the risk."

"Why, David, why?"

His face had changed color, at first flushed and then ashen-gray, as if he had aged fifty years in five seconds.

82

"Because," he said slowly, "because I believe, contrary to what you and your Red friends are saying, that it is not merely an inevitable struggle between rotten capitalist systems that sit back contentedly and watch this spectacle dispassionately. Their hour will come, and they'll have to wake up from that pleasant dream. They'll have to pay for dreaming as well, when the time comes. But I believe that this war is a fight waged against the greatest evil that has ever existed. I believe a man must fight. This war must be fought by all means, regardless of the chances of victory or defeat."

His voice became choked with emotion, and he stopped.

Tami looked at her feet and said nothing. David rose and began pacing the room.

"There are things such as Good and Bad," he said, "and I do not care if you call me a child, an imbecile, or an idiot. I believe in it. I know that for you there is only red pitted against the rest of the colors. Perhaps I am color blind."

"God—or whoever, whatever there is, will forgive me; or not. I do not care, believe me. And let me tell you, I am ready to take a lot of other sins on my conscience. You, of course, have no such worries since conscience is for you a bourgeois concept, invented by landowners and exploiters. The only sin you know is sin against the Party."

Tami stood up slowly. "David, I am sorry to say this: What do we have in common, you and I? Nothing. So what is the use? I won't even let you sleep with me. I do not think there is any sense in us meeting any more."

That was it, David thought. But she was right this time. It was I who was too weak to break it off. Why should we play on each other's nerves?

"All right, Tami," he said. "Be it as you say. I do not want to discuss it with you any more. Goodbye."

He did not expect it would be that difficult. It was as if part of his body had been cut out of him. He felt very sick that day, and the day after that. Mother took care of him.

"It is probably a cold," she said. "Some people suffer more

from a common cold than from a real, serious sickness. But if you do not feel better tomorrow, I think we should call Dr. Sacks."

Dr. Sacks, the family doctor, had been dead since June 1940. David and his mother had been much distressed when they had heard about it.

David said: "I'll be all right, don't you worry, mother."

Fate favored him, and he was spared the murderous task of telling his mother. They rounded her up in the first large-scale *Aktion* and carried her away with thousands of others. She never knew that her David had become a monster. If anybody had told her, she would not have believed it. Never. David, who was at that time still far from being perfect, had instinctively rushed after her when that tall SS selection officer motioned her with his thumb toward the waiting trams. Arthur, who was with him, struggled, and pinned him down, and would not let him go and be shot by this SS man, with a pleasant, smiling face. Arthur had surprisingly strong arms. David felt himself choking, bursting apart, disintegrating, but not one tear escaped his eyes. They were burning and dry.

Chapter eighteen

Dorka the prostitute distinguished herself in the turbulent river of a Ghetto street by a merry flash in her eyes. At that time, most people had worried faces, worn by suffering and undernourishment, and their eyes rolled incessantly and quickly in their sockets, on constant alert against the danger of a gray uniform. Nobody smiled, nobody laughed. Dorka conformed to the habit of gloom, but she was only half as nervous as the rest, and you knew immediately that a happy smile would flower out of that merry glint on the slightest provocation.

It had never occurred to David before that there could be whores in the Ghetto, where everybody's full time occupation was survival, leaving no leisure for such basic human activities as sex. And yet the professional wink he received was of such quality that there was no place for doubts. When he stopped, perplexed, she said: "Will you come with me? It is 20 zloty." He hesitated for three seconds, and within that time also thought that his great creation, his Frankenstein to be born, must have this knowledge. He went with her.

His clumsiness made him desperate, and amused her.

"Doesn't your girlfriend let you screw her?"

David dressed in a hurry, sweating, disgusted with himself. He pulled the shoelace and it tore. He cursed.

"I have no girlfriend."

"Don't be so nervous!"

Lying naked on the bed, she lit a cigarette for herself and relaxed, exhaling smoke through her nose.

"Say, it was not the first time for you, was it? You are not that young."

Standing with one shoe on, with the piece of string in his hand, David suddenly felt calmer. What the hell? Wasn't she sweet and kind, this tiny brunette with her friendly smile?

"You'll be surprised. It was the first time."

"Why didn't you tell me?"

"Why should I?"

"I would have given it to you on the house," she laughed, "if I had known I was taking your virginity. I give virgins special treatment."

"Well, now I am no more a virgin than you are." He laughed too, and sat down on the iron bed.

She shook her head. "My, my. And why? You are a good-looking boy. Do you want a cigarette? Here. Anyhow, you have a free ticket for the next time. But only for the next time; after that you pay like anybody else."

"Thank you. What makes you think there will be a next time?"

"The first-timers come back. Well, most of them."

David eyed her now with interest. She looked relatively well fed and healthy. "Is your business good? Do you make much money?"

"Whoring? So-so. Not bad. But I also earn money in other ways."

"How?"

"Why should I tell you? I'll teach you a lesson: never ask questions of whores. They'll lie to you, tell you what you wanted to hear to please you."

David flushed. "OK. I did not ask you."

"I might as well tell you," she laughed, "because of your virginity. I have a share in a smuggling business."

"Smuggling what?"

"What a baby you are! What do people smuggle here? Food, silly."

"Through the walls?"

"Through the cemetery." She extinguished her cigarette and started dressing. "I like it there, because of the fresh air."

The cemetery. He had not been there for years. When he was eight or nine, Father would say on Sundays: "It is a beautiful day. We'll go visit Grandpa in the cemetery."

In a forest of tombs his father would find Grandpa Reuven's grave, a slab of sandstone, and a vertical black granite stone with carved letters painted gold. An inscription in Polish, another one in Hebrew letters he could not read. David's father would stand there for a few minutes stern, angry, biting his lower lip and holding little David's hand. High up, on the swaying trees, birds were singing.

"Let's bow to the dead."

David politely lowered his head and saw Grandpa Reuven, whom he well remembered with his ragged white beard, accept his bow with a nod, in his grave. Then he looked up again at the treetops.

"There are no more trees there," Dorka assured him, buttoning her blouse. "They have all been cut down, and sold for wood. It was a hard winter."

"Who did it?"

"The grave-diggers, entrepreneurs, clerks. The dead would not mind. What are trees for them?"

"You go there often?"

"Once or twice a week. When they bring merchandise from the other side. Potatoes, vegetables. Water! They bring water!"

An old woman came in holding in both hands a basin with warm water. She did not look at David, put the vessel on the floor and went out. Dorka squatted over the basin and started washing herself.

"You see," she said. "You were in such a hurry before, and now you sit here quietly and watch me washing my pussy. Not that I mind."

David looked at the wall, embarrassed. Plaster was peeling off.

"When our Ghetto cops are there, and you know, they are not always partners in this business, there is quite a game of hide-and-seek among the graves." She laughed merrily. "Like when we were kids. What is your name, by the way."

"David."

"David. Give me that towel, please. Thank you. What are you doing?"

He got up quickly.

"No, no, sit down! I meant, what are you doing for a living?"

"Oh, I was a teacher. Now I go out on *placowkas* sometimes."

She stepped into a broad, red-brown skirt, and adjusted the elastic at her waist.

"All right. I am ready, let's go. What would you do if you were out of here?"

He was taken aback by the question.

"Out of here? Out of the Ghetto?"

"No, I mean, out of these times."

"I'd run."

"Where to?"

"To the end of the world. And back. And once again. And you?"

"The same thing I am doing now, probably. Minus the smuggling business. Come, come now, I can still find another man before the curfew. Give me a kiss if you want and remember never to do that with whores—you never kiss them. Anyway, I am healthy and you have a free ticket for the next time, as I told you. All right. Go now."

Chapter nineteen

The train rushed through the darkness with great speed, but the darkness, though still impenetrable, seemed thinner. The air was fresher, cooler, smelling of smoke, salt, wet wood, like in the mountains.

Grabowski pressed his face to the cold window for a moment.

This David Gordon, since his brainstorm in April, since things started happening, had had peculiar luck. First, a lot of people he was connected with died. Mother. Tami. Arthur.

Peculiar bad luck? A special quality to that man, David Gordon?

No. Grabowski did not think so. Just coincidence. Lots of people were dying in those days in the Ghetto. They were dying like flies. Starvation, sickness, suicide. Killed by Nazis. Tens of thousands perished in the first big campaigns, 'deported' like David's mother.

Tami was lucky to have died of typhus a couple of weeks before the German invasion of Russia started. She would not have survived the disasters of the Red Army in the first weeks of the war. Was it

89

better to die of typhus than of a broken heart? They told David that in her last hour she was happy. She kept speaking about the red children she saw on the red roof opposite, against the backdrop of a red sky.

How Arthur died, David never learned. He had banged on Ada's door for a long time and was about to leave, convinced nobody was in the flat, when the door opened slowly. He stepped back, like a man hit in the face. The old shaking woman in a dirty nightgown, with a crumpled, shattered mask instead of a face could not be Ada. Only the eyes, the huge eyes burned like red projectors. He felt his scalp shrinking.

"What do you want?" the hag croaked with a toothless mouth. "What do you all want? Go away! Arthur is no more!"

With great effort, David asked: "What happened? What? How?"

"Go away: He is dead!" She advanced one step. "You, too, are dead. Everybody is dead, even those who believe they are still alive. Stupid! Dead, dead, dead, all of you!"

The door closed with a bang. David stood in the staircase, sweating. Later, he met with some of the gang once more, they had no time for him. They were preoccupied with feverish preparations for weddings. Rudi was going to marry Martha in two days, and Bubi, Renia. In the madness of the dying Ghetto, young people were marrying by hundreds, as if this ceremony, performed in crazy haste, could save them in a miraculous way. David asked what had happened to Arthur, and they told him: "Arthur? Dead."

"How?"

Nobody knew exactly. Rudi thought for some reason he had hanged himself. Barbara said he had drunk himself to death. Nobody was interested, they were in a hurry, the world was going to pieces tomorrow, and they had to marry before that.

The *Volksdeutscher* in the compartment woke up suddenly, rubbed his eyes with his knuckles, looked around stupidly, and asked: "What? Where are we?" Grabowski moved in his seat. "I don't know. I think we have passed Graudenz."

The German struck a match and looked at his wristwatch.

90

"Past seven! We were supposed to arrive at four. Where are you going?"

"To the toilet."

"Wait. I'll go and have a piss too."

They went out together, passed the corridor running the whole length of the carriage. Grabowski saw the other compartments were full. Mostly sleeping soldiers with half-opened mouths, and rifles between the knees.

The iron wheels rumbled beneath his feet. Tiredness made him a little drowsy, but he felt a taste of satisfaction in his mouth. He was going north, towards the sea. Before the train stopped at the last station, David Gordon would disappear and Grabowski would be on his own, unburdened and with a clear purpose. Clear purpose, that was most important. And not badly equipped to achieve his aim, either. With that new confidence, he could endure David for a while longer.

Chapter twenty

David went back to Dorka a week later. Walking rapidly along the rotting streets filled with fear and panic, he thought suddenly that he wouldn't be able to find the place again. Then, somewhere mid-way, he was rocked by the suspicion that maybe they had taken her away. But that was unlikely, she was young and healthy, they had deported mostly people over forty, and the weak and sick ones.

He quickened his step. Breathless, he passed the few blocks of Gesia Street, until he was sure. He knocked, and listened to the thumping of his heart. He knocked once more.

The tall, old woman opened the door slightly. "What do you want?"

"Dorka? Is Dorka in?"

She moved her big face from side to side, scrutinizing him first with one eye, then with another.

"You have been here before?"

"Sure, yes!"

"Why don't you say so, then! All right, come in. Nowadays one must take precautions."

David caught her by the arms and shook her: "Woman, is Dorka in?"

She looked at him with contempt. "Oy, oy, what excitement! All men are pigs, *pfui!*" She spat on the floor. "Take your hands off me. Of course she is in! Why wouldn't she be?"

They were in the tiny kitchen now, with its soot-blackened, dirty walls, and she said, pointing with her elbow to the curtain: "You can go right in, she is alone, business is bad these days."

In the alcove, Dorka was on the bed, dressed, reading in the light of a candle. David, in all his breathless excitement, smiled. The tiny room was full of shadows creeping over the cracked, wet walls, peeling plaster, and the cobwebs on the ceiling. The light shone on Dorka's face and the open book, and deep shadows, like valleys in a bizarre landscape of frozen lava, flowed on the bed's green cover and the girl's dress.

"You have a customer," crackled the old woman from the kitchen.

She pushed away the book, and looked up.

"Your mother is not very friendly today."

Her dark eyes were bored. She yawned.

"Sarah? Oh! She is not my mother. What made you think so! She is my servant."

She sat up on the bed, reaching with both hands behinds her back, and bowing her head, started unbuttoning her blouse.

"Wait, Dorka. I did not come for…that, not this time. I want to talk business with you."

She looked up. "Ah! It's you! I did not recognize you. The ex-virgin."

"Well, how are you?"

"What are you reading?"

"A funny story by a French whore. Perhaps you know it? You look like a guy who reads books."

And you tried to search for the meaning of reality, you silly idiot. This young prostitute has more sense in one finger than you have in your whole crazy head. It is 1942, the great *Aktion* is in progress, they are taking out tens of thousands of Jews, the Ghetto is disintegrating, and Dorka, waiting quietly for customers, reads Colette. She is very real, Dorka. She smells of cheap perfume, and has remarkably smooth skin. You can touch it. You have a free ticket, you can even make love to her.

She reads, and it provokes her mind. She thinks thoughts, she functions, she avoids distortions. She has an old servant.

He explained to her what he wanted, and she listened carefully, and nodded. "Of course I can do it. Who told you I was dealing with that, too?"

"Nobody. I just thought— well, you mentioned smuggling, and the cemetery last time."

"You are a clever one," she laughed. "Well, baby, it costs money. Quite a lot. What do you have to sell?"

He had the papers in three days. Two pieces of paper: a certificate of birth and baptism, and an identification card.

"The certificate is genuine," Dorka said, "the identification card is not. It is forged, but most of them are, on the Aryan side. A normal, routine check-up cannot disclose it. It is a good forgery."

"And the man, the man himself?"

"Why, that's you now," she said seriously.

"I know, I know, but before?"

"The man is dead, I was told. He was a seaman, and he died in 1939. You don't mind, do you?"

"No."

"Well, at least that. With you one cannot know. You are funny. Now listen, boy. You learn by heart all that is written on these two pieces of paper, every word of it. And when you've finished learning, you learn it once more, and once more, so that when somebody whispers your new name when you are asleep, you wake up immediately and say: 'Here! That's me!' All right?"

"All right."

"When are you leaving? You want me to help you to the other side?"

"No. Not necessary. I'll go out on a *placowka* at the end of this week probably. Nothing keeps me here any more. What about you?"

"Don't worry. I stay here, meanwhile."

"Aren't you going to escape from here?"

"I can do it any moment, but I won't yet."

She shook her head, and said, almost merrily: "I am going to survive, you know."

"How do you know?"

"The same way I knew you'd come again. I feel it, very strongly."

"Nobody can image himself dead."

"Perhaps that is true, but I know I'll survive. Also a woman I know confirmed it."

"What woman?"

"A clever woman. She saw it in my left palm. So I don't worry and don't you worry. And listen, it really cost all that money. The prices have gone up in the last few weeks. You understand?"

"I believe you. I trusted you right from the beginning."

"I wouldn't cheat you. I cheat men frequently, it is part of my profession, but I wouldn't cheat you. You believe me?"

"I believe you completely."

"Good. Now beat it. I don't think we'll ever meet again."

"But you said you were sure you'd survive."

"And are you sure, Mr. Grabowski, that you will survive?"

They stood in silence for a full minute, and then she said: "OK. Go, and take care. One must try, anyhow. Goodbye."

He kissed her on her cheek, as he had done the first time they met.

Chapter twenty-one

And how did one actually die and be reborn in the same moment?

It was very simple. That is, under the circumstances, the easiest thing to do. There were very few *placowkas* by then, the Army and the Air Force on the local level were clearly perplexed and disappointed that the flow of free slave labor had stopped abruptly. The authorities that lead the depopulation campaigns in the Ghetto had not thought it necessary to keep them informed. The square in front of the former post office on Zamenhof Street, and the other one at the Community Center, which were already outside the Ghetto limits, looked almost empty in the early morning, but a few groups were still forming.

David looked for Weiss, but Weiss was not there any more. "You cannot choose much nowadays," a surly official told him. "Take it or leave it." He got a place with a group working with a German civilian subcontractor to the Army. They were dismantling machines of a Polish printing press.

It was a large building with two entrances on two different streets.

96

Thirty Jewish workers watched over by two unarmed civilian Germans pushed and pulled the heavy machinery on the ground floor. At ten o'clock, the foreman called: "Breakfast!" and they sat down to rest.

David got up, his heart beating, and casually walked to the entrance. The German, munching his sandwich, looked at him questioningly, and David put his hand on his trousers.

"At the end of this corridor, and to the left," the German said, "you'll find it, it is marked "oo" on the door."

In front of the toilet bowl, David said *alea iacta est* and smiled bitterly at David's persistent habit of using his Latin on every occasion. He then took off his white armband with the blue Star of David on it, rolled it tightly, wrapped it in a piece of newspaper, and threw it into the toilet bowl.

He transferred Grabowski's papers from his trousers into the breast pocket of his jacket, washed his hands, combed his hair, and opened the door. The corridor was empty. He walked without haste to the other end of it and found himself in a large lobby. Its glass door faced the street on the other side of the building. He stopped a moment.

"Grabowski," he whispered to himself, "Wladyslaw Grabowski, take courage. Here you go."

He pushed the door, went out, and started walking down the street.

Chapter twenty-two

Obviously, the first thing to do was to go to a barber. David's hair had grown too long. The last few weeks, men in the Ghetto had stopped visiting barbers for various reasons. One of them was that sitting in a barber's chair with a white sheet covering your body made you a sitting duck; you could not look out on all sides to avoid being caught by a German hunting party.

Grabowski chose a small shop on Chlodna Street. There were no other clients, and the barber set to work silently. Once he murmured something about "damn long hair." Grabowski remarked that he had spent a few weeks in the country, near Radom. "I don't trust these village barbers, you know," he laughed.

"Sure," mumbled the barber without interrupting his work, "they work on your head like with a scythe on the field. Food still plentiful and cheap there, eh? Maybe you brought something with you? I'd be ready to buy."

Grabowski looked at the big mirror opposite and was relieved to see his face: no dead Jew David Gordon. What he saw was Wladyslaw Grabowski. Whoever that personality might be, it had never

98

even met a David Gordon. He was not the type that associated with Jews.

He had his problems, naturally, as every Pole under the occupation, but they were of a different order than those of the Jews.

Aryan Warsaw had a different atmosphere than the Ghetto.

It was, in fact, another world altogether. There was electricity and water; garbage was collected. The streets were not crowded. Trams rolled on their rails and sparks spurted from the cables overhead on the curves.

But Grabowski made no comparison, because he had never been in the Ghetto. He just imagined what it might look like.

He walked the streets leisurely, absorbing new impressions, like a peasant arriving for the first time in a big city. In the center of the town, he saw many German soldiers: on Chmielna Street, although it was just early afternoon, more whores were standing in front of the shabby hotels than before the war. As soon as the association 'Dorka' started forming in his head, he pushed it away quickly and expertly.

So far, he had every reason to be well satisfied with himself. The main trouble was that in Grabowski's past, facts were so sparse! Father: Stanislaw. Mother: Victoria. Date and place of birth. Profession: Stoker. That was all.

Of course, you could build up a life history. History was based on facts, or on fantasy, but facts were too few, fantasy not developed, and the whole enterprise could be endangered by occasional failures of memory. Still, David Gordon provided character for him, and soon his behavior had become almost instinctively based on these premises.

He entered a small restaurant and ate a late lunch. While eating, he considered the possibility of visiting people in the city. Did Grabowski have friends or acquaintances in Warsaw? David Gordon did. But David was dead, and Grabowski stood up to the temptation.

There remained but one thing to do: sign up at the foreign workers recruitment office and leave the city forever, in accordance with a carefully designed plan. But he was unfamiliar with the procedure, did not know how one went about volunteering to work in Germany. Moreover, he did not know anyone who could tell him which questions he would be asked and which tests he would have to pass. He was taking the greatest risk imaginable. He went over his plan again and again while he drank tea and ate sponge cake—the typical war cake. His entire master plan was based on the next step and it was imperative that he try, no matter what happened.

He began to feel that someone was watching him. He lit a cigarette with confident fingers and leisurely turned his head. A man in a raincoat and a shabby felt hat was leaning against the wall, observing him with interest.

I don't know anyone in this city, Grabowski repeated to himself. Nevertheless, Jan Sulczynski, the Polish janitor David knew from a *placowka*, approached him, nodded hello and said: "I am happy you are here. Can I please have a light?"

As Sulczynski's cigarette touched his, Grabowski said: "Excuse me, I don't think we've met before."

Sulczynski inhaled until his cigarette was lit, and blew smoke out his nostrils. "Of course not," he said, "but in any case, I'm happy. At your age, it is difficult for a man to discern between good advice and bad advice, especially from a stranger. Do you plan to stay here?"

"No."

"That's good too. Don't stay. I could hide you, but this is a bad place and soon it will be a lot worse. Go as far away as you can. It is always safer inside the lion's jaws." He laughed curtly. "A paradox but true. Very true. There was nothing safer than the basement of the German officer's headquarters, was there? Here's my tram, number 17. Be careful."

He said goodbye with a nod of his head and, without hurrying, climbed onto the tram. Number 17 departed, its bell clanging.

Afterwards, Grabowski went directly to the main recruitment office for volunteers to work in Germany on Noby Sviat Street.

Transformations
Part II

Chapter one

Rosti's ship used to discharge its cargo of iron ore every two weeks in Weichselmünde Ost, which was one of Danzig's busy ports. This operation would usually take three days, and then the empty ship was moved to the other side of the canal. As soon as she was moored there, the loading would start with two big portal cranes dumping lumps of coal into her holds.

A dense cloud of coal dust hovered over the quay, covering everything with a shining layer of black powder. The fine dust settled on the ship's white superstructure, on her black decks, on the big Swedish blue-and-yellow flag painted on each of her sides, and, in spite of the tightly closed windows, penetrated to the cabins, staining the walls of the alleyways and tables in the messrooms, to the stewards' dismay. After the ship had left the port and started the voyage home, they had long hours of extra work to clean the whole mess up.

Rosti did not mind much. He felt very familiar with coal and coal dust. He was not a steward. His job was to spend eight or more hours out of every day in the stokehold of the ship, feeding its Scotch boilers. He took precautions, when going ashore, not to touch anything with his gloved hands, and not to brush with his navy-blue trench coat the walls or the handrails. Also, before taking shore leave, he would spend at least an hour washing his face and arms, using buckets of hot water and soap, so that no trace of dirt remained under his eyelids and around his nostrils. Those were the usual telltale marks of stokers and trimmers.

As a result of all these efforts, his appearance on the quay, immaculately clean, with shining black shoes and a fedora set at a slight angle, always misled the watchmen at the gangway. They never suspected he was a fireman. They always took him for captain, chief engineer, or chief mate. Accordingly, they saluted smartly, and were usually rewarded with a condescending smile, and two or three cigarettes.

"Thank you! Thank you very much, sir!" the watchman would murmur, looking stealthily around to check if anybody had been watching. Accepting presents from foreigners was forbidden. "Good cigarettes, not the lousy straw stuff we're being given here! Have a nice time ashore, sir!"

Rosti politely touched the rim of his hat. He walked to the ferryboat station, stepping carefully over the rail tracks, iron shovels, grabs, wires and all such junk as usually litters a coal pier.

A similar procedure followed with the port gate watchman; the harbor was well guarded. Then he stood at the small wooden platform, waiting for the ferry to come. Cold wind blew out of the darkness and an entering submarine whined like a small night animal.

Rosti, leaning over the wooden railing, was watching the slim shape of the coning bridge moving over the still water so intensely that he almost did not notice the ferry. Only when the deck hand called: "Hey mister! Are you coming or not?" did he jump onto the tiny boat. Five minutes later, he disembarked in Neufahrwasser.

He knew the place. He had been there many times. He walked confidently through the suburb's clean, tidy streets, badly lit by blue street lanterns.

Blackout, wartime. At the other end of his voyage, the Swedish ports were ablaze with lights.

Rosti passed the *Deutsches Haus* jammed with nostalgically roaring sailors and soldiers on leave, and went on, his hands in the pockets of his trench coat. He made two turns, and pushed the door of the Petroleum Bar, which was unofficially known as *Rio Rita*.

It was like coming home, except for the fact that Rosti had no home.

The three rooms of the establishment with deep, plushy armchairs more closely resembled a club, or the living quarters of a well-to-do merchant's apartment, than a harbor bar. The old artisans, retired officials, and pensioned sea-officers could feel perfectly at home in these surroundings.

Coal bricks burned in the fireplace. Old framed pictures hung on the walls: a schooner, running under shortened sail before a storm with dirty, vicious waves, and, on the opposite wall, St. Mary's Church—the *Marienkirche*—reaching skyward with its massive Gothic arm. Discreet lighting: well-polished brass ships-lanterns. Two stolid, veteran waitresses moving quietly and efficiently with large trays loaded with beer glasses.

Rita presided behind the counter in the central room. She said, "Well, at last!" and, switching over to Spanish, added: "Haven't seen you for a long time, *hidalgo*! Do you want a beer?"

Beer, thin and poor, real wartime beer, was actually the only thing she could offer her customers. At least downstairs.

Rosti produced a grin. She brought him the beer herself and sat down at his table: a powerful, stout, dark woman with a beautiful large face, perfect arches of eyebrows, sensuous lips.

Rosti took off his trench coat, hung it on a hanger under his hat, straightened the jacket of his charcoal suit, and sat down. Rita thought he moved like a cat: quiet, soft, elastic.

He offered her a cigarette from a fresh pack, and gave her a light from a silver lighter. They talked in Spanish but switched over to German when Biedermann, the young official from the local Gestapo Frontier Control, came in. He wore a leather coat—almost a badge of his profession—and shot a quick, sharp glance at everybody present. That was more habit than necessity. He knew each man there, all respectable people. He knew that their papers were in perfect order—even those of the two Poles from Wohnlager Narvik, sitting at the table in the corner.

"*'n Bierchen*, Hansie?" Rita asked.

He nodded. She extinguished her cigarette, rose majestically, and swung towards the counter to pour him a beer.

"The *Viking* is in," Biedermann said, looking at Rosti.

"As if you did not know," she said, laughing.

He laughed too. Of course he knew. He knew every foreign ship coming in or leaving. Swedes and Danes were the only foreigners and there were few of them.

In the corner sipping beer sat the short, stocky man with a mustache, whose nickname was Bleistift, the Pencil. He said to Grabowski in a low voice, in Polish: "Watch out, that one is, of course, from Gestapo."

Grabowski said innocently: "Well? Our papers are in order, aren't they? We're allowed to sit here, no?"

"All the same, remember, he is Gestapo. He can ask you about your '*P*' letter."

"But nobody does!"

"I know, I know. But he could. What I mean is, this man could make trouble for us if he wanted. Just remember that."

Biedermann had no such intentions. He drank his beer at leisure, listened to a song on the gramophone—*The Star of Rio*—and told Rita a rather bawdy joke about a tram conductress. He enjoyed Rita's loud laughter more than telling the joke itself. He paid, said: "*Heil Hitler*," and went out.

Rita returned to Rosti.

"You have business with him?"

She lifted high her eyebrows. "You know, I have been living in this town for the past twenty years. Bruno—may his soul rest in peace—has been dead since 1935, and I manage somehow alone. What can a poor widow do? I know everybody in this neighborhood. Hans is my client. Like all these people, like you."

She looked at him. He had eyelashes like an American movie star, she thought, and that eager, strangely quiet face.

"Like me?"

"Now don't be nasty, Rosti! Not exactly like you, but a customer, all the same. And you never told me what an Argentinian is doing on a Swedish ship in the Baltic Sea."

"He stokes the ship's boilers."

"Very well. And why?"

"Because they pay well, because it is relatively safe for a seaman in bad times like now. Because he likes you."

"Liar!" she exclaimed in German, slapping his hand and laughing. Her cheeks shook when she laughed. "Liar!"

"Woman," he smiled, "don't make me angry: I always tell the truth, only the truth. Or nothing."

Her eyes wandered to the clock on the wall.

"We close at ten tonight," she murmured.

"I know. I'll wait."

Rosti with his dreamy eyes. A seaman, a Latin man. Not exactly her own race or kin, but speaking the same language. Perhaps feeling a similar way. But she had spent many years among this placid, flat folk, she had adopted their ways, habits, language. She was a citizen of the Free City of Danzig and through a strange twist of fate—citizen of the Great Reich. Rita, the dark-eyed beauty from Seville. Thirty years ago, yes. Now, Rita Hemmcke, 53, of Neufahrwasser, Danzig. The owner of *Rio Rita*.

The two Poles got up from their corner table, paid, and said a polite goodnight. The law forbade them to say *Heil Hitler*. But they were clean, proper and correct, and Rita rewarded them with a smile, and a goodnight in return. They were customers, too. She knew they had to go at a quarter to ten to catch the last tram to Schellmühl. She knew, too, that they were forbidden to spend the night outside the residential camp, their Wohnlager Narvik. They were forbidden so many things by law. Poor things!

When the door closed after them, Rita passed majestically

107

through the two side rooms to see who was left. She hoped they would all clear out soon. Outside, Bleistift said to Grabowski: "You saw that dark man at the first table? He was from a Swedish ship."

"How do you know?"

"He had a package of American cigarettes on his table. That is a sure sign."

"Come, let's run, or we'll miss that tram." said Grabowski.

Chapter two

One of the two Poles," said Rita, "is looking for contacts."

"What contacts?" asked Rosti. He propped himself on his elbow.

They were lying in Rita's huge wooden marital bed, with brass bars on both ends of it, in the bedroom on the first floor.

Rita, in a silk transparent nightdress, raised one eyebrow. "One cannot be sure, but he makes an impression that he is in a hurry to get out of here."

"Is your friend—pardon me—your customer Biedermann onto him?"

"God, no! If he were, they wouldn't drink beer at my place!"

"So?"

Rosti was a bit impatient. He knew that he had to spend one night with Rita every time his ship called at this port, and that night was a necessary and unavoidable nuisance. She was at least twenty years his senior.

Conversations with her provided some kind of compensation,

for she was a witty woman, and had a sharp sense of humor. He enjoyed being with her, though not in bed. What he did not like were her far-stretched allusions hinting that she knew more about him than she really did. Or should.

"So?" he repeated.

"Maybe he wants to go to Sweden."

"Let him go. What do I have to do with it?"

"He might be willing to pay."

"Woman," Rosti said quietly, but she sensed that he was furious, "what on earth makes you think I'd do anything illegal? Do I look like a crazy man? One that is looking for trouble with police? With the Gestapo?"

Rita kept gazing at him, frightened, for a moment

"Ah, *bueno*," she said. "*Nada*. Forget it. I really have no interest in it. Tell me about Swedish women."

Rosti quieted down immediately. He grinned.

"Now you talk sense. Swedish women? Too cold for me. I like your bed better."

"Before you told me that you always talk the truth, or nothing. So keep quiet now. It is very early still. Let's get some sleep."

Chapter three

Wladyslaw Grabowski, an infant of one month, was growing so quickly that people could have taken him for a baby-genius. Two weeks after his arrival in Danzig, anybody living in Camp Narvik 2, when asked about him would say he had been there forever. A real old-timer. Two more weeks, and he was unanimously elected *Stubenältester,* the room representative.

Eight people were living in the room, sleeping in double-decked iron beds and Grabowski had the best bed, the lower one in the corner at the window and right next to the central heating radiator.

There were six such rooms in each barrack, and nearly seventy barracks in Camp Narvik 2, plus a huge dining hall, kitchen, boilers and machinery halls for central heating, and stores.

The camp as an entity, in its pure geometrical forms, was a very surrealistic proposition for Grabowski when he squatted occasionally on his haunches. From such a position, the barracks seemingly extended along lines of perspective converging at an infinitely distant vanishing point. Identical low wooden sheds, uniformly gray, under a uniformly gray sky, with an air of timeless solidity: They would stand there somber, simple, till the end of the world. Or, till a cosmic convulsion would twist the lines of perspective into spiral columns or snake like arabesques, shaking off the barracks into a heap of broken, splintered boards, and spilling their contents into a void.

Bordering with Narvik 2, but separated from it by a low fence, was Narvik—an identical camp, but inhabited by Germans and *Volksdeutsche*, with separate quarters for Italians, Belgians, Dutchmen and Frenchmen.

The camps had been erected early in the war to provide housing for the working force of Danziger Werft, Danzig's shipyard. Later, other camps, bigger still, were added in Langfuhr, another suburb. Cholm 1 and Cholm 2 housed, in slightly worse conditions, thousands of *Ostarbeiter*: Ukrainians, Russians and White Russians. The Schichau Yard, and the Port Authority, and the Wagonnen-Fabrik had their own, smaller camps. These new barrack towns had sprouted around every German industrial town like skin sores on a syphilitic's body. Here, the old Hansatown, surrounded from every side with rows upon rows of identical, drab barracks, shuddered till the spires of its Gothic churches and the tops of its narrow pointed roofs. At peak time, 1942, when a new submarine was leaving the port every three weeks, almost twenty thousand workers lived in the living camps.

Half of this population had come there voluntarily, at least in the strict, technical sense of the word. They had signed the contract papers in recruiting offices which were scattered in all major towns of occupied Europe, had mostly been asked no questions concerning their past, and had been required to produce a minimum of papers: sometimes a birth certificate was all that was needed. At least two thirds of these documents were forged, and the recruiting officials knew it. But the bureaucratic process had been cut so drastically because Germany desperately needed workers to man her huge war industry.

Grabowski smiled, comparing his recent experiences with those of others. They were, with minor differences, almost identical.

All these recruiting offices resembled closely those of the pre-war French Foreign Legion, complete with huge posters showing smiling men, beaming, radiating good health and satisfaction. The men on the posters loved working in Germany, for Germany's war effort.

The volunteer, signing quickly—without first reading the contract, which stipulated an unlimited time period, the termination to be decided only by the employer—shot quick glances over his shoulder. The police or Gestapo were usually on his heels. Since the volunteer knew well that the smiling man on the poster was a lie, and all he could expect were endless working hours, barely digestible food, bad living conditions, daily humiliation, and in addition to all that, the danger of Allied air raids, work in Germany was considered the last thing before suicide. Again, as before the war, the French Foreign Legion.

But such was the need for workers, that thousands were simply rounded up and brought to factories, mines, and shipyards, without being given a chance to sign a contract and be awarded the honorable title 'volunteer'. Once in Germany, in camps, their status was anyhow exactly like that of the volunteers.

There were no volunteers and no recruiting offices in the Russian-occupied territories. All *Ostarbeiter* were victims of large-scale manhunts. Then they were sold, wholesale, to the great industrial enterprises, or, individually, to farmers or private households. In provincial towns, the railway stations served as slave markets. At a certain time, the price of a female slave varied between 20 and 50 marks, depending on her age and strength.

The hierarchy of the camps, which Grabowski learned quickly, was complicated. The top authority was naturally the camp leader—the *Lagerführer*—with his small administrative staff. He was responsible only to the head of the manpower and to the top police officials. Where the division of various nationalities started, things became more complex.

The German and *Volksdeutsche* inhabitants lived in camps, took their meals there if they chose to do so, and were in all other respects equal to any other German town-dwelling workers.

Almost the same privileges were granted to Belgians and Dutchmen. They were even entitled to home leave for a week, once yearly.

The Frenchmen and Italians, up to the Italian Armistice, were constantly screened by the police. After the armistice there were no Italians at all. Their barracks and kitchens emptied out overnight. Before that, they had had the most distinguished privilege of separate kitchens with cooks of their own.

When Grabowski arrived in Danzig, the Germans and the Italians were still dear allies. Grabowski made friends with Giusto, a man from Trieste, with a round clown's face and blinking eyes, and sometimes got a plateful of yellow spaghetti with pieces of meat in it. Giusto looked on contentedly while he ate, and commented from time to time: "Fascist swine. Mussolini—pig. *Tfui!*" He spat on the floor.

Steam was hissed quietly in huge automatic boilers. Grabowski and Giusto sat at the table, reading newspapers, looking up occasionally at the pressure gauges and thermometers on the switchboard. Every two hours, Grabowski would go to the coal shed and load coal into a couple of big cylindrical containers. Then he pulled the containers on a special cart to a platform in front of the boilers, hooked them on one by one, and lifted them with an electrical crane to a special place above the oven. The coal would then drop automatically into the slowly moving grates.

He never knew how he had got that comfortable job, which had but one disadvantage: long shifts. Twelve hours a day, every day, one week dayshift, next week nightshift.

The job was too soft. It made you forget the war was on. It made you forget what you were born for.

Sometimes at night, Meister Göring would come in, stealthily. He never caught them sleeping with their heads on the table. One man kept watch, waking the other with a kick the moment the doorknob moved.

"Nazi swine," murmured Giusto after Göring's visit. "I wonder what makes him get up at two at night to spy on us. Perhaps his wife wouldn't let him fuck her. German shit!"

At four-thirty Grabowski woke the cooks. They were the camp's aristocracy. They did not live in the barracks but had tiny rooms in the kitchen building, which was right behind the boiler house.

The chef was a German, the minor cooks were Polish and French. The Italian was Mario, lame, hobbling on one leg. "That one is all right," Giusto explained to Grabowski, telling him the who's who of the Italian barracks. The big, square, bear-like Mario was arrested one day, long before the Italian Armistice, and handed over to the Italian police.

Two real tears rolled down Giusto's cheek, and he made a sign with his finger on his neck.—"Mario *kaput*, finished! Poor Mario!"

The dishwashers and cleaners were Russians and Ukrainians, men and women despised by everybody, the pariahs of the system. Pierre, the Frenchman, yawned and stretched his arms when Grabowski woke him. Fifteen minutes later, he came over to the boiler house to have his morning coffee with the stokers. A tiny, swarthy man, with a merry face, he liked to talk and to laugh.

"Had Olga, the Ukrainian with me tonight. Made her suck me. She was spitting and brushing her teeth for an hour at least after that. God, how funny! Said it was the first time in her life she had done that—you hear? What barbarians! Good people, but barbarians!"

He laughed, and smoothed his nice black mustache. "Take more cream, boys! There's more than enough to go round."

The camp's aristocracy. Grabowski lit a cigarette and went out. The night was thinning out over the fence of the women's camp. Long, pale, horizontal stripes cutting the canopy of darkness. War was far, non-existing. You could live a comfortable life here if you were a stoker, if your friends were cooks.

Sometimes, while loading coal in the shed, Grabowski saw, rising from behind the coal mountain, the pale face of the dead David Gordon. He threw pieces of coal at it. David whimpered like a wounded animal, and disappeared. Grabowski, cursing aloud, would finish loading, and push the cart to the boilers. He was great at cursing. That's where his real talent was. Polish is a great language for curses. He had perfect mastery of it.

Grabowski discovered that people seldom lived alone there. Usually they formed groups of three or four, sharing their tobacco, food, the occasional parcel received from home, if they had one. Helping each other.

But he had no buddy at that time. Since he expected his stay in Danzig to be a very temporary one, Grabowski chose to be a loner. He indulged in two activities: gambling, and trading in tobacco. Extra food obtained from the cooks was exchanged for black French or Belgian tobacco. From that cigarettes were hand-made and sold in the barracks. The profits were 200%.

As for gambling, it was almost the only pastime. The games were poker and Black Jack. Grabowski had phenomenal luck.

Nothing earned more status in the camp than daring in gambling.

The plate in the middle of the blanket-covered table was full with crumpled bank notes. "At least 500 marks in this bank," somebody commented in an awe-stricken whisper.

"All this dirt," Grabowski said, "and give me one card."

"All this? *Va banque?*"

Grabowski acted surprised. "Didn't I tell you clearly, man? What's the bloody matter with you? Give me one card, I said."

"Show me you can cover it. Sometimes it happens that one loses, you know."

He took from his breast pocket a bundle of money and put it on the table.

"If it is not enough," he added, "there are two new shirts I bought from the Frenchmen yesterday."

"Put them on the table."

"OK." He went to his closet, and tossed the new silk shirts on the table.

"Is it enough now? Give me my fucking card!"

The banker, a sullen peasant from Tuchola, peered at him, at the shirts, at the money on the table, and reluctantly gave him the card.

Tension rose rapidly and Grabowski enjoyed it for a while. Then he showed his cards: three aces, a king of hearts, and a king of diamonds.

"Good enough?" Without haste, he brought back the shirts to his closet, arranged bundles of notes on his right side, while cards were dealt again.

The next morning, the Polish barracks knew, and the news spread to other camps: "Grabowski is a real number. He has guts, that guy. Did you hear about the game last night? More than a thousand marks!"

Grabowski bought a money belt from a Dutchman, and carried his money with him. Why leave it in the closet and expose his mates to unnecessary temptations? He lived basking in his new glory, but refraining from boasting and showing off.

In the evenings, lying in bed, he read to them and translated the *Allgemeine Zeitung*. He was the only man in the room who could read German and they were eager for news, even as tinted as it was with propaganda. It was cozy and nice to lie in a warm bed and to read. They helped him fix up a reading lamp. Life was easy and nice.

From behind the window David Gordon, standing in the deep snow outside, showed his disintegrating face, tapped the window with freezing fingers. Grabowski folded the paper, turned off the light.

"Got to sleep now, gentlemen! Fucking work tomorrow—at five!" They moved reluctantly, but obeyed. Some whispered a short prayer.

"Wasn't he Wladyslaw Grabowski of the tremendous reputation? Wasn't he the *Stubenältester*? And he'll sure as nothing soon become the *Barrackenältester*. Glorious prospects. One has an excellent chance to survive the greatest and bloodiest war mankind has ever known. Grabowski, a stoker of the camp boilers, tough, witty, clever, respected—and soon *Barrackenältester*, officially responsible for 45 people to the German authorities. A social success.

How annoying that the ghost of David Gordon, so thoroughly

disposed of in far-off Warsaw, was hovering around, reminding him in most inconvenient situations, that he was not supposed to survive the war. He was explicitly created in order to fight it.

Grabowski shook himself and understood.

The next day he started making discreet inquiries.

Chapter four

It was Antoni from 37C who proposed, after a drinking bout one late afternoon, a joint excursion to Troyl. They had been drinking steadily since five o'clock. Men painting the submarine hulls in the yard supplied the stuff: paint-thinner with an alcohol base, filtered through layers of cotton wool. Grabowski paid for two liters. The booze stank of turpentine, but was praised as 'clean and safe'—no methylene alcohol in it. Grabowski drank comparatively little, and watched with interest how the fiery liquid made them gradually maudlin, babbling, bragging, aggressive, dreaming, and incoherent.

Stefan, who had transported the bottles under his jacket, had a high, bulging forehead and a Velásquez beard. He held Grabowski by the button of his shirt. "Wladek," he said, "you are a first-class fellow. A gentleman, that is what you are. Don't tell me anything to the contrary, because I know. I am not a Gestapo informer, don't be afraid. Everybody here can confirm I am no informer, isn't that right?"

He looked around with glaring eyes and demanded approval. They all shouted "Stefan is all right, he is no informer."

"Ask my cousin Bleistift, the crane-driver in Weichselmünde, he'll tell you who I am. Now, you, Wladek, are a gentleman, and I am one, too. That is my secret. Everybody here in these barracks—and not only us Poles, but every fucking foreigner, too—has got a secret of his own."

He lifted his finger high.

"Mine is, I am a gentleman and a painter."—

"Sure," somebody jeered, "smearing submarine hulls with red-oxide, we know!"

A roar of laughter. Stefan rose unsteadily to his feet. "Who laughed?" he demanded. "Who has got the goddamn cheek to laugh? Cattle! Swine! What do you know about an artist's soul? I am a painter. An artist! Wladek, you, are my friend, I can trust you, I'll show you my pictures!"

He fetched a sketchbook from his drawer, and Grabowski, smiling, looked at two soft charcoal landscapes and a red pastel nude.

"Look at her tits—that's your artist's soul, eh, Stefan?"

"Swine!" He brought his face close to Grabowski. The stench of turpentine was nauseating. "They don't know anything about art—how could they, poor bastards?"

It was then that Antoni suggested going to Troyl to see 'real stuff'. Only in the tram, through a black-gray mist filling his brain, a clear thought passed through Grabowski's mind—that it was not too prudent to go with all these people to the brothel. Not alone, either.

The Germans, a systematical, reasonable race, had not forgotten the foreigners' sexual needs. These had to be met and supplied, like food and soap, like lavatories and showers. The B-barracks in Troyl served the purpose. From the outside they looked like all the barracks in the camps. But a big crowd was already there. Grabowski noticed that most of the men standing there were Italians.

At a counter they obtained cardboard tickets, exactly like those of the railway. "Round-trip," somebody remarked, laughing. The tickets cost half a mark and a rubber condom was also supplied for that price. "Stand in that queue," instructed an old German, punching a hole in the ticket, "and wait for your turn." He had a ribbon of the Iron Cross from the First World War in the buttonhole of his jacket.

"Don't think that was all," remarked an Italian boy in front of Grabowski, shuffling constantly from foot to foot. "You pay the whore ten marks in addition to what you paid at the box office."

Right behind him Stefan, the painter, was swaying on his long legs with his eyes closed while talking to himself. The queue was moving slowly but steadily, like a caterpillar, and he had arrived at the porch by the open door to the waiting room. Through the doorway, he saw a short, dark girl wearing a black brassiere but no panties, passing a rag between her legs. She said, "OK, next."

The vapors of the poisonous spirit seemed to clear up in Grabowski's head. He was able to think reasonably again.

It was his last chance. Once in there, he could not escape any more. The Italian boy entered. Grabowski mumbled something, stepped out of the queue, went to the corner and, lowering his head, started vomiting. Nobody took notice. Stefan, with his eyes still closed like a somnambulist, simply took one step forward. That was it.

The next afternoon, when they were gloomily nursing nauseating hangovers in their room, Antoni asked: "Which one did you have, Wladek?"

"The short, dark one."

"I fucked her too," somebody said. "She was the best of the lot I should say. Jesus Christ, what whores! And the way they were urging you to hurry up! I hardly put it in her, and she says: 'Are you finished?'"

The others sadly agreed that Troyl B-Barracks was no good. War quality like anything else. The conversation passed easily to memories of other, better whorehouses before the war.

Grabowski participated in this talk actively, knowingly.

His status was intact.

Chapter five

Stefan's cousin, the one they called Bleistift, deftly rolled a cigarette for himself, licked the edge of the paper and tapped it on the table. He listened to what Grabowski had to say.

He was a taciturn man, a crane driver by profession. He was loading coal on Swedish ships in port.

He nodded a few times while Grabowski was speaking but said nothing. When Grabowski finished, he remained silent for a whole minute.

"I'll tell you what the procedure is," he said finally. "When I have to go on board for trimming or something, the watchman gives me a special token and I must return it to him when I leave the ship. So there is no chance of staying and hiding in some hole. He counts the marks at the end of his watch. One watchman is always on board or on the gangway, another one makes rounds. There are usually two, maximum three, Swedes and Danes, so his round is 200 to 250 meters."

"The Danes are no good."

"Of course not. But they are guarded the same way as the

Swedes. I don't know why, because the Germans sit there too, in Copenhagen. Now, when the ship is ready, the hatches are closed and battened up, they come on board with a search party—three, four, sometimes five men, with two dogs. They gather the whole crew in the mess hall and start looking for stowaways. A ship's officer goes with them. Sometimes they take it very easy and the whole search is finished in five minutes, a mere formality. Then they sit in the chief mate's cabin drinking Swedish schnapps. But sometimes they open the fucking hatches, and on one occasion we had to discharge the whole bloody cargo of coal we had just finished loading. They suspected something on the bottom."

"Did they find anything?"

"Not that I know of. But they thought it a great joke, they went away laughing."

"So, no chance that way?"

Bleistift opened his hands and raised his left, bushy eyebrow.

"You see for yourself. Now, if you knew somebody on board who would help you on, and hide you there, well, that's something else. But it is risky and you cannot buy them."

"Why?"

"Don't be silly. They've got everything, you've got nothing. German money has no value to them. Cigarettes, tobacco, booze? Man, they could bury you under a mountain of tobacco, drown you in booze. Their country is at peace—neutral they call it—and making good business out of this peace as well. So why should they risk their skin? For the love of you?"

Talking to Bleistift was a calculated risk. Nothing could prevent him from going straight to the police and telling them about Grabowski's plans. He would get a reward for it. But he felt this stocky crane driver was not that type. There was nothing to be afraid of from his side.

Grabowski said that he had a good job, but he might just do it, if there were a fair chance. "If not," he shrugged. "I can sit on my ass where I am, and wait till the end of the war."

The other man nodded. Then he added: "You go out sometimes? To town? We could go together to Neufahrwasser some evening. I know a decent bar there. I have almost no company here in this barracks. Most of them are from Tuchola, peasants. I am the only one from Warsaw."

Grabowski shook his hand. Bleistift said, while getting up: "If I had no family, I'd think about that thing myself. But you know—wife in Warsaw, two kid girls, what would they do to them if I bolted?"

They agreed on a day when they would have a beer together in town. But before that happened, Grabowski considered it necessary to travel for a day to the beach, in Weichselmünde. He thought he had a rendezvous there with the notorious, imperishable ghost of a certain dead Jew.

Chapter six

Wladyslaw Grabowski had been created by God's hand and by the late David Gordon's will for a specific purpose, and accordingly was equipped with certain qualities—daring, coarse resilience, physical courage—that would enable him to exist in a limited framework of space and time. But unpredictable events, like encounters with the dead, had not been taken into consideration in his planning. This, Grabowski thought, was very regrettable because already during the first short period of his existence, in fact, before he was two months old, he had had to face David Gordon three times. The excursion to Weichselmünde Beach was mainly intended to exorcise that ghost once and forever, to put an end to an unexpected and unwanted interference. Well, not forever, exactly. But at least for the time being. Grabowski felt that David could become more than an annoyance: at this stage, he could be outright dangerous. He was not prepared or conditioned to deal with him.

At six in the morning, he and Giusto were relieved by the day-shift workers. They washed their faces and went each one to his barracks. Grabowski changed clothes and left the camp. The day was snow-gray, but the cold was not penetrating. It was a soft cold, and there was no wind to whip it into a blizzard's fury.

Grabowski traveled first by tram, then by ferryboat. On deck he saw a Swedish steamer discharging iron ore in Weichselmünde West Harbor Basin. The blue square with a huge yellow cross loomed large on the ship's side.

He left the port and the village, and found himself at the seashore. The quiet, dark-green sea conveyed a message of tranquility and such power that Grabowski felt almost compelled to sit down on the coarse sand and stare.

Any memories, Grabowski? Memories of childhood, perhaps?

No sir. No memories. Grabowski was born at the age of 25, three years older than the deceased Jew who invented him.

No memories, but the brain was working, mental processes were intact, impressions were received and digested. Hence, the strange revulsion that momentarily took hold of him, for any intellectual activity, for that constant, lightning quick analyzing, dissembling, processing, without which Wladyslaw Grabowski could not have survived five minutes. The artificiality of his existence struck him with force. And yet, there was no other way. He had no doubts about it. Grabowski would be justified, if he succeeded. Success or failure, these were the only proofs of his existence. To pave a road, a bridge, over an impossible time period, for the immortal soul of David Gordon to be reborn in his next incarnation. Which would be that of a soldier.

Small greenish waves dissolved in an increasingly thin layer of water on the wet edge of land. The water seemed heavy like paint or glue.

Grabowski looked around. Three or four fishing boats were on the beach, heavy wooden vessels, leaning to one side, like dying sea animals. In one of them was a mast with a canvas sail furled around it.

The boats had no names. Each one had a number written in black paint on its bow.

In a sea like that, in a boat of that size, one could make a crossing to Sweden, he thought. How many days would it take? And what if a storm broke out? A small open vessel would quickly fill with water and sink like a stone. Or, on the contrary, if there were no wind at all? How long would he have to row?

These were not random associations of mind. Grabowski earnestly weighed possibilities, compared chances, and the conversation with Bleistift was recalled. It served as a kind of yardstick. One certainly had to take the boat as an eventual possibility.

He got up, walked over slowly, and put his hand experimentally on the wooden hull. The smell was strong, pungent, heavy. Tar, wood, rotting fish and weed, nets, and above all, the sea itself. The smell of the sea. The wood of the hull seemed dry, almost crumbling under the touch. The fishing gear, some ropes, a bucket, were thrown about carelessly, as if the owner had abandoned his vessel, disgusted with the whole business of going to sea for any purpose.

There were some low white houses among the trees, slightly further inland, perhaps two hundred yards from the shore.

That's where the fishermen live, Grabowski thought. He would like to see the men who owned these boats. He was not much surprised when, instead, he saw David Gordon sitting on a bench in a boat. He had put his feet on the gunwale and was gazing at the sea.

"Still here? I thought you'd be over there by now. Two weeks ago."

Grabowski shrugged. "You know it isn't easy. It won't do to rush on blindly, banging your head against the wall. You only break your head that way."

"That is not the worst."

"But that was not the purpose."

"The purpose was to get to the other side and start fighting. Or to perish."

"You are unfair. You know how damn difficult it is. I was just making up my mind to steal this boat, if I cannot manage it otherwise."

David slowly turned his head from the sea, and looked at him with derision.—"You couldn't even push this boat into the water. It is too heavy."

"I'll take somebody with me."

"Why don't you, then?"

"I told you. I want to succeed. I am trying to do it in the most reasonable way."

"Don't you think you should hurry up a bit, instead of living the good life?"

"The good life is relative, but give me some more time: three, four weeks."

David looked again at the sea.

"Three, four weeks is all right. But remember—the good life—even, as you say, relatively good life, is dangerous. You may easily forget what you are living for."

"Don't worry. I can't forget. After all, you created neither a hero nor a victim. You wanted me to accomplish something, no?"

"But quickly. Without much fuss."

"Good. And another thing. Kindly refrain from interfering with the workings of my mind. It has a retarding effect. It makes things more difficult. It hampers."

David did not answer immediately. After a long moment of silence, he said: "OK. I'll try not to. I understand that it's not useful."

"Then scram unless you have something more to say."

"Regards from Tami, Dorka, Arthur, and the others."

"I don't know what you're talking about. I've never heard those names before."

"Very good," replied the whisper. David had already disappeared but the words were still audible. "Very good: I'm almost proud of my creation. But remember your time is limited. Good luck to you."

Grabowski got up, brushed his trousers, and started walking back to the ferryboat station. From the gray sky snow started falling. Big, wet flakes descending slowly from the sky.

Chapter seven

Three kinds of posters were plastered on the walls. One was about the *Kohlenklauer*, a black, cat-like coal thief seen escaping with stolen sacks of coal. Propaganda for saving coal, since coal had become precious on the eve of the third year of the war.

The second poster showed a smiling soldier, bent a little under the heavy load of his gear, coming from or going back to the front from a leave, making his way to the railway, while disciplined civilians accompanied him with tender eyes, standing aside and letting him pass. The inscription read: *Räder müssen rollen für den Sieg! Er geht vor!* The wheels are rolling toward victory! He goes first!

The third poster was captioned: *Psst! Der Feind hört mit!* The enemy is listening!

Artistically, this was doubtless the most successful poster of the three. At night, on an abandoned road in a barren field, two men face each other. A match, lit by one of them, throws light from below on their faces. One of the men has a cigarette in his mouth. Perhaps he had just asked a passer-by for a light. Perhaps the other man had started a conversation, made a careless remark; perhaps the man with the cigarette was a spy, the enemy's agent. The night on the poster was dark-blue, and there was tremendous tension between the two men.

Many people stopped in front of the poster, gazing for a moment, not so much impressed by the warning in big black letters—*Pssst!*—but arrested by the magnetic field of the tension.

Grabowski, encountering Rosti for the second time, stopping him on an empty Neufahrwasser Street to ask him for a match, thought for a moment that to a secret observer, they must look exactly like the pair on the poster. But it was only a momentary reflection. Rosti shaded the burning match with his palm, Grabowski inhaled the smoke, and said: "Thank you. Could I speak to you somewhere for a few minutes?"

Looking up, through the smoke he stared into Rosti's unblinking eyes. Long lashed, almost like a woman's. Black, bottomless pupils. Strange expression on his face, a mixture of irony and compassion.

The voice was soft and low: "Sure, go ahead."

"Here? Could I invite you for a glass of beer?"

"Sorry, I have no time at the moment. What do you want?"

Grabowski took a deep breath. "I would like to escape to Sweden."

No muscle moved on Rosti's face.

"I have nothing to do with such things."

"You work on a Swedish ship, don't you?"

Rosti shrugged. "Indeed, I do, but I do nothing illegal."

"I'll give you anything you want if you help me."

Saying those words, Grabowski realized his task was impossible. How could he explain to this sailor the necessity, the ultimate, supreme necessity of escaping from Germany without bringing up the dead? Without involving David Gordon? Without telling the whole story? And how could he tell the whole story?

Rosti said, "I have everything I need; I don't need anything from you."

"I must leave this country."

"Must you? What nationality are you?"

"I am a Pole."

"I am sorry. I must go now."

"Could I see you again?"

Rosti hesitated a second. "I don't mind, if you wish."

"Tomorrow? At the Petroleum Bar?"

"Tomorrow. But not at Rita's."

"Anyplace, then. *Deutsches Haus? Alte Liebe?*"

"All right. Be at *Alte Liebe*. But remember I cannot help you escape from here. Goodbye."

Grabowski later recollected that Rosti had disappeared in an absolutely mysterious way, he had not seen him go, he simply was not there any more, and Grabowski stood alone on the wind-swept, ill-lit street.

Back in Camp Narvik 2, an endless sea of barracks, and every barrack a ripple under the sky of doom, Grabowski went to his room, took in the peaceful scene in one glance, and went to bed. The meeting tomorrow, he knew, would be decisive. He had to think and plan carefully. The man had left him a tiny bit of hope just by agreeing to meet him again. And yet, he had been very emphatic about his refusal to help him escape. Could he convince him tomorrow? The man looked strange, not like a Swede at all. But who knew better than he that a face was nothing, that a face was a hiding device and nothing more. Still, his eyes.

Somebody gave him the *Allgemeine Zeitung*. "Wladek, what do they write here?"

He pushed the paper away. "I have a bad headache, my whole fucking head is splitting, I cannot read today."

Piotr, the eldest man in the room, completely bald, with bags under his eyes which made him look dignified the way some old cobblers or tailors do, went to his drawer, took out a box, and untied the shoestring with which it was tied. He was clean, tidy, orderly. Systematic. Almost like a German.

"Take this, Wladek. It is very good headache powder. Real *Kogutek* from Warsaw."

131

Grabowski swallowed the bitter powder, washed it down with a cup of water. Mietek and Tadek Maliniak, two taciturn brothers, were sitting on opposite sides of the table, with a heap of tobacco between them, making cigarettes. Kazik, the man who wanted to know what was written in the German paper, watched them silently.

"Thank you, Mr. Waleski. Your powder is really excellent."

Piotr nodded solemnly. "I know. I bought these powders at home, the pharmacy was in the next building. On Wolska Street. They had all kinds of pills and powders, even foreign ones. I always bought red *Kogutek*. The pharmacist, a Jew, always recommended it. I've known him for years. What was his name, now?"

Water made gurgling noises in the central heating radiators. It was warm and cozy in the room.

"Many pharmacists were Jews," said Kazik. "Also doctors."

"The best doctors were Jews," asserted Waleski. "When my Genia was sick, we went to Meisel, an old doctor, an honest man. He put her back on her feet in two weeks, not the crooks from the hospital."

"Well, Tadek," the older Maliniak said, "now they are making ashes out of them, people say."

Stasiek, the redhead, made an impatient gesture: "They have had it good long enough. It is their turn to pay. That is how the world goes. You have to pay for everything, even a good life."

"I have had a fucking bad life as far as I remember, what do I have to pay for now?"

Everybody laughed. But Stasiek took issue. "It's not that. We all well know they were parasites, sucking our blood for God knows how long, and as much as I hate Germans, I cannot find much pity for the Jews. Perhaps it is just as well that they cleaned our country of them for us, our government would never had done that. When the war is over, you'll see. The best result from it will be that Poland will be free of Jews."

Stasiek was an able mechanic. His boss, though a fanatic Nazi, admitted reluctantly that the little red-headed Polack was a real exception, 'a smart guy, and diligent, too.' They were in a machinery-erecting team in the submarine engine rooms.

"If there will be any Poland at all," muttered Mietek Maliniak without interrupting his work.

Piotr Waleski scratched his bald skull. "They won't exterminate all of them," he said. "Some will survive."

"Poor chance. They closed them all in ghettos, and now they take them out from there, and…"

"Some will escape," insisted Piotr. "They are an ancient people, they have knowledge, experience. A Frenchman I am working with told me they found a Jew working you know where? In the Todt Organization in Norway!"

"How did they catch him?" Kazik inquired.

"An SSman saw him peeing and saw he had a circumcised prick."

They laughed again. Stasiek said, "Those are singular cases, I'm not talking about them. I mean the three or four million that were parasites before the war. I don't mind at all if fifty, or even a hundred thousand remain, provided they know their place and behave. What do you say, Wladek?"

There was no answer and they looked at the bed in the corner.

"Asleep already," said Piotr. "That *Kogutek* I gave him kills the pain no matter where it is—head, teeth—and makes you sleep as well." Stasiek got up and stretched his arms.

"Well, I'll turn in as well, I think."

Kazik followed.

Piotr knelt in front of his bed, and murmured a prayer. He climbed in, and covered himself with the blanket.

"I have it," he said after a moment.

"What?"

"The Jew, the pharmacist. His name was Gurfinkel."

Chapter eight

Grabowski came to the *Alte Liebe* half an hour before the appointed time. He was better known there than at Rita's; he visited that bar more frequently. It was a small place, very austere, and was run by Frieda. Tall and blond, fortyish, she wore a permanent grin of fatigue and contempt on her face. Something was wrong with the skin on her neck—sometimes she wore a shawl to cover the never-healing wound, sometimes she had it covered with a bandage and occasionally she'd wear turtleneck sweaters, which also had the advantage of emphasizing her generous breasts. Her husband was somewhere in the army, but she was vague about it; some people said she had never had a husband. She was a native of Danzig, and sometimes, when only trusted clients were around, and she happened to be in a good mood, she'd start a short conversation in Polish with Grabowski or with one or two other Poles who'd come to the bar. She spoke Polish with a heavy accent.

An old man in Tyrolean costume—short leather trousers, white socks, and a narrow-rimmed green hat with a feather—plucked the strings of a zither every second evening, and sang folk-songs in a shaky voice. Frieda's clients, lingering over their beers, listened to the performance with complete indifference, bordering on silent hostility. Yet, before leaving the premises, they'd put coins on the plate of the old Tyrolean.

Tonight, Frieda wore a green pullover with an amber brooch at her neck. Grabowski ordered a beer, treated Frieda to a cigarette, and sat patiently waiting. Patience was one of the most difficult things he had to learn.

The hands of the big old clock on the wall moved slowly. It struck every hour and half hour making a hollow metallic sound. The old Tyrolean plucked the zither strings with a thimble-protected finger but did not sing. He explained over and over again that he had caught a cold and was hoarse.

Grabowski sipped slowly the yellow liquid he detested, finished two big glasses, and ordered a third one.

This would be the last, he decided. If the Swede did not come, he would finish it, and go home. To Narvik 2. Well, and then?

Not to worry. There were boats in Weichselmünde on the beach. It was a cold, foggy evening, and the fog muted sounds from outside. The siren of a steamer in port roared hoarsely.

"He's got a cold too," one of the men remarked looking at the old man plucking the zither. He chuckled: "No wonder, in weather like this."

The depression numbed Grabowski's knees and elbows; he felt tired and drowsy. It was five past nine. Time to go.

Just then, the door opened and Rosti came in. He threw a quick glance all around, strolled over slowly to Grabowski's table, and asked: "Is this free?" Grabowski made a polite gesture. Rosti took off his wet trench coat.

Every movement was calculated, deliberate, soft, and the resulting impression was of natural ease and grace. He sat down, rubbed his hands together, and remarked that the weather was lousy. From the look on Frieda's face Grabowski knew that she was seeing Rosti for the first time. He ordered a beer, and they sat silently for a long moment listening to the old man playing what was intended to be a merry tune. When Frieda's eyes finally released Rosti, deciding that he was just another foreigner from the camps—probably a Frenchman or a Belgian—Grabowski said, "I had already decided you would not come."

Nobody could hear them talking. Rosti smiled, flashing a gold tooth in the corner of his mouth.

"Are you Swedish?" asked Grabowski.

He shook his head, still smiling. "I am from Argentina."

"How strange!"

"Why strange? The Swedes pay decently, I have been with them for a long time."

Again there was a long pause. They sipped their beer quietly.

"Are you a Pole?"

"Yes."

"Is the Gestapo after you?"

"Yes and no. It is difficult to explain."

Rosti nodded. "And where do you work?"

"In the shipyard. I am a stoker."

Rosti extended his hand, mockingly. "Shake. I am a fireman too. Colleagues." The hand was different from anything else about him. It was large, rough, calloused, with black lines deeply engraved in the hard skin from long hours of handling heavy shovels, iron bars, tools, coal.

"Let's talk business now," Grabowski said with a broad smile. Frieda, whose eyes swept momentarily over them, thought they were telling jokes to each other, the Pole and the Frenchman. She dismissed them altogether.

"I must leave this place, quickly. Could you help me?"

"I won't do it. Why should I risk my life?"

"It is a question of life and death."

Rosti, quiet and contemplative, took one of Grabowski's cigarettes and drummed lightly on the table, keeping rhythm with the old man's zither.

"Let me ask you once more. Why must you escape?"

They had been talking German, right from the beginning, and Grabowski thought that Rosti's command of it was rather limited.

So this, in addition to other things. If I could speak Spanish. If, if. Who could think of it? It is lost, thought Grabowski. I cannot bring David to him, he won't understand it, never. The whole thing would be incomprehensible to him, he has never heard of Warsaw, of Ghetto. He is living in another dimension, on another planet.

"Let me put it like this," he said. "I hate Germans very much. They are my enemies. I am their enemy. A great enemy."

All this was pitifully inadequate but that was as far as he could go. Again Rosti nodded. When he spoke, there was this sweet smile on his face again. "You see, it is very dangerous. They search the ship before it leaves. With dogs. Gestapo. Police."

Grabowski said nothing. Perhaps, he thought bitterly, the preparations for his creation had not been sufficient. He did not know how to handle this situation. There must be ways and he did not know them. Another man in his place would manage. He was impotent. Helpless, like that bastard in the Ghetto.

"As a matter of fact," Rosti said, "I thought you might help me. But it is dangerous, too." He paused, searching for words. "Everything you do nowadays is dangerous. There are various degrees of danger. Come, let us walk a little. I do not like sitting in these places. Is there still this fog outside?"

Grabowski did not understand.

"I will pay and go," Rosti said. "You stay here another five minutes. We shall meet at the corner. All right?"

Frieda accepted his money and a generous tip with a nod. He put on his trench coat, and left.

The Tyrolean put his instrument in its battered case.

"Enough for today. Sweet Jesus, what a bad cold I've got."

Grabowski, bitter, defeated, perplexed, sat staring at the advertisement on the wall opposite. *Aus gutem Grund ist Juno rund.* Juno cigarettes, unavailable for a long time. What did the man want? But if I can do him a favor, if I can help him, then perhaps after all he'll

137

agree to take the risk. But how, how could I help him? They have everything, Bleistift had said.

He got up without haste, paid, said goodnight, and walked out.

In dense fog, on the street corner, Rosti was waiting for him.

Chapter nine

In the weeks following his meeting with Rosti there were changes in Grabowski's life. First, he lost his good job in the camp's boiler house. He did not know why this happened but could only guess; some official in the shipyard personnel department must have decided the work was far too good for a 'Stateless Pole,' as he was defined on his new identity card. One day a pale, slightly lame German called Werner replaced him. Grabowski was told to report the next morning to Meister Claasen in the shipyard's Marine division. The redheaded Stasiek said he knew where it was, he would show him. They went together amidst the thousands of workers streaming to the yard. Many of them wore wooden clogs, which were heavy but cheap and kept your feet warm. The clippety-clop of thousands of wood blocks hitting the pavement made an eerie sound in the freshness of the early morning. They passed through the main gate, uniformed watchmen from both sides checking their passes and examining the round metal badges that everybody working in the yard had to wear on the right side of his jacket.

The shipyard was like a beehive. Workers swarmed over

scaffolds, on sections of submarines, over iron plates, on pieces of machinery.

Trucks, cranes, railway wagons were in motion. A feverish activity was felt in every corner. On the biggest floating dock, a sleek gray ship was resting.

"A real cruiser, that is. The *Königsberg*. Look at the guns!"

The great ship gave Grabowski an impression of an enormous lethal power. The big guns in their triple turrets were trimmed fore and aft. Flashes of electric welding blinked from under the ship's hull. A hundred cables connected its shark-like body with the shore. The four propellers looked tiny in comparison with the hull, but loomed huge over the heads of the men working beneath them.

Marine soldiers in heavy coats and steel helmets, with short submachine guns slung over their shoulders, stomped their boots on the three wooden bridges that connected the floating dock with the quay.

"What is she here for?" asked Grabowski.

"She got hit by a torpedo or a mine, they're changing some of the plating,"

Stasiek said. "That's what René told me; you know him, don't you? The Frenchie from Barrack 7; I buy tobacco from him sometimes. Well, over there is your Claasen's department. I'll bet you'll work on a tugboat, or on a floating crane. So long."

Meister Claasen had a thick, clipped beard and bushy eyebrows.

"Grabowski? Pole? Ah, you are the new stoker. Very good, my lad. Go to Pier No. 3, the Langer Heinrich is there now. What? You do not know what the Langer Heinrich is? Why, that's the 100-ton floating crane. They are taking a subsection on board there. Report both to Paul, who is the captain, and to Schultz, the chief engineer. To both of them, remember, and in that order. Off you go, boy."

He had a brisk but not unfriendly manner. Grabowski liked him.

On board the crane, stepping carefully over pieces of heavy gear, steel wires and hawsers, he looked for the captain. A big round cylinder—one of the middle sections of a submarine hull—was dangling from the crane's tall arm. Grabowski found the captain in a big cabin in the deckhouse, drinking his coffee from a thick porcelain cup.

"Grabowski, new stoker, sir. Reporting to work. Sent by Meister Claasen."

Paul wiped his mouth with the back of his hand, and nodded, barely granting him a glance. He was half-asleep still.

"Usually, it is forbidden to speak to me before I have my morning coffee but you couldn't know that. Go to Martin—I mean, Chief Engineer Schultz."

When Grabowski found Schultz, he was putting a safety pin through a thick flannel belt wrapped around the middle of his body. Schultz was a tired old man. He looked at Grabowski with round, bleary eyes.

"To keep you warm, there is nothing better than flannel," he explained. "And what is your business here?"

He listened to Grabowski, pulling up his trousers, tucking the ends of the jacket into them.

"That's all right," he said, straightening up finally. He took a few stiff steps in every direction, as if he wanted to make sure that no part of his body would fall off.

"Go down to the stokehold, what is your name again? Grabowski? Well, Grabowski, Wilhelm is there, he'll show you what to do. It is not complicated; simple good Scotch boilers we have here. Keep the fire going, watch the water gauge, and don't waste coal, that's all. Wilhelm will remain with you till Wednesday. He's been called up, poor thing, but that's how things are. We Germans have to go fight; the foreigners must replace us."

From that day on, Grabowski became a regular crew member of the self-propelled floating crane the Langer Heinrich.

He found the job satisfactory and extremely interesting, for this was a period of extraordinary elation, such as men experience only once or twice in their lives. In fact, he was so happy that he started worrying what would happen if his present situation were to end abruptly. But that was not likely. He worked hard, but of paramount importance was the fact that he was fulfilling, finally, the terms of his contract with David Gordon, and consequently had realized the purpose of his existence. Nobody but him knew this. David Gordon had disappeared completely and it was obvious to all that Grabowski had become even more cheerful, more helpful, wittier, and more social than before.

He decided that it was not necessary to be a loner any more and became fast friends with Kazik Pruszynski.

One day, through Kazik, he became acquainted with Bob and his wife Elena.

Chapter ten

Bob and Elena belonged to a very special category of foreigners. They both had Lithuanian passports. Lithuanians, Latvians, and Estonians, oppressed by Russians, were regarded as allies by Germans. Latvians were even incorporated into military organizations and assisted, actively and fruitfully, the SS, SD, and police forces in such complicated operations as the liquidation of ghettos in Eastern Europe. Their status was equal with that of the Italians before Bagdolio's treason.

But Bob was not really a Lithuanian. He was a Polish cavalry officer and received Grabowski just as a Polish cavalry officer would do. He opened his arms, embraced him warmly, and planted a kiss on both cheeks. "I knew you'd like him," Kazik kept repeating happily, "I knew it. He is a strange number, this friend of mine, this Wladek Grabowski, and I knew it!" Whereupon Bob repeated the procedure for the second time. The odor of alcohol was overwhelming.

"I am a Lithuanian by my passport only, Wladziu, you realize this, of course," he said, beaming genuine drunken happiness.

"I do," said Grabowski.

"She fixed me the papers," he pointed with his thumb at Elena, "because they caught me in Vilna."

"Bob. Bob. You are talking terrible nonsense, you are dead drunk, stop it."

"It is all right, Elena. I do not work for the Gestapo. I am not even a *Volksdeutscher.*"

"You are not even Grabowski," said Elena, "but that is your business. As Bob's business is to keep his bloody mouth shut."

Bob fell on his knees in front of her.

"Love, don't be angry. I know people. I know I can trust Wladek. And Kazik. They are my brothers. They are my brothers in suffering. You don't really know what a Polish cavalry officer's heart is like."

"I do know. I also know you are a bloody drunken big clown, Bob. Please, stop it!"

Bob jumped up, and brought a bottle from the cupboard. Real Polish vodka, not any self-made stuff, no turpentine or paint-thinner.

"Great God," said Grabowski. He looked at Elena while Bob smacked the bottom of the bottle with his flat palm to get the cork out. She was a beautiful woman. She had huge, luminous gray eyes, of great depth, and when she spoke, it was as if she were coming back, a bit reluctantly, from a great distance, from an unknown far-off place hidden there, in her eyes. Her brow was high, and broad, very smooth and clean, and he thought her whole body must be like that.

Beware, and be careful. None of it is for you. Before Rosti, perhaps, yes. Not now. Beware.

But Elena winked boyishly at him, showing with her finger that Bob, whose back was turned to them, was dead drunk. She smiled. She made the newcomer understand that she liked him, and he answered with a smile of gratitude, making her an accomplice of a shared secret. Still, beware.

During that evening Grabowski learnt a lot. Bob had studied at the Warsaw University before the war.

"Philosophy," he sighed, becoming momentarily dead serious. The ferment of alcohol in his mind stopped abruptly and his face changed. It was as if a curtain had accidentally fallen down in the middle of a theatre performance. Perhaps a stagehand had pulled the lever by mistake, perhaps he had leaned against it. They were silent. Bob, tall and lean, with silver hair on his temples, and sitting quietly with the bottle in his hand, said, "I want you to understand. Philosophy was not the subject of my study, it was my life, my great passion. A greater passion than Elena."

"Books of philosophy," he murmured, and lowered his head. "And I believed…"

Without any warning, the curtain rose again.

"Shit!" he exclaimed with violence. "Lies! Nothing there! Come on, let us drink! Wladek, you are new with us, you don't know yet how we drink here, eh, Kazik?"

He filled the glasses and downed his own before they had even brought theirs to their lips. He smashed his glass against the wall. Splinters covered the colored cloth on the little table. "That's how Polish officers drink!"

Elena withdrew completely into the unknown country in her eyes, and sat quietly with a smile.

"Wladek," Bob said, picking up with his fingers a slice of salami, "you know what have I become then? You won't believe it. A medical student. To hell with the mind, long live the body! Here's to the body!"

He was chief assistant to Dr. Krebs, the shipyard's medical director. The same notorious Dr. Krebs about whom Grabowski had already heard many horror stories. He would not accept the fact that a Pole or a Ukrainian could be sick, and as a result, unable to work. Krebs was, according to his own definition, first a Party member, then a German and then a war-plant employee. And only after all that a doctor, with a firm conviction that inferior races like East Europeans were immune to most diseases, but cursed with a hereditary biological inclination to laziness.

Bob lived in mortal fear of his superior, but tried secretly to help in more serious cases.

Elena worked as a typist in the planning department, and

constantly teased the drab, dull German girls working there. They had a two room flat in a barrack in the Cholm camp in Langfuhr. A young Ukrainian doctor—Krebs' protégé—and three sick-room workers occupied the other rooms of the barrack.

Throughout the evening Grabowski tried to drink moderately.

"You drink like a gentleman, Wladek. Kazik is a gentleman, too, but you are special." He put his arm on Grabowski's shoulder. "Wladziu, we don't ask questions here in these camps, and in these times, but I know you are a special gentleman, and a gentleman's son, and I am very happy."

"Bob, darling, you are terribly drunk. You have been talking nonsense almost nonstop."

Bob put his finger to his lips. "Psst! The enemy is listening! Have you seen those posters? Kazik, Wladek, have you seen them? They look like recruiting posters for the Intelligence Service, don't they?"

Grabowski stiffened inside while his face smiled. It was as if an alarm had sounded in his brain, while simultaneously his cheek muscles had contracted into a smile. Congratulations, Grabowski. You function all right, vodka or no vodka. You function properly.

Elena was now sitting on the bed, her long, slim, stockinged legs tucked under her, and Bob laid his head in her lap. Grabowski sensed a lull in the conversation, but Kazik started a long, complicated story about his quarrel with a Belgian who was working on the same lathe but on another shift, in one of the mechanics workshops.

Grabowski could relax now. He let his mind wander through Neufahrwasser's side streets with Rosti at his side in a fog so thick that the shadowy globes of dim light on the blacked-out street lanterns were all that could be seen. He could hardly make out Rosti's face as he spoke slowly, his head lowered, hands thrust into his trench coat pockets.

"I'll give you a try," Rosti was saying, "but there are two main conditions. One, you'll get money. Two, if something happens to me in this town, even by pure accident, even without a shadow of your interference or influence, you'll die."

It was strange, Grabowski recollected, while sitting in the armchair with a glass of vodka in his hand and looking at Elena's long legs—very strange to walk and listen to that low, stammering voice, hardly seeing the person who was talking. And the words were strange, too. How had David arrived here? It seemed like a pre-war spy movie. They reached a lamppost and he saw Rosti's silhouette, the jutting chin, the receding forehead. It was not a movie, after all. Nor a spy book read in bed, breathlessly turning the crisp pages.

Rosti was not a movie actor. He was waiting for his answer.

"I do not mind the second condition, although it is, I would say, unjust. More than that. It is absurd. A tile from a roof could fall accidentally on your head and kill you."

"Precisely, but I have no guarantees," said Rosti, "and I must have some. The entire risk is on my side."

"OK. I accept it."

"Because you do not value your life, isn't that true? Well, that's the wrong attitude. You must be very, very careful. I do not know enough words in German to tell you how careful you should be. Not for yourself but because the information you supply might be valuable? You understand?"

Grabowski nodded. "About the first condition, I do not like being paid for this. It will make me feel bad."

"That means nothing to me. I have sums of money to spend on this and you will have expenses, I think."

"Perhaps. One question—why do you do it?"

They passed the Scandinavian Seamen's Church. Rosti said: Have you tried there?" he pointed with his thumb, "Swedes certainly come there on occasion."

Grabowski shrugged. They were at the waterfront and it was completely dark. On the other side of the canal, lights were burning on the cranes loading coal onto Swedish steamers. Each light was surrounded by a halo of mist. It looked like a scene from behind frosted glass.

"I do it for money," Rosti said. "You can do it for your own reasons. But you must accept money from me. And remember—in

147

two weeks time, when I come back, you can either give me the information, and then you'll have to wait the additional two weeks till I tell you if the stuff has any value, or you can ignore me, and forget about having ever spoken to me."

Kazik was nearing the end of his story. "'I won't go to the *meister*,' the Belgian said, 'because you are a Pole, and he might send you to Stutthof for a month for that, but don't do it again.' So I said to him…"

"Bob is asleep, thank God," Elena said. "Will you help me put him to bed?"

They dragged the unconscious man to the other room, took off his clothes and put him under the blankets.

"He can't really drink, poor Bob," Elena said, "but he keeps drinking. Must be something in his blood. Is it the same with you?"

Kazik laughed. Grabowski grunted.

"You Poles are a strange race," she went on, "sometimes I can hardly understand your behavior, your way of living. You have drunk your country to ruin. Bob, with his brigade back in 1939, attacked German tanks on horseback! With sabers drawn! They must have been drunk too, all three thousand of them, including the colonel who led the charge."

Kazik sighed. "That is the way we are, Elena."

"Your bad luck. And mine," she said, but without bitterness. "You are welcome here, anytime," she added as they turned to go. "We have very few friends here."

On the way home Grabowski tried to master the new situation with Rosti, to organize. He put Elena on his list. He felt like a hero in a fable, entering a treasure cave, standing stunned in front of cases full of gold and diamonds. The planning department!

"You realize what is valuable and what is not," Rosti said in his strange sounding German.—"The U-boats and the submarines are most important. But all the other things you see in the shipyard are also interesting. One never knows. I cannot judge. I am only a messenger. You understand? Keep your eyes wide open, very wide."

Almost a week after that meeting, he started realizing that out of a thousand details—perhaps out of ten thousand—one could be of some importance. People working there, on the other side, must be flooded with details from all over the world. They must put together a huge jigsaw puzzle. It is not like in the books, Grabowski thought, when a daring agent steals great, decisive secrets.

Before they parted, he told Rosti, "I may need other people to collaborate with me in order to gather more information. Welders, electricians, painters working on the submarines."

"Yes," agreed Rosti, looking at the ships on the other side of the canal, "but be extremely careful, do not trust anybody. Pay them. I'll give you money. That is what the money is for. And remember, under no circumstances must they know about me. I do not exist for them. You exist, you are the address."

Then an idea occurred to Grabowski and he asked: "Have you other people here in Danzig?"

"That," Rosti said, "is none of your business. Don't ask me foolish questions." In the silence that followed, Grabowski's head was in turmoil. He tried to think in an organized way. It was futile. He could not.

Even Rosti thinks I really exist.

Then Rosti said: "I'll go now. You'll know me as Rosti. It is easy to remember. How shall I call you? Numbers are only good for spy books…"

"Wladek."

"Good. Wladek." He rolled it on his tongue. "Wladek. Forget about Sweden. Perhaps, after the war… You have important work to do here, now. If you want." They shook hands.

149

Chapter eleven

Somebody asked Kazik where he had been and Grabowski answered for him. "At Cholm camp visiting friends."

"We missed you. Will you join?"

A game was in progress, the usual game: a blanket spread on the table, cards, a plate with paper money, a bottle, cups.

Kazik looked at him and he nodded. One could not refuse, one should preserve one's status. He felt he'd lose money that night because he wasn't sharp enough, he had been drinking since seven and there were Bob, Elena, and Rosti in his head; but what is fifty or a hundred marks? He could afford it. They made room for them at the table.

By three o'clock in the morning, when the old German night watchman refused to be bribed, and demanded categorically that they turn off the lights and go to bed, he had lost seventy-five marks. Kazik had won twenty and a pound of tobacco. Since they were together and shared food and tobacco, they had not lost much. He slept like a stone till the time came to get up to work.

'Forget Sweden,' Rosti had said, before they signed the pact with a handshake. 'Forget Sweden' had become the slogan. He always had a slogan of some sort in his head. He could cheat, lie, and twist the truth like a piece of string and he could play very noble, straight, and absolutely honorable. Under all this, under the all-encompassing, universal hate, under the unquestionable will to fight, under the passion to avenge everything, even the misery and humiliation, when all was thought, said and felt, he'd prefer to be on the other side. To fight openly, together with all those who were daily fighting the Great Evil. Yearning for togetherness? Or a basic dislike of the cloak-and-dagger stuff. But it was a unique opportunity and Grabowski never forgot that. An opportunity to fight from where he was.

Probably more effectively than there. Yet, it was a solitary battle. He felt very lonely. Much more lonely since he had met Rosti. But hadn't he been conditioned by David, before his creation, to bear loneliness? And even before, hadn't David, young and inexperienced as he was, started discovering the basic facts of human loneliness?

It is one thing to study something theoretically, and another to practice. Oh, yes, they were different things. Grabowski, sitting in the crane's stokehold during the nightshift, listened to the low, steady hissing of steam in the ancient pumps and pipes, and stared at the bright flame of the carbid lamp. The fires in the boilers were banked, covered with ashes. Early in the morning, he would throw in a shovel full of fresh coal. The flames would spring up, come to life suddenly. Cleverly feeding them and cleaning, he would build up a roaring fire, raise steam, and when the dayshift fireman came at seven, he would find everything ready.

Right then it was quiet and peaceful there, and he knew that after midnight he could close the iron cover on the skylight entrance and lie down to sleep for a few hours on the bench. Claasen did not go for sudden night inspections like Göring.

A good job again, this floating crane. Apparently, his destiny was nice jobs.

Grabowski climbed the iron ladder and went on deck. A full moon covered the world with a semi-transparent layer of silver. Grabowski, walking on the broad iron deck, stopped to look at the submarine section secured there with wires and bottle-screws. A tube of thick metal, four meters in diameter, sealed with boards from both sides. In a few weeks, it would become part of a sleek hull of an underwater war vessel. Later, it would submerge, travelling thousands of miles with people living inside it.

A depth charge would tear the metal sheets apart. It would sink the submarine, suffocating the men inside. The downed vessel would stay on the bottom of the sea in eternal darkness, in complete silence and peace. Men would turn into skeletons; their bones would disintegrate and gradually disappear. How long would it take, down there? Ten years? A hundred?

Grabowski continued his walk, stepping over heavy iron cables, shackles, bottle-screws. He circled the dark deckhouse with its big funnel and dead windows, and started, on an impulse, leisurely climbing up the iron ladder along the crane's huge raised arm. In the lower part, a forest of girders surrounded him, like the Eiffel tower.

I have never been in Paris. Seen it on many pictures, though. A German sentry stands now on the Eiffel Tower and a red flag with a black swastika flies from its top. Poor chance I'll ever be there.

When German troops entered Paris, David Gordon, in the Warsaw Ghetto, fell ill. He ran a high fever, vomited. It lasted three or four days. Old Dr. Sacks with his dry parchment face, breathing heavily, touched his chest and back with his cold stethoscope.

"No," he said. "It is not typhus. It is nothing." He chuckled at his own inability to find an adequate description to reassure David's anxious mother. "I mean, he is really sick but many people fell sick on that day. The same symptoms, same sickness. Well, well."

Getting up, a tired old man, he added: "Don't worry. He'll recover. Young people are very resilient."

He left the German-infested Eiffel Tower and the old doctor. Instead he was climbing the arm of the Langer Heinrich in Danzig. The maze of iron girders, rivets and angle bars could support a hundred tons. Grabowski climbed on, taking strong hold of the round iron steps, lifting his body higher and higher.

At the top of the structure was a small platform. He sat down there and looked around. The shipyard was spread below like a plastic toy model in the moonlight. Roofs of workshops, welding sheds, three slipways with half-finished submarines on them, railway carts, canals with ships, tugs, and barges moored alongside, and directly beneath, the square of the crane pontoon itself.

Round, big, cold moon. Black sky tinted ghostly greenish around it.

"I can actively help to destroy all this," Grabowski said aloud.

A surge of power as he had never experienced before made his heart beat quickly. No stupid, childish bragging. Whatever I do, I help to annihilate this technological empire—the ships, the submarines, the modern machine workshops. I contribute my part, tiny as it may be. I am active. I fight.

David Gordon, may he rest in peace, during his philosophical year in the Ghetto, devouring philosophy tomes like a starved man finding himself, all of a sudden, through magic, in a well-stocked food store, had naturally encountered Descartes. He was more struck then by the elegant beauty of the discourse, than by its contents. But Grabowski, slightly advanced in time, and elevated some one hundred feet above the ground, said aloud: I fight, therefore I exist. Better than Cartesians. A real proof of existence. I disclose the mysteries of this place, and one day they will come and tear it apart, annihilate it with tons of bombs, with fire raining from the sky.

The vision inspired him with awe, fear and amazement. He could see fires spreading, buildings disintegrating in a rain of debris, sky-high explosions erupting like fierce volcanoes. Grabowski closed his eyes, breathed heavily, tightly clutching the iron railing of the platform. I will see the day or the night when the bombers will come, he whispered.

That day came much later, and Wladyslaw Grabowski was not granted the privilege of witnessing it.

Half an hour later, down in the stokehold, he closed the cover of the entrance, raised the flame of the carbid lamp, and cleared the small workshop table from rusty bolts, tools, and other rubbish with a dry rag.

From the breast pocket of his jacket he took out several sheets of paper, glanced over them, then wrote on the last page:

In the southeastern corner of the yard, across the small canal, marked on the attached plan "D", section 6 of a submarine is assembled. This section includes two engine room stores, a small workshop (there is a 1.30 meter-long lathe in it and a mounted electric drill), and a passageway below, leading to compartment N. 8. A hand-made sketch of the interior of this section is also enclosed, in three views...

He turned the pages again, and wrote:

On the 23rd of this month, the U621 went out for sea-trials. In addition to the crew and the shipyard's technical staff, some foreign workers participated in the diving trial: two riveters, a Belgian electrician, and two Frenchmen who were overhauling the main shaft carrier bearings. The ship remained submerged for almost two hours, and the trials seemed to be successful. The submarine was brought back to the Arsenal the same evening for loading torpedoes and ammunition. The U621 was brought to the shipyard for the second time on the 15th of October, part of her deck and coning tower destroyed. According to the story told by a crew member, the submarine was rammed by an Allied ship (a corvette, apparently) in Skaggerak on the 5th of October. She was towed first to Bremerhaven, and from there to this shipyard, for repairs...

The transport steamer 'Brake' left for Riga on the 22nd ... Three overhauled Tiger tanks, seven 88 mm guns in holds...

In Tuchol, 75 km south of Danzig, a square area in the forest has been declared out of bounds, several rows of barbed wire fence have been erected. Warning posters in German and Polish, saying anybody approaching the area will be shot without warning. Mines have been planted. A forester reported at night strong flashes of light visible in this part of the woods, accompanied by explosions. A railway siding was built on this place last summer. This reported by a Polish worker who came from Tuchol five days ago.

He stopped writing, and stared at the flame. Has it any value? Does it make any sense? Perhaps it is only his way of escaping? Of finding justifications? All these doubts, eternal doubts. Bad inheritance from that Jew.

Well, he could not know. He could not judge. Nor could Rosti. "I am only a messenger." Only the people on the other side could know.

The elation he had felt on top of the crane top had passed, but the decision to do good work persisted, he had to go on, to try to get more information.

Grabowski wrote for half an hour more, gathered his papers, put them in an envelope, which he placed in his breast pocket. He folded the jacket and put it on one end of the bench. Then he lay down to sleep, using it as a pillow.

Chapter twelve

Kazik had an overwhelming compulsion to confess to Grabowski. The urge had been swelling up inside him for a long time. A man must trust another man. Or woman. Women were not available (the whores in Troyl could not count as women. Elena certainly was a woman—and what a woman!—but she was Bob's). The friendship with Grabowski was precious. Kazik Pruszynski found the joy of sharing overwhelming. They had their evening meals together, black bread and margarine, thick marmalade. Sometimes a piece of cheese or sausage. All this spread on a clean towel on Grabowski's bed.

Eating in silence, enjoying the food, and the other man's close presence.

Kazik, who had been a college student in another life—in which he, too, had had another family name—yearned for human friendship. He could hardly find it with half-literate workers from the barracks in Narvik 2. Since the day on which, as a member of a Polish underground organization, he had to flee his native Warsaw, he had had two really happy days: when he met Bob and Elena, and when they became friends with Grabowski. He had obtained a new identity card—custom made, so to speak, because the organization had a forgery shop of its own—and jumped headlong into the German Foreign Legion.

"For the first week here, Wladek, believe me, I was afraid to sleep at night; for fear they'd come and fetch me. I prayed silently, at night."

He prayed. It gave him some comfort. Kazik was not religious, but would not reject the basic rites of the Catholic Church. "That's how we were brought up, you and I, and all the others, and our fathers and mothers. We are Catholics, aren't we?"

Grabowski nodded thoughtfully, puffing on his cigarette.

Kazik was an electrician's helper, carrying the toolbox for the tall, gaunt, elderly German from Langfuhr. They climbed through narrow passages in U-boat sections, installing lines, building switch boxes.

"Never dabbled in it before the war," Kazik smiled, "studying law, second year in the university. What did you study?"

A split-second decision. He almost heard the click in his head.

"History. But in Cracow."

Kazik laughed a short, dry laugh.

"I knew you were a student the moment you opened your mouth for the first time, I knew. I can smell an educated man a mile away. A man of culture."

He rubbed his forehead. "Two years! Two years, and it seems as if it were two centuries ago! Great God! In October, we did not study much yet, there was the usual fun of chasing the Jews around a little bit, demonstrations, monkeying around with the police. You remember those things, eh, Wladek?"

Grabowski nodded again. He did not remember, perhaps David would. Every year, numerous clashes at the universities, 'ghettos' in the lecture halls, two or three Jewish students killed, others with faces cut by razor blades stuck in a walking cane, the conventional weapon of a Polish student.

"Then this war, how did it happen, Wladek? Can you understand what happened? They crushed us like a mindless man would crush a tin toy under his foot. And there are no braver soldiers than Poles in the whole world."

"Easy, easy, Kazik. Look what they did to Norway, to France, and now to that giant in the east, Russia."

Kazik ground his teeth in a sudden rage: "For those bastards I have no pity. They stuck a knife into our backs, the fucking Jewish-Bolsheviks."

"Yes, but they still resist."

"Who knows for how long. The Germans are still advancing. And I tell you Wladek, if they were not such idiots with their theories about the superiority of the Germanic race, and the inferiority of others, if they did not treat all other people like dirt, they could easily rally the whole Europe against the Bolsheviks."

Grabowski said: "Don't be silly, Kazik. Even if they win, haven't they declared often enough their New Order for Europe? The Thousand Year Reich? Don't they exterminate Czechs, Poles? Especially the ones like us. They don't need a Polish intelligentsia, do they?"

Grabowski thought it was a bit silly on his part to deliver this speech, but it was still permissible. Calculating the times in terms of historical occurrences was all right for a student of history, but still—don't overdo it. Easy now.

"Sure, I know, I know. You don't have to remind me of all that, Wladziu. I know and hate them, those bastards. It is only that I don't like those Bolsheviks so much either. May they rot, dead or alive. Ah, Wladek, Wladek, what times we are living in. Darkness, darkness all around, not a flicker of hope."

"America is so far, and who knows how strong or how rotten they really are."

"How is your work?"

"Oh, that is the easiest part of it, believe me, although it is bloody cold in those submarine sections. It is like sitting in an iron barrel. And my Hans crouching, and looking for half an hour at the plan, and then drilling some holes, and laying cables. He is scared stiff too, that the cable is well fastened, connections right. And he shits his trousers full every time the engineer's assistant peers in. Some German Superman!"

Kazik spat and wiped his mouth.

"Now, that I am together with you, and I have Bob and Elena, it is easier, much easier. One should not complain, really. Come, let us have another lousy beer."

Kazik drank his beer, looked around, and said: "And how are you, down there in that floating sardine tin of yours, shoveling coal?"

"Oh, I'm fine. And it isn't very hard work, either, if the coal is good. And the crew is decent, as Germans go. Besides, it is moving from place to place, you know, the variety makes it much more bearable. Yesterday, moving sections; the day before that, loading tanks in Weichselmünde; and tomorrow night we are sailing to Gdynia to take some heavy pieces out of a ship there, I don't even know what. I always liked travelling."

Kazik sighed. "Well, we were not created for these things, not you, and not I, for certain. But what isn't one willing to do to save one's skin."

Sure. What isn't one willing to do to save one's skin. A great question. David Gordon, he was a learned young man, read a lot of philosophy, he'd answer that question for you. But not me. I was created very artificially, for one very specific purpose, and I am only trying to do that, period. Nothing more. I do not have to save my skin. I doubt if I even have a skin. Instead it is some kind of thin metal shell. David Gordon provided me with it. Inside, at the moment, is an apparatus for collecting information. My purpose is to gather more and better information in order to cause the most possible damage to the Germans. The more Germans killed as the result of this information, the better. Anything else is of no importance. How easy it is to exist with such a limited and well-defined purpose, with such wonderful limitations!

"You know what has drawn me so much to you from the very

beginning?" Kazik said. "It was your serenity. You seem to be in such wonderful harmony with yourself. You were so serene, so peaceful."

"Well," answered Grabowski, "I am serene."

"And, naturally, I knew you were an educated man."

Chapter thirteen

All of a sudden, everything exploded into frantic action. They were about to take Moscow any day. Ships were coming and going. Huge quantities of material were handled. Germany was making a last giant effort to win and to finish. The activity was feverish.

Grabowski's envelope was growing fat. He started understanding the framework of his job. It was clear that he had to have more people supplying information. He'd have to pay money, to distribute small presents.

Rosti would be coming in the next few days, and the days passed like a dream. Boilers, fire, water gauge, pressure gauge, sticking out his head through the skylight, looking, watching, counting... In the evening, he'd drink, talk, play cards and every second night he had a beer at the Petroleum Bar, visited the *Deutsches Haus*, and said hello to Frieda at the *Alte Liebe*.

He dared not try Elena yet.

* * *

Rosti took precautions. Before entering Rita's, he lit a cigarette on the street, and glanced casually in all directions. When he came in, Rita said:

"Well, well, here you are again. Welcome home!" He had a nice, sad smile for her, took off his coat, sat down, and waited for her to bring his beer. By the time she did that, he had already noticed everybody in the bar.

The Pole entered fifteen minutes later. He was all right, thought Rosti. Nothing moved in his face. He did not recognize him. He nodded to Rita, sat down at the corner table, and ordered a beer.

"What's new?" asked Rosti.

"Nothing," she said. "We seem to be winning the war. As soon as we take Moscow, it'll be over."

"Most likely. I understand the General Staff gave you this information?"

She slapped his hand. "Everybody knows it. Biedermann says the same."

"And how is he?"

"Very well. He hasn't got much to be worried about right now."

"And you?"

"Yes. That Rosti comes so seldom. Listen, perhaps you could settle down here in Danzig when the war's over?"

"In the Petroleum Bar?"

"Oh, what a nasty man you are today, Rosti!"

"I'm always nasty."

"That's not true."

One of the customers emerged from the men's room wiping his hands with his handkerchief. The Pole got up and went in through the same door. The customer sat down at his table and started folding carefully the soiled piece of colored cloth.

"This one's tidy," murmured Rita, following Rosti's eyes, "isn't he?"

"Everything is tidy in this country," he answered. "Let me make room for another beer."

He got up. Rita sailed to the counter.

Rosti, standing at the urinal, pushed slightly the doors of the two stalls behind his back. Both were unlocked. In one of them Grabowski stood, leaning against the wall, with one foot on the toilet seat. He gave Rosti the big, fat envelope, and Rosti put it in the inner pocket of his jacket.

From another pocket he took out a brown envelope and handed it to the Pole. "Money."

"OK."

"Be careful. Now go first."

Grabowski washed his hands. He crossed the cozy bar room in measured steps, and settled down again at his table. Rosti left the toilet after three minutes. Grabowski looked in another direction.

Somebody put *The Star of Rio* on the gramophone for the millionth time. Rita went back to Rosti's table and put her plump hand over his. Customers were coming and going. Grabowski had another beer and left. Rita was so busy in conversation with Rosti that she did not even answer his goodnight. He took the tram to the camp and half an hour later was in his bed, reading and translating the German paper to his comrades.

At eleven, they turned off the lights, and Grabowski fell asleep.

For the first time since he was born, he slept lightly. It was a strange lightness. Toward morning he had a dream of exceptional beauty. He dreamt he was walking in an orchard, with trees in white bloom. The sky overhead was a pure, transparent blue. From among the trees, a young girl in white stepped out. He had never seen her face before but she was very beautiful and her lips were full and blood-red. She took his face between her hands and kissed him on his mouth. He tasted cherries—large cherries, full of sweet juice and so dark red in color that they looked almost black. He thought in his dream that the girl had to be Tami; but how she had changed! Then he thought that she had Dorka's body. She kissed him again and again. He awoke with the distinct taste of black cherries on his lips.

Chapter fourteen

Some things were very personal. He carried the paper envelope in which he collected material for Rosti in a little leather pouch around his neck, and never parted with it. He constantly felt the touch of it on the skin of his chest and became so used to it that he thought it a part of his body. He had ordered a *kosa* the day before his second meeting with Rosti. Everybody in the Polish camp, and many in other camps, had one of these homemade long-bladed knives. It was carried in the left inner breast pocket of the jacket. Piotr made one for Grabowski from a broken steel file and reluctantly accepted the payment of a pound of tobacco.

"I'd give it to you as a gift, Wladek," he said, looking bashfully at his feet. "After all, aren't we in the same boat?"

"Then accept the tobacco as a gift, too." Grabowski said. A smile spread on the older man's hard face. They shook hands impulsively.

So he always had with him his 'good-luck pouch' and his shining knife, with a five-inch sharp blade and a wooden handle, lovingly

164

polished with the finest emery cloth to extraordinary smoothness by Piotr.

The tobacco for Piotr he got from René.

René from the surface-ship repair division was not an easy man to approach. Grabowski met him through Stasiek, whom he knew well. On the way, Stasiek volunteered some information about the Frenchman.

"He is strange. From Marseilles—or at least that is what he says—but you know, they are mostly volunteers like us, so one can never know. He went on home leave six months ago and came back another man. They say he found his wife in bed with a German sergeant. Since then, he keeps apart from others, hardly ever speaks to anybody. Makes good money on compressed tobacco. You must argue with him about the price."

Grabowski shook hands with a short, dark, broad-shouldered man. He had a great mane of jet-black hair, and the first impression he made was one of great physical strength.

René eyed him suspiciously. "He wants to buy a package or two of your black poison," Stasiek said.

"Is he all right?"

Stasiek laughed. "That's why I came with him. If he weren't all right, would I have brought him to you?"

"You, I know," mumbled René, opening the padlock of his chest, "but I don't trust any foreigners, especially the Polacks."

"Hey listen, don't you call me that," Grabowski said. "Fuck you! Nobody's going to call me a Polack. You can stuff your tobacco up your ass."

René looked up and a shadow of a smile crossed his face: "Oh la la, you are a hot-tempered one, aren't you?"

Stasiek said in Polish, "Are you crazy, Wladek?"

"I didn't mean to offend anyone," mumbled René.

"So say so," said Grabowski, "and don't use that word any more, eh?"

"Now that you are friends," Stasiek said, "I am going to fix my business in Number Four. There is a Dutchman there selling a leather jacket. See you."

René put some small dark-blue packages of tobacco on the table. "You want Ritz as well?"

"OK."

One of the Frenchmen in the room said something, others looked up and laughed.

"Want a drink?" asked René. He touched his throat lightly with his thumb. Grabowski nodded. René took out a bottle of wine. That was a surprise. He had expected the same stuff they were drinking in the Polish barracks, paint-thinner, methylated alcohol. It was red Bordeaux wine. One of the Frenchmen offered him a piece of hard yellow cheese on the point of a knife.

"To your health."

They drank slowly. The wine had a metallic taste, the cheese completed its flavor like two ingredients of the same dish.

"Nice. Now, how much are these?"

"Thirty marks for a cube."

Grabowski whistled. "That's a lot."

"You can make a hundred cigarettes out of it."

"Who'll buy cigarettes at that price?"

René scratched his head. "How many packages would you buy?"

"Two. Perhaps three, or even four, if you give a reasonable price."

He studied the Frenchman's face for a moment. "Let's walk outside a bit, eh?"

René stuffed the tobacco and the cigarette paper into his pocket. Outside, they stood in silence for a while, both of them looking at the bright, full moon.

"You work on that cruiser, yes?"

"Battleship, yes. Why?"

"Nothing. It has been here for a long time. When is she sailing?"

"Thursday or Friday, they say. What's that to you? I don't buy anything from the German swine of the crew, if that's what you're after."

"What's really wrong with that ship?"

The Frenchman turned his big head, which seemed to sit directly on his shoulders. He had no neck.

"You want the tobacco?"

"Yes, I'll buy. But I want to know more about that ship."

René was silent and Grabowski listened to the thumping of his heart. I take too many risks, he thought. But this man seems all right. What can I rely on, if not on my intuition? That strange feeling which somehow, by the strangest chemistry, transforms itself into coordinated thoughts, penetrates effortlessly from that other, unknown area onto the level of reasoning, calculations?

Grabowski took from his pocket a crumpled ball of bank notes and peeled off three of them.

"A hundred and fifty."

"Wait, I'll bring you the change."

"I don't need any. What was wrong with that battleship?"

"Take back your goddamn money," René said. "I can tell you everything I know about it, if you are really interested."

"I am. Take the money, I can pay for my tobacco. I have enough money."

René seemed to press his head deeper between his shoulders.

"So be it," he said finally. "She had an aerial torpedo in compartment number three, starboard, and another one, which passed too low, apparently, just touching No. 5, port side."

"Where did she get it?"

"Off the Norwegian coast. Five planes attacked her. They shot two down."

"Could you make a sketch of the damage, a drawing?"

"I can make it and give it to you, say, the day after tomorrow. Where will I find you?"

"You don't have to. I'll find you."

167

It was René now who sized up the Pole and looked at him through narrowed eyes. "I like the swine exactly as much as you. You Poles have no monopoly on it. No, sir."

It is easy, Grabowski thought later, with all those Europeans, because most of them hate. What power in hatred! It is easy, unless your luck runs out, and you encounter one who does not.

But you are making yourself too well known, too popular. Don't throw about too much money. If you want to live longer and be useful longer. If you want to fulfill your contract.

Now back to your barrack. Tomorrow, back to your floating crane. In the evening, to Neufahrwasser to visit two bars. Talk to Piotr. Talk to Kazik. To Elena. Try to find more connections. Make the envelope fuller, fatter.

He whistled a tune while walking with his hands in his pockets.

He stopped, surprised. He was whistling a melody Grabowski didn't know.

But David was another case altogether.

Chapter fifteen

He walked the almost empty streets of the old town. In the evening the shops were closed. Anyhow there was no merchandise to be bought, except what was rationed. A few pubs were open. In the blue half-darkness of the blackout, the old dignified houses loomed high with their decorated roofs. Higher still, above them, frozen in the silver of the moonlight, was the massive tower of the *Marienkirche* Cathedral.

The main gate was closed. Grabowski pushed a side door, low and heavy, and stepped inside. Why had he gone into the church?

The smell of the church stones attracted him. Stones have as many kinds of smells as flowers, he thought. Take burnt stones or defiled stones, with filth so thick on them that it becomes part of the stone. Or old wet stones covered with thick dark green moss. Those were, in fact, the same family as these church stones; the smell of time uninterrupted by births and deaths, ancient and powerful.

The church was huge and empty. Organ music flowed from somewhere above, pure but complicated, gently cascading down the steep, heavy arches and dark walls. The ceiling, high up, was invisible.

The huge chandelier, in which a solitary bulb was burning, might have been suspended from the clouds, or the moon.

Grabowski slowly walked along the stone floor. As his eyes became gradually accustomed to the semi-darkness, he discerned some elderly solitary people sitting near the altar. He sat down on one of the pews and closed his eyes.

Great peace enveloped Grabowski. The pew was dark solid wood, worn smooth by the passage of centuries. Music filled the whole Gothic interior, silver, cool, and precise, in several streams, which sometimes intertwined, forming a powerful flood, and then separated again. There must have been steep arches, balconies, galleries, but those were invisible. He could not even be sure there was a roof over these steep walls of black stone, damp and smooth. Three small candles were burning on the altar. The light was weak but steady. The air stood still.

Grabowski did not know how long he sat in the church, submerged in darkness, music, and peace. He thought he must have fallen asleep.

The music stopped abruptly. A man in a white vestment stepped up to the altar and blew out two of the three candles. Darkness thickened and Grabowski's heart sank. The peace was gone.

One by one the old people left the dark church. He got up and went out. Again he wandered aimlessly along the narrow, empty streets with a strange wonderful emptiness in his head. At a certain moment he found himself in the old, unused port, where once Hansa ships had been moored in the shadow of wooden grain silos. He leaned against a railing and stared at the black, motionless water. Then he headed back and lost himself in the labyrinth of old, cobble-stoned streets.

If I do not catch the last train from the railway station, I'll have to walk all the way to the camp, he thought.

I do not mind. My legs are not tired and I am light and still full of that wonderful music, although it is evaporating quickly.

Grabowski, no longer elated, but serene and quiet, was approached on the corner of the *Frauengasse* by a street girl. What was she doing there? What hope could she have of finding a customer where a passer-by was a rarity? He could not understand, but the fact was that she was standing there, in the dark doorway, whistling after him. When he stopped, surprised, she asked in a most professional way: "Well, love? Won't you come with me?" He came nearer and saw that she had a pretty, round, stupid face, and blond hair. She scrutinized him sharply, trying to place him in some category and found it difficult. She said, "I take ten marks, love." She clearly thought it a big sum of money. A pre-war whore, though she still looked young.

"OK, I am willing to pay."

She discerned his foreign accent and asked, "*Was für ein Landsmann bist du?*"

The punishment for a Pole having relations with a German woman was death, even if the woman was a prostitute. And Grabowski knew it.

But suddenly, he wanted the girl very much. He felt that in a strange way this would be the completion of the evening that had started so wonderfully in the *Marienkirche*, the fulfillment of a promise. The closest one could achieve to harmony.

"I am a Bulgarian," he said.

The girl nodded. She could read newspapers and she had listened to the radio. Bulgarians were allies.

She was very professional and made a mental note that Bulgarians were circumcised. She seemed to recollect having read or heard that some of them were Muslims, and Muslims were—or were they not? She dismissed the whole problem from her mind a moment later, asked the man on top of her if he had finished yet, and was given, in addition to the agreed fee, a generous tip. She said, "Thank you, you are a good man," and he nodded and said, "That's all right, you are a nice girl," and went.

Later, she mentioned this to a colleague in the trade.

"Ever had any Bulgarians, Trudi?"

The other girl shook her head.

"Well, I had one. Nice, and generous with money."

The matter of circumcision had been forgotten.

Grabowski, walking back through the night to his camp, was sad and disappointed. The promise had not been fulfilled. The girl had not fit the church and the music as he had hoped she would. He felt empty and tired.

David, clever and educated, would have labeled it *post coitum tristesse*.

Chapter sixteen

Rosti, sitting with him in the *Alte Liebe*, said, "I have a message for you."

"For me? From whom?"

"Have you got tobacco?"

"Cigarettes?"

"Not cigarettes—tobacco."

"Sure."

Grabowski produced his small tin box and Rosti gave him a booklet of cigarette paper.

"Don't use the first one, throw it away, take the next one and roll a cigarette for yourself."

He pulled out the first thin paper with the gummed edge and crumpled it in his fist, and then the next. Simultaneously he placed the finely cut French tobacco in the paper while reading what was written there in black ink in a very fine handwriting: *Thanks for valuable information. We are waiting for more, but be VERY CAREFUL. Priority one: anything concerning submarines.*

Grabowski finished rolling his cigarette, licked the gummed

edge and glued it together. He accepted a light from Rosti's match. He inhaled deeply.

A success. The paper quickly turned into blue smoke.

Rosti watched his face, smiling. "What was written there?"

"You don't know?"

"How could I? But somebody said some of your material was good. Is that what was written there?"

"Yes."

"Good. I'll give you the money at Rita's, same way as the first time."

"OK. I still have plenty. Money hardly buys anything here, everything is rationed." He thought a moment. "Could you bring me two or three wristwatches next time? Those are better than cash."

"Sure. Plenty of stuff this time?"

"Same as before. Perhaps a little more."

Then he changed the subject and, just to make conversation, said, "Seems the Germans won't take Moscow after all."

Rosti smiled: "They have lost the war."

"How can you know?"

"I know. I see both sides, you see only one. Besides, now America is in."

"So what? The Japs are beating the daylights out of them."

Rosti tapped his fingers on the table.

"You have never been to America, have you?"

"No."

"Well, I know America. They'll crush them. You'll see."

Naively, but with all his hope and desire, Grabowski said, "When?"

"It can take time. Maybe a year, maybe more, but it's definite. The Germans cannot win any more."

Later, at Rita's, with Grabowski's envelope in his pocket, Rosti waited till the bar was closed and followed Rita upstairs.

She left the room for a moment, for she never undressed in his presence, and when she came back he was already in bed, in the silk pajamas she had prepared for him.

"Come quickly, it's bloody cold."

"It is." She shivered. "Poor soldiers in Russia, what they must suffer!"

"Soldiers always suffer," answered Rosti.

"Hansie Biedermann isn't so optimistic any more."

"Well, he has reasons. You seem to have frozen fast there, before Moscow."

She sighed. "Rosti, don't include me in you, please. I am Spanish, you know."

He put his hand soothingly on her dark hair.

"I know, Rita. Just teasing you."

Rosti made love to Rita with difficulty, reluctantly. His mind was far away. When he climaxed, he was flying low over the gentle waves of the South Atlantic. It was ultramarine dark blue down there, with the faintest pale blue of the sky over his head. He even touched down fleetingly in Buenos Aires. But he was quickly back in Europe, listening to Rita's spasmodic breathing and, in the background, to the latest hit music from Sweden. Rosti had a girl in Malmö, another one in Gothenburg, and they were substituted for Rita, one after another. There was also a pretty, quiet receptionist in an embassy in Stockholm. He visited there but very rarely, once in four, five months, but whenever he came in, she gave him a long, deep look, and asked, "and whom shall I announce, sir?" "Rosti," he said, with a sad smile in his long-lashed eyes.

She said, "Just a minute," returned, opened the door for him, and murmured, "you are welcome, sir."

Rosti rolled off of Rita and fell asleep. He'd wake up later and ask her what Biedermann had had to say during the two weeks of his absence. Then he'd make love to her once more, remember the wristwatches he had to bring to Grabowski, and wonder in how many strange ways a man had to pay for knowledge.

Chapter seventeen

It was February again, and across Russia, from Finland to the Black Sea, millions were freezing, dug into earth that was like stone. The sky, too, was the color of stone. On the whole European continent, ice and fear paralyzed people in equal measure. A cruel fairy tale come true. From Grimm, perhaps, but enlarged in width and in depth. Not a kingdom, but a whole continent in troubled sleep.

Blood, too, flowed daily, and in the torture chambers of the Gestapo, sweat and urine. Blood, sweat and urine freeze quickly; the earth had no time to suck them in. It had lost its capacity to absorb, its softness. The fear-carriers that spread over Europe like armored cockroaches walked at night, in heavy overcoats and in large boots. Their stomping echoed in the frozen darkness of empty streets. Behind thousands of doors people did not sleep. They listened to the stomping on the streets, to the hollow echo of the staircases. Cold and fear took over. The world had turned into a stone.

The microcosm of the labor camps was part of this world. There was an outburst of violence in the Polish barracks. Michael broke a bottle on Karol's face and kicked him savagely in the chest and groin while others looked on silently. He had caught him cheating at cards. Later, the camp guards lead the dazed Michael away to the Gestapo, to Stutthof. They would never see him again. Karol was transported to the shipyard's hospital and released to go home after a month. Useless as a working force. Bob told Kazik and Grabowski: "His balls are smashed and he's blind in one eye."

On the wooden floor of Room No. 4 there remained a dark stain; Karol's blood. Scrubbing the floor did not help, the stain was there to stay. In the evening, the heating pipes humming, some men asleep, Piotr playing solitaire (he never played poker), the Maliniak brothers making cigarettes. Grabowski would lie in bed slowly turning the pages of *Adler*, the illustrated weekly of the German Air Force. Good photographs and drawings. Accounts of boundless heroism of the *Luftwaffe*. Clean, well-shaven, Nordic, courageous faces: men doing their duty to the *Führer* and the *Vaterland*.

Grabowski looked at the pictures, but his mind participated only minimally. He was busy with other things. Stasiek had brought him information about the Tiger tanks they were overhauling in workshop No. 7; René had told him about a destroyer they expected to arrive in two days for major repairs; a Dutchmen had talked about new torpedo warheads. People working during a war in a naval shipyard see and know a lot. He had also in his collection crude, hand-made, but quite exact plans of sections four and seven. These were built in Königsberg, others in Stetting, but most submarines were assembled and launched there, in Danzig.

Grabowski thought it would be nice to give Rosti a present of the assembly and launching schedule. It could be of real value. But those things were above the level on which he was working.

Sitting on a wooden bench in front of his fires, he polished the brass water-gauge guard with a piece of cloth, until it shone like real gold, and kept thinking.

177

The bad habit of continuous thinking he had inherited from that bastard David Gordon. He had to break it, there and then, otherwise it would show on his face. It also made his head tired.

He had already heard once or twice the question: "Hey, Wladek, what are you thinking so hard about?"

He had the quick response of his wits to rescue himself: "About cunt." The men would laugh, his popularity would rise, and a discussion about sex, that most inexhaustible subject, would follow.

But he could not react that way around Bob and Elena, and she sometimes probed deep into him with her large gray eyes. She would shake her head, sigh, and say, "Wladek, Wladek, I'd like to know what is going on in that crazy head of yours!" He would laugh. "You'd be greatly disappointed, I am afraid. Mine is not a very interesting mind."

He replaced the guard, screwing it into place on the front of the gauge glass on the boiler.

"You better take care that the glass does not break, son," Martin Schultz had warned him, "because the whole bloody stokehold will fill with steam before you can say *Pater Noster*. God knows if you have the guts to fight your way through that steam to close the cocks, and anyhow, you'll get roasted. I remember, in '32, I was working in the engine room on the Hamburg, when such a thing happened. No, wait, it was in '31."

He would spin a long story about it, and when others were present, they listened attentively. All of them had stories to tell. Grabowski was handicapped because he had no past, and no stories to tell. Sometimes, when he absolutely had to, he invented them, but he was not good at that. He thought his fiction was lame, lusterless.

In the evening the crane sailed across the bay from Gdynia to Danzig, a tugboat assisting its two ancient steam engines. On deck, near the stokehold hatch, some deckhands sat smoking and talking in low voices. Leo Mayewski, an old Kashub, was at the wheel. It was a huge steering wheel such as was used in the past century, and Grabowski, sticking his head out of the hatch, thought that they fit well together, Leo and the wheel. Leo must have been well over sixty.

He held the wooden spokes with his big hands very lightly, barely touching them. There was not much steering to be done on that floating crane, a square barge; the tugboat was keeping course.

"It was different on the *Monsoon* in 1910. It took two men to hold the wheel. Two!" Leo raised two fingers of his right hand to make Grabowski understand. Grabowski descended, tended his fires and popped back up on deck. He knew the chief and Bruno, the second mate, were asleep in their cabins. There wasn't anything for them to do on such a journey. But Leo was a very taciturn man, he seldom opened his mouth at all, so this was a unique opportunity. Not that anything he would say could find its way into Rosti's envelope; and yet Grabowski's interest surged. Simple human curiosity, which was for Grabowski a strange quality.

"Boy, on the *Monsoon* two men always held the wheel. A four mast steel vessel, two thousand nine hundred tons, carrying grain from Buenos Aires to Hamburg. A dangerous cargo, grain. It can shift."

Leo shut up like a clam.

It was wartime. There were almost no lights ashore, but one could still see the entrance to Neufahrwasser Harbor; they'd make it before complete darkness fell. Leo, powerful, bent over the wheel, gnarled hands resting on the spokes. Eyes straight ahead. Grabowski asked himself Elena's question directed at Leo: "I would like to know what is going on in your mind, Leo. Are you still on the *Monsoon*?" He spent his days on the crane without opening his mouth, and then suddenly one evening, he spoke several sentences. Grabowski wished to understand.

Paul, the captain, said, "Leo is from an old Kashub family, which is certainly not a compliment nor an asset to a man. He is one hundred per cent dotty, a fact that is not up for discussion. And he is also the only thousand percent seaman on board this crane."

"Perhaps Leo is empty inside?"

"Yes, he is. Still on the *Monsoon*, 1910, in the South Atlantic."

He grinned and turned his face to Grabowski: "One night there was a real gale. Landlubbers think that a gale means hell broken loose, clouds, rain, hail, snow. They don't know that sometimes it is different. Not one cloud in the sky, a full moon giving light like the sun, and a gale shrieking like a million demons in the rigging. Every sail taken down except two topgallants. The ship flying twelve, perhaps fourteen or more knots under those two pieces of canvas. A tilt of fifteen degrees, the starboard rail constantly underwater, and huge seas rolling like mad. A real gale. Two men at the wheel barely able to hold the ship." Leo fell silent. Grabowski made a quick dive to his stokehold. When he came back, the old Kashub unsealed his lips once more, in an astonishing pronouncement: "Such a gale makes you believe in God."

Sixty years old, most of them spent at sea. The body of a gorilla and the face of a sad bulldog, the quintessence of the wisdom acquired through these years.

"Makes you believe in God."

The end, or would he disclose something more? Before they entered the harbor, ten minutes later, Leo said, "I was young then. Had a family: wife, children."

Another silence. Deck hands took their places at the mooring winches, preparing for maneuvering. Paul walked out of the deck-house, rubbing the sleep from his eyes with his knuckles. Grabowski had to go down to the stokehold. As he was leaving, Leo said, "I even had a dog."

Chapter eighteen

Kazik showed him the note in the evening: *Come, I need help from friends urgently.* "It came from Elena this afternoon. Ljuba, Stasiek's Ukrainian girl, brought it."

"Well, we going?"

"I can't. I have to go to work at eight. Special nightshift. They're in a hurry on that section."

Out of habit Grabowski asked, "Why?"

"How could I know? Anyhow, you have to go there."

"I guess so."

Grabowski changed his clothes and went to Langfuhr. At first, nobody answered his knocking. He knocked again harder. Elena opened the door, a cigarette in the corner of her mouth.

"Where is Kazik?"

"Working nightshift. Do you want me to go?"

"Oh no Wladziu, come in please."

"The note was for Kazik?"

"The note was for both of you."

The room was in bad disorder. Remains of food and several

181

empty bottles were on the table. More bottles lay under the table. The wastepaper basket was overturned, and some garbage had spilled onto the floor. A crumpled sheet and blanket were on the couch.

"Where is Bob?"

"In the other room."

"Drunk?" he asked in a low voice.

She sat down heavily on the couch. Her face was white and tired.

"For the past five days without any interruption. He hasn't gone to work either. I told Krebs he was sick, so yesterday morning he came, personally, to see his assistant."

"And?"

"Oh, he was very polite. You did not have to be a doctor to see he had as bad a hangover as has ever been recorded. So Krebs said to me: 'Your husband has a bad case of stomach fever. I hope for his sake he'll recover and be back at work within two days. *Heil Hitler.*'"

Elena started to laugh but at the same time tears were rolling down her cheeks, big, heavy drops of transparent liquid.

Grabowski asked, "What set him off?"

"Perhaps it was I who did. We were discussing the situation at the front and Bob said Germany had lost the war. I said I'd commit suicide if the Russians came here. But he knew that; I had told him so many times. But this time he said that I was right. He'd do it together with me. He said he was fed up with the whole fucking world. So, till they come and while we still have some time, let's drink. We started with the bottle of the good stuff that I kept from your visit, but then he went to the Russian barracks and brought five bottles of a horrible *samogon*. I panicked and refused to drink it. Then the trouble started."

Grabowski listened while his eyes wandered aimlessly over the room to avoid Elena's eyes. Apparently, Bob had been violent. He had beaten her. He had called her names: 'Here's to your suicide, you bitch. They'll gang rape you and you won't have the guts to kill yourself. Who knows, perhaps you'll just spread your legs and like it. I, I can do it, I'll show you, and the Bolshevik apes, and the Nazi monkeys how a Polish cavalry officer knows how to die.'

The ghost of an infantry major walking calmly toward the German trenches with a drawn revolver, saying no bullets can touch me, flowed in front of Grabowski's eyes. He was annoyed. Such things should not happen.

Elena talked in a gray, toneless voice. No sobbing, no breakdowns. Strong stuff. Sausage skins and chunks of black bread on stained paper on the table. Grabowski looked at that paper and listened to Elena. She followed his eyes. "I brought some food from the shipyard. A girl in my office gave me German sausage—made of dogs, I am sure, the way it tasted."

"Do you want me to see him?"

"Have you the courage?"

"Go see if I can get in."

She went to the other room. Grabowski threw the food into one of the ashtrays and placed the crumpled, soiled paper in his pocket. It was a blue photocopy and across the top right corner of it was stamped in big letters: *Streng Geheim!* Top Secret!

Elena came back. "I think he is in a coma, I'm not sure."

"OK. I'll have a look."

To his surprise, he found Bob lying with his eyes open. He recognized him.

"Hello Wladziu," he whispered.

"Hello Bob. How are things?"

"Too much of a good thing, I'm afraid. My head is going to burst any moment. Little men with tiny hammers are banging on the inside of my skull, and two bastards with blowtorches are applying them to the inside of my eyeballs. Sheer Gestapo stuff."

"I know how you feel."

"I am not sure you do. It's horrible."

"It certainly is. Have you thrown up?"

"Nothing. I'm not that kind of a drinker. Old Bob can drink and drink."

183

And beat up his wife, Grabowski thought. Aloud he said, "Elena, can you prepare some coffee, the strongest stuff you have?"

"I don't want any coffee."

"I didn't ask you."

"Who the hell do you think you are?"

"I thought I was your friend and wanted to help you. Bob, stop this shit! Do you realize that tomorrow morning you have to be in Krebs' office, at work?"

"I can't, I'm sick."

"Like hell you can't. I'll fix you so that you can. If you don't show up there at eight sharp it means Stutthof for you. Do you understand?" Bob's eyes rolled helplessly. With a four-day beard and sunken cheeks, he looked like a dying man. He took Grabowski's hand.

"Wladek—aren't you a friend of mine? If you are, let me die. You can take that slut then. She can really screw."

"None of that shit. Get up."

"I can't."

"OK."

Grabowski closed the door to the other room and started taking off his clothes. Bob looked at him, uncomprehending, with maudlin eyes.

Down to his long underwear, Grabowski grabbed Bob under his arms, found him limp but light, and dragged him to the shower. Bob put up a little resistance at the door. "Jesus, Wladek, you're not going to do it to me. Leave me alone! Let me die!"

Heavy drops of sweat dripped from his forehead. "For Christ's sake, don't do it to me, I speak to you as one Pole to another!"

Grabowski pushed him violently into the shower and opened the tap. A stream of ice-cold water hit both of them. Bob wriggled but Grabowski kept him pinned to the wall. Bob started howling.

Elena burst in and turned to stone looking at them.

"Get out. Have the coffee ready."

She covered her face with both hands and ran out.

Bob stopped howling, a choking noise came out of his throat. A moment later he vomited while Grabowski held his head in his hands. I have to get him out now, thought Grabowski, or he'll have a heart attack. He closed the tap and said, "Enough!"

Five minutes later Bob was back in bed sipping the bitter black coffee. Grabowski, sitting on the chair, watched silently. He was cold and tired. Bob put his cup on the night table. "O.K. I am going to sleep now."

Grabowski got up and turned off the light.

"Shall I set the alarm clock for you?"

"No need. I get up on my own."

"Goodnight."

He went to the other room and closed the door after him. Elena was curled up on the couch.

"Well, I guess I'll go now."

"Wladek."

"Listen, if you want to commit suicide—both of you—because the Russians are coming, wait at least till they've come."

"Wladek."

She took his face between her long, thin hands, and moved her own close to it. "Is there something I can do for you, Wladek Grabowski?"

His heart started thumping. He pulled himself back, forcibly.

"Yes, you can do something for me, Elena. You can bring me from your office some German dog-sausage, wrapped in more paper like this."

She looked at the soiled, crumpled sheet of paper, not understanding for a full minute. Then her huge gray eyes narrowed, like a cat's. She gasped. "Wladek, Wladek, oh God, Wladek, do you know what you're doing?"

She sat up, uncoiling slowly. He noticed her long, stockinged legs. Her skirt rolled up a little, and he caught a glimpse of her garters. A hot wave rushed to his head.

"I don't want them for free," he said. "I'll bring you presents you'll like."

"You realize how dangerous it is, Wladek?"

185

"As dangerous as suicide?"

She was recovering quickly from the shock.

"Ah, Wladek, I knew, I knew when Kazik brought you here the first time—does he know?"

"Nobody knows anything. I don't know really what you're talking about. I am curious, that's all."

She nodded several times as she digested it in her mind.

"One moment," she said and went to the bathroom. When she came back, he noticed she had brushed her hair, put lipstick on, and penciled her brows. She had herself under control. She sat down next to him and again took his hand. They looked at each other in silence. She couldn't go any deeper than Wladyslaw Grabowski, he thought, clever and splendid woman that she was. If she did, his game was up.

"The curse," she said in a low voice, "is that I hate them almost as much as I hate the sub-humans in the East."

Abruptly she asked: "How old are you, Wladziu?"

"Twenty-six."

"And you look twenty at the most. I am much older, almost an old woman. Look here." She raised her head and touched the skin under her chin with her fingertips. "You see? That's where a woman's age shows first. I'm sure you didn't know that. Learn from Elena."

She sighed. "Ah, you could learn lots of things from Elena, even though you are a clever boy, Wladyslaw Grabowski. And you are very careless. If you don't watch out, you may not have time to learn. I'll see what I can do for you, Wladek."

She was silent, brooding.

"One thing is sure, you rescued that cavalry officer husband of mine this time. How did you know what to do?"

He laughed. "By watching others in my barracks. Did you think your Bob was the only Pole that drinks?"

"O.K., you are a sweet man. I'll do something for you. I'll bring you some German sausage. That young German cow that gave me this. You see, she and I are given stacks of this stuff to carry down to the cellar—they have a special oven there to burn it. The instructions are that you have to stay watching until everything is reduced to ashes. She just grabbed the sheet and wrapped the sausage so that nobody could see that she had given it to me."

"I'll go now," Grabowski said.

"Go. And be careful, for Christ's sake. God, you are so young, so inexperienced."

"I manage OK."

"I think that I am beginning to believe in miracles," she murmured. "Come, I'll give you a kiss."

He retreated.

"Don't be scared, silly. Not that kind of a kiss—a motherly kiss!"

She kissed him quickly on his forehead.

Grabowski ran out and slammed the door behind him. He stood for a moment under a low, starless sky. Then he started walking quickly to Camp Narvik 2.

Chapter nineteen

For several months life followed a routine. Its rhythm for Grabowski was the coming and going of Rosti every two weeks. Grabowski expected from the other side some confirmation, approval, of the papers marked *Top Secret*, but nothing came. He had no illusions about these sheets himself. They were mostly drawings of insignificant details in the arrangement of submarine machinery and armament. Even a single toolbox, a shelf, a rack for light weapons was marked thus, for the simple reason that, in accordance with a standing order, everything in the planning office had to be stamped *Top Secret*.

Still, he felt disappointed until at one meeting—again in the men's room at Rita's—Rosti asked him casually, "Where do you get those papers?"

"Which papers?" asked Grabowski to gain two seconds time for quick thinking.

"Those that are stamped. Marked."

"From a woman," he answered, "the woman that gets the stockings you bring."

"Careful with women," said Rosti, buttoning his fly.

"What about Rita?"

"Rita is something else. She probably works a little for Biedermann and a bit for me, one can't know for sure, but I know how to handle it: I am more experienced, believe me. So be careful."

"I will," Grabowski said.

The door opened and an old man came in and brushed shoulders with Rosti, who was already on his way out. Grabowski, sitting on a toilet seat in one of the two cabins, heard the old man sighing and moaning, and waited till he finished and left.

Then he too washed his hands and walked out. Rosti sat talking to Rita. Grabowski walked slowly to his table in the corner and ordered another beer. There was little excitement now that the procedure had repeated itself so many times. The envelope was in Rosti's pocket. He had three pairs of silk stockings for Elena and some cash of his own.

He'd give them to her tomorrow. After that evening, they had never discussed the subject again, though Grabowski thought he had detected a subtle change in her attitude toward him. There were hints of protectiveness. But in Kazik's and Bob's presence she teased him like she had always done.

In the well-heated room, she was wearing a light blouse with a daring décolleté. Kazik and Wladek shot frequent glances at her whenever she bent over the table, pouring ersatz coffee.

"Yes, yes, kids," she laughed. "Look, look as much as you wish, you'll see well the spot where my tits grow from. I know you'd like to see them totally, the tits, but they are out of bounds. They are Bob's. Not that he knows much what to do with them, but all the same, they are his. He bought them."

"Elena," Bob protested half-seriously, "stop goading them! You are not fair with them and not with me. Boys, you do not know what a woman she is. I have known her for three years and she still has surprises for me."

"If you don't like me, you can go to Troyl with Kazik and Wladek. They'll take you along gladly."

"Enough! Stop it!"

"Kaziu! Tell us—how are the whores in Troyl? Tell us, here and now, among friends!"

This is bad, Grabowski thought. This isn't fighting. It isn't doing. It is a fairly comfortable, almost normal life. If David were on hand, he'd say it is like life in the Ghetto, in 1940, or early 1941. It is like meeting Arthur, Bubi, Martha—like the intellectual circle. The same passive waiting, same idle talk, the same *let the world move and let me move together with it* attitude, or still worse, *let me perch outside and watch.* And the conditions are incomparably better here: no starvation, no epidemics, no fear of manhunts. A nice safe little corner. Collecting information has become a habitual thing. That's what it will be for the rest of my days. The way things look, with America taking beatings everywhere, the war could drag on for years, and the outcome was not at all clear yet.

Kazik veered away from Elena's question and said, as if reading Grabowski's mind, "There have been many long wars in history."

"Sure. Also a one hundred year war."

"You mean this one could last as long?"

"Easily. The Axis is dividing the world. America is badly mauled and shaken. If the Germans could finish the Russians this summer and turn their full might against Britain…"

"I don't know what you men are complaining about," Elena said. "We are all having a good time. We have work and a roof above our heads and bread. Some of us even have their own women. Others, less fortunate, have Troyl, which, while not first class, you must admit, is better than nothing. Occasionally we get presents: German dog-sausage."

Kazik and Bob laughed like mad. Grabowski succeeded in producing a grin. Shut up you bitch. Don't you dare open your mouth about that. He tried to convey a threatening telepathic message.

Elena was happy. "Wladziu, don't look at me like that! I can't show you my tits! Bob would protest!"

Grabowski, enraged, suffered till the end of the evening. He was silent on the way home but Kazik kept talking almost non-stop.

"Wladek, I think I shouldn't go there and see them too frequently. Not Bob of course, but Elena. When she starts that business, she drives me clear out of my mind. It's crazy. And what pleasure she has in teasing us that way! Naturally, she knows how hungry we are. It's not fair. Maybe we should tell Bob to tell her, eh?"

"What?"

Grabowski caught himself not listening to Kazik's chatter. A bad move, my friend. You should listen and be attentive. One day you may make a big mistake by just not listening.

"I mean tell Bob, but not to tell her that we have spoken to him about it, that he did it out of his own initiative, you know."

"Possibly," agreed Grabowski, "but I'm not sure she'll do what he asks her to do."

Kazik shook his head. "Sex drives me crazy."

Then he added, "You know, I can't even go to church. I find it impossible to confess to a German priest. Isn't it crazy? How about you, Wladziu?"

"Oh, I endure, somehow," Grabowski said. "One has to, no?"

Chapter twenty

In a big harbor town in western Sweden, Rosti enjoyed brightly-lit streets, healthy, well-clad people, elegant shops, and fresh air free of the pathological vapors of war. There was food rationing and sometimes at night, deep droning filled the darkness with vibration, whenever some of the war participants found it convenient not to respect Sweden's neutrality and sent bomb-laden planes high over the country's territory on their way to enemy territory. And even though everybody knew that no bombs would rain from the heavy darkness above, some people would shudder and cast anxious glances upwards. Two women had nervous breakdowns, the press reported. The government sent half-hearted, timid protests to the belligerents.

But Rosti had a sound nervous system and did not mind the droning overhead. He felt safe enough. He walked leisurely along the broad streets of the town center, glancing occasionally at his watch. His appointment was at eight. He climbed the few steps at the entrance to a small villa and pushed the bell button twice. He said a name in answer to the doorman's question. Next, a young woman appeared, and Rosti gave her one of his long-lashed, melancholy smiles.

"And whom should I report, sir?"

"Rosti."

He watched her slim body disappearing behind a heavy curtain.

Two minutes later, he was sitting at a desk, well lit with a strong table lamp, watching a young man perfunctorily sort out the contents of the envelope Rosti had given him. He read quickly and smiled. "He asks, if there is a possibility to be assisted in coming to England, to join the Armed Forces. Through Sweden, of course."

"That one. How is his stuff?"

"I am not the one who evaluates it; it seems routine. Not bad, not outstanding. He is trying hard, apparently. But we were thinking of giving you another assignment, Rosti."

He raised his brows, surprised, "What is it?"

The young man chuckled. It was an unpleasant, sharp sound, like bones rattling.

"A surprise: less dangerous, better paid, easier. You can almost regard it as a promotion."

"South America?"

The other man looked at him ironically,

"Do you think we're that stupid? We know that you can't go back there. We know some people in Argentina who wouldn't exactly welcome you with open arms."

He was playing with a silver pencil, leaning back in his armchair. Rosti watched him silently. Then he said in a deadpan voice, "I committed no crimes in Argentina."

"Of course not. It is Spain."

Rosti said nothing.

"Well, these are the directives. As a freelancer, a volunteer, you can of course take it or leave it. But I think our collaboration has been fruitful for both sides. By the way, how many men do you have there?"

193

"Two," Rosti said. I would like to know, he thought, how many men like Rosti you have on these Swedish ships. He almost asked, and you? But he checked himself in time.

"How big of a raise do I get when I go to Spain?" he asked. The man looked at some papers in a half-open drawer, and said, "It comes to about forty per cent more than what you are getting now. Is that all right?"

"All right," said Rosti. "Will you send anybody to replace me there, in Danzig, or do we cut the contacts?"

"That," said the young man, "should really not bother you."

For one moment Rosti visualized the big sitting room in Petroleum Bar, Rita, the dozing customers, Biedermann in his leather coat, and Wladek in the corner.

"What I mean is, it would be a pity in a way. The men over there are eager, dependable. One has the makings of a good agent. If the stuff I bring has any value."

The other man clasped his hands and examined his fingernails. "I told you, I do not know if it has any value: or, put it this way, everything has value. I only send it further on. I am simply your contact here, that's all. I make no decisions. Personally, I think it makes sense that they send another messenger to Danzig with you transferred to Spain."

"Do I make another trip still or should I pay off now?"

"You pay off now."

"So there's no way of telling them—the men in Danzig—about the change?"

The man made an impatient gesture and Rosti caught himself thinking, what the hell am I arguing about? Why should I worry about Wladek? Or Rita?

"We'll find ways of picking up the contacts, if necessary," said the other man, rising. His face above the halo of light from the table lamp looked like an African tribal mask in green.

"After you've paid off, come here tomorrow and we'll fix the details of the Spanish business."

There was nothing more to say. Rosti, prudent and rational,

got up and shook hands. He went to a movie theatre, picked up a streetwalker, and, before going to bed, thought that at least he wouldn't have to sleep with Rita any more. That certainly had been a nuisance.

Chapter twenty-one

When the *Viking* arrived again in Danzig's Weichselmünde Ost Harbor and started discharging iron ore, three people felt greatly concerned when Rosti failed to appear at Rita's.

Grabowski with his big envelope arrived every second evening at Petroleum Bar, taking care to spend as much time there as usual, and not one minute more. He would walk then to the *Alte Liebe*, and occasionally look in at the *Deutsches Haus*.

Grabowski's face showed nothing. He drank his beers alone, but one night, he met Bleistift there. The crane-driver looked around, and sighed. "Haven't been here for some months, but nothing's changed, I reckon. Have you made any contacts?"

"What contacts?"

"About what we were talking about then, do you remember? Going to Sweden."

Grabowski laughed. "I've forgotten about it. I'll tell you, I am so well satisfied with my present job on the Langer Heinrich, that it seems to me the best way is to sit out this bloody war."

Bleistift nodded thoughtfully. "That's what I figured out, too. Why risk my life needlessly?"

Grabowski agreed. If Rosti entered at that moment, he'd have to get rid of the man somehow, or arrange another meeting. It should not be too difficult.

Biedermann chatted with Rita and noticed that she was more nervous than usual. She did not smile even once, and kept glancing at the door. She passed her hand over her forehead: "Great God, what a headache!"

"Why don't you take a pill and go to bed?" he suggested sympathetically. "Can't Marga and Lise take care of business? You haven't got that many customers."

"I think I'll do just that."

Biedermann looked around and thought it would be nice to cheer Rita up. He really liked her. But he could not remember any one of the spicy anecdotes that usually had such an exhilarating effect on her.

"The *Viking* is in," he said. "Has your Spanish friend arrived yet?"

"Argentinian, not Spanish. No, I have not seen him this time."

"Well, he'll come, sooner or later, surely," Biedermann said and paid for his beer. "I do hope you'll be better tomorrow. Be well. *Heil Hitler.*"

It could be that he's got extra work on board, Rita thought when he went out. She indicated with her head to Lise to take over, and went upstairs.

In her broad bed it occurred to her that she could easily ask Biedermann to check the crew list of the Viking. Yes, she'd do just that. After all, it wasn't a secret, her friendship with Rosti. Nor was there anything illegal in it. As a bar owner, she had many seafaring friends.

The next evening, when she brought the subject up to Biedermann, he was only too eager to comply.

"But of course, Rita! There' s nothing easier in the world. Do you want me to check it now? I have the office keys in my pocket!"

"No, no, let's not exaggerate! I am hot, but not twenty years old, Hans! I can easily wait till tomorrow!"

"Just what was the name?"

"Rosti. Argentinian passport."

She received the information twenty-four hours later. Biedermann was thrilled by being actively involved in what he considered a romantic tragedy. His own life was devoid of such occurrences. Instead of leaning against the bar as usual, he chose that night to sit down at a table. "Rita dear, I am awfully sorry. There is no man of that name and nationality aboard that steamer."

"Are you sure?" She thought she had controlled the trembling of her voice. He took a list from his pocket.

"Firemen—look for yourself: Lars Gustaffson, Hugo Johannsen, Sven Kertvik, Jacob Olsen, Uve Maartsen, Eric Singvert—all Swedes. No foreigners aboard. Donkeyman—Martin Gullbranson.

"He must have paid off in Sweden," she whispered.

"He paid off in Sweden," confirmed Biedermann.

"Maybe he was sick."

"I could ask the captain, although to tell the truth, it is beyond our official business."

"Naturally." Rita collected herself resolutely. "Never mind, Hans. Don't bother. You have been a good friend, and thank you so much, thank you."

He waved his hand. "Don't mention it, Rita. It was nothing. I'd do any favor for you."

Her black eyes wandered over the faces of her steady clients, her *Stammgäste* whom she had known so well. Something had disappeared from her life, irrevocably, and she felt humiliation, then sorrow.

I am a woman of fifty-two, thought Rita, and he was probably my last young man. He preferred me to younger women, to girls, he always came here on his first evening in town, to make love to me. He had no other reason. But it's over now. He won't come any more.

He might send a letter, a note. It's still not too late. Oh, why delude myself? I know I'll never see nor hear from him again.

Biedermann saw how sad she was. He decided to be noble, the way a gentleman behaves: "He might have gone on leave and he'll come back next time. He might have been transferred by the company to another ship. They have several, you know."

Rita nodded. She wished he'd leave her alone. She'd manage better without him. As if telepathic, Biedermann rose. "I'll have to go now, Rita. Don't hesitate to tell me if I can be of any assistance to you."

"Bye, and thank you once more, Hans. I won't forget it."

"*Heil Hitler,* Rita."

Chapter twenty-two

Of all the men in Room 5, Stasiek the redheaded mechanic was the luckiest at least in one respect: he had a steady girlfriend. This enabled him to look with merry contempt at his less fortunate comrades and listen with smiling disinterest to the tales of their adventures in Troyl B-Barracks. The strange thing was everybody knew Stasiek had a girl, but only a few had seen her, or had seen them together. Yet, they met almost daily.

The Russian and Ukrainian women's camp was strictly out of bounds for men: Stasiek paid visits there, occasionally, never staying longer than 10 P.M. It was unthinkable that Ljuba should come to visit him in his room. Stefan the painter had once brought a Ukrainian woman, arranged two blankets on both sides of his bed as curtains and pumped her there to well over midnight, while all the others in the room were listening to their groaning and moaning.

While they were walking together to the yard in the early morning, Stasiek commented on this to Grabowski. "Would you believe a man like Stefan could behave that way? Like a fucking animal?"

"I don't know him well enough to be his judge."

"Animals screw in public, and not even all of them; some do it privately. And that dirty painter doesn't mind fucking that Ukrainian whore with seven other men around, watching."

"Don't exaggerate. The lights were out and he put up those blankets."

"But their squealing and groaning could be heard in the whole fucking camp." Stasiek spat.

For a while they walked silently, amidst the great human river of workers flowing toward the shipyard gate.

"Where do you meet with your Ljuba?" Grabowski asked.

Stasiek's small freckled face grew serious. "We meet in the open, outside the camps. Oh, you can find isolated places. Ljuba would rather die than to come to our barrack, and I'd never propose it to her. Do you think I am a fucking animal, like that Stefan? Besides, ours is a different relationship."

They still had a good ten minutes to go. In that time, Stasiek found it necessary to tell Grabowski some intimate secrets. I wonder, Grabowski thought, what is it in me, that makes people want to confide in me? What urged them to talk, to tell me things they'd rather hide in their hearts? David hadn't been like that, had he?

"She is a real, good girl, Wladek. I'll tell you something, but keep your mouth shut about it, for Christ's sake. Her father is a colonel in the Red Army. She is an educated girl. She's had more years of schooling than my three brothers and me together—not to mention my parents, who never went to school."

He stopped and hesitated, and looked around. They were walking in the middle of a group of Frenchmen, nobody could understand their conversation, even if they overheard it.

"Wladek, you work on this floating crane and you see all kinds of things. Well, she... Ljuba... she is very interested in these things... you understand?"

Grabowski shook his head.

"I tell her what I see on these warships I am working on. The destroyer that hit the mine in the Gulf of Bothnia. That kind of stuff."

"Why is she interested in that kind of stuff?" asked Grabowski slowly.

Stasiek was very excited now. He swallowed several times.

"Wladek, swear on Jesus' blood you won't tell anybody."

"I swear," he said.

"She says, once in a while, once in ten days, sometimes once a week—irregularly—a man comes to their room, late at night when it is pitch dark. He sits on her bed and asks her these questions."

Stasiek kept silent for a minute.

"She is a very patriotic girl, Ljuba. She says she'd do anything to help her country win the war. Once, in the beginning, she was scared and she struck a match to see who it was; but he blew it out before she could see anything and was very angry with her, made her promise never to do it again. But Wladek, may God strike me dead this very moment if I have told this to anybody, just to you. Keep your mouth shut about it, will you?"

"I will, I told you. And I can tell you what I see, so that you can tell it to your Ljuba, but there isn't much of interest, really. You know what I see, down there? Two big fucking Scotch boilers and a mountain of coal. That's what I see mostly. But all the same, if I see anything I'll tell you. I, myself, don't understand about these things. And you don't have to fear anything, I won't speak to anybody."

"Not even to Kazik?"

"Surely not about these things."

It is not likely, he thought, that what Ljuba tells the Man in the Darkness ultimately reaches Rosti. But Rosti was now two weeks overdue. One more week and he'd know. Perhaps he should give Ljuba the material, though the Russians probably worked on their own. He had two envelopes in his inner breast pocket, for they did not fit in the small leather bag, and he did not like carrying them with him. It felt like walking around with one's body not completely intact; as if some minor but persistent pain bothered him. Not really hurting, but making it impossible to ignore it completely, to forget it. He worried about what he would do with the material if Rosti failed to return, but he knew he could not trust Stasiek of all people, and felt resentful of his recent confidences, as if he did not have enough of his own problems already. Grabowski was annoyed.

The river of workers slowed down, stopped.

"What is it?"

"A strike," somebody joked. "The yard has been closed. They have enough U-boats," another joker suggested.

They started moving ahead slowly. There was a bottleneck at the entrance. Two additional guards made them step into a single line and were checking each identity card individually, comparing sharply the photograph on it with the bearer's face.

But after they had passed through the gate, another normal day in the shipyard started. The floating crane was transporting submarine section number four from the assembly shop to a steamer. During that week there was a gate-check twice more.

"They suspect something," Piotr said. The elder Maliniak said he heard that some British airmen had escaped from a POW camp near Thorn; they were looking for them everywhere. That seemed implausible.

Then on Friday morning, there was a great commotion. A ripple ran through the crowd at the gate. A shot rang, and people started running in panic in all directions. A wild stampede began.

"Halt! Halt!" somebody shrieked in German, and then two more shots rang. Grabowski, swept from his feet by the onrush of people, fell on the pavement: somebody fell on top of him.

Then everything was quiet. He heard the roar of a motorcycle, then of a car. He moved his elbow, and the man who was lying on top of him rose, and murmured, "Sorry," in Flemish. All over the big square people were rising, brushing the dirt off their clothes, and asking each other what had happened.

Grabowski saw two men pushing a stretcher with a body on it into an ambulance. Then the ambulance and two soldiers on motorcycles drove away and the workers started flowing again to the entrance. On board the crane, Martin Schultz, the chief, warmed his hands against the boiler door. Grabowski related to him what had happened and explained why he was late. The old man nodded. "Yes my lad. I know." He moved close to Grabowski, although there was nobody else in the stokehold, and whispered confidentially: "They say they shot a spy."

"A spy? What spy?"

"Psst! The Enemy is Listening!"

Grabowski wanted to laugh. The chief's puckish face resembled that of the *Kohlenklauer*—the coal thief—from the other poster.

"A Russian spy! Or perhaps a British one."

"Did they kill him?"

"Who can know? Who can know?" said Schultz. Then, hoisting his big body up the iron ladder of the exit, he added: "You just watch your fires and your water gauge, Grabowski, and close your eyes and your ears to anything else. We here just do our work, and do not want to know of anything. Listen to an old man's advice."

"Yes sir," Grabowski said.

"That's that. Good boy."

When Grabowski came back from work, the other men were all there. At the table sat Radecke, the camp leader's assistant, the camp leader himself, and a bespectacled man with a skull and bones on his cap.

"Oh!" Radecke said. "Here is our *Stubenältester*, at last!"

Grabowski became painfully aware of the two envelopes in his pocket. The man with the cap pierced him with his eyes. The lenses of the glasses sharpened the look.

"Grabowski, when did you see Stasiek last?" Radecke asked.

"Yesterday evening, sir."

"At what time?"

"Why, just before we went to bed, sir. Must have been around nine-thirty."

"What about this morning?"

"No sir. I got up earlier than the others, because I knew the crane was at the outer end, it takes longer to get there and I never arrive late to my post."

"Grabowski is a fireman on the Langer Heinrich," explained Radecke to the SS officer.

"I do not like his face," the man said in German.

Radecke shrugged slightly: "Well, he has nothing to do with it." He turned to Grabowski and said in Polish: "Look, we have taken all the belongings of this man Stasiek—what is his name? Ah, Kowalski. Stasiek Kowalski. He won't be coming back."

"What happened to him, sir?"

"Never mind." He turned again to the uniformed man. "Anything else?"

"Ask him who his friends were, said the SS officer, and Radecke translated the question into Polish.

"I think he was a loner, sir," Grabowski said.

"Come, come, he had a buddy, didn't he? All of you have, we know it."

"No, sir. I don't think so. Here, ask the boys."

A murmur of voices confirmed what he had said.

"Perhaps he had friends in other barracks, or even in other camps?" suggested the SS man.

"That might be," Grabowski agreed, "but he never told us, sir. He was a loner, one hundred per cent."

The two Germans rose.

"That'll be all, Grabowski. Send us two men with his mattress to the office, will you?"

"Yes sir. Do we get another mattress instead?"

The Germans looked at each other, and smiled.

"He is not very bright, this *Stubenältester* of yours," the SS man said.

"Yes," Radecke said laughing. "You'll get another mattress, Grabowski."

"He does not seem to know what happened," the SS man told the camp leader.

"Of course not. How could he?"

They left, and the Maliniak brothers took the mattress to the camp's office.

"They started cutting it with scissors as soon as we brought it there," Tadek Maliniak said when they came back.

"One thing seems to be sure. They were running after a spy. Stasiek was killed incidentally," Kazik said.

"Well, he was not a spy, that's also sure."

"How can you be sure?" demanded Stefan. "How can any of you be sure who is who, and what he is doing? We don't ask questions here. Nor do the Germans. Who really knew him?"

"He's been with us for a year," somebody murmured.

"Ask that Russian girl of his."

"Crazy! I wouldn't go near that camp for anything."

"Shall we go and see Bob?" Kazik asked Grabowski.

"I don' t know. I don't feel like it. Would you go alone?"

"All right. You going to bed?"

"I think I'll turn in. Quite a day, wasn't it?"

"Yeah. I'll ask them if they know anything about it. Maybe Elena does."

"Give them my regards."

Grabowski lay down with his clothes on and closed his eyes. He felt too restless to sleep. He got up half an hour later and took the tram to Neufahrwasser. He had a beer at Rita's, absentmindedly watching her while she chatted with Biedermann. Perhaps they had caught Rosti? There were too many things unknown for the moment. And yet he sat there like a man who likes his beer, likes the place, the quietness, the immobility of it, and, has plenty of time on his hands.

Then he got up and went to check the two other places. In the *Deutsches Haus* they were howling drinking songs. At *Alte Liebe*, Frieda, with a black handkerchief on her neck, sat down at his table. The place was almost empty. She spoke Polish. He looked at her large breasts and nipples like buttons beneath her blouse.

"Any chance of getting a bit of tobacco?"

He offered her a cigarette. "Home grown, or foreign?"

"You can make a mixture, half and half."

"Home grown and French?"

"Sure. I like it strong. I like everything strong," she leered toward him. He smiled. "How much would you like?"

"A pound. How much will it cost?"

"I'll make a special price for you."

"Thank you." She gave him a long look. "It is a pity you are a Pole, isn't it? Can't you try to be a *Volksdeutscher*?"

"I think I can't."

"A pity. All the young Germans are away. Fighting the war."

"I'm going now. I'll bring you the tobacco tomorrow."

Grabowski walked along the quiet empty streets of Neufahrwasser with his hands in his pockets. Two envelopes bulged slightly from the left side of his jacket. A great malaise was closing in on him. It looked and felt like shadows emerging from the walls of the fog, materializing in threatening forms, still too vague to be clearly perceived but coming on steadily. Something was cooking in this fog, something very evil, dark and silent.

Grabowski stopped to light a cigarette, and, shielding the match in his palms, looked around. On the nearby wall, he saw the big, dark blue poster: *Psst! Der Feind hört mit!*

Forgetting his own cigarette, he studied for a moment the two men in the picture, their faces lit from below by another match.

The match in Grabowski's hand had burnt out. The match in the picture was still burning. Grabowski lit his cigarette and continued back to Narvik.

Chapter twenty-three

The feeling of disintegration was becoming more and more persistent. Grabowski was still functioning without a hitch, but every day required more effort to carry on, to keep a straight face.

Kazik, his buddy, started noticing things. They had their meals in silence, Wladek absentmindedly staring into a void over Kazik's head.

"Anything wrong? You look worried, Wladziu."

"Me? Nothing wrong. Just tired, I guess."

"Never mind, it'll pass. I've had periods like those, I know the feeling. And the bastards are advancing on every front, as if they were going to win the bloody war. How triumphant they are! Onwards to the Caucasus, to the Middle East. And the Japanese drumming on the Americans. Sure, bad times. Nothing to be cheerful about. But what can we do, here, us little people?"

Grabowski continued going to Neufahrwasser, but he felt it in his bones that he would never see Rosti again.

"Come, there is a game going on in 31, come, Wladek, a bit of distraction will be good for you!"

The game had started early and when they entered there was

a big bank on the table of five or six hundred marks. People at the blanket-covered table made room for them silently. They played for an hour with indecisive luck. Grabowski looked at the faces around the table: heavy peasants from northern provinces, red with excitement and greed. Tense with expectation. And what were they expecting next? To grab the plate filled with paper notes. The sensuous joy of arranging them in neat stacks, folding them, putting them in their pockets. The room was dark with cigarette smoke.

And then what? What do they intend to do with their wealth? Grabowski never knew what to do with his, still had seven or eight hundred marks on him. Twice the monthly wages of the captain of the Langer Heinrich. He could buy clothes in the camp, or tobacco, or go back to the whore in the *Frauengasse*, the blond one who took him for a Bulgarian. She considered herself expensive. 'But I take ten marks, love.' The possibilities of exchanging this windfall for diversions seemed limited to him. He blamed David, for creating him with such a limited imagination for enjoying life.

Well, that was done with intention. He'd been created with a very clear purpose; not so the buddies around the table. They seemed so much freer, seldom burdened with thinking. Therein lies the great injustice, he thought: David could at least have spared me this. Yes, but on the other hand, how to fulfill this purpose, this destiny without the capacity to think? Therein lies the ambiguity of the situation. What would be the ideal solution? Selective thinking, perhaps. But this is impossible and David knew it. He was not so stupid, after all. As a palliative, he passed on this power of will, power of control. Grabowski felt he must keep things under control, including the thoughts, when they become insubordinate and start running in forbidden directions. Curb them.

He realized that they were waiting for him. It was his turn.

He looked at his cards: two queens, the rest nothing.

"Three cards," he said, and the man opposite him, with tiny hostile eyes, dealt them to him. Then he gave himself two cards. Grabowski mixed his cards and pushed the upper corners gently apart. He had now three queens, a seven of spades and a ten of hearts.

"Twenty marks," he said.

"Twenty and raise you fifty."

Grabowski looked at the other man for a long time, not able to decide if he should see him. Was the man bluffing? He did not look clever enough for that. He might be the cunning peasant, but he would flinch under his stare. At least that. And he had exchanged only two cards. He had to have a full house, or maybe four of a kind.

He shook his head and folded his cards. He put them gently on the table. There was a loud murmur in the room, as the man calmly took the bank. Grabowski rose, and stretched himself.

"Going now?"

"Why don't you stay some more, Mr. Grabowski? It is early yet! You've lost quite a lot, you've got a fair chance to win it back!"

He caught Kazik's eyes pleading with him to stay.

"No," he said. "It is not my night. I lost, so what? Another time I'll win. Don't you worry, you'll spit that money back. Not tonight."

The circle around the table had already closed. Another man had taken his place.

And how much in status did you lose, he asked himself. Do I really have to check every fucking gambler's cards? No, not that, but you should have stayed to teach him a lesson. "Shit," he said aloud.

The night was warm, and he decided to walk in the direction of the port. But as soon as he passed the cubicle of the watchman's hut at the entrance, a figure materialized out of the soft darkness, and approached him. It was dark, he could not see the face.

"Ljuba," a weak voice said.

"What? What do you want?"

"Ljuba… Stasiek's Ljuba."

"Ah! Ljuba! I did not recognize you."

He had seen her a few times before, fleetingly, with Stasiek. He had a recollection of a very thin, almost fragile girl with very high cheekbones. She had a handkerchief on her head, and old, worn out shoes on her feet, not the wooden clogs.

"You came on foot all the way from Langfuhr? That's a long walk!"

"I had to see you."

"Me? All right, let's walk."

He could not take her to a bar or to any place in town. The *Ostarbeiter* were even one rank lower than the Poles, all those places were strictly out of bounds for them, they were not allowed to go anywhere except to work in the shipyard and back to the camp. At nine, the camp's gates were closed.

"How did you get out?"

"There is a hole in the fence: I'll go back the same way, don't worry. I had to talk to you." They walked across the fields toward Langfuhr.

"I had to talk to you," she repeated for the third time, "because Stasiek said you were his best friend."

He almost cried out loud in the darkness but managed to remain silent.

"Perhaps it is so, or not. But I had to know. I know they shot him."

"How do you know?"

"Elena told me. Elena is a good friend. And I thought you might know more."

"Why should I?"

"Tell me everything you know about it, please!"

There was a great, swelling despair in her voice. It recalled for a moment the spirit of David and his one-time girlfriend Tami.

He shook his head and took her hand. "Look, Ljuba, I really know nothing about it. Only what they were saying in the yard and in the camp."

"What were they saying?"

"They said they shot a man at the gate. A man that was summoned to stop had started running."

"They shot him or killed him? Tell me, it is of great importance."

So it must have been true, he thought. She stopped and waited for his answer.

"I do not know for sure," he said, "but I think he was killed instantly."

"What makes you think so?"

This time Grabowski stopped. "Stasiek once told me you were a clever girl. If he were alive, in their hands, do you think you'd still be here?"

She hung her head low. After a while, she whispered, "You must be right. But somebody must have told."

"Not at all. Lately, they've been checking everybody at the gate. It could have been simple coincidence. He panicked and started running and they shot him. That's how I figure it."

They were in the cone of light of a single street lamp, and Grabowski took the opportunity to look at her face. Yes, she had high cheekbones and very slightly slanted eyes.

"Did Stasiek tell you anything about me?"

"He told me you were a very honest, very patriotic girl."

They walked in silence for five minutes. The lights of Cholm camp were now in sight. Grabowski felt he must say something before she went to her barracks. Even platitudes were better than silence.

"You must be very brave now. They are strong and victorious, yet they have not won the war. You must not lose hope."

He could not believe his ears. Ljuba was laughing. Not a hysterical giggle but real laughter.

"What did you say? Win the war? Are you joking? Did you really think the Germans had a chance to win this war as long as we have Stalin? They lost the war long ago, irrevocably. Stalin will annihilate them. Stalin will come to Berlin and plant the Red Banner where that criminal has his headquarters now. It is only a question of time. But that is of absolutely no importance."

"And what will become of us—of you—meanwhile?" He pointed at the huge, sprawling camp in which five thousand people were crowded.

She lifted her face. "This has no meaning, no meaning at all.

Russia is huge, we have millions of people. What happens to these poor wretches is completely meaningless. Don't you know that Stalin does not even recognize our existence? When they wanted to mediate with the Red Cross, he said, 'My people in Germany? There are no people of mine in Germany.'"

Shaken, Grabowski murmured, "So be it, Ljuba. All the same, take care of yourself."

"For what?" she answered coldly. "I will take care of myself only as long as I can be useful for our sacred cause."

He was sure that she had not slept with him. What a relationship it must have been—the ignorant, religious, anti-Semitic Stasiek, and this fanatic Russian girl. My God, what a strange girl!

"Be well, Ljuba. We might meet again, soon. Where is the hole in the fence?"

She showed him the place, and he looked around. She crawled in, easily and quickly, like a lizard. Inside the camp, she raised her hand. He made a sign and started walking back. It was too late to go to the port.

Chapter twenty-four

When Grabowski visited Bob and Elena the next time, he went there alone. Kazik was on nightshift again.

"Bob is drunk, Wladziu," Elena greeted him merrily. "I think it is his personal, original way of getting through the war. He invented it. Might as well patent it. I also had one or two or three. Would you like to have a drink, Wladziu? You look as if you need one," she chattered.

"Oh I don't mind having one, but not methylated, eh?"

"No, no, God forbid, civilized people like us! It is pure medical stuff, stolen from Dr. Krebs' dispensary, and Bob added something to it—juice, or something. Are you afraid of methylated?"

"Well, people occasionally go blind or die from it, you know."

She laughed, tossing her head backward.

"Of course I know, silly. I am teasing you. Here's to your health!"

They drank and Elena caught her breath. The alcohol was very strong.

"Are you afraid of dying, Wladek? Bob always talks about suicide. Naturally, he'll never kill himself. He is not the type. I am the real suicide type, chronic and persistent, and that will be the end of me. I know."

"Where is he?"

"Oh, he went with his Ukrainian friends and I am sure they'll bring him back when he is through drinking. Unconscious, naturally. He can drink with anybody, mind you. I cannot. But I can drink with you, Wladziu, because you are sweet. Have I told you before that you are sweet? No? Well, I say it now. To your health!"

I should get out of here, thought Grabowski. She is too drunk. I have no business with her. I just wanted to be with somebody. Because I've been worrying too much, thinking too much. Overdoing this business of thinking. Even now. Even when I was considering asking Rita about Rosti. I should stop thinking for a while. Normal people get drunk in such situations. But I, I cannot afford it. I am afraid of losing control.

But Elena drank merrily and did not care if she lost control. She looked at her smooth, maddening long legs and said, "These are beautiful stockings you brought me, Wladziu. I never asked you where you get them, but it is very obvious they are foreign stockings. They do not make things like that any more in Germany. By the way, you are no longer interested in these funny little papers I was giving you? Because I have some new ones. No? Then let's have another drink. I won't ask you embarrassing questions, Wladziu. I never do. A principle. I am a woman of principles, and that's why I am going to kill myself before the Russians come here."

Looking inwardly, going back in her memory, her eyes watching the tape of memory in her mind so that what he saw was only like a matted back of a mirror, she said, "Have I ever told you how we met, Bob and I? I was working in a pharmacy in Vilna then, late in '39, and was scared of that Jew."

Grabowski asked, "What Jew?"

"Lieutenant of the Red Army, Jacob Moiseievich Glaser, at your service." She saluted, and told Grabowski how Glaser had brought her enormous bouquets of red roses. God only knows where he had gotten them, in winter, in Vilna. Huge bouquets.

"Never saw anything so vulgar in my whole life. And I used to think that if this Jew touches my hand, I'd die."

Grabowski said, "Why?"

Elena poured from the bottle for him and for herself. They drank in silence, without toasting. "I don't know. I was brought up that way. We did not like Jews in Vilna. That's the thing we have in common with you Poles. It was the same in Warsaw, with you, wasn't it?"

Grabowski felt the inside of his body crumbling. Chunks of lungs, stomach, liver were falling apart, collapsing, disintegrating. Uncoordinated images swirled before his eyes and he thought he'd vomit his heart in a moment. He was choking. He fought it back and gasped and drank a little more.

"Then," she continued in a serious, confidential voice, "they have Mongols. Lots of Asians in the Red Army. They are every inch as bad as the Jews, though in a different way. In any case, I won't be touched by them either, while alive. When I am dead I don't mind."

Grabowski saw her hanging from the ceiling, her swollen tongue out, her face blue. He fought the nausea, and said, "Are you religious, Elena?"

She shook her head decisively. "Not at all. Not even a little bit. I do not even believe in God."

She added after a second, "The only thing I do believe in is rescuing Polish cavalry officers from the NKVD."

"They were after him?"

"What did you think? He was an officer, wasn't he?"

"And you did all this to escape from Jacob Moiseievich Glaser?"

Stop that, he ordered himself. Stop drinking, stop getting intimate with Elena and go home to Narvik 2 where you belong.

David, he said, David, something bad is happening to the

product of your creation. Something has failed; a malfunction, a breakdown. Maybe you made a mistake in your blueprint, in your planning. And you were so proud of it! You thought you had planned him so well, that you would be able to outwit the whole lot of them, the whole system: Gestapo, SS, SA, the Poles, the Russians, everybody.

"You are not listening, Wladziu! Where are you? You were very far away now, I know! And I was telling you important things. Telling you and myself as well."

"I am sorry, Elena. I won't do it again. I think I'd better…"

"I'll tell you once more, then. No, not only to escape from that Jew. I thought I was in love with Bob then. I probably was. Who knows what love is? Perhaps it is only something chemical, something stirring here"—she put her hand below her belly—"you know, secretions, hormones, all that stuff. I learnt something about it when I was studying pharmacology at the university. Not much, though. When I was a young girl." She stopped, and again her eyes looked backward, to those far-off times.

"It was one hundred years ago," she said, returning. "And now we are in the third year of the Great War, in Camp Cholm, and I have been married to Bob for almost three years, and I have just about had it. Let us drink and be merry. Let us look at it from the other side, Wladziu. We have a roof over our heads and electricity, and we have friends, Kazik and you, and even Dr. Krebs invited us last Sunday. Have I told you about it? What an evening!" She filled the glasses again and drank hers in one gulp. Grabowski only touched his with his lips.

"Do you want to hear about the evening at Dr. Krebs'? He has an apartment not far from here, in Langfuhr. What an apartment! And pictures on the wall, great God! Big, framed pictures, Wladziu."

Elena leaned forward and put her hand on his arm.

"Two kinds of pictures: reproductions of Dürer's woodcuts and reproductions of Rubens, big, fat women, with huge tits," she giggled helplessly. "His wife is that type. A real Brunnhilde but with a scowl. And above his desk, a real, genuine drawing by Daumier. Signed. His son sent it to him from Paris. Wladziu, guess what they have been talking about with Bob. Please, guess."

"I don't know," Grabowski said, painfully aware of the disintegrating process in himself but less distressed about it than before.

"After dinner—a real dinner with goose, wine, genuine coffee—she talked to me about the porcelain set the same son brought her from France, which, though pretty enough, was not as good as our Rosenthal. But the gentlemen, over cigars and brandy, talked philosophy. You know Bob once studied philosophy? Don't ever mention it to him; it hurts. There was also a woman at that time in his life—so don't touch it. I kept biting my lip so much to keep myself from laughing that the woman asked me if I had pains. Krebs kept talking about Spengler. I am sure Bob in his philosophy period never touched him. He knows as much about Spengler as I do about internal combustion engines, but he put up a fantastic performance. I would never have believed our Bob could perform so beautifully. He kept nodding his wise head and said yes at all the right places, Krebs talking and talking, never suspecting the truth. A lovely evening, and you know what he said when we were leaving? 'You are a young couple,' he said, 'and when this war is over at last, you'll have a position in life suitable to your birth, education, and living conditions that people like you deserve.'"

Elena laughed till tears were rolling down her cheeks, and Grabowski laughed too. Laughter is infectious.

She wiped her face with a handkerchief. "They have two slaves in the kitchen. Two Ukrainian girls."

"Bob is a great actor," she said. "Ah, what an actor my Bob is! ...Wladziu, why are you sad? You have troubles? Problems?"

"I have no troubles, no problems," Grabowski said.

Except that of falling apart, but that was a special problem, to be dealt with between David Gordon and Wladyslaw Grabowski exclusively. It could not be shared with anyone.

"Wladziu, would you like to sleep with me? Would it help you?"

She had moved very close to him and he felt the alcohol heavy on her breath and the warmth of her body, and it was difficult for him. She thought she'd die if Jacob Moiseievich Glaser touched her hand.

He gently pushed her away. "Elena, you should go to bed now... you have drunk a lot."

She nodded a few times. "Yes, yes. What a sad person you are Wladziu, but who knows..."

She got up unsteadily and Grabowski rose.

"You'll manage, Elena?"

"Of course, Wladziu, of course. Bob'll be back any moment. Have a good night, Wladziu."

He kissed her on her cheek, "Good night, Elena. Take care."

Chapter twenty-five

Three months after Rosti's disappearance, in June 1942, something incredible happened one serene afternoon in the old Hansestadt Danzig. For Grabowski, a fireman on the floating crane Langer Heinrich, it was the sign from Heaven for which he had been yearning so much. Even if he had believed in the theory that life is nothing more than a chain of coincidences, he would still have found it very strange that a decision of a few men in the far-off city of London could affect his life and his fate. But at that time, he was not thinking about philosophical theories, he was busy keeping the steam up in the crane's boilers. The poor-quality coal burned up quickly and left an enormous amount of slag, and Grabowski, half-naked, murmuring curses and biting the end of his sweat-rag, worked furiously with a long, heavy poker knocking the slag off from the far end of the furnace.

On the floating crane's broad deck stood a heavy Tiger tank that had been loaded in the shipyard. They were bringing it to Neufahrwasser to put it in the hold of the *Stettiner Greif,* sailing that evening for Riga. Led by a small smoking tugboat with a tall steam stack, the

Langer Heinrich sailed through the main channel. It was warm, and the whole crew sprawled on deck around Leo, who, as usual, was glued to the steering wheel, looking straight ahead.

Grabowski passed the rag over his face and climbed up the iron ladder.

He stuck out his head through the skylight, and inhaled deeply the fresh air. His eyes wandered over the tank, the crew leaning with their backs against its caterpillars, over the pale blue sky, already tinted with the warmth of the setting sun. Out of this sun five heavy planes appeared. They were flying low, in formation, and the noise of their engines grew from distant droning to a roar. Two of the planes veered to the left, two others northward, in the direction of the town, and one kept coming straight along the canal. As it passed low over the crane's tall arm, all heads jerked upward. They could see the plane's dark-brown belly and the colored circles on the wings.

"Great God, it…it isn't ours, it's a Tommy!" screamed Paul.

At the same moment heavy bombarding shook the air as the two bombers released their load over the Schichau shipyard.

Everyone ran for shelter to the deckhouse. Grabowski dived down to the stokehold. Only Leo remained at his wheel, turning its spokes frantically. The tugboat had released its towline and the floating crane was moving dangerously close to the shore of the canal. Other explosions followed.

In the stokehold, Grabowski sank to his knees and whispered, "Oh God, oh my God, bomb them dead. At last. Bomb them to annihilation. Destroy everything. Kill them all. Oh God!"

A frantic whistle came over the voice pipe, then the chief engineer, his old voice shaking with fear and emotion. "Grabowski, Grabowski, release the steam, do you hear me? Release the steam from the boilers! Grabowski, release!" Still no alarm, no sirens in Danzig. Not one shot from the aircraft batteries. He pulled the lever of the safety valve. Naturally, it was stuck. Never mind. He knew that old Schultz was scared stiff, fearing that a single bomb splinter could blow the boilers under pressure apart.

He ran upstairs again. The deck was empty. Only the Tiger

stood like a monument of impotence, and at the wheel, the motion-less figure of Leo the helmsman. The crane, pushed by its two small propellers, was moving very slowly in the middle of the canal. Leo had succeeded in keeping it on its course and avoiding collision. Over the roofs of the buildings in the yard, Grabowski saw two big pillars of smoke rising; three others over the town. Only then a siren somewhere started its hysterical scream, and others joined the wailing noise, rising and descending.

There were other dull bombardments further off, and then the anti-aircraft guns answered with their barking.

The same plane that had passed over the crane earlier returned from the north, but higher this time, and further inland. The small guns from the ships anchored alongside the canal opened fire on it, the tracer bullets climbing slowly on their trajectory and disappearing in the sky in small puffs of pink smoke. Grabowski saw four tiny dots detaching themselves from the plane's belly, floating downwards. For a moment, he thought that the plane had been hit and the crew had abandoned it. When no parachute flowered over the dots, he felt a sick pressure in his stomach. But the plane continued on its straight course, and when the four tiny sticks disappeared behind the houses, there were four more shattering explosions. It must have been quite close. Then everything was quiet.

He looked at his watch. No more than ten minutes had passed since the planes had arrived. The sun was a little lower, the sky serene and soft, and pillars of smoke stood motionless over the shipyard and over the town, like a permanent part of the landscape.

The first air raid on Danzig was over. Nobody in town had any idea what had triggered it or what considerations had caused the RAF to venture so deep into Germany at a time when Allied luck was at its lowest ebb, with German armies pushing into the Caucasus and push-ing forward in Egypt, with hundreds of Allied ships sunk every month by packs of U-boats. The raid could not have been foreseen.

One of the Wellingtons was shot down in Oliva, when, inex-plicably, it flew back and passed at no more than a hundred meters over an A-gun battery. The plane exploded on the ground and nothing remained of it or of its crew but pieces of strangely twisted metal and some coal.

The damage was slight. One storage tank in the municipal gas works had burnt down completely, but miraculously the other tanks had not caught fire. A bomb destroyed part of the welding shop shed and damaged a U-boat section standing there. Another one hit the embankment. A shore crane collapsed and fell on an empty barge moored nearby, crushing it completely. And a third one hit a slipway in Schichau. Two old houses in Langfuhr crumbled down. Three large bomb craters remained in Troyl, one in Oliva, and one in Weichselmünde.

Even though the *Danziger Vorposten* ran the headline the next morning *Our guns bring an air-pirate down*, disciplinary action was taken against the Civil Defense Warden, and against all the A-gun crews except that one. The strange raid brought war, which had almost been forgotten there, back to Danzig.

For Grabowski it brought war, two sleepless nights, and a decision.

Chapter twenty-six

In the days that followed the air raid, Grabowski did several things as if he were still true to his nature. At that time he was already far from the perfect, theoretical and monolithic being, that fabulous creation of David Gordon from the Warsaw Ghetto. But believing that the airplanes were an obvious sign from heaven, he had to be absolutely sure about Rosti before he left his post. That was how he considered his present assignment, and to dispel any shadow of doubt, any suspicion of desertion, he had to know. One thing was as risky as another; he had to take a chance.

He had this firmly in mind when one evening, having waited first till Biedermann had had his customary glass of beer and left, Grabowski approached Rita at the counter and asked her with a straight face, "Have you heard anything about Rosti?"

The shock for her was strong, but fortunately there were mitigating circumstances. He did not know it, but they improved his chances.

First, Rita liked Grabowski. She liked him the way one likes a shop window one passes daily on the way to work. He was extremely polite and clean, and he behaved very correctly in her bar. He was a young man with a definite charm about him, whom she would accept easily as her son. He could also pass for her lover if he were not a Pole. Second, Biedermann, whom she also liked, and who occasionally replaced Rosti in her broad bed with brass ornaments was, in general, a disappointment, mainly because of his regrettable habit of falling asleep immediately after lovemaking was over. Rosti would talk with her till sunrise if she felt like it, and occasionally there was more lovemaking before he left.

She suspected that Biedermann climbed the stairs to her bedroom when the boredom with his wife, Hilde, grew to the dimensions of an unbearable nausea.

Therefore, a growing sediment of resentment toward Biedermann was present, augmented by the bittersweet memory of Rosti.

Rita gave Grabowski one long, piercing look, leaned over the counter, and said, "Forget about Rosti. Young man, take my advice, forget about him."

She filled a glass of beer from the tap, cleaned the foam off the top with a wooden spoon, and said, "Drink it. It's on the house. Remember this: you never asked anybody about Rosti, you never asked me. You just wanted another beer, and you got it. Is that clear?"

Grabowski, controlling his shaking hand, drank. How much effort one had to use to control one's own hand!

When another customer came and stood next to him, planting his foot on the metal bar running at the bottom of the counter, Grabowski had a smiling face, and made a perfect impression of a man enjoying his drink leisurely. He put some coins on the counter, nodded politely, said thank you, and left.

He was not through yet with irrational moves on that night. He hesitated for a long while, and then went in the direction of the Scandinavian Seamen's Church. This was to be his last station in Neufahrwasser.

Chapter twenty-seven

In choosing a companion for a suicide trip to freedom, Grabowski had but one consideration—he was looking for physical strength. He and the other man had to push the heavy boat down to the sea. All other factors were irrelevant. In that, he was again true to his nature, as conceived by his creator. The chances of success in this enterprise, as he estimated them, were one to a thousand, but his partner did not have to know that. On the contrary, the less he knew the better. He'd have to find a very stupid man, strong, and sufficiently fed up with his life to be lured into this absurd adventure.

Unfortunately, that was the only question for which he had an answer. Grabowski had never been to sea. Could he handle the boat? Could he keep the course? Were the waters of Danzig Bay guarded? Or mined? What if he was seasick? What if he were picked up by a German ship?

Obviously, on the logical plane, it was a trip into the Absurd, into abstraction as well as reality. But other solutions were equally absurd. The only reasonable way would be to try to find another Rosti. But he had no time for that. He had wasted enough time. Grabowski's capacity for correct functioning was almost exhausted, he thought. He was not planned for a long existence. Time was running out.

The war against Evil was raging—very badly at the moment—and David Gordon had to participate in it, that was his destiny.

He found the man he was looking for in Barrack 24, one Waclaw Krzemienczuk, whose contribution to the German war effort consisted of scrubbing big pots in the camp kitchen. The scullion was officially listed as cook's assistant. There was no doubt that the working place was most suitable for him; he would hardly be able to tackle any other job.

Before he came to Danzig he had made his living carrying sacks of coal at a wholesaler's in a small town near Graudenz. He had a chest like a barrel, and arms the size of Grabowski's legs. He always wore a troubled expression on his face, which was the result—as those who were close to him learned—of his difficulty in grasping the reality around him. He liked working in the kitchen because it meant extra food, and he had an enormous appetite. He cleaned the huge, 200-liter steam pots very thoroughly and very slowly. Unfortunately, his superior, a tiny German named Hermann Stauber, was endowed with a sense of humor, and fed this sense with all kinds of practical jokes on the simpleton.

The constant teasing made life almost unbearable for Krzemienczuk. He was slow to understand the jokes but, oddly, he felt the injustice in them and the malicious intentions behind Stauber's bottomless contempt for a man of an inferior race.

Krzemienczuk had been a soldier in an infantry regiment in September '39 and hated the Germans because his sergeant had told him that he should. He failed to understand why Poles had lost the war: he had fought well, his comrades had been brave. He was released after a couple of months from the POW camp and was sorry that he had ceased to be a soldier. In the army he had always been told exactly what to do, and he did it well. He'd like to be a soldier again; he'd like to fight the Germans.

"Mister," he told Grabowski, "if I could only put my hands on that son of a whore Stauber! Believe me, it'd be enough to give him one good shake, that's all! He's a mean worm, that's what he is, and nothing more. One slap across his ugly mug, even with the back of my hand, and his fucking skull would break like an egg-shell."

"It is a very risky business, Waclaw." Grabowski still had some scruples, some doubts. "We do not have much chance of success in this trip. It would be like winning the first prize in the lottery."

"I want to do it," said Krzemienczuk. "Can't stand that Stauber's monkey-face any more. You live only once, the Russians say, and they are right. What the hell!"

Grabowski had his doubts. Waclaw might prove too stupid to pull an oar, although he certainly had enough strength to pull an oar on a slave galley. But the meanness of exposing the man to such danger, of putting him face to face with death, struck him suddenly.

The Gordon/Grabowski process of amalgamation, which he suspected had started some time earlier, was apparently under way; there were disturbing signs of it. Like the sudden pity he felt for Krzemienczuk. Like the last visit to Elena, which he well remembered. And he had premonitions.

But however it would be, he couldn't take a better man than that idiot. Kazik? Piotr? Piotr wouldn't go. Few people who had a fair chance of surviving the war in relative safety would dare such a mad step. Grabowski himself knew the philosophy of it by heart. He looked again at Krzemienczuk. If they caught them, what would he have to say in the Gestapo's cellar?

Krzemienczuk had a ready answer before Grabowski asked the question: "You know what I think, Wladek? It is not so dangerous after all. If they catch us, you know what we should claim? We should tell them we just took the boat for an excursion. Never dreamt about trying to escape. That's what we should say."

Grabowski sighed. He obviously could not tell him that he was not considering the venture in terms of success or failure. That he had chosen it for lack of choice. A blind alley. Such things do happen, commented David Gordon coolly, momentarily having taken over. Philosophically. Detached. Grabowski, on the other hand, was not sure. To hell with it, he said, like Krzemienczuk had done before.

"OK then," he said. "You remember about the food, eh?"

"No difficulty about that. What I've never been lacking in this camp is food!"

In an enthusiastic mood, he slapped Grabowski on his back: "Wladek, you'll see—we'll do it!"

Grabowski nodded. The slap was painful. Krzemienczuk was certainly a healthy, strong man.

Chapter twenty-eight

Dragging the boat took a great deal of effort, but went easier and smoother than expected. Grabowski thought it would take at least four fishermen to do it under normal conditions.

The tide was high that evening, breaking angrily on the shore in small explosions of foam, and spitting out long, green pieces of seaweed and driftwood. The thunder of the breaking waves was deafening, covering sometimes even the whining of the wind, the howling of the gale.

It was a full gale, with a wet western wind pushing the clouds overhead quickly, one after another, over the pale half-moon. The wind whipped the sea with growing fury.

Grabowski thought the weather was to their advantage. The westerly wind would assist him in moving north. In high seas, the Coast Guard might stay in the harbor and miserable weather would make it certain that the boat owner stayed at home and did not go out to look at the boat, which he had dragged high enough when the storm had started. With the exception of the last point, on all others he was absolutely wrong: the westerly wind, growing in force from hour to hour, would veer to northwest, thus making it impossible to sail out of Danzig Bay. Reaching Sweden with this wind blowing was definitely out of question. The whole bay was guarded, the seamen and the marines cursing the miserable weather but nevertheless staying out, and doing what they were told to do. But the fishermen stayed home behind bolted doors and windows. The boats were secure; it was weather suited to resting by the fire.

A fisherman by the name of Helmuth Riske chose to read the Holy Script; the storm brewing outside was a God-sent opportunity to do some studying. He never thought of looking into the howling darkness to make sure that no one was trying to steal his boat.

Waclaw Krzemienczuk, pushing the boat with his arms and shoulders, had some slight doubts whether it was the best time to escape, but he would not question the wisdom of Grabowski's decisions.

And Grabowski had absolutely no other choice but to try to escape to Sweden.

By sailboat. Through the stormy sea. Disregarding the weather, the Coast Guard, the Frontier Guards, disregarding all dangers and perils; perfectly contemptuous of his own life, and, much worse, that of Waclaw Krzemienczuk. David Gordon, absent on the scene but nevertheless capable of passing a moral judgment, certainly knew the problem and the offense. It was not easy. It was a real sacrifice, and as such a question of conscience—but Wladyslaw Grabowski was supposed to be a creature without scruples.

Two miracles happened that night. One was that Grabowski and Krzemienczuk stayed out at sea and survived for eight hours. The other was that the boat did not overturn in the shore breakers when stranded the next morning, seven miles down the shore. It was a very sturdy little vessel. The only damage it suffered during this trip was the loss of a triangular foresail, which a gust of the storm had torn away around midnight, and a broken rudder blade.

One huge wave lifted the boat, half-filled with water, and threw it beyond the line of the crushing breakers. It remained there, lying on one side like a mortally wounded sea animal.

Krzemienczuk, quite dazed from the shattering experience, still had enough common sense to calculate that they must be somewhere near Danzig and that if he caught a train or a tram, he might be able to reach the camp and report to work with only a few hours' delay. This would certainly earn him curses and threats, and possibly a certain amount of thrashing by the police but nothing more than that.

He tried to win over Grabowski to his plan, but in vain; Grabowski was as good as unconscious, still holding the tiller of the broken rudder in a grip as strong as rigor mortis.

Whereupon Krzemienczuk scratched his head and went alone.

The calculations concerning his own future proved to be amazingly accurate. About an hour later, when the pale sun stood higher, and it was just another gray stormy day, Grabowski woke up, climbed out of the boat, and walked slowly into the forest. His clothes were still drenched, his limbs were numb from cold and wetness, and his mind was hardly working.

He had no intention of going back to Camp Narvik 2.

Chapter twenty-nine

Some things were never discussed in the Wohnlager. The first among them was a person's past. Past was taboo, a strong, very deeply rooted custom grown on the simplest instinct of self-preservation.

The second taboo was not to mention a person's disappearance. Camp inmates occasionally disappeared, escaping to their families, their women, their towns or villages. Sometimes the Gestapo or police would take somebody away without any explanation.

Very rarely, one of those who had disappeared would come back, always a changed man. The camp's custom absolutely forbade asking questions. Nobody asked, nobody answered.

Grabowski's absence was noticed the next morning in his room, and never mentioned. The tension in the room ran very high but not a word was said. In the evening, Kazik spread out a clean towel in their corner on the table, where they used to have their meals together, and ate alone. Three days later, the camp leader's assistant, the *Volksdeutscher* Radecke, came to the room, and sat down heavily. He drummed his fingers on the table and watched the Maliniak brothers making cigarettes. Others were sitting silently on their beds or on the chairs.

"May I take one?" Radecke asked.

The elder brother pushed the box toward him. Radecke smoked in silence for a minute.

"Not bad, the tobacco, is it? No, no, I ask no questions. I am not a policeman, you know."

Then, all of a sudden, he exploded. "What kind of a room is this? One gets killed for nothing, another one goes off his rocker. Steals a fishing boat in a bad storm for an excursion at sea. For what?" he roared. "For what, goddamnit? Wasn't he well off here? He had a good job, hadn't he?"

They listened in silence; the brothers stopped making cigarettes.

Piotr asked: "What happened to him? Mr. Radecke?"

He shrugged impatiently. "You are a grown man. You know what happens in such cases: a few days with the Gestapo in Neugarten, then to Stutthof."

"How much does he get for this?"

Radecke looked up and gave Piotr a piercing look. "For theft? A boat? This is, in wartime, a sabotage on the country's economy. If the boat owner does not sue him separately, he'll get six months, at least."

Somebody whistled softly. "Whew! That is high! Nobody can survive that."

Radecke said, more in sorrow than anger: "Of course not. What did he have to do it for? For what?"

He glanced over their faces, one after another, then swiveled on the chair to look at those who were sitting behind his back.

"You, I've forgotten your name, Pruszyniak, no, Pruszynski. He was your buddy, wasn't he? He didn't tell you what was bugging him? What had got into his stupid head?"

Kazik shook his head. He had tears in his eyes.

"Not a word. Not one word and we have been sharing everything: food, tobacco, cigarettes, money. You know how it is."

"He did not say anything at all?"

"The evening he disappeared, we had dinner together, here, on this table. I brought the goulash from the kitchen. Here we ate. And not one word. Nothing. We finished eating, lit cigarettes. Then he said, 'I have to go. Meeting somebody in town. Be a good boy.' That's what he said: 'Be a good boy.' And I never saw him again."

Radecke looked at him for a long while. He nodded slowly.

"Oh, boys, boys. What stupid people you are! Stasiek gets killed, Dogalla from 29 goes blind from drinking paint thinner, and now this Wladek. And he looked so smart to me!"

Radecke got up. "Boys listen to me: stop committing idiocies. Use your brains..." He touched his temple with his forefinger. "Brains," he repeated, "and you can have such a quiet, good life!"

They did not move. Radecke, though a *Volksdeutscher*, was not really bad. He could not be trusted any more than any other German, they would not disclose anything to him, but as a camp leader's assistant, he was all right. He even said goodnight when he left.

Most people were in bed already. Kazik was still at the table, looking at the corner where Grabowski's bed was. They did not take away his mattress, and the reading lamp was still there, unlit.

Piotr, in his underwear, sank on his knees, and prayed in a feverish whisper for a long time. When he got up, he put his heavy hand on Kazik's arm.

"Go to bed, Kazik. It is late. I have prayed for him."

"And a lot of good it will do him, Piotr," he snarled. "The Gestapo has him!"

"A man in the Gestapo needs our prayers more than anybody else—I am a religious man, Kazik."

"Well, I am not. Leave me alone."

Piotr withdrew with dignity.

"Nor was Wladek," said Kazik in a low voice.

"Are you sure?"

He wanted to answer, but he realized suddenly that he did not know if Wladek was religious or not. In fact, he knew practically nothing about his partner, his comrade, his friend. For a moment he tried hard to recollect all his memories of him: from the day he arrived, confident, cock-sure, with his seaman's cap pulled back on his head; through all the evenings when he had read and translated for them what was written in the German paper, cheerful and clever, their joint visits to Bob and Elena, long card and booze sessions, and the last month, when Wladek had become taciturn and brooding.

It all added up to nothing. He knew nothing about Wladyslaw Grabowski. And he could not imagine what had made him steal a boat.

Kazik sighed and tried to brace himself for a long, solitary stay in Danzig. Miserable, he went to bed, and listened to the moans and snores of sleeping men. He tried to visualize where Wladek was, what he was doing at that moment. But even there he encountered a void.

Finally, late at night, Kazik Pruszynski, exhausted, fell asleep.

Escape

After three months of it, both Grabowski and Miller were tired of the game. They were in the same boat, and the game went on like this: the ship, that is the old *Marianne*, would call at a port, and Grabowski and Miller would attend to their duties, which were, respectively, those of a fireman and a chief mate.

After a day or two Miller would call the second mate to his cabin, and say, "Steinberg, keep an eye on the deck, will you? I have some business with the police ashore. I'll be back by noon, I think."

"All right, sir," Steinberg would answer, without changing the expression on his face.

"And tell the Captain, if he wakes up in the meantime, and asks about me, that I went ashore on official business."

"Yes sir. Very good, sir."

"OK, then, off you go."

Next, Miller would don his brown party uniform, which was hanging in the closet, knock on the door of his neighbor on board, the chief engineer, and say, "I am taking Grabowski for investigation ashore."

The chief, still in the comfortable warmth of his bunk, would grunt, which could mean approval as well as annoyance. Neither would make any impression on Miller, who then called Grabowski, and said, "Come on, we're going to set a few things straight."

And Grabowski's answer was, inevitably, "Yes sir, I'll be ready in five minutes." And when the time elapsed, they'd walk down the gangway, almost arm in arm, and head for the police station. If it weren't for Miller's brown uniform, they would have seemed like two buddies, shipmates, heading for the nearest bar.

That, then, was the game, and they were both tired of it.

The *Marianne*, an old rusty steamer of three thousand tons, was calling at various ports on the Baltic: Danzig, Gotenhafen, Königsberg, Lipau, Memel, Riga, Tallinn. It was the end of 1943. All these ports were German, or territories under German occupation.

Marianne—a vessel of the Merchant Marine—was chartered by the navy, and was carrying a variety of supplies to these ports. On return trips the cavernous holds would be loaded with broken tanks and other weapons in need of solid—not temporary—repairs, sacks stuffed with stained blankets, worn uniforms, and crates full of the most improbable junk, the inevitable waste and refuse of war.

These were melancholy trips: the Baltic, at best, is a bleak stretch of water, and the wartime ports of call were even bleaker; cold, dreary places, crowded with soldiers, and a civilian population tired of war and its deprivations, or numb with fear of what the next day would bring.

The people who kept the *Marianne* functioning were as diverse as the cargoes themselves. Contrary to most German vessels, which at that time had monolithic German crews, *Marianne* had five foreigners on board. The Germans, too, were a rather mixed lot. *Marianne*, of course, meant something different to every one of them.

For Captain Maximilian Roethke, age 49, she was his first command in life. When the war broke out, he was still a chief mate on the ships of the *Hanseatische Reederei* and everything seemed to indicate that he was likely to remain in that position for a long time to come.

Single, morose, and haunted by repeated attacks of jaundice, he had given up any hope of ever becoming a captain, for, in 1938, he had refused to blow his ship's whistle on the day of the Anschluss. Not that he had anything against the incorporation of Austria into the Great Reich: the subject simply did not interest him in the least. Consequently, when he was rudely awakened by a junior officer and told enthusiastically about the event, Roethke groaned, yawned, and barked, "Get the hell out of here!"

Then he tried to overcome his monstrous hangover. This happened in Bremen. The previous night was gay and tumultuous, and he could not understand why he should listen to the insane, joyous babbling of a subordinate at seven in the morning, in a matter which, as far as he could perceive through the red and black fog in his head, did not concern the ship at all. If it were a fire, an accident, or something significant—but the Anschluss?

He was very quickly made to understand what a bad mistake he had made. An official rebuke informed him in icily official terms that his very loyalty as a German was under suspicion from then on. This outrageous display of his lack of elementary, patriotic feelings will doubtless, the letter concluded, affect his further career as a naval officer.

Roethke very soon saw that it did, indeed. His name did not appear on any promotion list, from that time on, till a rainy day in the summer of 1943, when he was told in Danzig to pack his *klamotten* quickly, and to take over the *Marianne*, as her old man had had a heart attack and died.

In this way Roethke got his first command. He was too old, too sick, and too disillusioned to enjoy it properly.

Where the captain failed in his career, his chief mate, Walter Miller, was very successful in combining two careers simultaneously, one of seaman, and another of active Party member.

He was performing these combined duties with remarkable zeal. A chief mate at the age of twenty-eight was no mean achievement by itself, but his nomination to welfare officer on board the ship was—at least in his eyes—as honorable as that: as such, he was responsible for the welfare and political education of the officers and crew, for the upkeep of the patriotic atmosphere, for the preservation of the National Socialist spirit on board.

This was not an easy job on the *Marianne*. Miller, a bright young man, saw from the start that little could be done about the yellow-eyed master of the ship. He carried out his duties, that was true, doing not less, but certainly not more than what was expected of him. It was too late to kindle a fire of enthusiasm in the old, bitter man.

Worse than he were the other officers: apathetic, drunkards, or incompetent. The chief engineer was a sloppy fat man with half-closed eyes, occasionally responding to the name Neubauer, who, as far as Miller could discover, had but two passions in his life: beer, and Wild West stories. Stacks of fifty-pfennig paperback publications were piled high in his cabin, on his desk, on the untidy bed, and on boxes with empty beer bottles. Miller saw him daily going down to the engine room with a booklet sticking out of the rear pocket of his stained boiler suit. He was greatly apathetic to all other reality, but was always ready to discuss the wars of cowboys and Indians. He also had some hardcover books on the shelf: a deluxe edition of the Complete Works of Karl May. "Classics," he'd laconically comment to anybody who happened to show any interest in them.

Neubauer had his home in Stettin, was married, and had two sons, one of whom, aged fifteen, was still studying, while the other had received his Iron Cross First Class the year before, in Italy. When talking with Miller (these rare conversations were always sparked off by the chief mate), Neubauer was careful never to omit mentioning the son with the Iron Cross.

Well, the fat slob was an imbecile, no doubt about it, but Willi Steinberg, the second mate, was a whoremonger, which was worse. His mind must have been permanently flooded with sperm, Miller thought with disgust. This youngster (why wasn't he mobilized? he wondered occasionally) carried a small rectangular mirror and a comb in his side pocket, and, throwing stealthy looks on all sides, he'd always use both, trying to further improve his undeniably good looks. His tragic moments were when the burden of work on board happened to prevent him from going ashore to the whorehouses of the Baltic ports.

Then there was the crew, an odd collection of professional men, but almost without an exception overage, half-crippled ex-fishermen, the leading hand completely off his rocker, constantly talking to himself in a low voice: former longshoremen, retired firemen, and the likes.

Miller understood well that anything younger and better as human material goes had been drafted into the navy and only the scum of the ports was left to man the merchant ships, especially the ships of the *Marianne* category; he understood it well, it had been explained to him—unnecessarily, he thought, on many occasions in various party offices, and in official letters—and still he felt that this ship was especially badly handicapped. Because, on top of all this, he had five foreigners on board. Too much of the good for poor Walter Miller, industrious as he might be. Maertens and van Vogt, Belgians, and Clement the Dutchman could still be trusted, more or less. They, at least, proclaimed their loyalty to the New European Order louder and oftener than the Germans. Which, by the way, was not very difficult, Walter thought sadly. If only their zeal in work would somehow match their lofty words. Still, he felt he could tolerate, and even improve these seamen. Worse was the case of the firemen: Hrac, the Croat, and Grabowski.

Walter Miller very objectively gave allowance for the two Slavs: they were of an inferior race, handicapped by fate; it was not their fault, they were born this way. Consequently, not much was expected of them. Somebody had to feed the ship's furnaces with shovel-loads of coal, and to keep the steam up in the boilers. Ancient Romans and Greeks had their slaves pulling oars in the galleys: Miller thought it very proper that the modern equivalent of the job be carried out by the Slavs. Incidentally, the Croat seemed specially created by nature for this work, a heavy, muscular man. Still he hated the cunning sly look on his simian face.

Grabowski was another case.

From the very first moment he saw the man, with his bent spine, and long arms hanging loosely down to his knees, Miller felt an inexplicable aversion to him.

"Stand straight, man," he told him quietly, rather like a father reproaching a child. Grabowski raised his head, which did not improve his posture much. Miller looked at him for a second, then shifted his eyes to the papers on the desk. Apparently, he could not stand straight; his back must have been bent that way.

Miller read: Wladislaw Grabowski, born Warsaw, 1920. Father: Stanislaw. Mother: Victoria. Nationality: Stateless Pole. Profession: Stoker.

"You were a fireman on Polish ships before the war?" Miller asked in a mild, almost friendly tone.

"Yes sir."

"I see they sent you here from the Stutthof concentration camp. What were you doing there?"

"Six months, sir."

Evidently the cripple must have known beforehand the ship's discipline: he never missed the "sir" at the end of a sentence.

"For what?"

"Theft, sir."

"So you are a thief, are you?"

Miller now scrutinized the uplifted face of the man opposite him, and was shocked. Grabowski's skin was ashen, his eyes had almost no lashes and were unblinking. He was confronted by two gray discs with tiny, pinpoint black pupils. The Pole shifted the weight of his crooked body from one leg to the other, and rubbed the tip of his long nose with the back of his hand.

"I am a stoker by profession, sir."

Miller thoughtfully collected the papers. "Report to the *ober-heizer* and go to work. There is something wrong with you, and I don't know yet what it is, but I'll find out in time. Not now; we are sailing tonight."

"Yes sir."

He made a strange turnabout, and walked away on flat feet.

Miller spat on the floor. Goddamn it, he thought, there must be a limit to everything. Now they send us criminals from the concentration camps. What next? And there is something terribly wrong with this Grabowski. We'll try to clear it up in Riga.

The same evening, waiting on the raised forecastle for the orders to let the head-lines go, Miller, acting as chief mate now, thought again about Grabowski. And again, as before, an immediate feeling of uneasiness permeated him; it was as if tiny insects had started crawling under his shirt. He shivered, and the bosun, rubbing his gloved hands next to him, said aloud: "Bloody cold, sir. This fog penetrates right to the marrow of the bones."

When the ship was under way and everything was secured, Miller returned to his cabin. It was tiny, but very clean: the sheets and blankets on his bunk were tucked in tightly under the edges of the mattress; not even the tiniest crease spoiled the smooth surface.

On the desk stood a framed photograph of the *Führer*.

As was his habit, Miller slumped in the chair, propped his chin with both fists, and looked for a long moment at the picture.

There was Purity in this face, a superhuman purity such as mortals could never achieve. And Vision of great things to come: visions of victory, and a happy world for this race in the future. There was Wisdom in this face, too, and all-embracing, unlimited love for his People, a pure, self-sacrificing, altruistic, absolute love. The Leader loved all Germans, and every German individually: he loved Miller, Miller felt it distinctly here, on this old and rusty steamer lost in the darkness of a November night in the Baltic Sea, and Miller, in return, loved the stern man in the photograph more than anybody or anything in the whole world. He'd gladly die for him, right here and now. But he was already sailing an auxiliary cruiser, a big modern ship, somewhere in the South Atlantic, or the Indian Ocean, with a crew of dedicated, trustworthy seamen; they were sailing disguised as a merchant-ship, naturally, but when the fat British ship was in their range, the flag would quickly be changed, and the guns trained.

The treacherous British were quick on the trigger. Their ship, armed, like all ships in time of war, fired the first salvo. The whole crew of gun No. 1 fell victim to that first shot. They lay scattered on deck, in pools of blood. Miller jumped up, before anybody could grasp what had happened, before anybody could give an order. Or, perhaps—this would be a better version; he was actively trying to build up logical motives and explanations—another shot from the same first British salvo hit the bridge as well, wounding the captain. Yes, the captain should be wounded; otherwise he could not interfere. Miller manned gun No. 1 single-handed, fired, and immediately a cloud of black rose from the Englishman's bridge. Another shot and they were hoisting the white flag. Surrender. The crew cheered wildly. But he was back on the bridge in no time, taking simultaneous charge of the ship, the wounded commander, and not forgetting to give orders to fire once more from guns No. 3 and 4, to make sure that the white flag over there was not just a bad joke. We Germans can be as cunning as you bastards! Soon, a lifeboat would come over with a bunch of ragged survivors, pale and frightened all of them, and he would take them on board, and treat the British captain in a gentlemanly manner. "Captain, I am sorry I had to sink your ship, but it is war…" And then, much later, on a gray, rainy day, he'd bring the ship back to Bremerhaven, or Cuxhaven, standing in the rain on the bridge, a lonely figure in a gray leather coat, after sinking many, many other Allied ships. And after having broken through their blockade, they'd summon him to Navy Headquarters, and the bearded rear admiral wouldn't believe his eyes, "What, you are so young, acting as captain, Miller!" And then one day he'd be sent for, and go to Berlin, in a special plane perhaps, and then the moment would come that would crown his whole life even if he had to live till the age of one hundred, and no matter what else happened to him. The *Führer* would come out from the door on the left side (why on the left side, he never knew, but the door was always there on the left), escorted by many high-ranking officers and party officials. He would come up very close, look him deep in the eyes, shake his hand, and pin the Cross on his chest, and say, smiling, "In the name of the *Vaterland*, to which you have rendered such extraordinary services, Captain Miller, I thank you."

He opened his eyes slowly. He felt elated, the kind of feeling he had had as a child after attending a church service, or, later, when the last great chords of Wagner dissolved in the concert hall.

There was also an alternative story, involving a crippled submarine, but he did not like it as much as this one; evidently he was a surface-vessel sailor. Now, back in his cabin, he heard the asthmatic, idiotic thumping of Marianne's ancient engine, and saw another face in front of him: ashen-gray, with thick lips and unblinking eyes. Grabowski. He shuddered, and cried out, loud: "Tfui, verschwinde!" Disappear!

Obliging and always obedient, Grabowski vanished.

But the spell was irrevocably broken. Miller got up angrily, kicked the chair, and started to undress.

Step by step, Grabowski laboriously climbed down the iron ladder to the stokehold. It was very hot there, and the light was dim. It came from two small lamps placed near the gauge-glasses on the side of each boiler. There was also an additional source of light: the bright-red glare of fire in the ash hole, beneath the furnace.

The man whom he had come to relieve was already washing his face in a bucket of water in the corner. He was half-naked, a powerful man, with big muscles bulging under his skin. Grabowski nodded, and the man said, "Hi." He dried himself with a dirty towel, put on his shirt, and waited. Grabowski opened the doors of the furnaces with the tip of the shovel, saw that the fires were good and clean, glanced at the water gauge. Everything was as it should have been, and he said goodnight to Hrac. The other man climbed up the same way Grabowski had come down.

His colleague, relieved by Dietrich, followed him. Grabowski now nodded to Dietrich, took off his shirt, tied a sweat-rag round his neck, and started working. He had three fires to take care of. He opened the door of the first one, threw several shovels full of coal into the roaring flames very quickly, pivoted on his heels, closed the door with a bang, and opened the second door.

Here, he worked with a long iron bar, breaking the slag off the grate-bars, to let the air from below, from the ash hole, pass freely, and let the fire have the necessary draught. This was heavy work, requiring strength and a certain skill. The bar very quickly became so hot that he could only hold it with wet rags. But this time there was not much slag and cinder; the coal was of good quality. Grabowski worked on the third fire, then grabbed a bucket of water and poured it on the glowing slag on the floor, jumping back quickly: steam would fill the whole stokehold and you could get scalded badly if you did not jump back in time.

He now glanced at the manometer, making sure that steam pressure did not fall during the cleaning of the fires, then at the gauge-glass, and finally he checked the shade of the red glare in the three ash holes. That was it. He stepped back; he could afford to rest for some minutes now. He knew that Dietrich, who performed exactly the same work on his boiler, would also take a cigarette break at this moment. He knew, too, that he'd offer him half of his cigarette. As a German, he had more to smoke: his tobacco ration was twice that of Grabowski's.

They were now both directly under the ventilator pipes, letting the cold air cool the sweat on their bodies, and sharing the cigarette: Hugo Dietrich, a German fireman, a tiny, wiry man, whose hair was so blond it looked white, and Grabowski. Dietrich's moustache was like a piece of flax glued under his nose.

That was what arrested Grabowski's attention when he had descended to the stokehold of the *Marianne* for the first time. Everything was in terrible turmoil: the roar of the fires, the steam, the smoke, the heat. He was looking desperately for something to rest his eyes on for a second, for a point of salvation in this new hell, and he found Dietrich's flaxen hair and moustache.

"A Polack?" Dietrich asked. This was a nasty word, but the tone of his voice indicated he meant no offense. "Where did they dig you out of?"

"K.Z. Stutthof."

Dietrich nodded rapidly. "You look like you came from there. And I won't ask you why you were there, it is none of my business. You don't have to tell me. Can you keep up steam? Can you stoke?"

Grabowski did not answer. His eyes were now shifting from the German's face to the iron fire doors, where the flames roared, and terror was mounting again. Dietrich grew impatient: he stamped his small foot on the iron floor, but again, there was no trace of anger in his voice when he spoke. "If you can't, you'd better watch well what I'm doing, so that you can learn quickly. It's not a great art, but it is an art. Ever wanted to be an artist? No? Well, I did. You will learn. You don't really need superhuman physical strength, if you've learned the trick, and if the coal is not too lousy, of course. And remember, always keep the steam up, even if the bloody son-of-a-whore second engineer will make you regret you were ever born; or, he might even send you back to where you've just come from. Now watch."

For the first three days of Grabowski's stay on the ship, Dietrich worked for both of them, one tiny little man feeding six fires by himself, cleaning them, breaking them up, taking out the slag.

Grabowski ate, rested, and followed his every movement with pale lashless eyes. On the night watch of the third day he took the shovel, gently pushed Dietrich aside, and stood up before the boiler.

Dietrich, leaning on his shovel, looked at him working for a few minutes, then said, "Good, you can start now. Don't be afraid, you'll manage."

From then on he was on his own. In the beginning, he was much slower than Dietrich, and the German, after finishing his fires, would watch him work, and comment. "Grabowski, Poles are an inferior race: they are lazy, their brain has not developed properly. But after the war the Germans will teach them how to keep order and how to work, like I taught you. Not the Nazis, naturally. The Nazis are bastards: they want to stamp the little man into the ground, and mind you, while we are on the subject, the worst Nazi is not Hitler or Göring, but the political officer on this tub, Walter Miller. You watch out for Miller. He is a real piece of shit."

Grabowski listened and worked.

Once he mastered the art, and became a skilful—more than that—a dedicated fireman, he performed the ritual dance with the iron bar or the shovel in front of the boilers almost triumphantly. He stood straight, balancing the heavy shovel full of coal in his hands, half naked, his skin black with coal powder and glistening with sweat, sometimes chewing the rim of the sweat rag in his teeth. He could throw the coal with great precision in every corner of the long furnace, exactly where it was needed, and where he wanted it.

"You see?" Dietrich was saying. "Remember what I told you?"

He did not remember anything.

"Remember? You are only a dirty Polack, and what a regular fireman you have become! Upon my word, Grabowski, when this goddamn war is over we'll sail together on some fine ship, the same watch like here. But not an old bathtub like *Marianne*, no, sir! An elegant ship for us, my friend! Ah, I was once on the *Bremen*. Did I tell you about it? Twenty four boilers…"

He repeated the story of his glorious days on the elegant ship, before the war, interrupting for five minutes now and then, to tend his three fires, working in unison with Grabowski, so that during rest periods they could be together.

"You are a taciturn fellow, I must say," he would remark. "Don't you ever have stories to tell? I like to listen to stories and I love spinning a yarn myself. But you don't speak.

"You're all right though. Beware of that swine Miller. The chief engineer is all right, and the old man won't hurt you, and even the second mate will leave you in peace if the steam pressure is all right. But listen to Dietrich," he touched his sandy temple with his forefinger. "Beware of Miller. He is a troublemaker. What did he take you ashore in Memel for?"

"He went with me to the police."

Dietrich leaned on the shovel handle. "What for?"

"He wanted to check if my papers were in order."

Dietrich snorted contemptuously. "And?"

"They told him the papers were all right."

Dietrich opened the door of the middle furnace with the shovel, and threw ten, fifteen shovel-loads of coal quickly onto the fire. He glanced at the manometer, and looked at Grabowski. The Pole was working more slowly, but his movements were confident. He, too, closed the furnace door with the tip of his shovel, and wiped his face with the rag. Then he spoke, without being asked. "He said the Memel police are no-good buggers. He'll bring me to the Gestapo in Riga, they'll check."

"Grabowski, what has he got against you?"

"I don't know. He doesn't like my face."

"Fuck the bastard! Listen to me, if you've got nothing to hide, if you do your work well—and everybody is witness to it—you don't have to fear anything, not the Gestapo in Riga, either."

Grabowski nodded. He feared the moment the watch would be over and he would have to leave the stokehold and go upstairs.

The Gestapo official in Riga did not like the way Walter Miller talked to him in his station, but the brown Party uniform with the wide red armband made him tolerant toward the young man's rather brash manners. He listened politely to Miller's explanation, made no comment, and looked at Grabowski's birth certificate, worker's card, release card from Stutthof, and his sign-on paper from the Danzig shipping office, with the stamp of the Harbor Master, and the mark of the local Gestapo.

"I fail to understand, I am afraid," he said, "what is exactly wrong with this man."

"That's precisely what I want you to find out," answered Miller. "That's why I brought him here."

"These documents are in perfect order," stated the Gestapo man gravely. "And this is his photograph. If you want, we can check the fingerprints."

Miller shrugged with ill-concealed impatience. "It is really not my profession, all this. I only asked you to be so good as to check what is wrong with him. How you do these things is no business of mine."

The man behind the desk frowned, nodded at Grabowski, and opened the lid of a stamp cushion. Grabowski stepped nearer and extended his hand. He pressed his thumb and all fingers on the wet cushion, and left the prints on a sheet of paper.

The policeman took it, collected all the other papers, and said, "Just a moment." He left the room.

Miller and Grabowski stood before the desk. Grabowski looked up from under his brows and his eyes met the stern gaze of the *Führer* on the wall: distrustful, disapproving, deep-set eyes.

Miller was watching him from the side, trying hopefully to find a trace of some emotion on his face: hatred, disdain, fear. But nothing moved there.

"You don't like him very much, eh?" Miller said.

The Pole turned his head slowly toward him. "Sir?"

"I said, you don't like the man in the portrait very much, eh?"

Grabowski's eyes were gray, with tiny black specks of retina, either fathomless, or absolutely flat. "It is the *Führer*, sir."

Perhaps it is all a mistake, Miller thought. The man is obviously nothing more than an absolute idiot, a cretin. His brain has not developed properly. Or an evil genius of an actor. The greatest actor in the world. He sighed. He felt the other's eyes on his lips; and this, in itself, he found strange; from a distance of two or three yards he felt the other's eyes on his lips, not on his nose or chin, as if waiting for the next question to come.

Just then the Gestapo man returned. He sat down behind the desk and put the papers on it.

"They are all right, Mr. Chief Mate. They are genuine, and these are this man's fingerprints."

"Well?"

"Well, as I said, everything is in order."

"But I know it is not!"

"May I ask you how?"

"By—by intuition."

"So what do you want us to do?"

Miller felt he was again losing patience with these people: narrow-minded bureaucrats, all of them. "You don't think there's something special about this man?"

The policeman shrugged and threw a glance at Grabowski. "He looks like an idiot to me, but he is only a Pole, after all."

"Really?" Miller said with the heaviest irony he could put into the word. "Haven't you got any means of finding out the truth about people?"

The policeman looked him straight in the eyes, and suddenly it occurred to him that he finally understood what Miller wanted.

"Sit down," he said to Grabowski, pointing at the chair opposite the table.

Hesitatingly, the Pole obeyed. He sensed danger.

"Take one," the man across the desk held an open cigarette box in front of him. Again, Grabowski hesitated.

"Take one," ordered the policeman.

He took a cigarette, and put it between his lips.

The Gestapo man leaned over the table and his fist shot out like a projectile, crushing the cigarette and crushing his mouth: he fell backward with the chair. It was a heavy blow.

He laboriously got up from the floor protecting his injured face with his left hand. It was unnecessary. Nobody was thinking of hitting him again.

"Put the chair back in place where it was," said the policeman.

He obeyed, feeling his upper lip swelling badly, and blood trickling down his chin.

"Well?"

They both looked at Grabowski now, crumbs of tobacco and some cigarette paper mixed with blood on his face.

The Gestapo man laughed. "Pretty, isn't he?"

Miller shrugged. "Come. We'll go back to the ship. *Heil Hitler.*"

"*Heil Hitler,*" answered the policeman without getting up or raising his hand.

"I'm beginning to believe you're only an idiot," Miller said to Grabowski as he opened the door.

"Yes sir," said Grabowski through his swollen lips.

The man who was Wladislaw Grabowski had once been another man. As far as that went, Miller's supernatural intuition was right. Everything else he imagined or suspected in connection with Grabowski was wrong. Because the Polish fireman, who twice daily climbed slowly down the iron ladder to the stokehold of the *Marianne*, was not really a man any more, and as such, could not be dangerous to anybody, in any way, or suspected of evil-doing, nor even evil thinking. And the reason for this was that he almost did not think at all. The process of thinking had stopped some time before, when he was ultimately and finally broken, and this had happened even before a drunken capo in Stutthof slightly injured his spine with the handle of a shovel.

Grabowski, whose presence on board the *Marianne* disturbed Miller so much, was now a semi-human creature living in a tiny cube between the walls of fear on one side, and complete chaos on the other. An important factor in the working of his mind—though "working" is of course too exaggerated a word for anything that was going on in his head—was his almost complete amnesia, which blackened out practically anything that had happened before a certain date. However, he remembered very well his name and the date of his birth, his profession and nationality, indispensable details for his survival. He remembered them very well, for his will to exist, to live, remained, strangely enough, unimpaired throughout all his cruel experiences.

He also knew that he had been released from the Stutthof concentration camp, where he was serving a term for theft—an attempt to steal a boat, to be sure, but that detail was mercifully missing from the official release papers, as the German criminal code for foreigners simply did not differentiate between one kind of theft and another—in order to join a ship and perform useful work for the State and its supreme war effort.

Occasionally, very seldom, when the tumult in his head seemed to ebb a bit, when the feeling of a relative safety prevailed—as during his watches at the boiler—then, out of a complex maze, scenes would appear in his mind which belonged to the past. But he was not even sure it was his past. He would never name them his own experiences; but these visions were of extreme intensity, and he was deeply stirred by them.

He would perhaps call them fantasies if he had known the word. But Grabowski did not. Besides, these moments were rare, and the walls of sick terror on one side and of complete derangement on the other would soon threaten again to squeeze him to death, and he would need all his meager mental resources to fight against the danger of annihilation. And when another attack of these hostile and mysterious forces was repulsed, the fantasy was forgotten.

Another one was perhaps due in a few days. He had a weird sensation of it, but nothing more than that; expectations and longings were outside the realm of his thinking, far beyond his limits.

A man with that kind of mental deficiency was usually called "idiot" by others, but that was not Grabowski's nickname on board, not among the men with whom he came into daily contact (except for Miller, and even he in the beginning used the word more as an insult than a description of intellectual qualities), for he behaved in a normal way, worked well, and gave coherent answers to simple questions. When asked through the brass voice pipe, "Hey, what is the pressure on your boiler, Polack?" he'd glance at the manometer, and say: "Eight and a half, sir."

But he could hardly comment on Dietrich's remark, "What a lousy dinner they served last night, all greasy fat," because he simply did not remember what he had eaten six hours earlier. On top of that, he never seemed to pay any attention to what he was eating. Food was food, neither more nor less. Perhaps his sense of taste had been fatally injured in that far-off time when he was broken. But not his sense of survival.

"Never mind," the tiny fireman said, rubbing his hands together, "never mind, Polack. I've got something by way of compensation. Look here." With a grin, he showed him a bottle in the pocket of his jacket, which was hanging on a valve. "I lifted it from the chief personally.

And he'll never know. I substituted an identical bottle, just like it, but half-filled with water."

He laughed gaily, and slapped his hands on his thighs, and poked Grabowski in the ribs. The Pole looked at him with an expressionless face.

"Eh? Grabowski! We'll soon take care of that schnapps, you and me. And you know why I'm going to share it with you? Because you are my shipmate, and a good fireman, that's why. Even if you are only a stinking Polack. It's not your fault; you were born that way. But you are the best Polack I've ever known. Ever."

It was an easy watch. They had bunkered two days earlier, and the bunkers were full. There were two big mountains of coal in the stokehold itself, and it was good coal, and left almost no slag at all. Dietrich and Grabowski were working leisurely, and now and then the German took out the bottle, tilted his head, and took a big swig. He would then wipe the bottle with his hand and give it to Grabowski, who would follow his example. The liquid felt cool in his mouth and warm in his stomach.

"Good stuff, eh?"

Grabowski nodded. He was aware of a funny feeling in his head, a widening golden circle, sun-bright in the middle, with fire-red rims on both sides. With a push of the shovel he opened the door of the middle furnace and loaded some coal into it; the fire burnt perfectly. He looked for a long moment down the fiery flame tunnel before he closed the door. Again, he saw Dietrich's extended hand with the bottle.

"That's the last of it. Finish it, Grabowski."

Obediently he drank. The colors in his eyes grew brighter. Was it the glare from the furnace door? Grabowski took a step backward and sat down on the heap of coal. He was gazing at the bright red line in the ash hole.

What colors, he wondered. Even the iron black of the huge boiler was no longer black, there were many shades of black, very different from each other, not one of them comparable to the sparkling diamonds of the anthracite he was sitting on or the glistening black powder he was crushing with his boot on the iron floor plates.

Grabowski was taking it all in, with wide-open eyes, conscious of something happening in his head, but unable to register it as a sudden expansion of awareness. For the moment, the tiny crowded cube between fear and tumult disappeared, and then a strange picture came to his mind, almost from the Outside, as if somebody blew it through a straw into his skull. He saw a man walking in a forest. The wood was dense and silent, and the man was very hungry. He was so starved that Grabowski involuntarily swallowed saliva.

The oaks stood like temple columns, dark and solid beneath the thick roof of splendid foliage. The ground under his feet was soft, spongy, elastic, very wet from the rain.

He was thinking about eating roots; people sometimes ate roots to kill hunger, chewed them. He picked a stick and bit it. It tasted of rotten wood, saliva filled his mouth again, and he swallowed hard, but it did not affect the terrible emptiness of his stomach at all. His knees were weak, and he had an almost irrepressible urge to lie down on the moist moss, to rest. But then he saw mushrooms. Thousands of them, and he was surprised he had not noticed them before. They were white, or cream-yellow, but occasionally a dark brown mushroom popped out, bigger than the others, its cap glistening as if it had been oiled.

Mushrooms were food. But some kinds were deadly poisonous. And how to tell the difference? He crushed one of the fungi experimentally between his thumb and forefinger. He lifted his fingers to his nose: the smell was strong, dark and rich, bitter, and for the third time saliva flowed to his mouth.

Grabowski felt a hand on his shoulder: Dietrich was looking at him, worried. "Listen, chum, you're not drunk, are you? From that bit of schnapps?"

"No," he answered quietly. "I am not drunk. It's all right."

"Well, I thought... Because we still have half an hour till..."

Grabowski shook him off gently, and moved further into the

forest. Now he crouched low, and, sitting on his haunches, picked three, then four mushrooms, only the brown ones. The white ones, perched on their thin stalks had a more treacherous air. He chewed slowly and deliberately—heads only—and was surprised how quickly the terrible emptiness in his belly disappeared. If anybody would have asked him now if he were hungry, he'd answer in the negative, and yet he had eaten only a few crumbs of the caps!

The tiredness of his limbs was gone. After a few minutes he felt strangely light-footed. He could run. He felt an urge to run.

Dietrich was not in the forest, yet his presence was felt and could not be ignored. He was there, hovering somewhere outside this picture, outside this world, urging him to feed the fires, and for a few moments they were shoveling the coal in unison, each one standing before his boiler. Grabowski was impatient and a little worried that he might lose his woods and mushrooms in the meantime. He knew that once they were lost he'd never be able to return to that forest. He clung desperately to the taste in his mouth. The fires were again under control, and the flames were roaring, and he was back in the forest, which had changed a little. Low clouds bulged, all the colors were sharper. A hand had removed slightly opaque lenses from his eyes, which had blurred his vision before, and now the heavy stems of trees, the vast mass of green above, and the steel-blue clouds all shone with an intense light. They suddenly stood out clearly.

A thick shaft of sunlight, like a slanted tunnel, descended from an opening in the sky. A thin rain had begun. He did not mind. His clothes were still soaked, but it was not annoying. He was distracted by the brilliant clearness of his vision and by the radiance of the colors. He walked lightly among the trees, his feet treading the soft, spongy ground, till he arrived at a small clearing.

From here a rainbow rose, almost perpendicularly, in a giant multi-colored arch to the sky. Unhesitating, he moved forward, sinking immediately to his knees in red and violet shining dust. Submerged totally in warm soft colors, he started climbing up the structure. There was no need to move his arms and legs, the gentle current of the rainbow carried him up, higher and higher, above the treetops, to the summit. There the flow stopped, and he rested, for the first time in a long, long time, on the top of the rainbow.

There was a happy smile on his face, and his eyes were closed, and when he opened them, two guards were watching him with a peculiar expression, guns slung over their shoulders, their uniforms wet and heavy from the rain. He kept smiling, kneeling in the small clearing among the trees, and he was still smiling when Dietrich shook him by the arm. "Good God! Grabowski! It is time! They are coming, get up!"

So the happy watch ended, and the forest, the mushrooms, and the rainbow were lost, irretrievably. Next morning, in Königsberg, Miller told him, "Grabowski, come on. We're going ashore. Perhaps the Königsberger police can find out what's wrong with you."

The Königsberger police were as helpless as those in Riga, and those in Memel, and Lipau, and Stettin. Now and then, out of sheer desperation, and in order to get rid of Miller, they would beat up Grabowski, more or less severely; usually less, like the man in Memel.

Escorting him back to the ship one evening, Miller had to drag the Pole up twice, when his knees gave out under him and he collapsed on the street. He sprinkled some water from a puddle on Grabowski's swollen face, and the man came to, and opened his eye; the other was black and closed.

"Get up, man! We must be back on board by ten!"

Grabowski mumbled something, but got up heavily, and staggering, started walking.

Miller, tired and disgusted, thought that the next time perhaps he would send somebody else with the Pole to the police, perhaps the boson, the second engineer. After the investigation, the police would have to take the trouble of delivering him back to the ship. But he realized suddenly that he had no authority to order anybody on board to do this for him. Who would do it for him of his own free will? No one else was interested in this case at all, which gradually became the pivotal point around which his own thoughts revolved.

He remembered that a short time after Grabowski's arrival,

he had asked the chief engineer, "How's your new fireman, Neubauer?"

"Which new fireman?"

"The Pole, Grabowski."

"Never knew there was someone called that on board."

"What? You mean..."

"Bless your heart, Miller, did you really think I knew all my firemen by name? If there really is a Polack on board I guess he's all right, otherwise the donkeyman would report to me."

"Neubauer, don't you ever take a personal interest in your crew?"

"Never."

"On principle?"

"On principle. Besides, that's your job as welfare officer, isn't it?"

Miller answered grimly. "It is."

That was their attitude, all of them, with no exception. Narrowminded, egotistic, dumb. No trace of comradeship, cooperation.

Swine, bastards.

He exhausted his list of epithets, pushing Grabowski in front of him, and repeating mechanically from time to time, "On, on, man. We have to be back on board by ten." I wonder how he'll manage to work there, after that beating, he thought. He knew that Grabowski would have to start his watch at midnight. Apparently part of the indescribable something that was wrong with Grabowski was his toughness.

Near the entrance to the port they almost stumbled over a couple in a tight embrace. They could hardly be seen in the feeble light of a street lamp, whose glass was painted thick blue: blackout precautions were taken very seriously at the time.

"Excuse me," mumbled Miller automatically, and exclaimed: "Steinberg!"

"Sorry, Chief," answered the second mate, sheepishly. The woman was pulling up her panties, and averted her face.

"What are you doing here?"

"Well, you see, Chief…"

"Aren't you ashamed? Under a lamppost? Can't you go to … to some other place?"

"The captain only gave me half an hour off."

"Grabowski!" shouted Miller, for the Pole was walking slowly like a mechanical toy wound up with a key. "Grabowski! Halt!"

The man stopped obediently. Miller turned again to Steinberg. *"Pfui!* An officer of the Merchant Marines!"

Mysteriously, the woman disappeared, as if someone had pulled a string and hauled her up to the clouds.

"Who was the woman?" asked Miller, rage mounting in him.

But Steinberg recovered himself. "Who did you think she was, the Queen of England? A whore, a harbor whore! And you'd better leave people alone and stop being a nuisance!"

"Who's a nuisance? I warn you, Steinberg, it's my duty on board to look into people's activities…"

"Well, you have that Grabowski there," retorted Steinberg, turning his back on him and walking quickly away.

Miller, shocked, remained alone under the lamppost. Barely a hundred yards from him he could just make out Grabowski's black silhouette, standing like a monument.

A thin rain started again. A steamer's siren hooted. I have Grabowski, thought Miller, bitterly. A little damaged right now, but I have this Grabowski. "I'll teach that kid of a second mate a lesson," he said aloud. But in his head the same sentence repeated itself hollowly, as on a gramophone whose needle was stuck in the same groove of the record: I have Grabowski.

The police—or Gestapo—somewhere, somehow, sometime, might discover the terrible mystery of the fireman, penetrate to the core of his secret, if there was any, if his intuition was not wrong from the very beginning, and then Grabowski would disappear without a trace, like Steinberg's whore from under the lamppost. Suddenly, like a revelation it struck him: he might lose Grabowski one day. What would he, Miller, do then?

Perhaps dream about Grabowski the same way he was dreaming about heroic deeds on auxiliary cruisers and submarines? Terrible images started closing in on him from all sides. He felt the hair on his scalp bristling. "Grabowski!" he yelled.

And from the darkness came a muffled sound, "Yes sir."

"Oh, Grabowski…On, on, man. We must be back on board by ten…"

On some ancient church tower in Königsberg, an old clock started solemnly to strike the hour.

Grabowski liked it down in the stokehold better than anywhere else. If he could have smiled, there would have been a broad smile on his face when he climbed down the iron ladder. As it was, there was an equivalent of a smile, or all the ingredients of a smile inside him.

Outside, the world was cold, windy, rough. Walter Miller was there: police officials, party officers, Gestapo men. All those who were beating him up, kicking him, torturing him. A horrible tension was there.

In contrast, the stokehold, full of acrid smoke, was cozy: a haven of peace in a hostile world, a hiding place. In the back were the coal bunkers, and two small mountains of coal, like glaciers crawling down a Swiss valley. In front, two huge round Scotch ovens with fires roaring inside, and a red glare touching everything with warm colors. The place was small, enclosed. He had a feeling of security there. Nobody would come there, except Dietrich and himself. The other firemen disappeared when they came to take over the watch. And when the other two came back to relieve Dietrich and himself, they would leave, Grabowski reluctantly. He was always glad to come back there. But this time he came back with difficulty. His head swam, and there was a searing pain in his leg. The man from border police, enraged by Miller's persistence, had kicked him viciously with his boots.

Dietrich gave him one quick look and whistled. "Very bad this time, eh, Grabowski? Where did the swine take you? The Gestapo?"

Grabowski nodded.

"OK, buddy. Now you lie down here and rest a bit: you know

it's not difficult for me. No, don't protest! You can't work in this condition. Believe me, when the war is over, we'll work together on a decent ship, and there'll be no pig of a Miller upstairs, trying to do you in…and no Gestapo either…"

He continued for a while, but Grabowski did not hear him. His eyes closed in the same moment his body rested on the coal. It was soft coal, almost coal dust, no big pieces, and he felt comfortable.

He came to very quickly, and peered between the big iron bars of a railway wagon: the guard, dozing at the gangway of a Swedish steamer, changed his position suddenly; stamping his big boots, he walked a few steps toward the ship's bow, turned, and went back to the gangway. He had evidently not the slightest intention of leaving the place. Perhaps he had very strict orders. He was standing now with his back to Grabowski. The man lit his pipe and a cloud of bluish smoke rose above the heavy shoulders of his greatcoat and hood. Cautiously, Grabowski moved his arms and legs. It was painful. The weather was very cold and he had been lying under the wagon for a long time. Too long. This was hopeless, he knew, looking at the soldier, and at the ship with a huge Swedish flag painted on its side, all bathed in the bright, surgical light from the ship's mast-lights. The ship would sail very soon, some time tonight, and the guard wouldn't leave her till the last line was rolled up on deck.

And yet he stayed, hour after hour, until he heard the barking of the dogs in the distance. Then he knew for sure that he would not escape on this ship. They were coming with dogs to search for stowaways.

As the barking grew louder he slowly retreated, looking in all directions, till the darkness in the port took him mercifully under its protection. He turned back, only once, just in time to see the search party climb the gangway: four, five men, two big dogs tugging on their leashes. Then he felt a tin cup pressed into his hand and Dietrich said, "Drink, man, drink; it will make you feel better."

He raised his head a little, reluctantly, because it was so comfortable on the pillow of coal-dust, and took a sip. It burned his lips.

"Good, eh?" Dietrich chuckled. "It's half schnapps, half water. It will help, it will warm up your heart, if Poles have hearts. I must tell you frankly, I have no liking whatsoever toward your race. You're an exception. Well, drink man! I have no time: this bloody coal-dust produces quite a lot of slag, see?"

Grabowski drank half a cup, and moved his head away.

"Enough?"

He nodded.

"OK then. Keep resting. I have to work, or all hell will break loose."

Grabowski slumped back and closed his eyes. He was not back in the forest. The interior was white; it was a church.

"Pray with me," whispered the pastor.

"I'm not a Christian."

"Never mind. It does not make any difference."

"It makes all the difference."

"Not here. Not in the house of God."

The pastor closed his eyes and lowered his head, his lips moving. Grabowski looked at the black geometrical figure on the wall, but could not see Christ's face; it was too far. One thing was certain: the man on the cross was stone-dead; nobody could survive in the ringing silence of the white-walled hall.

The pastor opened his eyes and looked at him inquiringly. "Cannot pray?"

"Is it the prayer for the dead?"

"This is the prayer for the salvation of your soul."

"Then you gave up everything else of mine?"

"Listen, I told you already this church is under the constant surveillance of the Gestapo. I really cannot help you. I don't know if they won't come in here five minutes from now, and take you and me with them."

"No possibility of getting in touch with Scandinavian sea captains? They visit here sometimes, don't they?"

The pastor shook his head.

In the piercing, overwhelming silence, Grabowski said, "It really was the prayer for the salvation of my soul."

"Try to pray. It will give you comfort, and strength."

"No," answered Grabowski. "Comfort I'll never know, no matter if I live another day or a hundred years. The problem is strength. I'm afraid I'm not very strong now."

Perhaps another day in the "stand-up-cell" in Neugarten Gestapo headquarters would do the trick, or perhaps they should have left him hanging with his arms bound behind his back from the pole—the *slupek*—in Stutthof, for a few hours more.

But they did not, and he was victorious by the virtue of his unique achievement.

He chuckled, and Dietrich, wiping the sweat off his face with a rag looked at him. "I see you're quite happy, chum. We're almost finished, you'll be in your bunk soon."

Now, it was a face, but the name did not come through. The face was dark, with a receding forehead and a jutting chin. It was lit from below with a match. *Pssst! The enemy is listening!* He gave the man a big, fat envelope, and the man took it, and smiled.

The match went out, the night was very dark and immense, expanding.

The name was there, near, somewhere, behind his eyes, on the back of his tongue. He opened his mouth to say it, and he could not. He made a conscious mental effort now, a labor he had not performed for eons of time, and sweat burst out on his face. His hands were shaking.

Dietrich looked at him, worried.

Something is happening to him, something is very wrong with him, he thought. Then, once more, the Pole opened his mouth.

"Ro -o -o -sti!" he shouted. "R o -o o -o -sti!"

He roared with a wild laughter, that shook his whole body, a waterfall of roaring laughter, cascade after cascade, again and again, until he collapsed on the heap of coal.

The evening before the arrival of the *Marianne* in Danzig, the

265

officers were sitting in their tiny messroom, drinking coffee. This was almost a ritual, because the coffee served at 20:15 in the messroom was real coffee, not the ersatz stuff, which nobody could get used to, and which everybody was drinking daily, cursing aloud, or in the depth of one's heart, according to one's boldness.

They, the officers of the Merchant Marine, were among the most privileged, they could still drink real, genuine coffee once a day. They were duly aware of their privileged position over the unfortunates ashore, and the drinking was done in silence, like a prayer.

The captain smacked his lips and put his cup on the saucer. He lit a cigarette, drew in the smoke deeply, and again raised the cup to his lips. The smell of coffee, the smell of good tobacco, almost as it was in peacetime. Miller, opposite, scrutinized closely. How old this man looked! There were many wrinkles on the captain's dour face, and his hair was dull gray. How would he behave in an emergency, Miller thought, a man who complained every day about the pains in his back, and whose hand was shaking badly, even now, while holding the coffee cup? He should retire, thought Miller. But naturally there was no retirement in wartime. If he quit the sea, they'd send him to the front. Eastern front, most likely. A wreck.

The question is, thought Captain Roethke, what will happen to me when the war is over? Will they keep me on or not? They may or they may not. There will be a shortage of ships, and a lack of able men, worse than now. Look at your present shipmates: the chief engineer's eyes were almost closed. He was drinking, naturally. He had not enough booze to get properly drunk, but the few glasses daily kept him in a kind of half-drunken stupor. Look at your chief mate: a swashbuckling kid, flies in his head, and busy with his silly Party business more than with his job. Luckily, the bosun was competent. And then this bunch of foreigners. The captain shook his head involuntarily.

"Tomorrow at eight, Danzig, eh?" he said, just to push himself away from his gloomy thoughts.

"Yes. Sure. I'm taking Grabowski to the Gestapo there. For investigation." Miller said, louder than necessary.

266

The chief engineer woke up and chuckled. The captain grinned.

"I must say, Miller, it is strange, your dealing with that Pole, kind of an obsession with you, isn't it?" he said. "What do you suspect him of? What do you think? He's an Englishman in disguise, or a Russian spy?"

"To me, he sometimes looks more like a Jew, or a Gypsy, with that crooked back of his," added the chief engineer.

Idiots, Miller thought. Both absolute idiots. A Jew! A Gypsy! A Russian spy! He shook his head. Both men were his superiors in rank, he couldn't allow himself to forget it.

"I wouldn't think so," he said. "I was told by specialists that Grabowski is actually from a noble Polish family, kind of a minor aristocracy. You'd hardly expect to find any Gypsy or Jewish blood there, eh chief? Nor Russian. Certainly not English. Your ideas are rather strange, gentlemen."

The chief laughed hoarsely. "Then what are you after, for goodness sake? The man is doing his job, I am told, and he looks like a degenerate, which is not his fault. Agreed, perhaps he is one. I don't expect superior intelligence among my firemen."

How silly they were! He was sure they were jeering behind his back, laughing at him, and yet he tried to explain to them: "I really don't know what it is, gentlemen, but I do know, deep in my heart, call it intuition or feeling, or call it whatever you like. I know there is something wrong with that man. I'm not a professional investigator, and that's why I drag him to the police, to the Gestapo, to the people who should know how to get at the truth. That's their job, isn't it? Unfortunately, they have a strange attitude in this case. I'm sorry to say, many of them are not very competent. If I, for instance, went about my work in the same way these men go about theirs, this ship would have been at the bottom of the sea long ago."

The captain and the chief engineer touched wood simultaneously. A pompous fool, the captain thought bitterly. He really thinks he's running this tug!

Infantile, thought the chief engineer. No use arguing. He said

"Anyhow, if you get him off in Danzig, Miller, and the Gestapo detains him, do see that I get a replacement in time."

"Let the Harbor Office worry about it, chief," retorted Miller icily.

The captain got up slowly, and groaned. "My poor back! The weather will change in a day or two," he said. "We'll probably get the report at the end of your watch, Miller. Maybe a bit later. Good night to you."

Good night, Captain," said the chief engineer.

"*Heil Hitler,*" murmured Miller.

Three Lancaster bombers were flying blind as bats. It was bitter cold in the planes, and the pilots and gunners were freezing in their flying jackets, staring into the black void.

As they plunged deeper and deeper into the night, invisible in the impenetrable darkness, the air-raid warning sirens sounded an alarm in Bremerhaven, in Bremen, Hamburg, and Lübeck.

By the time they flew somewhere north of Lübeck—only the navigators had the vaguest notion of their whereabouts—the all-clear signal was given in Bremerhaven, Bremen, Hamburg, and countless people deep in shelters gave a sigh of relief, and went upstairs to continue their interrupted sleep in bed.

Past Lübeck the three Lancasters flew, over the stormy Baltic Sea, and the alarm was given now in Swinemünde, Stettin, Danzig and Gotenhafen.

Up in the dark void, the instruments on board the planes told the crews they had reached their target. Blindly they dived, through many layers of clouds, till the fat bellies of the planes almost touched the rolling waves. Then they dropped their loads, and turned back, climbing quickly up again. Their mission was accomplished. An all-clear was given a half an hour later all along the coast of Germany.

No bombs fell on this rainy, windy night, and the anti-aircraft guns never went into action.

But the heavy sea mines, each one weighing almost a ton, splashed into the sea, and traveled like rocks, forty fathoms down to the bottom. There, an anchor dug itself into the ground, and each mine climbed back up slowly on a steel cable, until it reached a point some two yards below the surface. There it remained, bobbing slightly, its four deadly fingers pointing outward, treacherously awaiting the ships to come. The explosion, which occurred at 4:20 A.M., swept Walter Miller, the officer on watch, off his feet. He was standing on the left wing of the bridge trying to shake off the drowsiness of sleep still heavy on his eyes, in the damp, cold air.

He saw a flash of blinding fire-like lightning, heard the thundering noise, and fell onto the deck, smashing his left hand against the iron railings. He lost consciousness a moment after he felt the nauseating pain. The helmsman felt the floor disappear from under his feet, but clung to the spokes of the wheel, and knew that nothing could release the iron grip of his hands: it was like rigor mortis.

The *Marianne* stopped her progress through the water, some forty miles northeast of her port of call, Danzig.

Captain Roethke, up on the bridge two minutes after the ship struck the mine, thought it was surprising that she had not broken in two and sunk immediately. She was sturdier than anybody had thought, yet it was clear she was going to sink. The initial list to the port side was increasing gradually.

She must have a great big hole in her side, the captain thought. And then, bitterly: it had to happen to me.

In deep darkness, he acted blindly, automatically, did all the things that had to be done. He sounded the general alarm, but it failed to work after two seconds, like the last groan of a mortally wounded animal.

Then, hearing voices of people running upstairs, he laboriously climbed to the starboard side, on all fours, because the inclination of the deck was growing. It was as if he was walking up the side of a wall.

The crew was all right, after all, he thought. They did not panic, they swung the only usable lifeboat over the side, a few sailors were already inside, but most of them were crowded near the rail waiting.

Then a strange thing happened. The ship did not heel over

more to the wounded side, as one would have expected; instead, her bow sunk deeper into the sea. The captain, looking forward, thought he saw a few men running from the forecastle quarters toward the central deckhouse, where the boat was. Miller, on the bridge, remained unconscious only for a minute or two. As he came to, *Marianne* straightened herself a little, but the bow sank deeper, lower. Miller rose slowly to his feet, just in time to see the raised forecastle already covered by water, and the seamen running toward the masthouse. It was difficult, for the ship was steadily inclining, and they had to climb the steep slope of the deck.

Miller could hear the boat being swung out on the davits, somewhere behind him. He heard excited human voices, but, inexplicably, he kept watching the struggle of the survivors from the forecastle in their desperate attempt to reach the lifeboat.

"Miller?" the captain's voice boomed. "The boat is out. Come along!"

"There are some men from the forecastle trying to get to her. Let's wait a second."

"Are you crazy? She'll go down any moment!"

Grabowski must be one of the three men, Miller thought. Grabowski must get into the boat for investigation tomorrow in Danzig.

The ship stopped moving for a moment: Grabowski must be saved. He could not afford to lose Grabowski. "I'll run and give them a hand," he shouted. "Wait one moment with the boat."

He did not wait for the captain's answer. He was already climbing down the ladder to the main deck. Once there, he realized he could not reach the men, and that they had no chance to get to the deckhouse. Apparently, they had finally understood it at the same time, for Miller saw them mounting the bulwark slowly and jumping into the sea, one after the other. He decided to follow them, but the *Marianne* lurched violently forward. He lost his grip, and slid on his back the length of the slippery iron deck, until he banged his head hard on a bulwark stanchion.

Grabowski was the last of the inhabitants of the forecastle to jump overboard. He saw the others do it, desperately, and still he hesitated. He saw the outline of the deckhouse, the silhouette of the boat swinging on the davits, and beyond, the unnaturally raised stern, towering over the whole length of the ship. A wave leaped over the low bulwark. He jumped.

I should know who is still missing, thought the captain. Count them. But there was no longer time for it. The ship started sliding down, and those who were still on deck jumped into the boat.

"Let's go! Let's go!" somebody shouted.

"She's sinking!"

So finally, he too jumped, and the lifeboat lurched and hit the side of the sinking ship several times, but at last it was afloat, and jumping high on the waves, the men working the oars frantically.

There was a deafening noise as the boilers tore down from their trestles and rushed forward in the belly of the ship, smashing bulk-heads. Then they saw quite near, and towering high, darker than the black sky, the stern of the ship, her rudder and propeller, and they were pulling on the oars in a fury, to get away from it. Finally *Marianne* turned over and plunged into the depths with a horrible roar.

The lifeboat danced as on a carousel, caught in a huge whirlpool. Somehow, they were not sucked in.

"Pull hard," cried the captain, and they pulled with supernatural force, to drag the boat away from destruction.

"Easy now," Roethke said after a minute.

Now that the last of the *Marianne* had disappeared beneath the surface, everything seemed suddenly much quieter to the people in the boat. They stopped rowing and looked around with dazzled faces.

Roethke's leg hurt badly—he had fallen on his knee when jumping from the deck—but he started feeling it only now. He thought it must be broken.

"Who is missing? Is anybody missing, men?"

A confusion of voices; they started looking at each other, touching each other. Up till now it was only the sinking ship, the whirlpool, and the oars they were pulling. The sea was almost calm, the boat was rocking gently. Out of the crew of twenty-four, five men were missing: the second engineer, the Croatian fireman Hrac, the Polish Grabowski, the able-bodied Belgian seaman Maertens, and the chief mate Miller.

"Look out! Look sharply. They may be swimming around here." Roethke gave this order because he knew that this was the order to be given. He knew with certainty that there was no chance of finding anybody in practically total darkness. Besides, the water was ice cold; nobody could survive in that sea for more than a few minutes.

"Look out! Look sharply, men!" called Roethke again. Pieces of flotsam were now on the surface, as if the sea, having swallowed *Marianne*, vomited part of its prey. Planks, pieces of broken furniture, papers, rags, emerged slowly from the depths.

"Here! Here! There is something there! There!" The man pointed excitedly at a black-brown-white blotch a short distance away, and the boat moved toward it.

It was difficult to haul it in, because the three components were joined together strongly, as if welded: a half-broken door, a man in long underwear with half of his body spread on this door, his legs dangling in water, and another man, clutching to the first one's thighs.

Hard as they worked, the men in the boat could not pull apart this bizarre trinity. The boat keeled over up to the gunwale and others hurried to the opposite side to counterweigh and prevent it from capsizing. They pulled it in, finally, unseparated: the wooden door, Grabowski on it, and Miller holding his legs.

Roethke, from his position in the stern of the boat at the tiller, asked, "Who's that?"

When they told him, he mumbled under his nose: "He's bringing him to investigation, most likely."

He waited a few minutes, before he gave an order. "Steinberg and two others, take care of them, and the rest of you, keep on the look-out! There could be more of them!"

And the boat moved slowly again, amid the floating wreckage, crossing the place of the disaster.

"Are they OK?" asked the captain.

"The Pole's dead; the chief mate is still alive, I think."

"Try giving him some brandy...Keep on looking, men...perhaps we can still find the others!"

Dietrich, kneeling over Grabowski, felt the man was ice-cold, as cold as the water. There was no sign of breath: his heart must have failed after a few minutes in the water. The dead man's eyes and mouth were open, which made his face grin sardonically.

"Dead, poor bastard," said Dietrich, more to himself, than to anybody else. Miller was still alive, paradoxically. Submerged in water, he must have kicked like a mad fool, and this had kept his circulation going. The Pole must have rested immobile on the door and frozen to death.

But Miller was unconscious, and there was a big gaping wound in his head, surrounded by coagulated blood. His breathing was coming in rapid, rattling sequences, and when Steinberg tried to force some brandy through his clenched teeth, it spilled on his chin.

"Drink, you bastard," hissed Steinberg, and the two men who were rhythmically moving Miller's arms and legs stopped for a moment.

"Who told you to stop?" barked Steinberg angrily, and the men resumed their work hastily.

"Better try rubbing his skin with something, Steinberg," said the captain. In the same moment, Miller opened his eyes.

"He's alive, captain," Steinberg said.

Miller moved his lips feebly. Steinberg again took the bottle of brandy, but Miller let his head roll over to one side. His eyes were now opposite Grabowski's white hand, not more than two inches away. Then his head rolled back, and he whispered, "Grabowski?"

"What?" said Steinberg, leaning over him.

"Grabowski?"

"Grabowski's dead."

"Impossible!" Miller's eyelids drooped.

"Stone-cold dead, Miller."

From the stern, the captain said: "How is he, Steinberg?"

"I think he's fallen into a coma again, sir. But he is alive."

"Go on working on him."

These, again, were the proper commands, he knew. Already he could hear the questions they would ask him ashore, and his answers. Up till now, he knew the answers. He had behaved in this critical hour in accordance with all the rules. His ship was torpedoed, or had struck a mine—one could never be sure—and had exploded. She had sunk within—he looked at his wristwatch and tried to calculate—say, fifteen minutes. They had lowered the only boat available. Yes, he left his ship last. Yes, they had circled the place for an hour. One body was recovered, and one survivor: a dead Polish fireman, and the chief mate. The search had continued for an hour. No other survivors. Set course for Danzig. Mast and sail rigged, a weak wind blowing north by northwest, which helped a bit. Wind force? Perhaps 3–4. The crew took turns rowing. Arrived at Hela at 15:00. Three o'clock in the afternoon. Thank you, captain. The inquiry will continue tomorrow, at nine o'clock. Yes, sir. Thank you. That's all. *Heil Hitler.*

The sky very gradually changed its color to dark-gray, and rain started falling. The men in the lifeboat were cold, wet, and very miserable. The sea was almost calm, and the boat slid slowly on its surface in silence.

The big sail flapped in the weak breeze and the waves under the wooden bottom of the boat made a strange lapping noise, like a big animal drinking greedily. The oars were moaning rhythmically in the tholes.

Roethke's knee was hurting badly. He hoped that Steinberg could relieve him at the tiller so that he could lie down on the floor and doze for perhaps half an hour.

"How is Miller, Steinberg?" asked the captain.

But just then, Miller started coughing violently. It sounded like the dry barking of a little dog, but the coughing fit shook his whole body. His face grew red, and he started beating the floor with his heels.

The two seamen moved slightly aside. Only Steinberg kept

kneeling over the chief mate, watching, fascinated, what was happening.

It did not take much time. Suddenly Miller's whole body stiffened, he opened his mouth, and a loud sigh escaped from it.

"How is he, Steinberg?" repeated Roethke after a minute.

"Dead, sir."

"Are you sure?"

The Anatomy and Death of a Dream

Things were simpler once I'd reconciled myself to the thought that the deformations of my mind were a direct result of short circuits in the Broca and Wernicke areas of my brain. To tell the whole truth, when I finished writing *Distortions or Variations on the Theme of Broca and Wernicke*, I was convinced that it was the very last piece of writing to emerge from my pen. I thought that I had ten books to my credit and it was certainly enough for a minor writer of my stature. I had never craved fame.

I stopped accusing my wife of accelerating the tempo of my life (accusing the person nearest to you is a natural impulse hardly to be resisted), since it had dawned on me that this acceleration was not prompted by her ill will or hostility toward me, but was an objective phenomenon with an explanation possibly in some Einstein equation I was unable to understand because of my total ignorance of the principles of higher mathematics and physics.

Mind you, what I am talking about is the acceleration of the tempo of life. These days I watch a lot of TV and it has occurred to me that the images on the screen have been flitting in front of me more quickly than in the past, or could this be just another distortion?

This observation applies especially to commercials. There are only two possibilities: either the people who made these ads think they should be shorter and thus more profitable (more money for less time) or the perception of the general public, the reactions of their eyes, nerves or brains is speedier than mine. That would be sad, because it would confirm the theory of the brain's distortions. At this moment my concern is the velocity of the TV images—a purely technological aspect of the small screen—but other aspects are a completely different story.

For example, I could question the ethical or moral validity of an ad that presents American teenagers devouring hunks of fried chicken, an ad that interrupts a documentary film about starvation in Sudan—skeleton children and dying adults covered with festering wounds and flies.

It prompts me to ask myself if any moral standards are applied to TV programming (including advertising) or if profit is the sole and all-embracing motive of the tube. Just before writing *Distortions*, I had minor surgery involving a local anesthetic. Well, it wasn't a joyous experience, but less annoying than I had anticipated. Since it involved an intravenous connection, a tricky procedure because my veins are brittle, I had to sign a document allowing the doctors to apply a numbing device to my throat and releasing them from liability should anything go wrong. Then I was told to lie on my left side and try to sleep, which I did. During the following half an hour, the doctors dilated my esophagus and removed scar tissue from a previous operation that interfered with swallowing food. I felt no pain. An obedient patient, I slept during the operation. But it was not a peaceful sleep. Only when my wife brought me home did I sleep a proper sleep, complete with dreams.

As usual, the beginning of the dream was a sea journey, this time on a trawler at night along the southern coast of Israel. Unusual, however, were the sounds and smells that proved to be the main features of the dream, since there were no people in it. I was standing on the trawler's deck, deeply inhaling the fragrance of the orange groves ashore, which were in full bloom. In spring, the breeze carries the scent a considerable distance over the water to the ships traveling this route. The scent of orange blossom, pervasive in its volume and strength, is absolutely intoxicating, bitter and sweet at the same time, sexual, and almost painful in its unbearable loveliness.

There were also sounds in this dream. Unless you happen to be a sailor I doubt you are familiar with the swishing sound made by a ship's prow as it cuts through the water. I would lean against the trawler's low bulwarks and listen attentively to the murmur the water made passing along the ship's sides. I learned many secrets that the sea whispered to me during the soft, moonlit nights fragrant with the scent of citrus flowers and now, as I was not able to sail anymore, they returned to me in my dreams, for which I was grateful.

Reader, kindly bear in mind that I am an old man, and my several strokes and cancer operation have confined me largely to an investigation of the mind (and I admit that such investigations are apt to degenerate into a very egocentric or even misanthropic quest). Thus I became fascinated by the nature of the mechanism in my brain which lets me replay to myself the music of a Mozart piano concerto without opening my mouth or even uttering a sound: where is this knowledge stored? And now, the music in my dream, which brought me to the sound of the water, heard fifty years ago. A mystery I might have understood had I studied neurology in my youth instead of having had to deal with Adolf and the ships.

I have mentioned my fascination with Einstein before, a man who could perhaps explain the phenomenon of the acceleration of the world. But even here my ignorance is an obstacle. All I know about Einstein is that he overturned classical Euclidean planimetry and sterometry that I had been taught in school by introducing Time as an additional dimension. Later I read somewhere that, angered by Brown's particles experiment and the principle of determinism, Einstein said, "I refuse to believe God plays dice with the world he created." This on the cosmic scale. But based on the experience of my own long life, I am inclined to believe we are very much like Brown's particles: we are accidents, we simply appear by no choice of our own. As Saul Bellow says, we make what we can with the means available. We must accept this mixture as we find it: the immunity of it, the tragedy of it, the hope of it. "The impurity of it," Bellow says, and I think I can put under this heading my dreams, which pervade so much of my writing. Bellow says the soul escapes from the body during sleep, though I am not convinced it is so. I am rather inclined to believe that the dreams are a mirror reflecting the soul's remembrance of things past. For example, I vividly recall an important episode in my life featuring strange occurrences and an individual named Rosti. These memories returned often in my dreams, distorted as in a fading mirror, until many years later something happened to help me get rid of that particular dream, since it never appeared again.

I was living at my kibbutz then and was temporarily in charge of volunteers from abroad who arrive in spring and stay till late autumn with the regularity of migrating birds. They then leave for India or Nepal or Thailand where grass is both more readily available and cheaper. One morning a man arrived in my office, and said, "I'm from Buenos Aires."

He was a swarthy man of middle height, had a shirt that looked like an explosion in a paint factory and a pair of very faded jeans. He also had a cleft chin, a narrow, receding forehead, bushy eyebrows and large ears. He reminded me so much of Rosti, who had played a dominant role in my life in an unforgettable year, 1943, that I felt tempted to ask him if Rosti were his elder brother, or maybe his father.

But the illusion ended abruptly when my eye noticed the tiny Star of David dangling from a gold chain below his prominent Adam's apple. He could have been no relative of Rosti, for Rosti's chain sported a golden cross and his signet ring a likeness of St. Christopher.

Amazing the details I remembered, after forty years, how I had pondered if I could trust a man I didn't know with my story, telling him that I had escaped from the Warsaw Ghetto to flee to Sweden then to England to fight the Germans. Let's return for a moment to

Einstein: dice or no dice, the mathematical probability of a meeting between me, going then by the name Grabowski, a recent escapee from the Warsaw Ghetto, and an Argentinian called Rosti, were one to four hundred billion. Given the circumstances and the time of meeting, multiply this number by another two hundred billion. And yet we did meet, and did whatever we did successfully, and it was a good thing, and perhaps the only one that matters in the final count.

At the time, the element of communication was of paramount importance. I spoke no Spanish; Rosti knew a little German and a little English and that's how we managed to talk at this first meeting, which took place after I chased him for a couple of nights. I understood he was scared, how could he know I was not one of the Gestapo men, the whole port area of Neufahrwasser and Weichselmünde was swarming with them. Aware I was tailing him, he had his beer in the Petroleum Bar, switched over to *Zur Hütte*, and finally to the *Deutsches Haus*. Even after this meeting, he insisted that the *Deutsches Haus* was the safest meeting place. In the vast hall, three hundred seamen of the German *Kriegsmarine* were screaming *Denn wir fahren, denn wir fahren nach Engelland!* The noise was deafening. Nobody could overhear our conversation.

I said conversation, but now I realize that talk was actually a minor part of it. There were long silences between us in the hellish noise of the place and deep looks into each other's eyes, looks which seemed to penetrate the retina and the eye nerve deep into the human soul—if and wherever such a thing exists. And yet, between the silences and the deep looks and the random talk in half-broken German and half-broken English, Rosti had succeeded in convincing me to give up my dream of escaping to Sweden and ultimately England and to stay where I was, in Danzig.

"If you hate the Nazis as much as you say you have a much better chance to fight them here. I know people on the other side, in Gothenburg, who would be delighted to have steady information about what ships are being repaired in the Danziger Werft: how many U-boats are being constructed, that sort of thing. Do you think you can supply that kind of information?"

283

I tried for the last time. "So you won't help me to escape to Sweden?"

He moved that strange head of his in a negative motion. "And the information?" he asked after a while.

"Seems to be my fate," I answered glumly.

"My ship sails on Friday," he said.

"I'll bring you the stuff on Wednesday night," I said.

"But we must meet on the street," he responded. "We'll find a quiet little street; remember this is the real thing, dangerous."

"I'm not afraid," I said.

"I am," he answered.

"Let me ask you one last thing, Rosti. Why are you doing this?"

He shrugged. "Money," he said. "Gothenburg pays me well. Don't forget that I'm just a poor Argentinian stoker on board an old Swedish steamer."

"And I'm just a Jewish stoker with false papers, a stoker on a floating crane in Marine Waffenbetrieb of the Danziger Werft."

"Don't we just make the perfect couple?" he laughed.

We shook hands and I left. He stayed. How perfect a couple we were I saw when we met on Wednesday night on a blind side street ending directly on a river canal, where some barges were moored. The place was dimly lit by a single gas lantern. It was snowing heavily but not too cold. From the bar just around the corner we could hear the yelling of the drunken soldiers and seamen of the *Kriegsmarine*. Occasionally a siren of a submarine passing on the main canal or the hooting of a tugboat were heard, the only other noise was the snow that crunched under Rosti's feet when he arrived for the rendez-vous.

On the wall, as in all the port area, were the war placards. One said, *'Räder müssen rollen für den Sieg! Er geht vor!'* (Wheels must roll for the victory! He takes priority!) In the picture was a soldier with rifle and backpack, obviously on leave, flanked by family and friends. Clearly the waiting civilians were happy to let him go and be virtuous and patriotic. The other poster was very different *"Psst,"* it said, *"Der*

Feind hört mit" (the enemy is listening). Pictured were two men on a dimly lit street, one of them lighting the cigarette of the other, who was handing him a thick envelope. The atmosphere was murky—that of secrecy, implying clearly that some kind of unsavory business was going on here. Rosti grinned, pointing to the poster when I handed him a thick envelope, which he put away immediately in his pants pocket.

"See?" he said, "exactly like the picture."

I said, "Not exactly. Where is the cigarette?"

"You're right," he said, producing a packet of Old Gold and lighting a cigarette for me and one for himself.

It was of this scene that I dreamt so often, till I met the young Jew from Buenos Aires in my kibbutz many years later. But never after that. Once the recollection of the actual event had been restored, its reflection in the dream died. Oddly, the image of Rosti's face faded gradually into complete oblivion, but I was able to remember the most minute details of the affair. I know for sure it was Old Gold cigarettes and not any other brand. I remember the poster on the wall, I even remember the contents of the first envelope I gave him on that night and the taste of the cheap beer we drank later in the Petroleum Bar. I recollect how anxious I was for him to take the envelope to his ship, but he was very calm and said, "Don't worry, it will be on board in my cabin tonight."

This first envelope was very amateurish, I realize now. In it were detailed drawings of three sections of a submarine under construction, a list with dates of tanks and heavy artillery pieces unloaded by my floating 100-ton crane, and a description with drawings of the damages suffered by the heavy cruiser *Königsberg* (in the stern by a torpedo and just below the bridge by a gun shot.) I delivered such envelopes to Rosti every three weeks and on one occasion received confirmation that they were delivered to the British Consulate in Gothenburg. Then the deliveries of iron ore from Sweden, and German coal to Sweden in return, ceased towards the end of the war and

I never saw Rosti again. I never overestimated my activities during this period; my contribution to the victory over Nazi Germany was probably less than that of a single infantry soldier on any of the many fronts. But for me the experience was one of elation. I felt that at least I was doing something instead of surviving the war first in the safety of the German *Handelsmarine* and then in the Danziger Werft. Later, I indulged in visualizing the information I had supplied to Rosti spread on a huge jigsaw table, mixed with countless other pieces—there must have been thousands of people like me in Nazi-occupied Europe—and many men and women busy trying to obtain some clear picture of the enemy's plans and intentions and using this information to fight the diabolic rule of the Nazis.

Once I stopped dreaming about Rosti and the remembrance of these past days survived my cerebral strokes and remained as pure memory, labeled as the years 1942–43 on the chronological calendar, I was ready to lay it aside: I didn't return to it daily or nightly, but promised to write about it one day. Mind you, reader, my bag of memories is huge and I remember well almost everything in it, from my first sexual encounter at the age of nine. What I don't remember is where the hell I've left my reading glasses. Immediate memory is definitely weak, but maybe that's normal in a man of sixty-seven.

The question I asked myself when I embarked on the adventure of writing "Distortions" in the mind of Wladislaw Grabowski was whether anybody would be interested in reading this piece of writing or was I doing it purely for my own satisfaction. A literary friend of mine offered me a critical evaluation of these images. He told me I'd written a statement, not a story or an essay. I wholeheartedly accept this but am ready to fend off attacks by future critics pursuing the same line, trying to force me to define what the subject of writing was. I had written in the past tense. What is it, they asked: a novel, an essay, a short story? But these are only your ideas. And what were you expecting, my nail clippings?

And you think people will read this? Only if they want.

An ancient Jewish anecdote comes to mind. A Jew is caught on a border trying to smuggle a bag of tobacco.

"What do you have in this bag?" asks the border guard.

"Food for the birds," answers the Jew. The guard rips open the bag. "The birds will eat this?"

"Only if they want," says the Jew. "I won't force them."

I think this joke is very characteristic of the bitter Jewish sense of humor. We are a very ancient people and should be treated as senior citizens of the world along with the Chinese and the Egyptians. Paradoxically, the concept of Senior Citizen is unknown in Israel. An approximate equivalent frequently in use is the Yiddish *Alte Kacker*, or Old Crapper; and as to the nature of my future, prospective readers—many of whom will be Sabras (the 'fruit of the prickly pear'), Jews born in Israel—I define them as prickly on the outside and bad-mannered on the inside.

I ended the first part of Distortions with a dream and a prayer. I think that as one firmly believing in dreams, and as someone also convinced that Time is circular and not linear (this is what Marxists believe, don't they?) that I, Wladislaw Grabowski, should finish this exercise in self-disclosure with another dream, a dream from this morning which I remember in its entirety.

We were living in New York City in a flat on the 25th floor and I had a conversation with a man I had sailed with for a long time and liked. His name was Gershon and he has been dead for three years; I eulogized him at his burial. Then Gershon disappeared (have you noticed how effortlessly the dead disappear?) and I was watching a long coastline deep down below and noticed some dolphins, or whales stranded there in the surf. The window of the 25th floor was open and my dog was barking wildly. I told my wife she'd better close the window, the dog might jump down to the dolphins. He won't, she answered, he knows it's very far. Then I woke, wishing so much that these dolphins or whales wouldn't be stranded and that they'd find their way back to the open sea, to the liberty of the open sea.

After reading what I'd written up to this point, on "The Anatomy of a Dream", my wife (who is also the first person to whom I show anything I write), asked, "What was it you were trying to write, a diary?"

287

Robert Graves once warned me that a man should have his breakfast alone. We were sitting in the thin early morning sun on the terrace of Canellun, his home in Deya Mallorca. He said, "In the morning a man is half-asleep and still wrapped up in his dreams and should not be disturbed. Notice that most quarrels in the family occur mainly in the morning." Well, I didn't, and that was the result.

"A diary!" she said.

So be it. I'd be in very good company. Stendhal, Dostoevsky, Rimbaud, Baudelaire, Camus, Conrad, even Montaigne, who kept writing for his pleasure only; and isn't Don Quixote really Cervantes' diary? And what about Joyce and his Bloom diary spanning one complete day in Dublin? Then there are the people who have no talent for writing novels yet the urge to write a novel drives them nuts. They remind me of the poor nineteenth-century composers desperately trying to produce an opera. No matter how much wonderful music you composed, you were nothing if you didn't write an opera. Debussy finally created his *Pelléas* but, lovely as it is, I'd rather have three dozens of his Preludes. But it is only a matter of taste, and the ancient Romans advised us not to discuss taste. I bow my white-haired head before their wisdom.

Yet as I embark on this journey (perhaps ultimate, perhaps penultimate, one never knows) which seems to attempt to clear up certain problems of reincarnation, I pray and invoke the blessing of an ancient writer whom we Jews call *Kohelet*, known to the rest of the world as Ecclesiastes.

I've already stated that in my opinion we are definitely accidents and so is everything that happens to us. The other day I was flying to Philadelphia, by accident of course, and after releasing my seat belt at the altitude of some 28,000 feet started to watch castles of cream-colored cumulus clouds far below. Contrasted with the flawless blue of the sky above them, they were an eerie sight; triggered by some ancient shadow of a memory, I repeated with my inner ear the musical theme of Debussy's *Nuages* and wondered what music he would have composed had he been able to see what I saw at that moment. I decided that he wouldn't change a note of it, nor would

I. The fact that I performed the unnatural feat of flying above the clouds instead of watching them below, shouldn't change anything in the nature of things.

Watching the endless progress of these cumulus castles toward the ever-evasive distant horizon, it occurred to me that my life, as I lived it now, was only a reflection of some previous life, lived perhaps by someone else, perhaps by a relative of mine or maybe myself, but in such a remote past that what I remembered of it was only a vague shadow of remembrance. But there were parallel developments in both lives—similarities, repetitions, analogies in the behavior of the protagonists—if they were indeed two different characters, and not the same character seen from a different angle and in a different time frame. Was each cumulus castle really different, or were they only endless repetitions of themselves ad infinitum?

At any rate, I thought that in this present life I have spent a number of years hiding myself behind some other person, assuming this person's character, manner of speech, personal documents. For six years I was a Polish seaman, a stoker: I made a credible performance of it and thus saved my life, for what it was worth. I thought now that this was but a repeat performance. I must have done it 500 years ago for the first time and after a moment I started remembering this first time.

Earlier, I invoked the assistance and a wish for a blessing from *Kohelet*, not only because he is my favorite chapter in the Bible, but also because he says there is a season and a time to every purpose under heaven. "A time to be born and a time to die, a time to weep and a time to laugh..." This list goes on to include almost every human activity.

These lines from Ecclesiastes are particularly fitting in setting the parameters of a seaman's life; a symbiosis of a sailor's existence with that of his ship in defined and very concrete limits: time between the Sign-on and the Pay-off. I must have participated in these ceremonies at least a hundred times; a glance at my seaman's book confirms it. My name and that of my captain are recorded there in the proper rubric. This procedure was so deeply embedded in naval tradition that even in wartime the Germans insisted on preserving it in all details. Thus, my signature is affixed on the articles of the good ship *Marianne* opposite the signature of Captain Karl Schmidt.

The occasion was hilarious as well. I was brought to the captain's cabin by police escort until I'd officially signed-on. "Well now, he's all yours," the policeman said with relief before leaving. I was booted down to the stokehold. That was my first sign-on; at least a hundred followed in the next year, but who could know that then. I must digress here to explain that even people with a reputation for thoroughness like Germans sometimes get confused in their bureaucracy. In 1940, no Polish seamen were allowed to work on German ships. By 1941, due to the acute shortage of German men—they'd all been mobilized—this directive was annulled and they were searching for Polish seamen in prisons and labor camps. I was serving a sentence for the theft of a boat in Straflager Stutthof when they discovered my stoker's card during a routine checkup. Stutthof was a camp for Poles and Germans; while it had a separate section for *Untermenschen*—mainly Jews and Gypsies—it never earned the reputation of Auschwitz or Treblinka. The two sections were strictly separated.

So I worked on the *Marianne* until she was sunk and then on the *Brigitte*, and in the end of 1941 they changed the rules once more and transferred all the Poles to land jobs in the shipyards. Both *Marianne* and *Brigitte* were old tubs sailing to Baltic ports under German occupation: Memel, Riga, Tallinn, Helsinki. As stated, two sections of Stutthof were strictly separated, the Straflager Stutthof and the K.Z., the concentration camp. Stutthof just shared a name but I, having had a glimpse of the other installation, often wondered what it was that protected me from joining the other crowd behind the double barbed wire. Just a piece of paper saying that I was a Polish seaman, son of Jan Wladyslaw and Victoria Krukowski and that I had been baptized in a church on Chlodna Street and that this birth certificate was duly registered in the church's archives. On the basis of this fraudulent document, other papers were issued which served me well till I was signed on in Danzig, on the *Marianne*, and even after that. Nobody cared to check what had happened to the son of

Jan Wladyslaw and Victoria in 1939. Had they checked, they would have discovered that in September of that year he had been drafted into the Polish Navy and had been killed on the 30th of September, fighting for Westerplatte, the Polish free zone in the former Free State of Danzig. Once I started impersonating this dead man, things were relatively easy: I spoke German and Polish fluently, I knew the slang and the way my Polish colleagues lived, knew their games, knew how to drink and how to swear. The only danger was that I had at all costs to avoid appearing naked in front of my Polish and German shipmates. The disclosure of my circumcision would have been my death sentence.

Once I was very near to it.

It was a routine medical check-up of the seamen in Königsberg. We were standing in a long line and each man whose name was called had to step up on a little platform in the middle of the room and a young woman doctor examined his genitals. The moment she said 'all right' a weary port police official affixed his stamp to the man's papers.

"Next" she said. I stepped up. She was very young, probably just out of a medical school in some German university. I was sure she had never seen a circumcised male member in her life. I looked down at her, she looked up at me, our eyes met at the level of my hips. Then she let me live and said, "All right. Next." The bored policeman didn't bother to glance at the man whose papers he had just stamped.

And so I lived on, protected by my papers and an incredible *chutzpah*. I would often think about this episode in relation to one of my previous reincarnations in Spain, around 1500. Papers would not have saved me then because I hardly knew how to read. Circumcision was not such a deadly peril as it was in Germany and Poland in 1940. Especially not in Sevilla, where I lived after being separated from my parents in the great Jewish Expulsion from Spain in 1492. Many Spaniards in the south, recently under Moorish rule, had been circumcised, and nobody would have accused a man of being a Jew in disguise on the evidence of his circumcision.

As a young Spanish sailor at the end of the fifteenth century, I had no difficulty in joining the ship of a conquistador, Captain Vincente Yanez Pinzon, on his fourth voyage to the New World. It was a dangerous trip. What I remembered of it were the cramped quarters, stale food, lack of water to drink and a miracle: four days before our landing, the water in the ocean ceased to be salty and became as sweet as that of a mountain stream in Spain. This miracle was the direct result of the fervent prayer-vigil, lasting the entire night, by the captain to Jesus Christ. After all, the captain said, Christ had changed water into wine in the Holy Land, so changing salt water into sweet would be just a minor miracle.

Many years later I used to tell this story to my children in Salonika, Greece. They hardly believed me: the young mistrust old men in just the same way that children do in this present year, 1989. Apparently this is the way of the world. But now, when my zest for living equals zero on the scale from one to infinity, I see, perhaps too late, how right was old *Kohelet* in declaring that all is vanity. Not for nothing was he pronounced the wisest of mortals.

Newton, July 1989

Episodes in Autobiography

These episodes, loosely connected to each other, can be compared to fragments of a broken mirror shattered by the blows of life, which I try to collect and preserve for whom? For posterity, perhaps for my grandchildren.

According to ancient Jewish wisdom the average life span of a man is three score and ten, so at the age of seventy and after what may be called a turbulent life, the summing up cannot be very far. My wife, to whom I dedicate these lines, would like me to live forever, but I prefer to be damned to hell for eternity rather than live this mess again. At any rate not in this life, perhaps in the next reincarnation, preferably as my own dog. The cerebral strokes which have hit me repeatedly in recent years have restricted my activities and made it difficult for me to deal with many aspects of reality. On many occasions I do not know exactly where I am and why. It may be that my reluctance to live my present life could be traced to the fact that for five years I had to live two lives: one of Jan Krokowski and one of John Czeslaw Auerbach, a most unpleasant experience, probably well known to those of you who have read Dostoevsky's *The Double* or

295

Conrad's *Secret Sharer*, not to mention those who still remember R.L. Stevenson's "Dr. Jekyll and Mr. Hyde" read in a remote youth.

At any rate, I cannot avoid returning to this period of my life when recollecting my past and this is how, yesterday, I came upon a fragment which I now call an error of judgment, which reflects the predicaments of my life during World War II.

It is unimportant for this narrative how I got on board this self-propelled floating crane in Danziger Werft, a huge shipyard producing mainly submarines for the German navy. The narrative starts at the moment I am stoking fires under the big furnaces of this crane and am interrupted by a cry from the deck: "Hey, Polack, open the door and catch this!"

The cry came from Wilhelm Mach, who had just stolen a bottle of Aalborger Aquavit from a Danish steamer and found himself quite exposed with the stolen bottle sticking out of his pocket on the huge deck of our swimming crane. Wishing to get rid of the stolen goods he spied the open door of the stokehold leading to the deck and yelled to me.

I must explain a few things to those readers who might be ignorant of the characteristics of a shipyard in wartime.

Our floating crane, called the Langer Heinrich, with a lifting capacity of 100 tons, was the tallest structure in the yard. The Langer Heinrich was indispensable for the construction of submarines, which arrived in eight separate sections that were then welded together with the help of our crane. Submarines were the only product of Danzinger Werft at that time.

The Langer Heinrich was registered as a sea-going vessel and as such it carried a full crew: a captain, a chief engineer, a helmsman, seven able-bodied deck hands, two stokers and a donkeyman. I was a stoker, Wilhelm was donkeyman. The other stoker was Ernst, a German from Bremen. The door from the stokehold to the deck was open most of the time, because the stokehold with its two huge furnaces was very hot, and besides I loved to steal a glimpse of what was going on outside whenever I could leave my post for a moment.

There were others, too, who were interested in what I could see of the submarines on the deck of the Langer Heinrich. They were in the British consulate in Gothenburg. I had been submitting a bimonthly detailed report of what I had seen from my crane, along with other information. My contact was an Argentinian sailor on a Swedish ship plying regularly between Danzig and Gothenburg.

I would meet him in the harbor bars and always give him a fat envelope, and the other side confirmed their satisfaction with the information, asking for more and urging me to continue the good work. As to my contact, Rosti the Argentinian seaman, he once told me, "I do it for money. They pay me well. No complaints."

Now we are talking about Wilhelm Mach, the donkeyman—*oberheizer* they call it in German—and the aquavit bottle he stole and which he later shared with me in our boiler room.

I liked Wilhelm. The other crew members didn't. He never cursed me like the others. You must remember, I was an inferior being, a Polish stoker, and in addition, having recently been released from the Straflager Stutthof I was supposed to wear the letter P sewn on my shirt. Nevertheless, I must say I was a little surprised when Wilhelm walked in and said, "OK, Jan, let's kill that bottle!"

I moved the bench so that the table was between us and so that where I was sitting I could watch the water gauge and the manometers. I put the bottle and two glasses between us. I also noticed that Wilhelm had brought two bottles of ordinary beer to serve as chasers. I prepared a box of domestic tobacco and cigarette paper so that we would be able to smoke as much as we wanted. I was still wondering what made Wilhelm prefer me as his drinking companion to another crewmember or the casual clients of some Neufahrwasser drinking hole. Wilhelm went to business immediately. We touched our glasses and he started talking. "Look Jan, I'm celebrating my forty-ninth birthday today. I have no immediate family. The crew of this vessel don't like me. You know it. I am not exactly anybody's buddy on board. So even if you are a Polack I decided to spend this evening with you. I hope you don't mind."

My mind wandered for one moment to the stern section with its deadly torpedo tubes right now on our deck. Tomorrow I was scheduled to report to Rosti, but meanwhile Wilhelm kept talking.

"A man's memory is like a garbage bag. Twenty years ago I was *oberheizer* on the *Bremen* liner. Of course you have heard of the *Bremen*, the blue ribbon for almost two years, the fastest ship to cross the Atlantic from Hamburg to New York. After that the Italians took it with their *Rex*. Yessir, I was *oberheizer* on that ship. You know, Jan, the officers wore the insignia of their ranks always on their sleeves and shoulders. Always. Because of the passengers, they said, but it was not true, Jan. They were just swollen up with pride for being officers of that ship." I banked the fires, checked that they were covered properly with ashes and returned to my bench opposite Wilhelm. He said, "I was dismissed from the ship when the second machinist, a party member, accused me of stealing money from his pocket." Wilhelm slapped my thigh and laughed. "Well, I learned my lesson. I joined the party a year later. But they refused to reinstate me on the *Bremen*, so I moved to Danzig, started working in the yard." Our bottle was half empty but Wilhelm rambled on. I felt fairly drunk but he seemed to me absolutely sober and keen on telling me the whole story of his life.

Through a time distance of half a century I watch that night in the stokehold of the floating crane in Danzig and agree with Wilhelm. Each man's memory is like a garbage bag and serves the same purpose.

Wilhelm launched into a detailed story of his service on the *ss Bremen* twenty years earlier. "Do you remember things, Jan?" asked Wilhelm. "That depends," I answered. "I prefer to remember pleasant memories, to push the unpleasant ones into forgetfulness, beyond memory, beyond awareness."

Wilhelm finally spread his huge arms and hands on the table and rested his head on them, the alcohol starting to work on him as well; at any rate he stopped talking for many minutes and there was silence in the stokehold. I started wondering if Wilhelm could know what was going on in my head, but he was silent. I don't know if it was the longing for the sheltered life I had been living till now, or the alcohol, or the combination of both, that made me do what I did.

Wilhelm seemed fast asleep for half an hour or so, and it was past midnight when suddenly I blurted, "You know, I am really a Jew who escaped from the Warsaw Ghetto and is now stoking fires on a floating crane in Danzig." Wilhelm stirred and mumbled, "Jan, I didn't hear what you just said."

When Ernst came at seven to relieve me, Wilhelm was not in the stokehold. Ernst first checked the fires, then noticed the bottle and glasses. "What went on here?" he asked.

"We had a little drinking party, Wilhelm and I."

"A very violent man, Wilhelm, very violent."

"With me he is always OK," I said.

"Come with me," said Ernst. We went together to the officers' quarters on the main floor and he opened a closet marked Wilhelm Mach, *Oberheizer*. Inside hung a freshly ironed black S.A. uniform, complete with a red armband and a swastika on it and black boots beneath it. "Well here is the real Wilhelm Mach for you," said Ernst, "in case you didn't know."

The months after the drinking party were dominated by fear. I knew that at any time they could take me out of my stokehold and return me to Stutthof. At night I woke with this nightmare. On another level I kept functioning almost normally. I kept my fires burning well.

I met Rosti every time his ship was in port, delivering to him a heavy envelope with drawings and sketches and dates and information about the shipyard activities. On one occasion Wilhelm reappeared on the scene. He entered the stokehold, glanced around and said, "It seems the *Führer* and the *Vaterland* cannot manage without the help of old Wilhelm. I am almost fifty years old and yesterday they called me up!"

Two months after the capitulation of Stalingrad, a heavily mustached man appeared on the crane. "I am Wilhelm Mach's older brother," he told Jan. "I don't know if you've seen yesterday's obituaries, but I thought you should know. Wilhelm fell in the line of duty for the *Führer* and the *Vaterland* on the eastern front."

My wife, whom I have mentioned before, is a professional theater director and perhaps this is the reason I cannot refrain from comparing my wartime experiences and transformations with some of the actors in her theatre. My situation was infinitely worse. The actors can always consult the script and ask the director for additional instructions.

When I escaped from the Ghetto and became Jan Krukowski I had in my hands only a certificate that Jan Krukowski was baptized in All Saints Church on Chlodna Street in the presence of his parents, Wladislaw and Victoria Krukowski on 11 December 1917. I had to reconstruct the life of this individual from the beginning to the end in order to become a viable double. I had no clues as to what he was or who he was. But who knows, perhaps this is the main difference between theater and real life. In any case, we should consider ourselves lucky that the only rewind button on the videotape of life is that of human memory, and that is, as Wilhelm Mach said, a garbage bag, and serves the same purpose.

December 1991, Kibbutz Sdot Yam

The Border Incident

Even before he married his second wife, and long before his strokes, David's life was dominated by memories. They were bad memories: he was a survivor of the Holocaust.

"Let's play the document game," said the stranger in the leather coat on the train. "I'll show you mine and you will show me yours," he said, and produced an *Ausweis* of the Gestapo, with a bird which brought luck to nobody: it was a German eagle holding a swastika in its talons.

Whereupon David showed him an identity card of a dead man, stating that the bearer was a Pole and a Catholic. Whoever wished to verify the truth of these particulars could have challenged David to unbutton his trousers, which would have revealed him to be a circumcised Jew and thus terminated his existence. In fact, the Gestapo agent did not require verification and so prolonged David's life for some 47 years. But David's semi-subconscious fear of all police and state officials persisted.

His marriage to Lillian had added another dimension to his life: she was a theater director of renown, a widely recognized teacher of acting, and an American. Living with her, David discovered a new world, the existence of which he had never suspected. He was rather well educated, but his heritage was the culture and civilization of Europe, very slightly mixed with a Jewish background; hers, however, was American through and through: Second generation American.

Actors, many of them homosexual, kissed one another on the mouth; in the period between world wars in Warsaw, where David had spent his youth, gentlemen were still kissing ladies' hands. These actors embraced onstage and off and were knowledgeable about the latest reviews and productions on and off and off-off Broadway, as well as their Israeli equivalents. Their talk was peppered with exclamations: Divine! Marvelous! Horrible! What a flop! It will simply kill him! It'll slay her!

David and Lillian lived in Israel. Lillian taught in an Israeli university, but when she was offered a job in America for her sabbatical, they moved to a large city in New England. Toward the end of this period an opportunity offered itself for a weekend excursion to Canada.

"Oh let's go darling, it'll be fun, you'll see. Look, I was born in Manhattan and never went to Canada before, isn't it a shame?"

David, who was not feeling too well, timidly objected. "Look, darling," he said, "you with your American passport can travel practically all over the world without bothering about such things as visas and permits. But I, with my Israeli passport, am only a guest here, with my visitor's visa."

Acknowledging her husband's atavistic idiosyncrasies, Lillian phoned the Canadian consulate and was told that a bearer of an Israeli passport with a valid visa to the u.s. could visit Canada. "No problem whatsoever, ma'am."

They made the trip in their car, with a couple of their friends. All the way through New England, David recalled events in his life connected with crossing borders and displaying his travel documents to border policemen and various immigration officials. These documents were sometimes genuine, more often false. He remembered that while employed bringing Jews illegally into what was then Palestine, he once crossed four borders in Europe on various multi-colored passports, issued for individuals with names like Rafael Sarto, Franz Masaryk, Jan Wladyslas Krukowski—names he had to memorize before crossing and to forget as soon as he had crossed.

But now he had his good, genuine, passport with his real name on it, his photograph and his signature. In this passport there was also an American visa, valid for multiple visits to the United States. Nobody bothered to stop them as they crossed the line between the USA and Canada. The American side seemed to be abandoned; they evidently were not concerned with anybody leaving their country. The Canadian side was different. A policeman peered in and asked, "All of you American citizens?"

His friend, who was driving, answered "All but one, who is the bearer of an Israeli passport." David held up the dark blue passport.

"Would you please step into the office?"

Inside, a woman official examined his passport. It took a long time and David smiled and said "I'm sorry, it goes from right to left in the Hebrew alphabet, you know."

She lifted unsmiling eyes, which gave him the opportunity to have a good direct look at them—tiny, dark gray metal discs—and said, "That's all right. I'm familiar with all kinds of passports."

She wore no makeup and her complexion was as gray as her eyes. She had blond hair. Separated from her by the table, he experienced her as a mixture of hostility with high tension—a volatile mixture—that might explode under the slightest provocation into hysteria.

She had tiny pearl studs in her ear lobes, but to David, the large porcelain insulators used to transmit electricity on high-tension lines would have been more fitting. Automatically, he glanced to see if no electric wires were attached to them.

As to the rather contemptuous hostility, he did not think it could have been provoked by his Israeli passport (all Jews are paranoid to some degree, they have good reason to be); rather, it had something to do with the fact that he was a man, accompanied by a woman and another couple. Being Americans, both the woman and the other couple were untouchable.

She looked at David once more. "You're in trouble, sir," she said. "You can enter Canada at your own risk. You have no guarantee that the Americans will allow you to return after your three-day excursion."

"But I have a valid multiple-entry visa into the United States," said David.

"You will be regarded as a potential new immigrant to the States unless you can prove the contrary."

"What do you advise me to do?"

"Give up the idea of leaving the u.s. and visiting Canada, unless the Americans give you a guarantee that they'll readmit you after three days."

Lillian intervened. "Look here," she said, "I'm an American. I teach at an American University."

"I can confirm this," added David's friend.

"All this has nothing to do with this case," said the Canadian passport inspector. "If you return now to the Americans, I'll prepare a document for them." As they left, a tourist bus arrived and she was busy processing the newcomers.

At the American checkpost there were no visitors. The atmosphere was relaxed. Two men were telling jokes, a girl was laughing almost hysterically, tears streaming down her cheeks. The immigration officer glanced at the paper the Canadian had sent. He snorted. "She knows damn well we can give no guarantee to anybody. Show me your passport," he said, taking it from David's hand. "This is perfectly fine, with a valid visa. I can see no reason for any problem with reentry. My advice is to go have a good time in Canada and forget the whole business. You'll see, no problem."

At the Canadian checkpost the woman was not convinced. "You see, they would not guarantee it. I told you. I can give you a visa for a few days but I'm warning you, you're taking a big risk. If they refuse to readmit you, we cannot keep you here." Her hand rested on a big stapler waiting for his decision.

David smiled. "I'll take the risk." She lowered her hand and stamped *Immigration Canada, visa, expires April 21* in David's passport.

They drove to Montreal, which was like any American city, attempting but not quite succeeding to be another New York, and then on to touristic Quebec. They had a good time, as Lillian had promised, eating well and enjoying themselves. The nights were huge and David perceived the vastness of this huge country from the St. Lawrence seaway to the Pacific coast thousands of miles away, and the infinity of this continent stretching all the way from Labrador to the Gulf of Mexico.

They returned by way of Maine. At the border a girl in the uniform of the u.s. immigration services asked, "All Americans?"

"All but one," replied the driver.

"May I see your passport?" she asked David.

"OK" she said, in a moment. "Have a nice day."

Newton, April 1987

About the author

John Auerbach

John Auerbach was born in Warsaw in 1922, and served as a soldier in the Polish army at the beginning of the Second World War. During the German occupation, he escaped from the Warsaw Ghetto and worked on German ships as a stoker under a false identity. He was caught trying to escape to Sweden in a stolen boat, and sent to the Stutthof concentration camp. After the war, he went to Sweden and worked on Swedish ships. Here, he joined the Mossad *Aliyah B*, and transported refugees to Israel for three years. He was captured by the British and was detained in a Cyprus camp for two years.

On his release to Israel, Auerbach came to Kibbutz Sdot Yam, where he was a skipper of fishing boats. After officer's training in Acre, he served as a Chief Engineer in the Israeli Merchant Marines for fifteen years. Upon the death of his son in the 1973 Yom Kippur War, he left the sea and returned to the kibbutz, where he wrote and published twelve books of short stories and novellas (translated into Hebrew). His short story, *The Owl*, was awarded First Prize in the PEN/UNESCO Awards in 1993. He died in November 2002, as this volume was in preparation.

Other works by John Auerbach
also available from *The* Toby Press

The Owl & Other Stories

The Toby Press publishes fine fiction,
available at bookstores everywhere. For more information,
please contact *The* Toby Press at www.tobypress.com